ADVANCES IN HEALTH EDUCATION AND PROMOTION

Volume 2 • 1987

ADVANCES IN
HEALTH EDUCATION
AND PROMOTION

A Research Annual

Editor: WILLIAM B. WARD
University of South Carolina

Volume 2 Guest Editors: SCOTT K. SIMONDS
University of Michigan

PATRICIA D. MULLEN
University of Texas, Houston

MARSHALL BECKER
University of Michigan

VOLUME 2 • 1987

 JAI PRESS INC.

Greenwich, Connecticut   *London, England*

EDITORIAL BOARD FOR VOLUME 2

v

Donald C. Iverson
Associate Director
Cancer Control Science Program
Division of Cancer Prevention and
   Control
National Cancer Institute
Bethesda

Senendu B. Kar
School of Public Health
University of California
Los Angeles

Marshall Kreuter
Director
Division of Health Education
Center for Health Promotion and
   Education
Centers for Disease Control
Atlanta

Frances Marcus Lewis
Department of Community Health
   Care
School of Nursing
University of Washington
Seattle

Zora T. Salisbury
Project Director
Research Development and
   Marketing
American Red Cross National
   Headquarters
Washington, DC

Heather Walter
American Health Foundation
New York

Richard A. Windsor
Director
Division of Health
   Education-Health Behavior
School of Public Health
University of Alabama
Birmingham

Jane Zapka
Division of Public Health
University of Massachusetts
Amherst

CONTENTS

LIST OF CONTRIBUTORS

Marshall H. Becker

Department of Health Behavior
and Health Education
The University of Michigan

Noreen M. Clark

Department of Health Behavior
and Health Education
The University of Michigan

Janet L. Collins

IOX Assessment Associates
Culver City, California

Leonard H. Dawson

Department of Health Education
University of North Carolina

Rocco A. De Pietro, Jr.

Department of Communication
University of Michigan

Nancy E. Epstein

Austin, Texas

Brian R. Flay

John Stauffer Pharmaceutical
Sciences Center
University of Southern California
Los Angeles

Robert M. Goodman

Department of Health Education
The University of North Carolina

Lawrence W. Green

Center for Health Promotion,
Research and Development
The University of Texas
Houston

Alan C. Henderson

Department of Health Sciences
California State University
Long Beach

Barbara A. Israel

Department of Health Behavior
    and Health Education
The University of Michigan

Frances Marcus Lewis

Department of Community Health
    Care
School of Nursing
University of Washington
Seattle

Patricia D. Mullen

Center for Health Promotion
    Research and Development
The University of Texas
Houston

Judith M. Ottoson

Center for Health Promotion,
    Research and Development
The University of Texas
Houston

Gilbert Ramirez

Academy of Health Sciences
Fort Sam Houston, Texas

Irwin M. Rosenstock

Department of Health Behavior
    and Health Education
The University of Michigan

Kathleen A. Rounds

School of Social Work
University of North Carolina

Scott K. Simonds

School of Public Health
The University of Michigan

Allan B. Steckler

Department of Health Education
The University of North Carolina

Cynthia J. Stewart

School of Nursing
University of Michigan

William B. Ward

Department of Health
 Promotion and Education
School of Public Health
University of South Carolina

Elanna S. Yalow

IOX Assessment Associates
Culver City, California

INTRODUCTION TO VOLUME 2:

INTEGRATING POLICY AND THEORY WITH RESEARCH AND EVALUATION

William B. Ward

Volume 2 of *Advances in Health Education and Promotion* assembles an exciting collection of manuscripts that add to a body of literature indicative of the evolving nature of the two overlapping fields of health education and health promotion. The authors of the chapters in this volume are to be commended for the excellent interpretation they add to the existing literature. At the same time, it must be mentioned that their efforts would not be possible were it not for the legion of practitioners who have helped empirically to determine needed directions. The chapters included in Volume 2 make major contributions to *Theory Building, Theoretical Construct Development, Operationalizing of Theory for Programming*, and *Strategies for Evaluating Research*.

THEORY BUILDING

Health educators have been in search of a theoretical framework that represents the eclectic nature of their field (see Becker & Rosenstock, this volume). Many of the behavioral theories that have been proposed to date for application to health education deal with only a small corner of the health educator's world. As a result, there has been recent excitement with social learning theory, seen by some (Parcel & Baranowski, 1981) as having the potential for integrating the diversity of theoretical, measurement, and program variables (Green & Lewis, 1986) with which educators are confronted.

Although there are questions about ways to apply systematically the various components of the social learning theory (SLT) paradigm to health education programming, it is apparent that in spite of the relatively limited number of SLT evaluation studies identified by Clark in her chapter (this volume), the theoretical paradigm warrants additional attention by health educators. Close examination of SLT (Clark; Becker & Rosenstock; in this volume) strongly suggests that it adds to the development of mega-theory that, in combination with other paradigms (the Health Belief Model for example), will enhance health educators' ability to influence beliefs, attitudes, social norms, environmental constraints, the constraints of previous experience, and habitual behavior relevant to changing health practices.

Clark is surprised to find, in her review, a relatively limited number of research studies that state as their intent the testing of aspects of the social learning paradigm (vicarious learning, the use of cognitive symbols, self-regulation, reinforcement, self-efficacy and outcome expectations). However, based on a detailed review of a number of the more prominent studies of the SLT paradigm, Clark concludes that these few studies represent a broad range of age groups, ethnicities, and income levels and, therefore, have the potential for generalizability.

Although Clark found a lack of published comparisons of SLT applications with those of other theories, Becker and Rosenstock provide a conceptual comparison between social learning theory and the Health Belief Model.

THEORETICAL CONSTRUCT DEVELOPMENT

At the same time that the health behavior theories discussed by Becker and Rosenstock and Clark help, increasingly, to explain why people take the health actions they do, focus on a single construct (for example, Raven & Litman-Adizes' "Social Power and Influence," in Volume 1, 1986) can assist researchers and practitioners in fine-tuning their programmatic interventions. Lewis, in her review of the literature of the construct "Control," discovered that while education on "what the patient will feel during an endoscopy" proved useful in limiting disability, focus on "what procedures will be carried out during endoscopy" seemed to increase fear about the process. The growing understanding of how to fine-tune health-education programming as a result of the increased understanding of concepts such as "Control," when added to relatively comprehensive health behavior paradigms being developed, such as SLT and the Health Belief

Model, which help to delineate multiple factors influencing behavior, promises exciting opportunities for health promotion and health education.

Based on the chapter by Israel and Rounds, providers of health services should consider ways to draw upon the social network as a tool supportive of the actions they wish the client to take. Types of social-support mechanisms available to them include: "home visits, training of significant others outside the home, structured reinforcement and contracting, and group support." Israel and Rounds add a caveat, however, in indicating that providers of care must ascertain that the social-network resources to be drawn upon are employed in an appropriate fashion, so that applications match the needs of the problem to be solved (financial, self-esteem, social competence, etc.).

Another conceptual construct, self-efficacy, is defined in the chapter by Yalow and Collins as "individuals' beliefs in their abilities to engage in specific behaviors." Thus, according to the authors, it is quite different from generalized measures, such as locus of control and self-concept. In addition to its ability to enhance the prediction of health-related behavior, the construct described by Yalow and Collins should reduce the tendency to "blame the victim" in that those with abilities inadequate for a prescribed task should receive support rather than criticism. This seems infinitely more fair than blaming such individuals for a lack of motivation to act.

OPERATIONALIZING OF THEORY FOR PROGRAMMING

A problem that will challenge health educators for some time to come is the increasing demand for breadth in training, coupled with the growing need for a recognizable specialization, a problem not fully addressed by the Role Delineation Project Committee (see Henderson, this volume). Health-educator roles can be site-specific (hospital, school, etc.), content-specific (maternal and child health, cardiovascular disease), or method-specific (counselor, planner). A method-specific area of potential specialization is that of marketing. With the realization by hospitals that a part of their customer base is slipping, health educators and promoters are being hired to recruit new customers into community outreach activities (fitness and weight loss programs, screenings, and employee assistance programs).

At the same time that the educator is developing marketing skills, s/he must be aware of strategies for the successful implementation of organizational and/or societal policy to deal with challenges from those previously having vested interests in the status quo.

As the various health behavior paradigms become part of an overall theoretical framework, and suggest new areas of the literature with which the health educator must have familiarity, it is apparent that a realignment must be made between the broad array of needed skills and the typical one and a half to two years master's program for the professional health educator. Mullen and Ramirez raise the question that it may not be whether or not a given intervention is effective, but rather the extent to which educational quality is or is not a part of the intervention. Flay and Lewis provide summary evidence that we are not sure why changes occur, to whom, and by whom, and that there are numerous mediating variables that are yet to be identified so that their impact can be assessed. This suggests that health education as a profession must move to greater specialization. Implications for the training (Stewart, this volume) and credentialing of such a trend in specialization must be addressed in the near future.

STRATEGIES FOR EVALUATING RESEARCH

Significant advances have recently been made in evaluating health education and promotion literature. The chapters by Flay and by Mullen and Ramirez in this volume are major contributions to this process. Mullen and Ramirez demonstrate how the information-synthesis approach can be used to assess findings from research studies where previous writers, using less exacting methods, came to unfortunate conclusions by giving undue attention to only a few cases, using simple counts of studies with positive and negative outcomes, or missing interaction effects by ignoring the impact of interventions on subpopulations within the studies.

The Mullen and Ramirez chapter offers direction for both the researcher and the practitioner. A number of examples of the meta-analysis process are included in enough detail that the researcher might replicate them in carrying out similar examinations of published and unpublished studies. A series of seven steps provides the reader with clear instructions on actually conducting such a synthesis. Finally, the authors include a set of twelve guidelines to be used by researchers and evaluators in determining what to include in a report of their findings so that other scholars will have less difficulty in interpreting study results. It is suggested further that the process of reviewing and evaluating the literature might well consider an examination of the historical development of a field of research as is done by Flay in this volume when he examines the changes that have occurred over time in smoking prevention.

Although Flay does not consider his review to involve meta-analysis, he does examine a number of methodological issues for each study: "the experimental comparisons attempted, the number of units assigned to each condition, what those units were, whether or not they were randomly assigned, whether or not pretest differences were reported, the time of the longest follow-up, whether or not individual students could be tracked over time, the extent of attrition (which proved to be a significant issue), and whether or not there was biological validation of self-reports of smoking and its nature." Flay's check list of quality control procedures for the review of studies, coupled with the statistical analysis examples provided by Mullen and Ramirez, goes a long way to suggesting the type of rigor with which studies should be examined before reliance is placed on their findings.

CONCLUSIONS

Volume 2 of *Advances in Health Education and Promotion* has three major themes. These themes are: directions for professional training and certification, the concurrent building of megatheories and explication of components of these theories, and the increasing rigor of health education and promotion research studies. That such topics dominate this volume attests to the fact that the fields of health education and health promotion have come of age. That the themes cut across the boundaries of the three sections is evidence that the profession, the theoretical base, and research strategies are interactive and that the field is growing, to a great extent, because of this interaction.

There are a number of key points within the text that demonstrate the remarkable advances made in health education and promotion within the very recent past. Now there exist several theoretical paradigms that bring us close to the comprehensive theoretical base long sought after. SLT, in the words of Becker and Rosenstock, provides us with behavioral explanatory power beyond that of the Health Belief Model (HBM). At the same time, it is was pointed out that the HBM covers concepts not dealt with by other paradigms. It should not be long before the various pieces are put together in a framework that more closely approximates a megatheory.

At the same time that we are moving toward this megatheory of health behavior, researchers (as evidenced in chapters in this volume by Lewis, Israel & Rounds, and Yalow & Collins) have begun to define the nature of some of the more ambiguous components and constructs of the existing theoretical paradigms (control, self-efficacy, and social networks and social support). This is in response to increasing evidence that research studies often fail to operationalize components of health behavior theories in any consistent fashion. Flay's historical examination of four schools of smoking prevention research points to a way to ensure that different research groups use the same measures for the same concepts. With advances in component definition, it becomes possible then to develop the sociometrics required for measurement and continued definition of the constructs and for comparing particular components of the various health-behavior theories.

However, as Flay has written and Clark has inferred (both in this volume), we still do not know why change does or does not occur in a given situation. Flay proposes the need for more long-term, large sample studies on the one hand, and more short-term, small sample experiments on the other. While these obviously are needs, Mullen and Ramirez suggest the possibility of a more rigorous evaluation of studies in the existing literature, a procedure that could enhance the ability of future research to address more clearly important research questions and to make current research more cost effective. To facilitate this, Mullen and Ramirez have taken to the establishing of criteria for information synthesis as an important step in their chapter.

The implications for health education and for the health education specialist are that the existence of a megatheory will serve as a guide to the systematic improvement of the fields of health education and health promotion. Then, in addition to being able to "plug-in" components of theories of related fields such as marketing, it will be possible, as suggested by Israel and Rounds, to pick the appropriate social-support technique for a given patient, or, as indicated by Lewis, to determine whether the issue with a given group or individual is the strenthening of cognitive as compared with contingency control. Then, as stated by Flay, we may begin to focus on enhancing the quality of our interventions rather than using a shotgun approach to programming, as has been the reality in much of health education and health promotion to date. These are heady days for educators and promoters of health.

REFERENCES

Green, L.W., & Lewis, F.M. (1986). *Measurement and evaluation in health education and health promotion*, Palo Alto: Mayfield Publishing Co.

Parcel, G.S., & Baranowski, T. (1981). Social learning theory and health education. *Health Education 12*, 14–18.

Raven, B.H., & Litman-Adizes, T. (1986). "Social Power and Influence" *Advances in Health Education and Promotion*, Volume 1. Greenwich, CT: JAI Press Inc.

SECTION I:

POLICY IN HEALTH EDUCATION AND PROMOTION

INTRODUCTION TO POLICY DEVELOPMENT AND IMPLEMENTATION

Scott K. Simonds

The policy section of this volume, building as it does upon the policy section of the 1986 edition, addresses four issues that call for the attention of the profession of health education, and of others involved with health education and health promotion. The four articles are entitled:

- Policy Advocacy: Three Emerging Roles for Health Education
- Continuing Education in Public Health
- Developing a Credentialing System for Health Educators
- A Marketing Research Approach to Health Education Planning

The issues raised here are ones of concern to those who prepare health educators, to those who employ them, as well as to health educators themselves functioning in community and organizational settings.

By themselves, the four articles constitute important statements about key issues in health education and promotion. As a group of four papers, they deal with substantive issues of much wider focus such as strategic planning for health education's future. The papers also direct the reader's

Advances in Health Education and Promotion, vol. 2, pages 1–4
Copyright © 1987 JAI Press Inc.
All rights of reproduction in any form reserved.
ISBN: 0-89232-617-4

attention to the state of the art in health education and raise questions about how health educators relate to each major issue.

The first article, "Policy Advocacy: Three Emerging Roles for Health Education," by Steckler, Dawson, Goodman, and Epstein, provides a useful background for the entire section as well as a focus on issues in policy advocacy itself. The authors propose a logical method of determining the scope of policy development and suggest ways health educators can relate to that general process by serving as (1) citizen participation advocates, (2) as policy analysts, and (3) as policy administrators. It suggests that these are all relatively new roles for health educators.

Placing the topic of policy advocacy within this framework, the authors demonstrate clearly that rapid changes in the political, economic, and social environment have impact on the health care system, which in turn sets the stage for new policy functions for health educators. The profession, through the Role Delineation Project, envisioned a rather significant increase in policy roles for health educators that the authors identify as harbingers of an important trend. Readers will find here not only a new view of how health educators contribute to policy development generally, but also a view of the conditions leading to improvements. Health education has not traditionally functioned in the policy arena, and it is clear from the views of Steckler et al., that movement in this direction is long overdue.

The second article, "Continuing Education in Public Health," by Stewart, provides an analysis of key issues in the development and maintenance of professional competence. It is generally accepted that the half-life of a professional curriculum is no more than five years, thus the need for professions to keep up to date is essentially a continuous process. In public health, the problems are particularly complex because many disciplines are involved.

Difficulties in dealing with credentialing, mandatory continuing education, assessment of educational needs, evaluations, and accelerating costs of continuing education are reviewed in detail by Stewart. Health educators particularly are concerned with continuing education of health professionals because frequently they are requested to plan, help implement, and evaluate continuing education programs and to participate in organizational change activities. One would anticipate, based on documentation in this article, to see increased demands on health educators to play roles as trainers in health care and public health settings.

The third article in this section entitled, "Developing a Credentialing System for Health Educators," by Henderson, focuses on one of the most pressing problems in health education, namely "quality assurance." Credentialing of health educators has been of great concern to the profession and continues to focus the energies of professional organizations in the field.

Henderson reviews the essential steps required of occupational groups en route to professionalization, and traces the steps that health education has taken to fulfill those requirements. He places this development within the larger context of how professions develop in society and the alternatives open to health education.

Of the many routes to professionalization, the author discusses credentialing as the preferred route in contrast to accreditation or registration or licensure. Henderson makes it clear that efforts must continue to be directed to quality assurance, legal and regulatory issues, and political and economic issues involved in development of the profession. He also recognizes the need for a National Commission for Certifying Health Educators to direct these efforts.

The fourth article, "A Marketing Research Approach to Health Education Planning," by DePietro, examines the increasingly significant interaction between health education and marketing within the context of health care or health service settings. While one must acknowledge the very substantial increase in attention given to marketing in hospitals and health maintenance organizations, the roles of marketing in health education and health education in marketing have not yet been clearly defined. The extensive documentation of the contribution of marketing to health services supports the point that health educators increasingly need to acquire marketing skills and be able to work creatively with individuals trained in marketing and marketing research.

The article discusses a marketing approach as essentially involving five major elements: (1) emphasis on research-based planning; (2) formal treatment of the external environment; (3) user orientation and usage situations; (4) emphasis on behavioral change; and (5) positioning in the market and price. It is likely that marketing as an analytic and planning process will be increasingly relevant to health educators working in health promotion programs.

Methods used by marketers to pretest programs and services such as focus groups, which may be more cost effective than alternative procedures used by health educators, are likely to find their way into health education practices according to DePietro. He also suggests that conjoint analysis, a technique whereby consumer preferences for programs and services having multiple attributes can be determined, will also find its way into practice.

The four papers together make major statements about health education policy in 1988—namely that:

- Policy roles for health education are expanding and gaining in importance.
- Health educators are becoming more aware of the policy dimensions of their professional roles.

- Continuing education of the public health professions recognizes a vital concern to health education and an area in which health educators can make an even greater contribution.
- Quality assurance of the health education profession requires new strategies for institutions preparing health educators and new leadership in the profession itself.
- Health education must add marketing research techniques to its professional armamentarium, particularly in the area of health promotion.

Policy development provides a way of thinking about health education within a larger framework. It focuses the reader's attention more on macrolevel issues and on those political environments in which these issues occur.

Each issue in this section is one of current concern to the field; each one represents an area where theory, research, and policy development interface.

POLICY ADVOCACY:

THREE EMERGING ROLES FOR HEALTH EDUCATION

Allan Steckler, Leonard Dawson,

Robert M. Goodman, and Nancy Epstein

POLICY-ADVOCACY ROLES FOR HEALTH EDUCATORS

In a previous article we argued that "health educators should view policy development as a unit of professional practice analogous to the individual, the small group, the community, and the organization (Steckler & Dawson, 1982). The impact of policy on other units of practice and on people served by health educators is too great and the competition for scarce resources for health and human services is too keen to be disregarded. An increasingly active role in the policy process is, therefore, vital to the profession. The previous article went on to present some key policy definitions, a model of the policy development process, and sixteen suggested policy roles for health educators. These sixteen roles are depicted in Figure 1.

The present article, which builds on the foundation laid in the prior one, is divided into four main sections. The first section contains a summary of some of the main ideas included in the first article, and focuses on the model of the policy-development process. The remaining sections, which include the main points of this chapter, discuss three additional policy roles

Advances in Health Education and Promotion, vol. 2, pages 5–27
Copyright © 1987 JAI Press Inc.
All rights of reproduction in any form reserved.
ISBN: 0-89232-617-4

Type of Involvement	Role Category	Role
Indirect Involvement		
	Source of Information	1. Identify relevant sources of information
		2. Communicate information
	Technical Assistance	3. Consultation
		4. Policy analysis
		5. Writing implementation guidelines (regulations)
Advocacy		
	Organizing	6. Citizen participation
		7. Coalitions with community and professional groups
	Influencing Policy Makers	8. Identifying influence networks
		9. Influencing policy-maker selection
		10. Direct contact with policy-makers (lobbying)
		11. Board Training
		12. Use of mass media
	Political Action	13. Referendum and initiative
Direct Involvement		14. Party politics
		15. Political appointment
		16. Public office

Figure 1. Health education policy roles.

for health educators, not emphasized in the first article: the health educator as citizen-participation advocate, as policy analyst, and as policy administrator.

Rationale for Health Education Involvement in Policy Development

The nature of health problems that professional health educators confront in their practices is changing rapidly, and as a result, the profession of health education is currently in a period of rapid development. As we move into the last decade of the twentieth century, we face problems of chronic diseases with multiple, complex and unknown causes. These diseases not only have intricate chemical and biological etiologies, but also interact with complicated behavioral, social, organizational, and political factors. To meet the challenges wrought by these and other complexities, health education as a professional field must continue to grow and develop. Particularly ripe for development are the areas of political action and policy development (Miller, 1976; Freudenberg, 1978). As members of a profession, health educators must actively endeavor to influence those policies that not only determine the kind and amount of resources allocated for health education programs, but also consider the larger policy framework under which health education is subsumed.

There is an interest among professional organizations that represent health educators for consolidation and amalgamation, partly to increase their collective political effectiveness. Also, there is a renewed prominence accorded health education as a result of the burgeoning interest in the health promotion movement. As a consequence, the health promotion bandwagon is attracting many other professional groups that enter the competition for scarce resources. Health educators therefore must include in their theoretical and practical armamentarium not only concepts of health behavior, community development, and program planning and evaluation, but also concepts of policy development and policy advocacy that reinforce and facilitate approaches consistent with sound health education principles.

We previously suggested that health educators should consider policy development as a unit of professional practice. While we continue to see policy development as a separate unit of practice, we also believe that there is a policy dimension to all levels of health education practice.

Units of Practice refer to the levels of social organization at which health education interventions are directed. Units of practice are not necessarily the social levels that are the ultimate targets of change. That is, to ultimately affect one social level, it may be necessary to actually direct a program or a part of a program at a different but related level. Units of practice are divided into the social levels of individual, family, social networks, community, organizations, and large populations. Among health education program planners it is becoming increasingly common to design interventions directed at multiple units of practice (Green et al., 1980), but it is not yet common practice to analyze and plan simultaneously for interventions at policy levels. For example, patient educators plan and implement health education interventions directed at individual patients and their families, but they rarely analyze how hospital policy affects program objectives.

The idea of health educators becoming active in policy arenas has also been suggested by other authors (Collin, 1982–3; Gottlieb, 1985; Minkler & Cox, 1980; Coreil & Levine, 1984–5). Henderson (1982) in his monograph entitled, *The Refined and Verified Role for Entry-Level Health Educators*, which is the final report of the Role Delineation Project, suggests five policy roles for health educators: "1. participates in identifying needed policy changes, 2. articulates the need for policy change to others, 3. organizes support for policy change, 4. assists in developing action plans for change, 5. provides leadership in effecting needed change." In this chapter, we build upon these roles by providing a more detailed analysis, and by delineating how these roles might be operationalized.

In an article entitiled "Training Health Educators for Social Change," Freudenberg (1978) also suggests increased training for health educators in policy action and particularly in policy analysis. The Surgeon General's report entitled *Healthy People* (1979), and the companion volume *Objectives for the Nation* (1980) lay the conceptual foundations for the health promotion and disease prevention movement. Both include substantial sections on needed policy changes. While these two documents are not directed exclusively toward health educators, they imply that health educators, as well as other health professionals, will have to become active at policy levels if the health promotion objectives are to be met.

The three policy roles for health educators suggested here, i.e., citizen participation advocate, policy analyst, and policy administrator, can be seen therefore as part of a larger movement that is attempting to increase health education involvement in policy arenas.

THE POLICY DEVELOPMENT PROCESS

"There is nothing as practical as a good theory," is an assertion usually attributed to Kurt Lewin. Theory provides a framework and direction for action; theory guides and informs action. Without theory professional actions appear as random, unconnected events—a lot of smoke but little fire. The conceptual model of the policy development process discussed below is presented as an heuristic one. It is a model developed for teaching purposes and does not represent any one reality. Rather, it is an amalgamation of many realities; that is, it depicts policy development in many different types of settings, ranging from a rural health center, to a hospital board, to a state legislature, to the United States Congress. The utility of this model is that it suggests to the health education practioner multiple avenues and arenas for influencing the development and implementation of policy, as well as providing a conceptual framework for understanding policy as process. The model (Figure 2) is presented here only in summary because it has been presented in detail elsewhere (Steckler & Dawson, 1982).

Problem Awareness and Identification

At the problem awareness and identification stage, a particular issue is brought to public attention and begins to be recognized as an important and legitimate problem that should be addressed by policy. This stage of policy development is often more political than rational, since at any given time there are usually multiple interest groups vying for attention and competing to have their "problem" recognized as the most important policy issue deserving of immediate attention. The competition for attention and recognition at this stage is often quite keen. The process of waxing and waning of issues at the problem awareness and identification stage has been termed "the issue attention cycle" (Downs, 1972).

Problem Refinement

Once recognized as a policy issue, a problem is usually stated in broad, general terms. From this broad, nonspecific statement, the problem must be refined and policy objectives must be set. The intention at the problem-refinement stage is to move from the subjective to the objective, from the irrational to the rational, and from the political to the analytical. At this stage the problem, to the extent possible, is quantified. The process of problem refinement, though analytical, can be politically charged, especially for controversial issues. Opposing groups will often present conflicting and contradictory data and interpretations that support their political philosophy and values.

Setting Policy Objectives

Once the parameters of a problem have been identified and refined, and once there is a workable consensus about the nature and extent of the problem, then policy objectives can be formulated. Policy goals and objectives are not the same as program goals and objectives. Unlike program

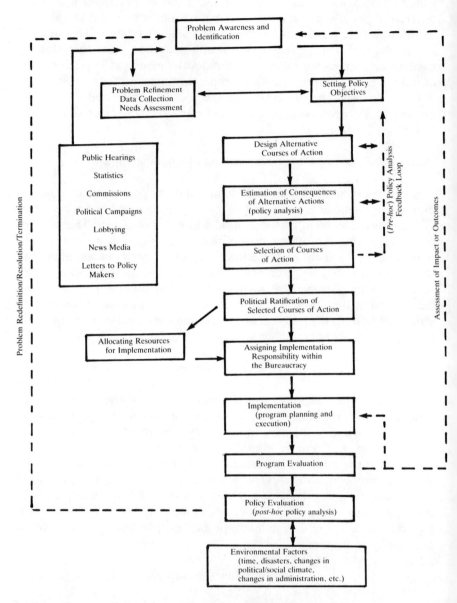

Figure 2. The policy-development process.

objectives, policy objectives are usually stated in very broad terms that are intended to satisfy as many competing groups as possible. Sometimes policy goals are purposefully vague and even contradictory because of necessary political compromises.

Designing Alternative Actions

Because of the often vague and contradictory nature of policy objectives, multiple solutions and courses of action are usually suggested. Often a lot of energy, thought, organizing and "politicking" go into the design of alternate courses of action with the hope that at least some part of recommended actions/solutions will be included eventually in the final policy and/or the subsequent implementation.

Estimating Consequences of Alternative Actions

Concurrent with, or after, the development of suggested alternative courses of action, the next stage of the policy development process is the critical examination of the various proposed programs. Such *pre hoc* policy analysis involves asking and answering certain predetermined questions about each suggested alternative to determine both intended and unintended consequences of each. The role and methods of policy analysis are discussed in greater detail in a later section of this chapter.

Selecting a Course of Action and Allocating Resources

Once the *pre hoc* policy analysis stage is completed, a specific course(s) of action is adopted, assuming that any action is taken. (It is quite conceivable, even usual, that no action is taken, and many proposals have "died" in the policy development process.) The policy-making body, after considering and debating all of the proposed courses of action and the intended and unintended effects, selects a course that is typically a compromise and amalgamation of several proposals. Once the course of action has been chosen, it generally goes through a political/administrative ratification process in which key interested and influential groups or individuals are allowed to suggest modifications. While a course of action is being finalized, resources for implementation are usually allocated.

In the resource-allocation phase, policy advocates are often willing to accept fewer resources than necessary to implement a policy fully because they feel that "half a loaf is better than none." They gamble that during the next policy cycle they will be able to return to the policy making body for additional resources for implementation. The dilemma posed by this "incremental" approach is that by the next policy cycle new problems may have arisen that are demanding attention, or a new administration is in office and the previous problem no longer commands policy makers' interest and support, and so additional resources may not be forthcoming.

Assigning Implementation Responsibility

There are two major components of implementation: the first is assignment of implementation responsibility within a bureaucracy. The second, with which health educators are most familiar, is local program development. Assignment of responsibility for policy implementation within an organization is critical for eventual programmatic success. A policy assigned to an indifferent or even hostile agency (or unit) may be worse off than never adopting it in the first place. Since policies are often purposefully vague, implementors have a great deal of latitude in developing program guidelines, regulations, and rules that are essential in determining whether and how a program is eventually implemented. After having survived the pounding waves of the policy process, many health and human service programs die on the rocks of inadequate implementation.

In the following sections, three roles are suggested that can mitigate against inadequate policy implementation, and that can enhance health educators' opportunities for influencing the policy development process. These health education roles are those of citizen participation advocate, policy analyst, and policy administrator.

THE HEALTH EDUCATOR AS CITIZEN PARTICIPATION ADVOCATE

Democracy as a Basis for Modern Citizen Participation

Health educators should not view democracy as immutable or static, but rather as a growing, changing, and developing political philosophy that embodies the values of freedom, equality and participation. What we call citizen participation has strong philosophical roots in concepts of democracy. Emphasis on citizen enfranchisement has had a major impact on health education principles and practice.

The modern concept of citizen participation has its roots in democratic ideals and theory. The word democracy joins two Greek words—*demos* and *kratein*, roughly translated as "the people" and "power," respectively. In theory, democracy means that the people have political power, but how the people get that power and how they exercise it are sometimes unclear. In modern political thought, democracy is often defined through explaining certain values that democracy is thought to embody, e.g., liberty, equality, and participation (Riker, 1982). Participation is frequently equated with democracy, the implication being that the greater the participation in political decision-making, the greater the democracy (Schaller, 1984).

The increasing enfranchisement of the American electorate is often used by political scientists to symbolize the broadening of citizen participation. Suffrage in the United States has expanded from only property-owning white males in 1789, to universal white male suffrage in 1840, to blacks in 1870, to women in 1920, and to eighteen-year-olds in 1971 (Boone, 1977). The expansion of the franchise is still continuing, the latest group embraced being the homeless.

Voting is a form of indirect political participation. It is indirect in the sense that voters select representatives who participate in policy-making on their behalf. Since the 1960s, more direct citizen participation has been required by law. Most students of citizen participation trace the beginnings of direct participation mandates to the "War on Poverty," in which poverty was believed to be due, at least in part, to inequality of access to policies that govern key social institutions such as education, employment, voting, housing, health care, and legal justice. It was believed further that ethnic and racial minorities, women, the poor, the elderly, and the rural had been systematically excluded from these institutions. To increase accessibility to these social institutions the government mandated an expanded voice for those disenfranchised groups in how agencies provide important social services.

Since 1965 the idea of direct participation of client groups in agency policy-making has grown (Checkoway, 1981). Today, almost every federally funded health program mandates some form of citizen participation (Koseki & Hayakawa, 1979; Bond & Steckler, 1985). State and locally funded health programs also often require some form of citizen participation in program policy development. Long-term trends toward broader enfranchisement and open meeting laws (sunshine laws) will tend to mitigate against efforts of the current administration to de-emphasize citizen participation.

Even though the impetus of social change historically favors an expanding role for citizens' participation in shaping agency policy, the realities of organizational dynamics and pressures brought to bear on an agency by various vested interests can weight policy decisions away from citizen concerns. Goodenough (1965) provided an organizational framework for conceiving how competion among vested interests can work against those of consumers. This framework, depicted in Figure 3, will also be used in exploring policy analysis and administrator roles.

Goodenough observed that health agencies are beholden to several constituencies that he labels "sponsoring," "target," and "entailed" publics. The sponsoring public " . . . finances the agency as an instrument for ac-

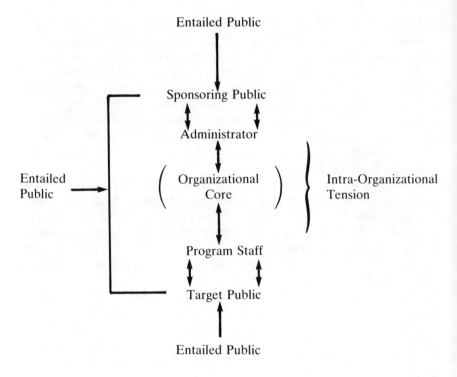

Figure 3. Interactive forces among administrators, program staff and sponsoring, entailed and target publics.

complishing certain broad objectives that it—the sponsoring public—deems good." The target public " . . . is the object of the sponsoring public's concern and of the agency's program." The entailed publics are " . . . those additional publics whose interests are liable to be affected by the agency's activities." These various publics, and their subsets, can be considered special interests with vested concerns in influencing the scope and direction of policy.

A premise of social legislation in the past twenty years holds that citizen participation generally can be enhanced by inclusion of the target public (and in some instances entailed publics) in the policy process. Goodenough notes that since agency administrators are held accountable for the success or failure of their organization, they are apt to be most responsive to the sponsoring public (funders). Considering the adverse consequences that the sponsoring public can bring to bear, policy decision-makers usually defer to fiscal and legislative pressures above all others.

Implications for Health Education

Health educators have served traditionally in the role of a linkage or interface between communities (target publics) and professionals. Health educators have also served to stretch boundaries and remove barriers between client or community groups on the one hand, and professional groups (entailed publics) and governing, fiscal and regulatory bodies (sponsoring publics) on the other hand.

The role of the health educator as citizen participation advocate within policy development arenas is an extension of the linkage role between client and professional groups. As democracy itself expands and as opportunities for direct participation increase, an important role of the health education professional is to help citizens develop the knowledge and skills necessary to gain leverage; that is, to be effective policy participants, and effective representatives of their communities. (Messinger, 1982).

It appears as if, at least in an historical sense, opportunities for citizen participation will continue to grow and that power will at least be shared with citizens, clients and consumers (target publics). But such power sharing will not come without struggle, nor without adequate preparation. The role of the health educator is to help citizens understand where, within policy development processes, opportunities for leverage exist, and then how to exploit those opportunities. The role of the health educator is not to represent client nor citizen groups in health care decision-making, but rather, first to open up the system to their participation and, secondly, to ensure that they themselves are effective participants. Community organizing theory has always included community capacity building, and leadership development skills as objectives. The concept of the health educator helping citizens enhance policy-development skills is an extension of this community organizing principle to the policy realm (Kramer & Specht, 1969).

Specifically, health educators can help citizens understand the process of policy development in the abstract, to generalize to various policy making bodies (as presented in the preceding policy development and organizational models, see Figures 2 and 3). Citizens can also be helped to understand the policy development process in relation to particular policy-making bodies. The understanding of this process should proceed from the most accessible arena that offers the fewest barriers to successful entré, to the least accessible policy arena.

Secondly, citizens can be aided in developing those skills necessary to gain access to the policy process. Skills at the problem awareness and identification stage might include how to:

1. Articulate needs and problems.
2. Gain access to sympathetic influentials or population segments for a broader support base.
3. Build coalitions with other target and entailed publics experiencing the same or similar needs.
4. Apply pressure on public officials (sponsoring publics) to gain an audience and/or to acquire endorsement/sponsorship of a needed policy.
5. Use media and other informational strategies.

Skills in relation to problem refinement might include how to:

1. Secure documentation to specify the nature and extent of the need/problem.
2. Testify before a policy group to highlight, through specific cases, the magnitude, severity, and results of a need/problem in personal/human terms.
3. Compete with groups with other or similar needs.

Skills in relation to setting policy objectives focus on achieving the target publics' policy objectives. Specifically, this might entail how to utilize professional expertise germane to each policy area. Skills related to the design of alternative actions also might entail how to utilize appropriate professionals, as well as how to articulate preferred courses of action as a function of social, cultural, or political factors, past experiences, and accessibility. Those skills related to selecting a course of action, allocating resources, and assigning implementation responsibility are similar to skills mentioned previously under problem awareness and refinement. An important point to consider at this stage in policy development is that pressure still must be brought to bear so that adequate resources are allocated, and that implementation is assigned to an empathetic unit of the bureaucracy.

There are obviously many barriers to enacting citizen influence within policy development. Most policy systems historically have not been open to direct citizen influence, consequently systems themselves present inherent barriers. But also citizens, by and large, have not actively pursued direct political participation. The desire has not been there, and there is, in many cases, the belief that "you can't fight city hall." Furthermore, if you could, it would take too much time, energy and money, commodities just not readily available. In linking citizens to the policy process, the health educator's role is, on the one hand, to help citizen groups overcome these social, psychological and economic barriers, and on the other hand, to work with citizen groups in pressuring the system for greater accessibility, participation, and balance in the overall process. Citizen participation is, after all, in the finest tradition of American democracy, as epitomized by Thomas Jefferson's assertion that:

> I know no safe depository of the ultimate powers of the society but the people them-selves; and if we think (them) not enlightened enough to exercise their control with a wholesome discretion, the remedy is not to take it from them, but to inform their discretion. (Letter to William Charles Jarvis, September 28, 1820)

THE HEALTH EDUCATOR AS POLICY ANALYST

What is Policy Analysis and Why is it Important?

Policy analysis provides valuable information and critical review of al-ternative courses of action to those policymakers responsible for adopting new policies and revising old ones. *Pre hoc* policy analysis entails an as-sessment of the alternative courses of action with regard to citizen input, costs, desired outcomes, populations to be served, and the levels of effort required to bring about the desired outcomes. *Post hoc* policy analysis examines the degree to which desired policy objectives and outcomes have been met once a policy is implemented.

Policy analysis examines the interrelated factors affecting a problem. These factors may include the causes of the problem, the extent to which different population groups are affected, and the political realities in which the problem exists (Gil, 1973). A health educator working as a policy analyst must weigh evidence that is often conflicting, and that may be provided by groups with different perspectives and varied recommenda-tions on what to do about the problem. It is important to understand as many perspectives on the problem as possible so that the analysis of al-ternative courses of action can be complete and thorough, and result in effective policies. The analysis process also includes examining-related pol-icies and services already in existence that deal with a problem, and the degree to which they are meeting the need. This approach creates the need for simultaneous *pre hoc* and *post hoc* policy analysis.

Policy analysis highlights the checks and balances of policies and pro-grams already in place, as well as those proposed for future action. It underscores further inclusion of citizen input to the development of policy options by considering factors such as availability, accessibility and ac-ceptability of services to target publics. In some cases, bureaucratic rules may be consistent with policy, but the ensuing implementation of programs falls short of adequately serving the target population and achieving the desired outcomes. Estimating the consequences of proposed courses of action enables the policy analyst to incorporate appropriate checks and balances thus ensuring that resulting programming does not deviate from addressing target public priorities (House, 1982).

In the final analysis, well-directed policy cannot assure adequate programming if insufficient resources are allocated. Resource allocation is not as much a function of tightly knit checks and balances as it is a function of the political process. This dichotomy illustrates the relationship between policy analysis and the valuing of citizen advocacy. Target publics that are skilled in politicizing their needs are more likely to influence the allocation process. Complete policy analysis, therefore, is not limited to constructing checks and balances, but also includes strategies assuring citizen competency in monitoring implementation. In a sense, the enfranchisement of the target public in keeping policy on track serves as an additional check and balance augmenting policy analysis.

Policy Analysis Roles for the Health Educator

For health educators to assume a role in policy analysis, it is not necessary to be employed as an "analyst," although such a formal position does enhance the amount of time and resources available to study a problem, and propose remedial courses of action. In the past, health educators have been predominately program-oriented rather than policy-oriented. Yet many of their skills, such as conducting community diagnoses, and developing and evaluating programs, are well suited to policy analysis. Health educators can use their skills to influence policy in a range of ways spanning from voluntary assistance to citizen groups, to working as staff members of a legislative body.

As a staff health educator one could play a policy analyst's role within an employing agency by:

1. developing a credible relationship with the agency administrator, thus enhancing the opportunities in which the administration will seek the health educator's opinion on policy issues;
2. serving on the management team of the agency, thus formalizing input into the policy analysis process;
3. interpreting policy alternatives to the agency's board;
4. serving as staff to the board with the specific objective of assisting them in sharpening their policy analysis skills;
5. providing leadership to the agency by analyzing new or existing policy for its impact upon the target public;

6. assuring that educational needs assessment data are included in
   pre hoc analyses; and
7. using program evaluation data in *post hoc* analyses, thus assuring
   that new policies (or changes in existing policy) consider the successes or failures of previous experiences.

For example, the authors are familiar with a health educator employed
by a local mental health center whose job title is "Coordinator of Prevention Services." Through her own initiative, this health educator's responsibilities include serving on the management team that formulates policy
alternatives for the agency's board of directors. In addition, she is responsible for board training, and for providing staff services to the board and
its committees. Through these activities this staff health educator has had
a significant impact on the policies of her mental health center.

In relation to the sponsoring public (see Figure 3), the policy analysis
role for health educators might include:

1. advocating to the sponsoring public the inclusion of target public
   representatives and their analyses in the policy development
   process;
2. interpreting policy options to the sponsoring public;
3. communicating program evaluation data to aid the sponsoring
   public in selecting appropriate policy alternatives; and
4. interpreting consequences of existing policy, or proposed policy,
   on the program, target, and other competing publics.

In reference to the entailed publics (see Figure 3), a health educator's
actions might include:

1. raising professionals' awareness of the value of policy analyses;
2. organizing a group of professionals who would be available to
   participate in policy analyses in appropriate areas; and
3. coordinating leadership among professional groups so that they
   may stay abreast of policy issues.

The target public offers numerous opportunities to the health educator
to function in the role of policy analyst:

1. promoting target public awareness of the need for its participation
   in policy analysis;
2. assisting the target public in acquiring the skills necessary to do
   policy analysis;

3. helping the target public focus on the consequences of policy alternatives upon those affected;
4. promoting target public self-advocacy for participation in policy analyses within the agency/program, and with the sponsoring and entailed publics ensuring that its views are adequately considered in weighing policy alternatives; and
5. promoting target public self-advocacy for resource allocation.

The "bottom line" for the target public is embodied in the following analysis questions:

- Are our needs being addressed?
- Are they being addressed adequately?
- Are policy alternatives viewed from the perspective of the target public to assure availability of, accessibility to, and acceptability of allocated resources?

Clearly, the above roles are not exhaustive, and overlap one another. They are intended to illustrate that it is neither necessary to have a job title of policy analyst, nor to work for an organization whose primary mission is policy analysis, to perform policy analysis roles. Rather, these roles can be operationalized in a variety of ways and settings if the health educator conceptualizes policy analysis as a legitimate professional role.

While it is not the most typical occurrence, health educators do function as analysts for policy-making bodies. The authors know of two health educators who worked for the Texas state legislature. One was an analyst for the Senate Interim Committee on Hunger and Nutrition, and the other was with the Joint Committee on Autism. In each case the health educator conducted a policy analysis that became the basis for legislation (Epstein, 1984; Untermeyer, 1982).

Another example involves a health educator who is the primary staff person to the North Carolina Senate Sub-Committee on Health. His responsibility is to provide staff services to this subcommittee, and to coordinate analyses of health issues under subcommittee consideration. A third example of a health educator functioning in a policy-analysis position involves a professional who served as health analyst in the Office of the Governor of North Carolina. In that capacity his role was to advise the governor on health issues in the state and to provide him with background information, policy alternatives, and position papers related to health issues under consideration.

THE HEALTH EDUCATOR AS POLICY ADMINISTRATOR

This section provides a theoretical, philosophical, and practical rationale for examining an often overlooked policy role for the health educator: that of administrator. Parlette et al. (1981) cite surveys tracking the careers of health education graduates from the School of Public Health, University of California, Berkeley that indicate that over 50 percent of those graduating before 1965 now hold administrative positions. Agency administrators play a pivotal role in the policy process. Administrators are responsible for planning and guiding program implementation, which in a sense is the final stage of the policy development process (see Figure 2). Moreover, they are frequently sought for input on policy matters by other administrators, by funding sources, and by vested interest groups.

It is our contention that one way for health educators to become policy actors is in the role of agency/program administrator. It is from this vantage point that health educators gain more influence in opening organizations to meaningful citizen involvement in the policy process. In essence, the health educator as administrator is in a unique position to have an impact on policy that other roles do not provide. But to appreciate better how the health educator/administrator can best accomplish this, an overview of factors affecting organizational leadership is presented below.

Factors Affecting Organizational Leadership

Theorists of organizational leadership commonly emphasize the pivotal role administrators play in shaping and influencing organizational culture. Methods of influence include promotion of organizational values, resolving ethical issues for the agency, invoking symbols, and managing environmental conditions both internal and external to the organization (Burns & Becker, 1983). Administrator characteristics that have been studied with reference to organizational innovation include administrator ideology, referent groups for professional ideas, propensity toward activism in support of agency goals, political orientation, age, and agency tenure (Becker, 1969; Mohr, 1966; Mytinger, 1968).

Administrator disposition (attitude) is one of the most critical determinants of how hospitable an organization is to any given program, and the likely direction that program will take (Gentry et al., 1970). This is true particularly for nontraditional and innovative programming.

Administrator disposition in shaping organizational culture and program direction is complicated further by environmental influences on the administrator. As noted earlier, Goodenough observes that the administrator is most responsive to fiscal and legislative pressure of the sponsoring public.

In contrast, line-staff operating agency programs often form empathy and allegiance toward the target public whom they serve. The dichotomy between administrator and staff creates intra-organizational tension, further exacerbated by the lobbying efforts of various entailed publics (vested professional interests). These relationships are depicted in Figure 3.

It is the administrator's role to maintain a balance between the sponsoring public's expectations for the fiscal solvency and survival of the organization on the one hand, and the target public's needs for services on the other hand. It is often the staff's desire to maximize agency locus of decision-making to target public needs. When "push comes to shove," the administrator is likely to favor decision-making toward sponsoring public desires, often to the chagrin of line-staff, since they fund the agency. Both administrator and staff often believe they are serving the agency's best interests and often find it difficult to appreciate the pressures influencing the other's point of view.

An additional factor that complicates administrator dynamics is the increasingly complex and uncertain environment enveloping public health programming. Contributing factors include the proliferation of health-related agencies and health professions, regulations, funding mechanisms and interest groups, and the predominance of environmental, social and behaviorally related health pathologies requiring costly technological solutions. Environmental complexity and uncertainty of solutions have blurred the lines among publics and have increased competition among vested interests, making it more difficult for the administrator to manage. It is our contention that the well-trained health educator is vested with both a professional ethic and skills that are required to manage creatively the various publics and agency staff, thus enriching the policy process of the agency.

Implications for Health Education

Because the health educator is invested with a professional ethic that stresses a community-oriented perspective, those health educators who successfully move into administrative roles not only gain greater access to organizational resources that can insure community based programming, but also situate themselves in a position to shift organizational culture toward a greater emphasis on a community-directed perspective. This is not to say that the health-educator-turned-policy-administrator can ignore the desires of sponsoring (funders) and entailed publics (vested interests). But empowerment as a policy actor means that the educator can exert more of a countervailing professional attitude by promoting a different perspective.

There are a number of avenues available to the administrator that can aid an organizational shift toward a greater community orientation. This is accomplished through the policy process by skillfully balancing the various agendas of the various publics and agency staff. Most health and human services agencies are governed by a board that has responsibility for developing policies within which that agency operates, and the administrator is charged with the implementation of the policies that the board adopts. The administrator must help the board analyze proposed policies, and their likely impact upon the survival of the agency client groups. He must guide the board in developing policies that will facilitate the acquisition of adequate resources for employing competent professional personnel to provide the organization's services effectively.

Policies of external funding sources (sponsoring publics) must be adequately interpreted to the board in terms of their compatibility with existing agency policies and goals. Policies related to agency function and structure must be analyzed and perhaps changed due to the policies of the funders.

Policies of the board must be interpreted to agency staff to achieve their compliance. Likewise agency policies must be interpreted correctly and fully to the entailed public (interest groups) and the target public (clients). This can be accomplished best by creating an open system for policy development, whereby the agency seeks the input of all affected groups in policy formulation.

Responsibilities to the funders include not only communicating program evaluation results, but helping them understand where and why successful implementation of their policies occurred, and where changes should be considered. The funders also need to be aware of the clients' perceptions of effects, and their level of satisfaction with policy implementation. The administrator can play a key role in guaranteeing that effective communication occurs between these two groups. To facilitate this, the administrator might help client groups acquire skills in

1. articulating their needs and priorities;
2. organizing and mobilizing;
3. building coalitions with other target publics; and
4. analyzing policy.

Client groups can also be aided in developing an understanding of

1. the policy process and how to access it;
2. the nature of competition in formulating policy priorities;
3. trade-offs that occur in the policy process; and
4. strategies for competing in advocating their needs and concerns to increase their influence and power base.

The administrator as an actor in the policy arena must also manage the vested interest groups that are composed of other agency administrators and professional groups. Such management requires buffering the entailed public's various agendas with those of the other publics by

1. assuring a mutual understanding of the policies and goals of respective agencies;
2. effecting coordinated planning and programming for shared client groups;
3. assuring mutual access to respective agency policy processes;
4. minimizing competition through coordinated endeavors when priorities are directed at the same target groups; and
5. training the entailed publics to increase their understanding, skills and commitment to mutually beneficial policies.

Finally, the administrator must buffer line-staff affinities for client group priorities with those espoused by funders and vested interests. This is accomplished by an open-administration style that communicates to staff the extents and constraints of the agency when translating policy into program implementation. At the same time the administrator needs to buffer those special interests that can compromise program effectiveness at the expense of the target public by insuring that policy development and implementation does not veer from its expressed purposes.

CONCLUSION

ealth educators traditionally have not been trained to envision a role in the policy process. While many of the philosophical perspectives, social values and change agent skills inculcated in health education training are germane to the policy process, the application of those virtues has been directed at effecting cognitive, affective, and behavioral changes rather than at policy processes. This is partially a consequence of professional vision, but also is a result of imposed political and organizational constraints. While we acknowledge these factors as common conditions, they serve as a starting point for the health educator interested in making an impact on agency policy. These common constraints contribute to developing a perspective of the organization that is political in tone and strategic in approach. The basis upon which the creative and dynamic health educator can surmount such obstacles once identified and analyzed is inherent in the educator's training and professional development.

The professional health educator is distinctly qualified to be an effective actor in the policy arena. The three roles explicated above are a means toward realizing that goal. The role of citizen participation advocate with the objective of empowerment of citizens to have a greater and more effective influence on the policy process is a logical transition for the professional health educator. It is a role that is congruent with many of the existing professional values inherent in community development, and the mobilization of citizens for greater capacity building. In the health field, health educators are distinctive in their orientation to participatory planning. The extension of this orientation to the policy process is a small one conceptually, but a large one for professional practice.

Incorporating policy analysis among the health educator's professional roles is again a logical transition. Health educators can enhance their credibility and effectiveness through the application of planning, community diagnosis (including needs assessment), and evaluation skills in the policy arena. When those skills are also applied to target publics they facilitate capacity building of citizens. The roles of policy analyst and citizen participation advocate are then mutually reinforcing and drive each other for greater impact on the policy process.

Similarly, health educators functioning in an administrative role are in a formal position to shape both the structure and function of the agency/program and also the wider, increasingly more complex, environmental milieu in which health organizations operate. They can also shape the nature and extent of the organizational response to the acceleration of technological innovation, to new organizational arrangements, to rapidly changing health conditions, and to shifting constituencies. Balancing the various publics can be orchestrated to create an open system of policy development, and the health services driven by those policies. Perhaps most importantly, the application of a behavioral, social and political paradigm to the health policy agenda can result in greater mutual benefits to the competing publics through creative and innovative policy responses.

In summary, the three roles posited for increasing health education involvement in the policy process are intertwined and mutually reinforcing. They do not require a new model for the professional training of health educators, but rather a higher vision of professional practice. The risks are no greater in the policy arena, but the potential payoffs are of a much greater magnitude than can ever be realized from practice of lesser vision.

REFERENCES

Becker, M. H. (1969). Predictors of innovative behavior among local health officers. *Public Health Reports, 84*, Dec., 1063–1068.

Bond, B. A., Steckler, A. (1985–1986). Effects of the federal risk reduction education grants on state health education units," *International Quarterly of Community Health Education*, 6:1, 31–43.

Boone, R.C. (1977). *American government*. New York: Barnes and Noble Books. pp. 61–62.

Burns, L. R., & Becker, S.W. (1983). "Leadership and decision-making." In S.M. Shortell, & A.D. Kaluzny (Eds.) *Health care management: A text in organizational theory and behavior*. New York: John Wiley and Sons.

Checkoway, B. (Ed.) (1981). *Citizens and health care: Participation and planning for social change*. New York: Pergamon Press.

Collin, D. F. (1982–83). Health educators: Change agents or techno/peasants? *International Quarterly of Community Health Education, 3:2*, 131–144.

Coreil, J., & Levine, J. S. (1984–85). A critique of the life style concept in public health education. *International Quarterly of Community Health Education, 5:2*, 103–114.

Crawford, R. (1977). You are dangerous to your health: The ideology and politics of victim blaming. *International Journal of Health Services, 7:4*, 663–680.

Downs, A. (1972). Up and down with ecology: The issue attention cycle. *The Public Interest, 28*, 38–50.

Epstein, N. (1984). *Faces of hunger in the shadow of plenty*. Senate Interim Committee Report on Hunger and Nutrition to the Texas Legislature.

Freudenberg, N. (Winter, 1978). Shaping the future of health education: From behavior change to social change. *Health Education Monographs, 6:4*, 372–377.

Gentry, J. T., Kaluzny, A. D., Glasser, J. H., and Sprague, J. B. (1970). Perceptual differences of administrators regarding the implementation of health service programs. *American Journal of Public Health, 60*, 1006–1017.

Gil, D. G. (1973). *Unraveling social policy*. Cambridge, MA: Schenkman Publishing Co.

Goodenough, W. H. (1965). Agency structure as a major source of human problems in the conduct of public health programs. *American Journal of Public Health, 55*, 1067–1074.

Gottlieb, B. H. (Spring, 1985). Social networks and social support: An overview of research, practice, and policy implications. *Health Education Quarterly, 12:1*, 5–22.

Green, L. W., Kreuter, M. W., Deeds, S. G., & Partridge, K. B. (1980). *Health education planning: A diagnostic approach*. Palo Alto: Mayfield.

Henderson, A.C. (1982). The refined and verified role for entry-level health educators. *The Eta Sigma Gamma Monograph Series, 1:1*.

House, P. W. (1982). *The art of public policy analysis*. Beverly Hills: Sage.

Koseki, L. K., & Hayakawa, J.M. (1979). Consumer participation and community organization practice: Implications of national health legislation. *Medical Care, 17:3*, 244–254.

Kramer, R. M., & Specht, H. (Eds.) (1969). *Readings in community organization practice*. Englewood Cliffs, NJ: Prentice-Hall.

Messinger, R.W. (1982). Empowerment: A social worker's politics. In Mahaffey, M., & Hanks, J. W. (Eds.), *Practical politics: Social work and political responsibility*. Silver Springs: National Association of Social Workers.

Miller, C.A. (October, 1976). New demands for health education. Paper presented before the *Society for Public Health Education*, (unpublished).

Minkler, M., & Cox, K. (1980). Creating critical consciousness in health: Application of Freire's philosophy and method to the health care setting. *International Journal of Health Services, 10:2*, 311–322.

Mohr, L. B. (1966). *Determinants of innovation in organizations*, Ph.D. Dissertation, University of Michigan, Ann Arbor.

Mytinger, R.E. (1968). *Innovations in Local Health Service*, PHS Public. No. 1664.2, Washington, DC: Government Printing Office.

Parlette, N., Glogow, E., & D'Onofrio, C. (1981). Public health administration and health education training need more integration. *Health Education Quarterly, 8*, 123–146.

Riker, W. (1982). *Liberalism Against Populism*. San Francisco: W. H. Freeman & Co.

Schaller, S. M. (1984). *The people disassembled*. Masters Thesis, University of North Carolina, Chapel Hill, NC.

Steckler, A., & Dawson, L. (Winter, 1982). The role of health education in public policy development. *Health Education Quarterly, 9*, 275–292.

Untermeyer, E. (1982). *Autism an intricate dilemma*. Joint Committee on Autism Report to the Texas Legislature.

U.S. Department of Health, Education and Welfare, Public Health Services (1979). *Healthy people: The surgeon general's report on health promotion and disease prevention*. Washington, D.C: U.S. Government Printing Office.

U.S. Department of Health and Human Services, Public Health Services (1980). *Promoting health/preventing disease: Objectives for the nation*. Washington, DC: U.S. Government Printing Office.

CONTINUING EDUCATION IN PUBLIC HEALTH

Cynthia J. Stewart

INTRODUCTION

Health care in the United States is undergoing tremendous change in response to ever-expanding knowledge, new technologies emerging from this new knowledge, new occupations arising to apply the new technology, and new organizational systems (Begun, 1985; Houle, 1980; Scott & Lammers, 1985). In addition, the by-products of new technologies, such as toxic substances and hazardous wastes, have added to the complexities. Concurrently, there is a growing concern about keeping professionals up-to-date and competent in their practice in the face of these changes. As a result, continuing professional education has become a focus of public interest and professional concern. For some professionals, continuing education is mandated by state law. Guiding these developments is the view, held by many, that continuing education is a mechanism for quality assurance of health care (Suter et al., 1981).

Much of the literature addressing continuing education in health care speaks to the issues and concerns of professionals involved in direct patient

Advances in Health Education and Promotion, vol. 2, pages 29–58
ISBN: 0-89232-617-4

care. However, public health is concerned not only with the health of individuals, but also with the health of populations. To accomplish the tasks of disease control, prevention of disease and disability, and enhancement of health, public health enlists a diverse group of occupations and professions from within the health care field and from fields outside of health. The breadth of public health concerns, the diversity of public health workers, and the changes occurring in health care present challenges to those responsible for continuing education of public health professionals. Knowledge about the concepts and issues in continuing education, about continuing professional education developments in those professions from which public health draws, and about what is happening in public health is essential in meeting the challenges. This review looks at some of the general issues in continuing education, some specific issues confronting the health professions and public health, and the role of the public health educator as a key professional in the provision of educational services.

Day-to-day pressures may require the health educator to respond to administrative requests for staff in-service education, to organizational commitments to provide continuing education for practitioners outside the organization, to administrative directives to use continuing education programs for income generation, or to practitioner requests for educational activities that satisfy their particular interests and goals. How one deals with these requests is shaped by specific contexts. However, several principles and processes have been enunciated in the literature concerning continuing education that can strengthen whatever activity is undertaken. There are many decisions that must be made: Who is to be reached? How are their needs to be determined? What are the relevant outcomes to be achieved? Who is to make these decisions? Who should do the instruction using what methods? Who should evaluate the activity using what methodology? And what are the costs involved and how will they be met? These crucial decisions rest on a bedrock of other concerns about continuing education and adult education in general. Although these general concerns may not be an explicit part of day-to-day activities, they shape how we think about continuing education and, more importantly, what we do about it.

CONTINUING PROFESSIONAL EDUCATION

Overview

Continuing education, of which continuing professional education is a part, goes by many names—adult education, lifelong learning, inservice education, recurrent education and, more recently, human resource development (Stubblefield, 1981; Knowles, 1980). Concomitant with the multiple labels, there are multiple definitions. Cross (1981) cites 17 descriptions or definitions of lifelong learning, noting that it is "variously described as a slogan, a process, a set of activities, a conceptual framework, a rallying cry, and a philosophy of education" (p. 253).

Boissoneau (1980) notes that there is no generally accepted definition of continuing education, although this may change in the future. In 1984 the Council on the Continuing Education Unit published the *Principles of Good Practice in Continuing Education* with the hope that the principles would be widely accepted both by providers and consumers of continuing education services.[1] In that document, continuing education is defined as

> formal education programs/activities for professional development and training, or for credentialing, for which academic credit is not awarded, or of personal interest to the learner, for which academic credit is not awarded (p. 7).

This definition deals with the formal relationships between the educator and the learner and excludes informal self-learning, the most common form of adult learning (Cross, 1981; Houle, 1980). On the other hand, the definition of continuing education for health care professionals by Suter et al. (1981) not only encompasses formal and informal education/learning, but also includes the outcome to be achieved through continuing education:

> . . . processes aimed at the improvement of health care outcomes through learning either by individual efforts or as a part of CE provider unit developed activities, products, and services. Learning may result in the maintenance or enhancement of professional competence and performance or in health care organizational effectiveness and efficiency (p. 691).

The strength of this definition is the incorporation of outcomes. However, both definitions have limitations. The one given by the Council on the Continuing Education Unit deals only with formal programs, is limited to nonacademic credit activities, and is silent on the outcomes being sought other than professional development and training. The definition does recognize multiple reasons why individuals may seek continuing education and provides some structure to the range of activities subsumed under the term "continuing education."

The Suter et al. (1981) definition includes both formal and informal learning activities focused on professional competence and performance. It is silent on whether or not academic credit is awarded for the activities. This definition places stress on individual and organizational outcomes, which in public health, may be difficult to specify.

For purposes of this review, continuing education will be defined as *those activities formally organized by a continuing education provider for the purpose of developing and enhancing professional competence and per-*

formance. This definition does not address who bears the responsibility for continuing education. Houle (1980) emphasizes that continuing education, to be continuing, must be self-directed. This clearly places responsibility for continuing education on the learner-cum-professional. At the same time there must be opportunities for education that include structured learning activities. Here, questions about the adult learner become important. Why and how do adults learn? What motivates their learning?

Theoretical Foundations

Cross (1981) has noted that "one of the most underutilized vehicles for understanding various aspects of adult learning is theory" (p. 109). Others have found little agreement among learning theorists about the major components of their respective theories and scant research on the linkages between learner characteristics and learning outcomes (Pennington et al., 1984). However, there are principles that have gained acceptance:

- Adults can learn and are motivated to continue their learning.
- The motivation to learn is derived from the immediate or current situation.
- The learning sought is that which is directly applicable to what it is they are doing.
- Participation and learning are strongly influenced by an individual's past experience.
- Efforts to improve the conditions of learning can influence the outcomes of continuing education. (Knowles, 1980; Cross, 1981; Pennington et al., 1984).

Although motivation to continue learning is posited as a professional attribute, some scholars note that individuals must be taught how to continue their learning and encouraged to do so (Pennington et al., 1984). Cordes (1984), concerned with the motivational factors involved in health professional continuing education behavior, describes four models that he believes to be of value for those concerned with continuing professional education:

1. The Boshier Model where the congruence between the learner's self-concept and key aspects of the environment determines participation in CE;
2. The Dubin and Cohen Model, a systems model, where multiple factors operate to lead the professional to update knowledge and skills;
3. The Cross Model, COR (chain-of-response), where participation

in CE involves a sequence of linkages and a chain of responses beginning with self-evaluation and ending in participation; and

4. The Mager-Pipe Model, where there is an analysis of what is and what should be, and, if there is a performance discrepancy, determining its importance, why it exists, and then taking the appropriate action.

All the application models "emphasize the importance of attending to what the learner values. In day-to-day practice of CE, this requires identifying what learners value . . . and, in turn, designing ways of providing what learners value" (Cordes, 1984, p. 68).

It is clear that there is consensus that continuing education for adults must be learner-oriented rather than teacher-oriented, that the learner bears responsibility for his/her own learning, and that the education sought is a process that is learner- and problem-centered and application-oriented. However, the goals of continuing education may reflect a complex set of factors that determine how the problems become defined.

The Goals of Continuing Education

Continuing education is viewed as an integral part of being a professional (Houle, 1980) and imperative for maintenance of professional competence (Boissoneau, 1980). The need for continuing education is rooted in the rapid expansion of knowledge and technology that is altering the content and context of professional practice. Concurrently, emerging new occupational groups use continuing education as one of the ways to establish, maintain and strengthen professional standing (Houle, 1980). In addition, several other goals of continuing education have been put forth.

Houle's (1980) model of professional education has a lifespan orientation that emphasizes continuing education following specialized education and certification of competence. At this time, continuing education can be undertaken for several purposes: maintenance and modernization of basic professional abilities, preparation for change in career lines, induction into new responsibilities, or refresher training (Houle, 1980). These purposes address maintenance and development of competence, but do not include explicitly the expectation of improved health care outcomes.

Suter et al. (1981), on the other hand, see the aim of continuing education as the improvement of health care outcomes, with learning resulting in maintenance or enhancement of professional competence or organizational effectiveness and efficiency. However, others argue that delivering continuing education that ensures improved patient care is not the responsibility of educators or education alone, noting the responsibility of the profession as well as the range of other variables that affect patient care, e.g., organizational and social policies, funding, and inadequacies of measurement (Caplan, 1983a; Chambers & Hamilton 1981). The Council on the Continuing Education Unit (1984) takes an eclectic position, stating that

> A generally accepted purpose of continuing education programs/activities is to help maintain, expand, and improve individual knowledge, skills (performance), and attitude and, by so doing, equally meet the improvement and advancement of individuals, professions, and organizations (p. 3).

Thus multiple constituencies have a stake in continuing education and purposes may vary, depending on the particular set of actors. However, there is agreement that competence, for whatever goal is being sought, is the central purpose of continuing education.

Competence

Competence, as a subject, contains its own set of issues—how to define it, how to measure it and how to ensure it. The three major sources of influence on professional competence are: (1) the profession, through accreditation, licensure, and/or certification, and training programs; (2) society, through governmental policies aimed at cost containment and quality assurance, malpractice litigation, increased consumer interest in and knowledge about health and disease, and consumer demands for greater involvement in health care activities; and (3) research and development, through technological advances in how medicine is practiced and research on health care outcome measures and quality assurance (Neufeld, 1985a). However, multiple concepts of competence exist. For example, competence is seen as a quality or state of being according to one perspective (Lane et al., 1983; Short, 1984) and as attributes (knowledge, skills, attitudes, and judgement) needed to function as a professional by another (Suter et al., 1981; Norman, 1985). In addition, competence is seen as being determined by the situation in which practice is performed (Gross, 1983; LaDuca, 1980).

This multidimensional nature of competence, with its meaning shaped by the context of practice, presents challenges when attempting to measure it. Norman (1985) and Levine (1978) review the strengths and limitations, including reliability and validity, of the following methods: examinations— oral and written, direct observation, simulations—written and computer, record review, global rating scales, and rating forms/scales of activities or performance. Both conclude that no one method is adequate to measure all dimensions of competence, either because of biases inherent in the method or as a result of its limited focus. In addition, there is the issue of test-taking competence influencing the measure of professional competence

(Middleman, 1984). Given the advantages and limitations of each method, the one(s) selected should be dictated by the purpose(s) of the evaluation. Benner (1982), pointing out that practice is more complex than that which our current test methodology can measure, cautions against defining practice downward to the capabilities of our measurement tools.

Although there is much discussion of competence and its measurement, Pottinger & Goldsmith (1979) note "some consensus . . . about several important aspects of the concept [competence]: that it is desirable, that it can be taught, that it can be measured, and that it is rarely the true basis of teaching, learning assessment, accreditation, certification, or job access" (pp. vii–viii). If this is the case, what part does formal and continuing education play?

Preparation for initial competence is the function assigned to professional programs in higher education. Academic credentials are usually requisite for licensure and/or certification and, in some fields, the only requirement for employment. However, academic credentials do not predict practice performance (Pottinger, 1979; Hogan, 1979a; Gross, 1984). One reason for this has been attributed to the emphasis on development of cognitive skills with relative neglect of affective and behavioral competence (Hogan, 1979b). This is a particularly salient criticism if student selection criteria are geared primarily to evaluation of those competencies that predict academic success rather than practice success (see, for example, Berner & Bender, 1978).

Others have expressed doubts about educational institutions either being able to measure or to foster competence (Peterson, 1977; Short, 1984). Further, there are the problems of educational differentiation in competence levels, that is, undergraduate, graduate and continuing education, with different components of competence emphasized at each level (Neufeld, 1985b). Compounding educational differentiation are performance differences between novice and experienced practitioners, because through experience actions become much more situationally defined (Benner, 1982). Consistent with this Peterson (1977) argues that:

> . . . certification of competence occurs on-the-job and after a predetermined amount of experience has been accumulated. Consequently, a terminal academic degree does not imply possession of competence. Educational institutions provide only educational experiences which allow individuals to master the knowledge and essential skills (attainments), required for entry into the profession (p. 9).

Despite such doubts, the focus on competence has led to the development of competency-based education/learning designed to achieve specific performance outcomes. Nursing educators have found that competency-based learning seems to have merit (Scott, 1982). Del Bueno et al. (1981) successfully tested a competency-based education model that emphasized outcomes, used self-directed learning activities, allowed both time and flexibility for achievement of outcomes, used the teacher as a facilitator/resource, and assessed both learning styles and previous learning.

To be able to implement effectively a competency-based (Benner, 1982) or attainment-based (Peterson, 1981) learning model several prerequisites have been identified:

1. Identification of competencies in specific roles or definition of behaviors and products that relate to specific goals or outcomes;
2. Establishment of minimum performance levels;
3. Valid and reliable assessment techniques to measure the degree of attainment or to predict competent performance in actual practice situations;
4. A flexible, efficient, and adequately funded instructional delivery system that enables students to achieve the desired outcomes; and
5. Faculty who have the knowledge and skills to perform more specialized roles in the teaching/learning process.

These prerequisites also can serve as limitations to competency-based education. Benner (1982), writing about nursing, notes: (1) the existence of few well-defined behavior domains and outcomes[2]; (2) confusion between attainment objectives (skill objectives without consideration of specific goals, contexts, and outcomes) and competency statements (actual performance in specific roles); (3) problems with the predictive validity of certain measurements; (4) difficulty in testing some of the dimensions of competence thought to be important; (5) lack of guidelines for determining the relative importance of task categories generated through job-function analyses; and (6) inability of task components to lead to evaluation of total performance in relation to the demands of the job situation (pp. 305–306).

Competence in total performance in the job situation and the role of education are extremely important issues for those concerned with continuing education, especially in determination of educational needs and interventions. There is a need to understand not only what professionals bring into their practice from formal programs of preparation, but also what the setting demands of the practitioners, what they learn from it, and how they learn it. Houle (1980) and Schön (1983) are concerned with the nature and source of practice knowledge, or the art of practice. Houle attributes this source to introspection and Schön attributes it to "reflection-in-action." Introspection, according to Houle, has not been fully recognized for its educational importance. This kind of learning occurs in response to uncertainty about how to handle a problem, or to failure, or to development of an habitual detached viewpoint on one's work and conceptions and, from that perspective, examination of the uniqueness of each case dealt with, however routine it might originally appear to be (Houle, 1980, p. 5). This introspection is basic to self-monitoring, the refinement of technique, and problem solving, and takes the practitioner "as close to mastery of the profession as it is possible for him or her to get" (Houle, 1980, p. 210).

Schön (1983) is concerned with the "artful practice of the unique case." He believes that because professional knowledge and competence are modeled in terms of application of established techniques to recurrent events (p. 19) they are

> ... mismatched to the changing character of the situations of practice—the complexity, uncertainty, instability, uniqueness, and value conflicts which are increasingly perceived as central to the world of professional practice (p. 14).

The ability to *set* problems and to choose among competing paradigms of practice for dealing with them constitutes for Schön the core of professional competence. This ability is derived from knowledge gained from practice and, in the absence of a systematic understanding or recognition of the realm of practice and the knowledge that it generates, the definition of competence is incomplete, and remains a fundamental issue in professional education.

The definition and measurement of competence and the problems these present to education are also basic issues surrounding certification and assurance of continuing competence after completion of an academic program. It is in this arena that their importance to continuing education is most apparent and pressing.

Licensure and Certification

Formal educational programs, through the awarding of academic credentials, play an important role in the certification of practitioner competence since academic credentials are usually required for licensure and certification. Licensure and certification, in turn, are the major mechanisms the professions employ to certify practitioner competence.[3] However, scholars have noted that licensure and certification do more for the profession than for assurance of practitioner competence (Collins, 1979; Jago, 1984; Gross, 1984; Gaumer, 1984).

Licensing, based on law, sets minimum levels of competency and serves as a basis for making predictions about future behavior (Shimberg, 1983). Certification restricts the use of a title to those who have met the standards of the certifying body, a governmental body or voluntary organization. Although current systems of regulation have not effectively controlled initial or subsequent competence of professionals (Gross, 1984; Gaumer,

1984), the concern for continuing competence has led to much discussion of and some action to require relicensure and recertification (Shimberg, 1983; Gross, 1984). Relicensure and recertification of practitioners as ways to ensure competence are being criticized on the grounds that:

> ... The same types of instruments used for the initial certification are now being used (in the absence of anything better) for recertification ... these tools have not yet been demonstrated to possess adequate validity for certification ... [and] it is highly doubtful from a methodological point of view whether we are ready for [recertification] (Neu-feld, 1985a, p. 11).

Gaumer (1984) believes that, because of the lack of reliable credentialing methods as well as problems created by professional specialization and concurrent obsolescence, "the only demonstrably reliable way to monitor continued competence and remedy deficiencies is through the use of 'output monitoring' and corresponding deficiency-oriented training" (p. 407). However, Gross (1984) notes that "monitoring of continued competence has not progressed beyond the questionable mandating of continuing ed-ucation" (p. 155).

Mandatory continuing education, the most common basis for recreden-tialing, has been characterized as big business, generating income for in-dependent consultants, businesses, universities, and professional associations and as the least threatening and least anxiety-producing type of regulation (Gray, 1984). The most basic issue, however, is the relation-ship of continuing education to professional competence. That continuing education has a positive impact on professional practice is subject to doubt (Shimberg, 1977; Houle, 1980; Tugwell & Dok, 1985; Gaumer, 1984; Gray, 1984) and there are second thoughts about the cost-benefit of mandating such participation (Edwards & Green, 1983). Hogan (1979b) has recom-mended that relicensure should only be concerned with whether or not an individual is competent to practice; how individuals maintained their com-petence should not be the concern of licensing boards (p. 375).

Although Bertram and Brooks-Bertram's (1977) influential review of the literature on evaluation of continuing medical education (CME) did not clearly demonstrate the effectiveness of CME, in part owing to method-ological weaknesses of the evaluations, subsequent work has found a pos-itive impact (Lloyd & Abrahamson, 1979; Stein, 1981; Davis et al., 1984; Haynes et al., 1984). Davis et al. (1984) also found some positive effect on patient outcomes, although these findings were inconsistent or often statistically insignificant. Gosnell (1984) found that evaluation studies in continuing nursing education gave minimal support for any relationship between continuing education, professional practice, and patient out-comes, but that there was evidence of gains in measurable cognitive learn-ing and positive opinions.

The major work on linking continuing education to outcomes has been done in medicine, but the need for more research has been identified, since CME is "the only link between health care research on the one hand, and health care outcomes on the other" (Davis et al., 1984, p. 281). A paucity of evaluative research in continuing education has been noted in other health fields, e.g., nursing (Oliver, 1984; Greaves & Loquist, 1983), and dentistry (Chapko et al., 1984). The lack of a clear and compelling demonstration of the relationship between continuing education and improved practitioner performance or competence has not been attributed to a failure of continuing education, but to the failure of educational designs or evaluations (Suter et al., 1984). To clarify the issue of efficacy, those who design and evaluate continuing education activities must assume greater responsibility and encourage, if not conduct, relevant research efforts.

CONTINUING PROFESSIONAL EDUCATION IN PUBLIC HEALTH

Continuing professional education in public health faces special challenges for the goals of public health are often articulated in terms of health rather than disease. The lack of agreement on the definition of health makes determination of practitioner performance competence levels difficult, if not impossible (Gross, 1984). Further, many public health professions, organizations and institutions change activities in response to changing technology and social values (Sheps, 1976). The literature on continuing education for public health personnel is scant and the amount of continuing education available to them is difficult to determine. In fact, defining the role boundaries of public health personnel is problematic because of the uncertain boundaries to public health itself, the lack of consistent, discrete definitions of the public health occupational categories, the lack of credentialing requirements, the variation in public health jobs, and the diversity of educational and training institutions (U.S. Department of Health and Human Services, 1983).

Who to include in the public health target population for continuing education is a major concern. The American Public Health Association lists 72 occupations plus an "other" category from which members identify themselves. These occupations include the natural sciences, social sciences, health professions, non-health professions, and technical occupations. The U.S. Department of Health and Human Services 1982 report on public health personnel identified a primary and secondary public health workforce. The primary public health workforce, those who perform public health functions full time or work for public health agencies, was estimated at about 250,000 and included 17 categories of personnel containing several professions/occupations, e.g., epidemiology, health statistics, health education, environmental health scientists and engineers, sanitarians, occupational health, medicine, nursing, veterinary medicine, dentistry, laboratory personnel, health services administration (including nursing home administration and hospital administration) (U.S. Department of Health and Human Services, 1982). The secondary public health workforce, more than 250,000 other persons working as technicians or performing public health functions occasionally or part time, was equally diverse. These workers were employed in health agencies and departments, clinics, hospitals, industry, and schools of public health, as well as in other health or health-related organizations.

With such diversity the issue of competence in public health is complex. Although there is accreditation of educational programs and schools of public health, many public health workers do not have formal training in public health. Most public health specialties have not adopted competency mechanisms and credentialing in public health is rare (U.S. Department of Health and Human Services, 1982) although many workers obtain credentials through their basic discipline (e.g., medicine, nursing, dentistry). Furthermore, job and occupational mobility are common, with many career paths into public health, and "the multiplicity of workplaces generates many specialists, different sets of responsibilities and functions . . . [and] occupational standards are the exception" (U.S. Department of Health and Human Services, 1982 p. 300).

The lack of a system of credentialing and occupational standards created concern about the accountability of public health and its insurance of practitioner competence. As a result, efforts were initiated by the federal government to involve some of the public health specialty groups: environmental health, health education, health services administration, as well as other health professions, in role delineation studies (Henderson, 1982; this volume). These studies, the first steps in determining standards for practice on which credentialing depends, were seen as having three outcomes: a systematic credentialing system, development of learning materials and formal continuing education programs, and resource materials for faculty to define relationships between curriculum development and job performance (Lane et al., 1983).

The results of role-delineation studies have been reported by the National Environmental Health Association (1980), public health nutritionists (Sims, 1979), and the specialty groups within health services administration. Lane et al. (1983) compared the role delineations for hospital administrators, nursing home administrators and group-practice managers as published by their respective professional associations and, although they could identify eight composite categories, there was considerable variation in the specific areas and the role expectations. This led them to conclude that the design of curricula for health services administration should be based, in part, on the knowledge and skills required to perform desired roles in particular types of settings. They also identified a number of issues that remain to be resolved: the relationship of professional education to on-the-job competence, the relationship of professional education to credentialing, and the relationship of formal education programs to informal education in the development of practice competence. They also questioned whether or not knowledge and skill statements delineated by the professional group's role definitions can be developed into measurable competencies for learning outside the classroom (Lane et al., 1983). This is an important question for those interested in continuing education, as well as those interested in competency-based education.

Health education as a specialty was involved also in the role-delineation studies. Health education faces many of the same issues faced in other public health disciplines: multiple entry points, multiple settings in which to work, diversity in preparatory educational programs and standards, uncertainty about qualifications, lack of manpower data, and lack of quality assurance for consumers (Henderson et al., 1981). In addition, three major areas of specialization of health education—community health education, school health education, and patient health education—are expanding and other specializations are developing, e.g., education related to environmental health, occupational health, substance abuse, and human sexuality (Hamburg, 1980). In response to what was happening in the profession, the Role Delineation Project was established in 1978 to look at what the entry-level health educator should be able to do, what the prospective employer should look for when hiring a health educator, and what the standards should be in both preparation and demonstrated competence (Henderson, 1982).

The roles and competencies defined assign no explicit continuing education function to entry-level health educators although their stated skills would enable them to be involved in such activities. The emphasis on theory-based educational diagnosis, intervention and evaluation as central to their roles places them in an important position to assume a role in continuing education for public health personnel. Simonds (1984) has noted the shift within the health education profession to focus more on the training and continuing education of other health personnel, and health educators are being asked to design, implement and evaluate continuing education programs for health professionals (Smith et al., 1982).

The final report of the role refinement and verification for entry-level health educators places responsibility on the health educator for his/her own professional development and improvement of professional competencies (Henderson & McIntosh, 1982). Responsibility is also placed on professional preparation programs and professional associations to develop practitioner continuing education programs that reflect the refined and verified role. (Henderson & McIntosh, 1982). Thus, the role of the health educator is twofold, to be both a provider and consumer of continuing professional education.

Continuing Education Programs

As a provider of continuing education in public health, the health educator is confronted with the implications of the diversity previously described, the multiple issues in continuing education, and the changing nature of public health. The immediate concern is to identify the group to be reached through the activity. The variety of work settings, the many specialties—often with only a few of some specialties in any given locality, and the range of responsibilities each individual may have (e.g., management and direct work with clients or client groups), shapes the definitions of target populations. Decisions may be made on the basis of profession/occupation, workplace, e.g., school, hospital, health department, industry; function, e.g, staff, middle management, top management; or on the basis of the content to be transmitted. Complicating the decisions is the fact that, within any given specialty, there may be individuals with and without formal public health preparation, some with specialty training at the baccalaureate level, and others with graduate training, all of whom may hold similar job titles. Geographical dispersion of those in the intended audience may make the activity too costly and thus necessitate reaching a wider audience. These factors may be used singly or in combination and each decision carries with it educational implications in terms of needs assessment, activity design and expected outcomes.

The importance of continuing education, and the prediction that an increasing number of professions will, through licensure laws or professional association certification, obligate continuing education (Ruhe, 1982), has placed more emphasis on formal types of continuing education because of their ease of documentation. Several recent publications (Knox, 1980; Green et al., 1984; Council on the Continuing Education Unit, 1984; Adelson et al., 1985) are available on how to plan, organize, present, and evaluate a continuing education activity and the reader is referred to these sources. However, there are issues that shape the planning and implementation of continuing professional education in addition to those already addressed. These issues concern needs assessment and evaluation, rising costs and increasing fiscal constraints (Ruhe, 1982), and who is and who should be providing continuing professional education and the standards governing these providers.

Needs Assessments

Multiple kinds of need exist (Smith et al., 1982) and the lack of consensus about the meaning of the concept of need has created a confusing variety of uses of the term (Brackhaus, 1984). However, there is agreement that educational needs assessments are a crucial part of developing continuing education programs. Educational needs may exist in response to deficiencies in individual or organizational performance, introduction of a new technique or procedure, organizational change, or in response to personal interests (Council on the Continuing Education Unit, 1984).

Cross (1981) describes professional people as active self-directed learners who usually know what they need to learn. However, Flournory (1984) cites a study of registered dietitians that found that most (80 percent) of the study population indicated no desire to assess their learning needs and plan their own continuing education and were depending upon the professional association to offer programs that would satisfy registration requirements. How true this is of the other professions is not known. These findings do, however, underline the importance of provider-initiated needs assessment.

The purposes of a needs assessment are to (1) insure that an education intervention is an appropriate approach (CCEU, 1984); (2) determine the nature, extent, and priority of educational needs (Levine et al., 1984); (3) provide a rational basis for decisions (Brackhaus, 1984); and (4) develop continuing education projects that address the identified needs, thereby increasing the likelihood that the project will be successful (Brackhaus, 1984; Levine et al., 1984).

Needs assessments may be done in a variety of ways, e.g., formal questionnaire surveys, interviews, observations, medical record reviews/patient care audits, and meetings with formal and informal groups made up of representatives of the intended learners or experts or both. Levine et al. (1984) and Adelson et al. (1985) discuss how to approach the process as well as the techniques available. However, some of these techniques have been limited to medical and nursing practitioners in patient care settings and their applicability to public health professionals has not been reported.

How an assessment is done must relate to its purposes, the target population, and the resources, money, and time available to carry it out (Smith et al., 1982; Levine et al., 1984). The cost of conducting an assessment is frequently cited as a problem. In addition, there are methodological concerns in terms of reliability and validity, and, perhaps more importantly, there are political considerations (Brackhaus, 1984). At issue is how to select topics for a course and develop the course to be general enough to appeal to a large enough audience while, at the same time, sustaining the interest and involvement of professional people who may have highly focused problems (Cross, 1981).

Caplan suggests that an empathetic and imaginative program planner can be effective without the necessity of much formal needs assessment as long as there is effective communication with content specialists (Caplan, 1983b, p. 56). This is at variance with the primacy of the learner and learner-centered continuing education (Cross, 1981; Houle, 1980), particularly if content experts are uninformed about the learners' educational needs in the practice setting. If content experts are academicians, their goal of transmitting knowledge may not accommodate the learners' goal of applying new information/knowledge, thus reducing the effectiveness of the continuing education activity. Others also have some doubts about the requirement for formal needs assessments and suggest other ways to identify learning needs, e.g., participant feedback on other learning needs, direct requests for programs, costs, and talking with practitioners and faculty (Headricks, 1983).

As with many other areas in continuing education, there is a need for more research on identification of learning needs of practicing professionals (Manning, 1981; Chernoff et al., 1983; Headricks, 1983; Brackhaus, 1984). Some information concerning continuing education needs in public health has been published that is helpful, but would require additional information on the specific group to be reached (Clemmen & Bertrand, 1980; Monroe et al., 1980; Applied Management Sciences, 1983).

Educational Interventions and Providers

The needs assessment results are the basis on which the continuing education activity objectives and program design rest. The activity outcomes are believed to be enhanced if the program planning involves learners (individuals in the target population) in not only identifying their deficiencies, but designing their own learning activities and evaluating the impact of the learning on their practice (Suter et al., 1981). A client-centered planning model for continuing education was implemented in a school of public health (Nichols & Stewart, 1983) and actively involved public health professionals in needs assessments, program planning, implementation and evaluation. In this involvement, practitioners and professional continuing education staff worked with faculty, both academicians and practitioners, to facilitate focus on application rather than mere transmission of information. A major function of the professional staff was liaison between practitioners and university-based faculty. Program evaluations consistently showed positive results regarding the overall relevance of the material presented (Nichols & Stewart, 1983). Other planning models, involving both content and process experts, are also described in the literature (for example Grosswald, 1984). Whatever the planning model, however, careful assessment of needs appears to be critical to program outcomes.

The actual content of the continuing education activity is one facet guiding program design. Other motivations may operate that will influence the impact of the activity on the learner. Continuing education programs provide peer reinforcement and interaction that contribute to learning (Manning, 1982). Also, attending programs may be one mechanism participants' use for professional networking. To the extent to which these processes are desired, programs should be designed to facilitate them.

Multiple educational methods can be used in continuing education and helpful analyses of various instructional methods and strategies, as well as information about designing educational activities for groups, are available (Grosswald, 1984; Moore, 1985). There is also a developing literature about the use of computer technology in continuing education and competency-based education (for example, Lee et al., 1982; *Mobius* Special Issue, 1983; Gullion, 1984). Computer application methods that can be used include computer-assisted instruction, video/computer interactive systems, data banks, teleconferencing, computer-enhanced learning, and computer-assisted diagnosis (Gullion, 1984). The problem is how to select technology from among the increasing alternatives of communication that will contribute to the continuing education outcomes sought. To what extent such technology is in use for public health continuing education is not known.

Costs

The costs and funding of continuing education are central to the enterprise, and yet there is limited information in the literature concerning the costs (Houle, 1980; Shannon, 1982). The work of Anderson & Kasl (1982), on their study of the costs and sources of payment of adult education in different kinds of settings, and that of Sparks (1985) dealing with budget planning are useful in understanding the problems and procedures. Shannon (1982), based on three years' experience of continuing education in pharmacy, reported that direct costs could be covered by program income but that indirect costs had to be met through institutional sources. A similar experience was reported by Stewart (1985). Examination of full costs, classroom, administrative, and overhead, is essential for evaluation and planning (Anderson & Kasl, 1980; Shannon, 1982; Sparks, 1985). Multiple sources of revenue are used to meet these costs and vary according to the provider. Volunteer time, release time provided by employers for individuals to attend programs and to volunteer, adds to the costs, but is seldom computed. When all the costs are computed, the continuing education activity may cost much more than that covered by program fees. This shortfall must be met through other sources. The issue of who should pay has not been fully resolved, although there seems to be some consensus that it should be shared by all who benefit—the individual participant, the employer, the profession, and society (Houle, 1980; Shannon, 1982). Issues such as the cost-benefit of various teaching modalities on learner outcomes and the cost-effectiveness of various provider organizational arrangements on learner outcomes have yet to be addressed.

Evaluation

The costs of a program are one dimension of evaluation. However, much of the literature concerning evaluation deals with the shortcomings of designs and methods as the major issues. Three broad explanations for not achieving the intended outcome of a program have been suggested: (1) program failure: inadequate performance of the program; (2) theory failure: the theory upon which the program was based was inadequate; or (3) measurement failure: the program was well conducted, but there was a failure to detect a program effect (Green & Lewis, 1981; Quantrano & Conant, 1981).

The Council on the Continuing Education Unit reported that in 1982–83, multiple continuing education evaluation methods were used in the health sector—in hospitals and clinics, and in other health-related organizations (Activity Report, 1984). Almost all respondents to the Council study reported using participant satisfaction questionnaires or rating forms, and over half of the hospitals and clinics reported using participant self-ratings (both pre- and postinstruction) and exams (both pre- and postinstruction). Few used attitude measures. In addition, at least half of the hospitals and clinics used follow-up approaches: participant self-report of utilization of instruction, supervisor report of utilization of instruction by participant, and post-instruction improvement in productivity or service quality. Other health-related respondents used fewer approaches, with satisfaction rating the most common approach. None of the respondents reported using attitude measurement, and fewer than half used follow-up approaches.

Abrahamson (1984a) noted that most continuing medical education programs include some evaluation. Although some of these evaluation efforts are still limited to "happiness" indexes, he found fairly widespread use of pre- and postprogram testing, a substantial increase in the number of attempts to examine physician practice performance, a steadily growing concern for and interest in the connection between continuing education of the physician and patient outcomes, and increasing use of more sophisticated statistical tools among professional evaluators (Abrahamson, 1984a).

The general impression conveyed by these articles is that evaluation is being done and there is improvement in how it is done.

However, how to evaluate the impact of continuing education on professional practice and patient outcomes is complicated by the context of practice. Changing participant performance requires both upgrading the learner's competence and restructuring the work environment to allow expression of and reward for the competence (Griffith, 1981). Cervero (1985), influenced by Griffith and the "diffusion of innovation" theorists, has proposed an evaluation model, as yet untested, that attempts to incorporate characteristics of: (1) the educational program, (2) the individual professional, (3) the proposed changes, and (4) the social system in which the behavioral change must occur. He argues that unless the working environment allows the proposed changes to take place, it is unlikely that the continuing professional education program will result in behavioral change on the part of the learner. Cervero (1985) argues that learning whether or not continuing professional education is effective is not too useful. Rather, we need to learn *why* some learning activities are more effective than others.

This argument is particularly salient for public health. Multiple practice settings, variation in job expectations for those with similar job titles, and geographic dispersion make it difficult to specify outcomes in terms of competence. These factors influence the acceptability and feasibility of certain evaluation protocols. In addition, absence of occupational standards, competency specifications, and job-function analyses in much of public health limit ability to establish competency outcomes for a continuing education activity. However, for those groups that have done role-delineation studies, attainment statements can be developed. Further, sound follow-up evaluation protocols may be facilitated if the activity is "in house," where all the participants are employed in the same organization to which the continuing education provider has easy access.

Several problems in the conduct of continuing education evaluations have been identified: limited resources (time, personnel, money); participant resistance to performance appraisal; participant diversity in terms of education, experience and interests; minimal faculty-learner contact time; and last-minute changes in programs (e.g., enrollment size, location, speakers/faculty) that modify the conditions for learning or disrupt the evaluation plan (Mitsunaga & Shores, 1977). Although problems exist, evaluation of the continuing education activity is both possible and essential.

Evaluation is essential on educational grounds and, if continuing education credit is to be awarded to participants, evaluation is required for continuing education program approval. For those professions/occupations that are obligated to have continuing education for relicensure or recertification,[4] the requirements for program approval present special challenges. If health specialties do not define public health functions or practice as a part of professional competence, it is more difficult to obtain program certification for award of continuing education credits. Often it is deemed crucial to replicate the interdisciplinary nature of public health in the educational activity. However, the individual professions may require representation of the profession on the planning committee, a given percent of the profession in the audience, and members of the profession involved in the teaching. Blockstein (1983) notes that "no one group in the several health professions yet has either a national or local scheme for interdisciplinary continuing education accreditation" (p. 69). Knowledge of certification requirements is essential for the continuing education provider and the lead-time and costs for applications are a factor to be considered in the planning process.

Abrahamson (1984b) has summarized the key points in evaluation in the following way: (1) evaluation of continuing education programs usually involves ongoing educational activities; (2) political pressures always accompany attempts to evaluate real, ongoing programs; (3) it is essential to decide why to evaluate at the onset because (4) the reason(s) to evaluate influences the design of the evaluation; (5) evaluation is a simple concept, but a complex process; (6) evaluation is easy to design but difficult to execute; and (7) evaluation is demanded but not financially supported (pp. 18–20).

Continuing Education Providers

In addition to the evaluation of particular continuing education outcomes, there has been growing concern about the need for evaluation of continuing education providers and the absence of standards by which to to judge their quality. The publication of *The Principles of Good Practice in Continuing Education* (Council on the Continuing Education Unit, 1984) is an attempt to establish such standards. The 18 principles put forth address identification and analysis of learning needs, specification of learning outcomes that are related to situations outside the learning environment, program/activity agendas, learner- and outcome-oriented learning experiences, instructional staff, evaluation, and the administrative structure of the provider organization. The process embodied in *The Principles of Good Practice in Continuing Education* is shown in Figure 1. Clearly, it is a learning-oriented approach to continuing education and, although the "state of the art" is less than we desire, assessments of learner needs and learning outcomes carry equal emphasis with learning experiences. It is too soon, however, to determine the extent to which the standards have been adopted or to assess their effect on provider quality.

These principles are not provider-specific and continuing professional

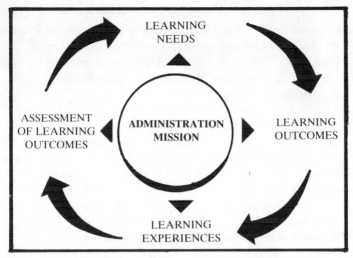

Figure 1. CE components and the provider's administrative mission.

Source: Principles of Good Practice in Continuing Education, (1984) Council on the Continuing Education Unit, p. 4.

education is a growing field with many providers. Houle (1980) identifies seven dominant provider forms: autonomous groups, e.g., journal clubs, physicians' round tables, professional associations, professional schools, universities, employers, independent providers of learning opportunities, and purveyors of professional supplies and equipment. The most powerful and pervasive of the providers are the professional associations, professional schools, comprehensive university programs, and controllers of employment settings (Houle, 1980). However, universities have been criticized for their less-than-desirable acceptance of responsibility for continuing professional education (Frandson, 1983; Queeny, 1984). Because of (1) their education mission, (2) their being the greatest single source of new knowledge, (3) and their preparation of individuals to enter the professions, there must be collaboration of universities with professional associations, regulatory agencies, and employers if continuing professional education is to contribute to practitioner competence (Queeny, 1984). Queeny (1984) indicates the care with which this collaboration must be established, as we know very little about cooperative relationships in continuing education and providers may not know how to cooperate (Hohmann, 1980). The extent to which the advantages to collaboration are viewed as being greater than the disadvantages will determine the receptivity to collaborate.

The professional associations have a responsibility for providing resources to practitioners for self-assessment and continuing education (Gray, 1984) and are both providers and purchasers of continuing education services (Hohmann, 1980). Hohmann (1980) suggests three tentative organizational models of current practice and their implications for cooperative relationships:

1. The service model, the classic form, responds to the knowledge needs of practitioners, yet these needs are ultimately determined by the program developer. The organizational stance is reactive. Program evaluation is limited and quality is determined by what works in the marketplace. This model should foster complementary relationships between the professional association and university insofar as they do not view one another as a competitor.
2. The marketing model, a rapidly developing proactive form, emphasizes program packaging to market segments, and has the same orientation to evaluation and quality as the service model. "The ultimate measure of success is the solvency of the operation and the number of participants" (p. 91). This model is seen as fostering competition.
3. The performance model emphasizes learner outcomes and self-learning. The organization/institution assumes a supporting role. This model should foster cooperation.

The third model is seen as absolutely essential to survival of the professional associations but not "the first choice for the majority because of the required investment of money, time, and staff" (Hohmann, 1980, p. 91).

Multiple providers are active in the public health community. Professional associations, governmental agencies (e.g., state and local health departments, the Public Health Service/Centers for Disease Control), schools of public health, hospitals, and other health agencies are among those involved. Schools of public health are involved in providing continuing education services (Roulhac, 1982) as well as serving as a resource for other providers. These schools follow four general patterns of operation:

1. The state capitation model, where the state provides economic incentives to a state-supported school to encourage and sustain the provision of continuing education opportunities for state and other public health personnel.
2. The consortium model, where schools located in a particular geographic region pool their resources and talents to jointly develop and offer continuing education courses and opportunities.

3. The university extension model, where a school establishes a continuing education program through an existing university extension service.

4. The autonomous in-house model, where a continuing education director or coordinator within a school serves as a broker between the faculty who actually provide the continuing education services, consumers-client agencies and public health personnel, and various other groups and organizations which may share interest in marketing and developing continuing education (Roulhac, 1982, p. 9).

These models do not attempt to describe all continuing education providers in public health, but help in understanding the variation among the public health professional schools. Professional associations and governmental agencies are very active in continuing education, and further development of organizational models as proposed by Hohmann (1980) and Roulhac (1982) would be helpful. Especially useful would be an examination of the formal and informal relationships among the key providers, and how productive the various arrangements are in meeting continuing education needs and at what costs.

Continuing education offerings in public health are not systematic, and often must compete with programs of other health specialties. Participation of the public health workforce in continuing education, their frequency of participation, the kinds of activities in which they participate, and the providers of those activities, is not known, and would probably be difficult to ascertain. However, professionals are eager to participate, especially in those activities that are explicitly geared to the public health community.

SUMMARY AND CONCLUSIONS

Continuing professional education is complex and challenging. The definitional problems reflect a field that is changing and growing in importance. Theoretical bases for the practice of continuing education require development and testing, while at the same time the demands for continuing education are increasing. The basic issue for professional education, both preparatory and continuing, is practitioner competence. How it is defined, taught, measured, and sustained are pressing concerns to the professions and to the public. Continuing professional education is one mechanism that is mentioned consistently in discussions of maintenance of competence. The contribution of practice to competence, and how we organize and use the knowledge that it generates, will become increasingly important to understand. Licensure and certification, and relicensure and recertification, are the major mechanisms used to recognize professional competence, but they are subject to much criticism. Continuing education, mandatory and voluntary, is viewed as the way to deal with insuring continuing competence. The planning, implementation, and evaluation of continuing education, however, raise other issues: needs assessments, determining educational interventions relevant to practicing professionals, costs and evaluation.

Continuing education in public health is a part of these broader educational issues. The diversity in public health, the goals being sought and values held merely add to the complexity. Some of the special issues in public health continuing education involve the relative and appropriate role of the public health worker, the employing agency, the school of public health, the professional groups, and government in setting priorities for continuing education and insuring its provision. Furthermore, in light of the diversity in public health, there are issues surrounding the definition of the scope, intensity, and duration of continuing education need and how accurately, economically and timely it can be appraised (Roulhac, 1982). To be a provider of continuing education services in public health, one needs to be aware of the broader issues while recognizing the diversity that will shape the kinds of activities offered. The public health educator has a role to play, both as an education expert and as a consumer of education services. It is an exciting and challenging field that presents more questions than answers.

The research needs in continuing professional education are many. And so too are the research needs in public health. The agenda should include the development of needs assessment methods applicable to the many specialties in public health, examination of the impact of interdisciplinary vs. single discipline continuing education on learning outcomes, the relationship between continuing education, practitioner behavior, and organizational behavior and, more basically, the relationship between public health practitioner behavior and the community's health status. Because of the diversity of people in the public health workforce, the delineation of contribution of practice to the development of competence in public health can benefit not only continuing education but also the programs that provide academic preparation.

The future may see the development of yet another public health specialty, that of individuals especially concerned with continuing education for maintenance of professional competence. This may be an emerging role for public health educators. However, the ultimate responsibility for continuing education remains with the individual practitioner, since " . . . each professional must be the ultimate monitor of his or her own learning, controlling the stable or shifting design of its continuity" (Houle, 1980, p. 13).

ACKNOWLEDGMENTS

The author is indebted to Helen A. Bielous for her assistance in the development of the material and to the unnamed reviewers of the manuscript for their helpful suggestions.

NOTES

1. The Council on Continuing Education of the Association of Schools of Public Health defined both adult education and continuing education in the context of schools of public health (Roulhac, 1982). However, the Council and the Association of Schools of Public Health have accepted, in principle, the *Principles of Good Practice in Continuing Education*, and have recommended that the schools follow the recommendations therein (House, 1986).

2. Nursing is not alone. Neufeld (1985a) notes the "sobering evidence that many health outcomes are not directly attributable to what physicians do" (p. 11).

3. Privileging, another mechanism for ensuring competence, has been described by Ball (1984) and Porter (1984). This mechanism is used by organizations which grant privileges, for a set period of time, to qualified individuals to carry out specified procedures/activities within the organization. These privileges are renewed upon demonstrated competence.

4. The requirements for application for award of continuing education units of various health specialties have been compiled by Korb & Carden (1983).

REFERENCES

Abrahamson, S. (1984a). Evaluation of continuing education in the health Professions. *Evaluation and the Health Professions, 7*:1, 3–23.

Abrahamson, S. (1984b). The future: An educationist's perspective. *Mobius, 4*:4, 113–120.

Activity report of council members, 1982–83. (1984). *CCEU Reporter, 7*:3, 6–8.

Adelson, R., Watkins, F. S., & Caplan, R. M. (1985). Continuing education for the health professional: Educational and administrative methods. Rockville: Aspen Systems.

Anderson, R. E., & Kasl, E. S. (1982). The costs and financing of adult education and training. Lexington, MA: D. C. Heath.

Applied Management Sciences, Inc. (1983). Workshop on health promotion/disease prevention: Impact on health professions education. Summary prepared for Health Resources and Services Administration, Bureau of Health Professions, Division of Associated and Dental Health Professions. Contract No. 240–83–0024. Rockville, MD.

Ball, J. R. (1984). Credentialing versus performance—a new look at old problems. *Quality Review Bulletin, 10*:3, 75–80.

Begun, J. W. (1985). Managing with professionals in a changing health care environment. *Medical Care Review, 42*:1, 3–10.

Benner, P. (1982). Issues in competency-based testing. *Nursing Outlook, 30*:5, 303–309.

Berner, E. S., & Bender, K. J. (1978). Determining how to begin. In Morgan, M. K., &

Irby, D. M. (Eds.), *Evaluating clinical competence in the health professions*. St. Louis: C. V. Mosby.

Bertram, D. A., & Brooks-Bertram, P. A. (1977). The evaluation of continuing medical education: A literature review. *Health Education Monographs, 5*:4, 330–362.

Blockstein, W. L. (1983). Interdisciplinary continuing education. *Mobius, 3*:3, 60–75.

Boissoneau, R. (1980). *Continuing education in the health professions*. Rockville: Aspen.

Brackhaus, B. (1984). Needs assessment in adult education: Its problems and prospects. *Adult Education Quarterly, 34*:4, 233–239.

Caplan, R. M. (1983a). Continuing education and professional accountability. In McGuire, C. H., Foley, R. P., Gorr, A., Richards, R. W., & Associates (Eds.), *Handbook of health professions education*. San Francisco: Jossey-Bass.

Caplan, R. M. (1983b). A fresh look at some bad ideas in continuing medical education. *Mobius, 3*:1, 55–61.

Cervero, R. M. (1985). Continuing professional education and behavioral change: A model for research and evaluation. *The Journal of Continuing Education in Nursing, 16*:3, 85–88.

Chambers, D. W., & Hamilton, D. L. (1981). Continuing dental education: Reasonable answers to unreasonable questions. *Mobius, 1*:2, 28–34.

Chapko, M. K., Milgrom, P., Bergner, M., Conrad, D., Skalabrin, N. (1984). The effects of continuing education in dental practice management. *Journal of Dental Education, 48*:12, 659–664.

Chernoff, R., Lindsay, C. A., & Kris-Etherton, P. M. (1983). Continuing education needs assessment and program development: An alternative approach. *Journal of the American Dietetic Association, 83*:6, 649–653.

Clemmen, D. I., & Bertrand, W. E. (1980). A model for the incorporation of alumni-faculty feedback into curriculum planning. *American Journal of Public Health, 70*:1, 67–69.

Collins, R. (1979). *The credential society*. New York: Academic Press.

Cordes, D. L. (1984). Relationship of motivation to learning. In Green, J. S., Grosswald, S. J., Suter, E., & Walthall, D. B., III (Eds.), *Continuing education for the health professions*. San Francisco: Jossey-Bass.

Council on the Continuing Education Unit. (1984). *Principles of good practice in continuing education*. Silver Spring: The Council.

Cross, K. P. (1981). *Adults as learners*. San Francisco: Jossey-Bass.

Davis, D. A., Haynes, R. B., Chambers, L., Neufeld, V. R., McKibbon, A., & Tugwell, P. (1984). The impact of CME: A methodological review of the continuing medical education literature. *Evaluation and the Health Professions, 7*:3, 251–283.

del Bueno, D. J., Baker, F., & Christmyer, C. (1981). Implementing a competency-based program. *The Journal of Nursing Administration, 11*:2, 24–29.

Edwards, R. L., & Green, R. K. (1983). Mandatory continuing education: Time for re-evaluation. *Social Work, 28*:1 43–48.

Flournory, I. C. (1984). Planning for continuing education: Goal setting and self-assessment. *Journal of the American Dietetic Association, 84*:8, 926–928.

Frandson, P. E. (1983). The case for a market consciousness in continuing education: Implications for long-range curriculum planning. *Mobius, 3*:1, 43–54.

Gaumer, G. L. (1984). Regulating health professionals: A review of the empirical literature. *Milbank Memorial Fund Quarterly/Health and Society, 62*:3, 380–416.

Gosnell, D. J. (1984). Evaluting continuing nursing education. *The Journal of Continuing Education in Nursing, 15*:1, 9–11.

Gray, M. S. (1984). Recertification and relicensure in the allied health professions. *Journal of Allied Health, 13*:1, 22–30.

Greaves, P. E., & Loquist, R. S. (1983). Impact evaluation: A competency-based approach. *Nursing Administration Quarterly, 7*:3, 81–86.

Green, J. S., Grosswald, S. J., Suter, E., & Walthall, D. B., III (Eds.), *Continuing education for the health professions*. San Francisco: Jossey-Bass.

Green, L. W., & Lewis, F. M. (1981). Issues in relating evaluation to theory, policy, and practice in continuing education and health education. *Mobius, 1*:2, 46–58.

Griffith, W. S. (1981). Developing a valid data base for continuing education in the health sciences. *Mobius, 1*:2, 83–91.

Gross, S. J. (1983). The professional as regulator and self-regulator. In Stern, M. R. (Ed.), *Power and conflict in continuing professional education*. Belmont, CA: Wadsworth.

Gross, S. J. (1984). *Of foxes and hen houses: Licensing and the health professions*. Westport, CT: Quorum Books.

Grosswald, S. J. (1984). Designing effective educational activities for groups. In Green, J. S., Grosswald, S. J., Suter, E. W., & Walthall, D. B., III (Eds.), *Continuing education for health professionals*. San Francisco: Jossey-Bass.

Gullion, D. S. (1984). 1984 and beyond: A panel discussion. *Mobius, 4*:4, 100–103.

Hamburg, M. V. (1980). Concepts and trends in the preparation of health educators in the U.S. *International Journal of Health Education, 22*:2, 82–86.

Haynes, R. B., Davis, D. A., McKibbon, A., & Tugwell, P. (1984). A critical appraisal of the efficacy of continuing medical education. *Journal of the American Medical Association, 251*:1, 61–64.

Headricks, M. M. (1983). Needs assessment: Sense or nonsense? *The Journal of Continuing Education in Nursing, 14*:5, 13–15.

Henderson, A. (1982). The refined and verified role for entry-level health educators. *The Eta Sigma Gamma Monograph Series, 1*:1 3–40.

Henderson, A., & McIntosh, D. V. (1982). Role refinement and verification for entry-level health educators. Contract No. HRA 232–80–0014, Division of Associated Health Professions, Bureau of Health Professions, Health Resources Administration, DHHS, August 22.

Henderson, A., Wolle, J. M., Cortese, P. A., McIntosh, D. V. (1981). The future of the health education profession: Implications for preparation and practice. *Public Health Reports, 96*:6, 555–559.

Hogan, D. B. (1979a). Is licensing public protection or professional protectionism? In Pottinger, P. S., & Goldsmith, J. (Eds.), *New directions for experiental learning: Defining and measuring competence*. San Francisco: Jossey-Bass.

Hogan D. B. (1979b). *The regulation of psychotherapists. Volume I. A Study in the philosophy and practice of professional regulation*. Cambridge: Ballinger.

Hohmann, L. (1980). The professional associations. In Frandson, P. E. (Ed.), *Power and conflict in continuing education*. Belmont: Wadsworth.

Houle, C. O. (1980). *Continued learning in the professions*. San Francisco: Jossey-Bass.

House, R. (1986). Chairman, Council of Continuing Education, Association of Schools of Public Health. Personal communication, January.

Jago, J. D. (1984). To protect the public: Professionalism vs. competency in dentistry. *Social Science and Medicine, 19*:2, 117–122.

Knowles, M. S. (1980). *The modern practice of adult education*. Revised edition. Chicago: Follett.

Knox, A. B. (1980). *Developing, administering, and evaluating adult education*. San Francisco: Jossey-Bass.

Korb, R. H., & Carden, J. A. (1983). *Sourcebook for continuing education units in healthcare*. Chicago: American Hospital Publishing.

LaDuca, A. (1980). The structure of competence in health professions. *Evaluation and the Health Professions, 3*:3, 253–288.

Lane, M. S., Smith, I. L., & Oldak, R. (1983). Review of professional society role delineations for health services administration curriculum design applications. *The Journal of Health Administration Education, 1*:2, 151–174.

Lee, E. E., Watson, D. R., Argo, J. K., Kalish, R. A., & Catlin, P. C. (1982). A model for competency-based, computer-managed instruction in allied health. *Journal of Allied Health, 11*:2, 106–114.

Levine, H. G. (1978). Selecting evaluation instruments. In Morgan, M. K., & Irby, D. M. (Eds.), *Evaluating clinical competence in the health professions*. St. Louis: C. V. Mosby.

Levine, H. G., Cordes, D. L., Moore, D. E., Jr., & Pennington, F. C. (1984). Identifiying and assessing needs to relate continuing education to patient care. In Green, J. S., Grosswald, S. J., Suter, E., & Walthall, D. B. III (Eds.), *Continuing Education for the health professions*. San Francisco: Jossey-Bass.

Lloyd, J. S., & Abrahamson, S. (1979). Effectiveness of continuing medical education: A review of the evidence. *Evaluation and the Health Professions, 2*:3, 251–280.

Manning, P. R. (1981). Development and demonstration center: Continuing education for the health professionals. *Mobius, 1*:1, 54–59.

Manning, P. R. (1982). Continuing education in the health sciences: Can we change the paradigm? *Mobius, 2*:2, 5–7.

Middleman, R. R. (1984). How competent is social work's approach to the assessment of competence? *Social Work, 29*:2, 146–153.

Mitsunaga, B., & Shores, L. (1977). Evaluation in continuing education: Is it practical? *The Journal of Continuing Education in Nursing, 8*:6, 7–14.

Mobius (1983) Special Issue: Technology and future of continuing education. *3*:3, 6–93.

Monroe, L. B., Tuttle, D. M., & Lorimor, R. J. (1980). Job-related activities, academic preparation, and continuing education needs of graduates of schools of public health. *American Journal of Public Health, 70*:1, 70–73.

Moore, D. (1985). Designing instructional strategies. In Green, J. S., Grosswald, S. J., Suter, E., & Walthall, D. B. III (Eds.), *Continuing education for the health professions*. San Francisco: Jossey-Bass.

National Environmental Health Association (1980). *The sanitarian in environmental health: Responsibilities and competencies*. Denver: The Association.

Neufeld, V. R. (1985a). Historical perspectives on clinical competence. In Neufeld, V. R., & Norman, G. R. (Eds.), *Assessing clinical competence*. New York: Springer.

Neufeld, V. R. (1985b). Implications for education. In Neufeld, V. R., & Norman, G. R. (Eds.), *Assessing clinical competence*. New York: Springer.

Neufeld, V. R., & Norman G. R. (Eds.) (1985). *Assessing clinical competence*. New York: Springer.

Nichols, W. H., Stewart, C. J. (1983). Assessment of the client-centered planning approach in continuing education for public health professionals. *Mobius, 3*:3, 12–21.

Norman, G. R. (1985). Defining competence: A methodological review. In Neufeld, V. R., & Norman, G. R. (Eds.), *Assessing clinical competence*. New York: Springer.

Oliver, S. K. (1984). The effects of continuing education on the clinical behavior of nurses. *The Journal of Continuing Education in Nursing, 15*:4, 130–134.

Pennington, F. C., Allan, D. M. E., & Green, J. S. (1984). Learning theory, educational psychology, and principles of adult development. In Green, J. S., Grosswald, S. J., Suter, E., & Walthall, D. B. III (Eds.), *Continuing education for the health professions*. San Francisco: Jossey-Bass.

Peterson, G. W. (1977). Attainment rather than competence: A legitimate basis for the certification of learning outcomes. ERIC document ED 145 766.

Peterson, G. W. (1981). Performance-based education. *Journal of Higher Education, 52*:4, 352–368.

Porter, S. F. (1984). Ensuring competence: Toward a competency-based orientation format. *Critical Care Quarterly, 7*:1, 42–52.

Pottinger, P. S. (1979). Competence assessment: Comments on current practices. In Pottinger, P. S., & Goldsmith, J. (Eds.), *New directions for experiential learning; Defining and measuring competence*. San Francisco: Jossey-Bass.

Pottinger, P. S., & Goldsmith, J. (1979). Editors' notes. In Pottinger, P. S., & Goldsmith, J. (Eds.), *New directions for experiential learning: Defining and measuring competence*. San Francisco: Jossey-Bass.

Quantrano, L. A., & Conant, R. M. (1981). Continuing competency for health professionals. *Journal of Environmental Health, 44*:3, 125–130.

Queeney, D. S. (1984). The role of the university in continuing professional education. *Educational Record, 65*:3, 13–17.

Roulhac, E. E. (1982). Continuing education programming among U.S. schools of public health; 1975–76 and 1980–81. Baltimore: Johns Hopkins School of Hygiene and Public Health. (mimeo)

Ruhe, C. H. W. (1982). What is the status of continuing education for health professionals? *Mobius, 2*:2, 8–14.

Schön, D. A. (1983). *The reflective practitioner: How practitioners think in action*. New York: Basic Books.

Scott, B. (1982). Competency-based learning: A literature review. *International Journal of Nursing Studies, 19*:3, 119–124.

Scott, W. R., & Lammers, J. C. (1985). Trends in occupations and organizations in the medical care and mental health sectors. *Medical Care Review, 42*:1, 37–76.

Shannon, M. C. (1982). Budgetary considerations in planning pharmacy continuing education programs. *Mobius, 2*:4, 39–47.

Sheps, C. G. (Chairman) (1976). *Higher education for public health: A report of the milbank memorial fund commission*. New York: Prodist.

Shimberg, D. S. (1977). Continuing education and licensing. In Vermilye, D. W. (Ed.), *Relating work and education*. San Francisco: Jossey-Bass.

Shimberg, B. S. (1983). What is competence? How can it be assessed? In Stern, M. R. (Ed.), *Power and conflict in continuing professional education*. Belmont: Wadsworth.

Short, E. (1984). Competence reexamined. *Educational Theory, 34*:3, 201–206.

Simonds, S. K. (1984). Health education. In Matarazzo, J. D., Weiss, S. M., Herd, J. A., Miller, N. E., & Weiss, S. M. (Eds.), *Behavioral health: A handbook of health enhancement and disease prevention*. New York: Wiley.

Sims, L. S. (1979). Identification and evaluation of competencies of public health nutritionists. *American Journal of Public Health, 69*:11, 1099–1105.

Smith, I. K., Smith, J. O., & Ross, G. R. (1982). Needs assessment: An overview for health educators. *Mobius, 2*:2, 52–59.

Sparks, P. (1985). A systematic budget process for CE programs. In Green, J. S., Grosswald, S. J., Suter, E., & Walthall, D. B. III (Eds.), *Continuing education for the health professions*. San Francisco: Jossey-Bass.

Stein, L. S. (1981). The effectiveness of continuing medical education: Eight research reports. *Journal of Medical Education, 56*:2, 103–110.

Stewart, C. J. (1985). The University of Michigan School of Public Health, Center for Continuing Education of Public Health Professionals. Final Report to the W. K. Kellogg Foundation.

Stubblefield, H. W. (1981). What should be the major focus of adult education? The focus should be on life fulfillment. In Krietlow, B. W. & Associates (Eds.), *Examining controversies in adult education*. San Francisco: Jossey-Bass.

Suter, E., Green, J. S., Grosswald, S. J., Lawrence, K. A., Walthall, D. B. III, & Zeleznik, C. (1984). Introduction: defining quality for continuing education. In Green, J. S., Grosswald, S. J., Suter, E., & Walthall, D. B. III (Eds.), *Continuing education for the health professions*. San Francisco: Jossey-Bass.

Suter, E., Green, J. S., Grosswald, S. J., Lawrence, K. A., & Walthall, D. B., III (1981). Continuing education of health professionals: Proposal for a definition of quality. *Journal of Medical Education, 56*, 8, 687–707.

Tugwell, P., & Dok, C. (1985). Medical record review. In Neufeld, V. R., & Norman, G. R. (Eds.), *Assessing clinical competence*. New York: Springer.

U.S. Department of Health and Human Services (1982). Public health personnel in the United States, 1980. DHHS Pub. No. (HRA) 82–6. Washington, DC: U.S. Government Printing Office.

U.S. Department of Health and Human Services (1983). Survey of public health/community health personnel. Contract No. HRA - 232–81–0056 Public Health Service, Health Resources and Services Administration, Bureau of Health Professions, June.

DEVELOPING A CREDENTIALING SYSTEM FOR HEALTH EDUCATORS

Alan C. Henderson

BACKGROUND

During the past several years, concerted efforts have been made to address fundamental issues in the preparation and practice of health educators (Cleary, 1983; Criteria and guidelines, 1977; Green, 1976; Hamburg, 1980; Henderson, 1982; Simonds, 1984). It has been evident that no reliable system exists to inform the public, health professionals, employers, policy makers and other constituent groups of the quality and value of services performed by professional health educators. Moreover, for those who wish either to become health educators or to develop health education services, no mechanism exists that assures reliable information to assist them.

The impetus for a credentialing system stems from conditions in the health education profession and in the social environment. Professional activities of health educators have broadened as more becomes known about influencing health behavior through reported field experience and research in a variety of contexts. Research advances in behavioral science have been complemented by increased knowledge about behavioral con-

Advances in Health Education and Promotion, vol. 2, pages 59–91
Copyright © 1987 JAI Press Inc.
All rights of reproduction in any form reserved.
ISBN: 0-89232-617-4

tributions to primary causes of morbidity and mortality (McGinnis, 1982; Taylor, Denham, & Ureda, 1982; Vaupel & Gowan, 1986). Changes in the age distribution of the population, economics, and the political climate have significantly heightened awareness of the extent of personal and social control over health status, the health aspects of socially defined quality of life, and implications of increased longevity. Other factors stimulating the development of health education have been the expense, complexity and impersonal qualities of medical care, and, in conjunction with reactions against complete control over health by experts, a growing impetus toward self-care and activated consumers as users of health care services (Blum, 1982). Social and environmental concerns, now recognized as public health issues having significant behavioral components (Matarazzo, 1984), have been granted more attention by the public and policy-makers. These concerns include indoor air pollution, accidents and violence, influences of electronic media on violence and consumer behavior, and growing evidence of associations between dietary patterns and major causes of mortality (Segal, 1984; Taylor et al., 1982). Public fears over industrial toxic wastes and resulting potential disease and genetic mutations demand more informed individual and collective decision-making and actions. As more becomes known about behavior and health, emphasis has been increasing on quantifying the benefits of health education services, which demand, because of advances in the field, greater skills in planning, implementing and evaluating health education programs.

Because of the broad scope of health education programs, health educators have lacked a defined territory of practice. Health education is implied in the roles of all health professionals who serve clients, patients and students. Health educators have become an occupational group because the need for health education arose out of ever increasing complexities of knowledge, technology and specializations in health and medical care. As long as it appears that many health and education professionals are fulfilling their consumer education functions, health educators will have difficulty in establishing authority over their field of practice and subsequent public recognition.

In short, health educators need to decide which direction the profession as a whole will take. To remain unrecognized as professionally authoritative has certain consequences: a select number of individuals and groups in certain practice settings will retain their reputation for excellence, despite a lack of professional organization and a system of quality assurance. Most health educators will have to compete with other more established professionals for territory.

Historically, professional groups have banded together to protect their typically hard-won territory from actual and potential competitors. As Selden noted, this process is analogous to physiological reactions of organisms to intruders (Selden, 1971). Such self-protection may be viewed as self-centered and self-indulgent. Another view is that this internal focus may afford health educators the opportunity to develop an internal consensus as to the core purposes and functions of health educators. At the same time, health educators can work to establish norms and standards for the profession. These codes and practice norms are a significant means for others to judge the legitimacy of health educators' claim to their professional domain. As Starr has pointed out, internal consensus and recognized expertise are two basic elements for would-be professions to establish authority (Starr, 1982). The key to establishing the legitimacy of the health education profession is to win support from outside the group's own membership, which is not easily done. Competition for existing professional territory, blurring of practice areas by new knowledge and technology, increasing bureaucratization of professional work, developing consumer skepticism toward professions, increasing numbers of health occupations, and increasing resistance by policy-makers, employers, and third party payers to professionalization and its accompanying rising costs contribute to strong countervailing forces that resist efforts toward professionalization of health education.

It should also be pointed out that within the field there are health educators who may actively or passively resist efforts for formalization. Active resisters are those who typically are considered superior and inferior practitioners. Superior practitioners have established their competence by dint of their own excellent performances. Formalization of rules and standards would not enhance their status. Indeed, added formal processes may only complicate their own abilities and performance. For inferior performers, consensus and standards can represent a threat to be imposed upon them. Added formalization would only highlight their deficiencies and, thus, would threaten their ability to maintain their careers. Passive resisters are those who "go along for the ride." These are practitioners who would benefit from elevated status that could accrue from consensus and standards efforts by the group (Gaumer, 1984). This type of resister has no compunction to participate because benefits can be gained without effort.

Evidence of this scenario of the development of a profession can be taken from Starr's *Social Transformation of American Medicine*. In citing the origins of the American Medical Association, it was noted that leadership for the organizing convention of 1846 came from younger practitioners with an expressed interest in elevating the profession's status. The convention was noted by its absence of eminent leaders in medicine, as well as resistance from certain groups (Starr, 1982). While it is unlikely that health education would repeat this historical process, it is quite possible that this kind of leadership will be necessary for any formal process to develop.

The alternative either to the status quo or to a vigorous pursuit of formalization of standards can be found in the work of Levi (1980). Levi opines that there are basically two ways to move upward socially and economically. The first is to acquire an education and to pursue personal attainment. The second is to raise the status of one's job and, as a consequence, raise the practitioner's status. Further, Levi characterized "semi-professions" as those with aspirations of raising their status that have the following features:

- They are comprised primarily of women.
- They work in bureaucratic settings.
- They have little control over the numbers of new practitioners being produced.
- Their failure to control the labor supply results in excess supply of job applicants with two significant consequences: First, acceptable substitutes are available for any one practitioner, and, second, many people can perform the same functions of the practitioner.

What Levi depicts is a situation in which a health occupation has developed, but cannot achieve the kind of control necessary for sustenance of the profession's direction and self-determination. Yet this perspective on "semi-professions" is imperfectly applied to health education. A semi-profession, according to Levi, is one that demands accurate and efficient service delivery consistent with established guidelines. That is, a semi-profession does not require creativity, sound judgment and an ability to inspire trust. Health education practice requires qualities that go beyond a semi-profession as Levi defined it. Yet some of the features of semi-professions are applicable to the health education profession.

Given that health education has some collective decisions to make through its leaders and practitioners about its evolution as a distinctive field, what follows is a description and analysis of the steps to be taken and issues to be resolved for health educators to control the future. A systematic development of a quality assurance process for preparing capable practitioners can provide access for practitioners and consumers to benefit from quality health education services. Through a credentialing system, constituencies served by health educators have the potential of acquiring needed information about health education specialists and, as a result, about the services they offer. Ultimately, a credentialing system will be evaluated by the degree to which credentialed health educators will be accepted by consumers, other professions, employers, policy-makers and the public.

RATIONALE FOR CREDENTIALING HEALTH EDUCATORS

A premise for establishing a voluntary certification system for health educators is that the unregulated practice of health educators may result in harm to the public from unscrupulous or incompetent practitioners due to the perceived lack of recognized standards (Background statement, 1980; Baron, 1983; Cohen, 1979; Havighurst, 1983a, b; Henderson, 1982; Reid & Deane, 1982). For health educators and other professionals, harm is difficult to identify and measure precisely. Nevertheless, credentialing can be a useful means for establishing strong practice standards among practitioners and useful for ensuring quality services to the public. Historically, the evolution of professions and public delineation and acceptance of credentials has occurred in an uncoordinated fashion. No single pattern can be discerned, but elements of a profession have been identified. Most notably, Freidson has characterized attributes found among professions that have publicly recognized privileges to function autonomously to include the following:

1. A service orientation.
2. A prolonged period of specialized training.
3. A distinct body of knowledge.
4. Determination of standards of education and training.
5. A practice regulated by licensing and control over licensing by members of the occupation.
6. A professional organization (Freidson, 1970).

None of these attributes can produce social legitimacy. According to Freidson, all would-be professions must be able to gain full autonomy over the work they perform. Health educators often have their professional practice determined within the settings in which they work. This seriously limits the opportunities for health education to emerge as a profession. If Freidson's conceptualization of a profession is accepted, health educators need to gain control over their professional roles and responsibilities. Whether attempts for control derive from a motivation for better public service or for enhancing economic gain, it is the nature of the resulting credentialing system that will determine the nature of the benefits to the public and health educators.

Credentialing forms and methodology fall into distinct categories. Credentialing mechanisms are both public and private. Probably the most familiar public form of credentialing is licensure. Licensed professions come closest to Freidson's conceptualization of self-directing autonomy. Licensure is enacted by state legislatures to restrict the use of title and function to a professional group. Legislatures delegate authority to an agency charged with the responsibility of ascertaining credentials of candidates for a license, developing and implementing licensing standards, investigating complaints, and disciplining those practitioners found to be substandard (Background statement, 1980; Department of Health Education and Welfare [DHEW], 1977; Gaumer, 1984). Licensing agencies are most often governed by practitioners within the discipline being licensed, with these potential results: Restricting competition through controlling the supply of practitioners, impeding mobility among professional categories and across state lines, and failing to adequately police the ranks of the profession to remove or restrict substandard practitioners (Baron, 1983; Cohen, 1980; Gross, 1984; Reid & Deane, 1982; Zufal, 1981).

Private or voluntary credentialing practices often support licensure (Background statement, 1980; Cleary, 1986; Cohen, 1979). Accreditation of an institution, school or college, or program is frequently required for eligibility by licensing authorities (Beckes, 1981; Brodie & Heaney, 1978; DHEW, 1977; Larson, 1980). Accreditation is completed by a nonprofit organization that attests to the quality of education of those it accredits. General accreditation is done by regional accrediting bodies, such as the North Central Association of Schools and Colleges. Specialty accreditation is completed for schools, colleges or programs within a university. The most influential and accepted accrediting bodies are recognized by the Council for Postsecondary Accreditation (COPA). COPA recognition is important because the U.S. Department of Education uses COPA membership standards to help determine the eligibility of universities, schools, colleges and programs for federal grant and contract funding (Young, 1976; Young, Chambers, & Kells et al., 1983).

While accreditation has value for health educators, an attempt to develop an accrediting mechanism for health education programs is problematic. Among COPA members, only the Council on Education for Public Health (CEPH) has specific program accreditation for graduate programs in community health education. The National Commission for the Accreditation of Teacher Education (NCATE) accredits schools and colleges of education that often include health education programs (Gray, 1984). NCATE criteria do not address programmatic concerns such as health education. As only 6 out of an estimated 131 graduate health education programs outside schools of public health are accredited by CEPH (Cleary, 1986), with no undergraduate program accreditation, CEPH does not apply to the universe of health education programs. SOPHE has embarked upon an approval process for undergraduate health education, but is not recognized as an accrediting agency (Criteria and guidelines, 1977). Moreover, activities by professional associations in accreditation and other forms of credentialing have been criticized as self-serving, where professional groups limit the supply of professionals to produce some economic and job security (Arnstein, 1979; Baron, 1983; Brodie & Heaney, 1978; Fallows, 1985). Whether or not these concerns are appropriate for health educators is not at issue.

College and university leaders are concerned about the proliferation of specialized accrediting, related expenses, and the perceived usurpation of control over academic decision-making by outside agencies (Arnstein, 1979; Brodie & Heaney, 1978; Henderson, 1982). Thus, colleges and universities have become resistant to additional specialized accreditation; and some have dropped specialized accreditation while retaining the process of self-study and peer review that are central to accreditation mechanisms (DHEW, 1977; Jung, 1979; Orlan, 1980). Even if health educators could incorporate existing accreditation efforts into a new design for health education programs, the number and diversity of preparation programs would result in the accrediting of large numbers of programs at a level where quality would be an issue, or few programs that would not be representative of the field (Starr, 1982). Neither future scenario is desirable. Therefore, it is recommended that health education leaders continue to develop and disseminate the preparation standards for programs and existing accrediting bodies. Furthermore, the recommended credentialing system for health educators should include educational program development in conjunction with constituent organizations concerned with health education.

Like accreditation, certification is a private endeavor that often serves a public function. Certification focuses on demonstrated proficiency of an individual with respect to a number of qualifying standards, including some form of an examination, as does licensure (Background statement, 1980; DHEW, 1984). Certification can be developed for state or national levels. National programs are predominant since they can be used for state credentialing purposes as a substitute (Larson, 1980).

Certification allows restriction to the use of a title, rather than function as in licensure. The title should represent information important to consumers and employers. In some instances, required state licensure and national certification coexist (Cohen, 1980; DHEW, 1977). Social workers and physician's assistants are examples. The hypothetical title, Certified Health Educator (CHE), should represent evidence of proficiency that will aid the title holder to gain employment or to secure third party reimbursement for services or for other purposes. In return, those served by a certified health educator should be able to expect at least an acceptable level of quality for planning, implementing and evaluating health education services that benefit consumers and employers. Health educators required to have a state license, such as those teaching in schools, would be able to add certification, should they so choose, as evidence of their abilities. Furthermore, school health educators might promote certification to boards of education as a criterion for recruiting new teachers for health education classes.

Another advantage of a certification system is its potential for enhancing status. Employers, policy-makers, consumers and other professionals would have access to explicit standards of professional conduct, thus facilitating decision-making about using health education services. Third-party payers would have standards upon which to reimburse for health education services, where applicable. Certification would enable practitioners to remain geographically mobile in contrast to restrictions that would be imposed by state licensure (Cohen, 1979; Cohen, 1980; Fox, 1979). Certified practitioners would also have an opportunity to move within the profession by allowing career changes among the various settings in which health educators work, depending upon the level of entry for the individual practitioner within each setting. Career paths and mobility would be based upon a common foundation of professional identity and standards around which preservice and continuing education could be planned. A basic unity would provide direction to the development of the profession and establish a basis for developing relationships with other health professions.

To assure quality, certification practices typically rely upon more than one measure of proficiency. These include education, testing, supervised field experiences, and disciplinary practices (Henderson, 1982; National Commission for Health Certifying Acencies, or NCHCA, 1980). Education and training characteristics are often used as criteria for eligibility (NCHCA, 1980; Weisfeld, 1981). Without access to programs to assure eligibility, or to require an individual to return to higher education solely to gain eligibility, certification can be seen as restrictive on the supply of practitioners. Often evidence that justifies such restrictions is lacking. It is preferable, therefore, to develop opportunities for potential candidates to acquire the training necessary to perform adequately. Another measure typically used is an examination that tests knowledge and personal attributes. However, while great advancement has been made in developing tests of behavior, the lack of broad-based experience with such tests has yet to demonstrate their efficacy in identifying proficient practitioners (LaDuca, 1980; Olson & Freeman, 1979). An alternative certification measure involves ascertaining appropriate professional behavior through direct observation by experts (NCHCA, 1980). Various professions use evaluation of practicum, internship, and externship experiences to recommend a trainee for certification eligibility. Many preservice health education programs require similar training for their students, but the experience is not universal in the field, and such apprenticeship experiences are limited in scope (Cleary, 1986; Henderson, 1982). A procedure for disciplining certified members of the profession who are performing at a substandard level is necessary for encouraging public acceptance. Policies for receiving, processing and taking action on complaints about practitioners need to be included in a certification program. Active disciplinary standards help to maintain a reputation for quality and to avoid the appearance of substituting self-service for public service.

Since 1976, the NCHCA, an organization for health certifying agencies analogous to the Council on Postsecondary Accreditation, has emerged (NCHCA, 1984; Weisfeld, 1981). The Commission has developed certification practice criteria for certifying agencies wishing to become members. The criteria call for specific information about the certifying agency's organizational structure and credentialing practices, including the measures used for certification. The NCHCA has provided certifying bodies with a commonly accepted basis for certification procedures without dictating the content of the profession's practice. Thus, a well-developed framework for designing appropriate measures to certify health educators is in place to guide creation of the systems. The system should encourage public responsibility by health education practitioners while improving the identity and status of the profession.

In summary, a voluntary certification system for health educators will enable the profession to emerge as a valued contributor to the public's health, recognized by consumers, employers, policy-makers and other health professionals. The system, using several procedures, will establish a basic quality-assurance mechanism needed by, and missing from, the field. Of all credentialing methods, certification is the most readily adaptable and appropriate to the professional development needs of health educators. The certification system will provide information essential to informed decision-making by potential users of health education services that is currently unavailable. In return, the public will be directed to certified health educators as a reliable resource for information and services. The system will also establish a common foundation for developing preparation and practice standards for the challenges health educators face now and in the future.

CREDENTIALING ISSUES

Contemporary debates over the relative merits of credentialing practices have produced a wealth of literature. To take advantage of the experiences of many groups, credentialing issues can be divided into a number of interdependent themes: political (Arrow, 1985; Brodie & Heaney, 1978; Cohen; 1979; Cohen, 1980; Fox, 1979; Larson, 1980; Rottenberg, 1980), economic (Begun, 1980; Begun & Feldman, 1981; Hershleifer & Riley, 1979; Levin, 1980; Stigler, 1961; Stigler, 1962), legal and regulatory (Barney, 1983; Benham & Benham, 1975; Gaumer, 1984; Havighurst & King, 1983a, b; Peterson, 1983; Rottenberg, 1980), and quality assurance (Bausell, 1983a, b, 1985; Beinicker, 1984; Brook & Lohr, 1985; Donabedian, 1985; Farrington, Felch, & Hare, 1980; Gonella, 1983; Levine, 1985; Luke & Modrow, 1982; Matek, 1974; Mattson, 1984; Robertson & Martin, 1981; Schwartz, 1985). Note that despite considerable criticism and doubt about the validity and reliability of credentialing mechanisms, credentials are a well-accepted feature of our society. Furthermore, it is unlikely that reforms in credentialing will substantially alter current practices (Audent & Johnson, 1985); exceptions may be made for individual professions. Important decisions are made about personnel and services largely on the basis of established and accepted credentials. While it may seem difficult to establish a credentialing system, the ultimate and most difficult test of any credential is its acceptance by the public. It is rare that the public insists that credentials be created (Larson, 1980; Levi, 1980; Starr, 1982). Rather, it is the experience and expectation of society that occupational groups seek credentialing as they attempt to elevate their status as a profession.

Quality Assurance

Quality assurance has been defined as a system of organizing and controlling one's activities with the purpose of ensuring that the best possible services are received. Quality assurance selects standards to compare with results (Brown, 1985; Mattson, 1984).

Health services professions have been the subject of analytical studies conducted to establish definitions of and goals and objectives for quality care even before Donabedian formulated an analytical framework of structure, process and outcome (Bausel, 1983a; Donabedian, 1985). Structure refers to elements such as physical and organizational arrangements of health services and personnel characteristics. Process refers to the methodologies and services performed within the health service context. Outcome features include those of changes in health status resulting from health service delivery (Bausell, 1983a; Beinecke, 1984).

Ordinarily, quality assurance would form the foundation for rationalizing the need for credentialing specific health professionals. Yet most of the literature on quality assurance has emphasized either process or outcome criteria to evaluate quality of care (Donabedian, 1985; Farrington et al., 1980; Mattson, 1984). There is an apparent assumption in this literature that the competencies of health personnel are given (Levine, 1985). This situation is further complicated by uncontrolled growth of health occupations and of technology as well with subsequent impact upon scopes of practice. One major result is that job titles and credentials do not indicate accurately what is done by whom (Weisfeld & Falk, 1983). Another complication arises from the autonomy of licensed professions. Professional autonomy makes it difficult for sufficient information to be gathered from confidential interactions between consumers and health care providers. The result is a serious lack of data for evaluators to maintain accountability and assess quality of care (Luke & Modrow, 1982).

Schwartz, in reviewing the establishing of quality standards for health educators, notes that ihe competence of providers is essential for assuring quality (Schwartz, 1985). To evaluate competence and to assure quality, it is necessary to either evaluate a health educator prior to entering the field if the potential for consumer harm would entail unnecessary risk. Otherwise competence could be assessed based upon process and/or outcome measures from experience with program delivery (Komaroff, 1985).

Quality of care may be only tangentially related to knowledge and skills typically assessed by credentialing mechanisms. Methods employed by health educators may have little to do with outcomes of programs. It is also realized that outcomes are not easily evaluated in that health services received are only one set of numerous, and possibly more important, influences on outcomes: physical and social environments, personal attitudes and habits are examples (Mattson, 1984).

Despite limitations noted, quality-assurance mechanisms and investigations have improved in the recent past (Donabedian, 1985; Komaroff, 1985). Continuing development of evaluation strategies and technology will begin to explain the relationships between and importance of quality indicators. As Mattson succinctly stated, quality-assurance programs should be able to identify those practitioners operating outside of acceptable norms, by appropriate measures, and to improve the average practitioner's quality of care (Mattson, 1984).

Legal and Regulatory Issues

As concern has swelled in recent years about quality of health services, so has interest in the governmental role of licensure of the professions. As previously mentioned, the increasing ranks of new and existing health occupations combined with new knowledge and technology serve to increase the complexity of attempting to assign role definitions through legal and regulatory means. Existing state laws licensing certain health professions have been seen as inadequate for defining contemporary scopes of practice and as too vague to be meaningful (Baron, 1983; Didier, 1981; Gaumer, 1984; Gross, 1984).

The significant interest in pursuing licensure can be ascribed to the autonomy that this form of credential gives to licensed professions. Among the benefits licensure confers is a basic public recognition of prestige and legitimacy. Economic benefits can also be measurable (Begun & Feldman, 1981; Benham & Benham, 1975). Such qualities cannot be appropriated by any would-be profession, but must come from society. As Freidson conceptualized autonomous professional qualities, legal restrictions on who may practice a profession are controlled by licensing boards made up of the same kinds of practitioners who practice the profession (Brodie & Heaney, 1978; Freidson, 1970; Gross, 1984). Autonomy is granted by society in return for public service uncompromised by the self-interest of members of the profession.

Most occupational groups have not been able to achieve professional status. The nature of their work, perceived importance by the public, technical complexity, and notion of public service are not construed to be as significant as those acknowledged for the professions. Most aspiring professions lack a philosophy of public service, interpersonal qualities and autonomy in their activities (Levi, 1980; McCready, 1982). Even existing licensed health professions are finding it difficult to maintain autonomy. Dependence upon organizational facilities and other health personnel to perform their tasks has tended to bureaucratize health care (Larson, 1980; Nyre & Reilly, 1979). This has been reinforced further by the reimbursement requirements mandated by government and private third party payers (Weisfeld & Falk, 1983).

The desirability of a license and the large volume of occupations seeking licensure have raised interest in an analysis of governmental regulation of the professions. Many of the governmental licensing issues that have been uncovered are summarized by Rottenberg: Licensure is promoted by providers; enhancement of quality is suspect; licensure dampens the rate of innovation; licensure reduces the dissemination of information; licensure permits anticompetitive practices; licensure increases costs; licensing boards can control entry into the profession; licensure restricts the number of practitioners; and licensure restricts geographic mobility (Rottenberg, 1980). In addition, licensure affects the relationships among professions, reimbursement patterns for services rendered, educational programs, continuing competency after entry, and public accountability (Matek, 1974; Weisfeld & Falk, 1983; Zufall, 1981).

Related to licensing are the gaps in public policy within and between states. The Department of Health and Human Services recommended a moratorium on new state health profession licensing in the 1970s (DHEW, 1977). More than one author has indicated that proliferation of licensure systems is accompanied by a lack of clear public policy on the part of state legislatures and licensing boards to encompass acknowledged interrelationships between educational program content, credentialing and practice performance. And, critics note, licensing boards have traditionally been comprised of licensed professionals from the regulated disciplines, setting up the appearance of a conflict of interest, if not a conflict in fact (Gaumer, 1984; Rottenberg, 1980). Autonomous self-regulation is seen as anticompetitive, by its effects on controlling entry into a field, on limiting geographic mobility, and on lowering quality of care through failure to enforce compliance with established practice standards established among peers (Cohen, 1979; Cohen, 1980; DHEW, 1977; Luke & Modrow, 1982; Reid & Deane, 1982).

As imperfect as state licensure systems are, they are substantially influenced by federal government programs. Federal statutes and regulations restrict reimbursement for services to specific licensed professionals. The federal government funds many health profession education programs. In addition, federal programs have promoted the development of credentialing systems and have helped new health occupations to become more professional (Weisfeld, 1981).

It is not surprising, then, that the potential payoffs of autonomy, social prestige, economic gain, and a degree of job security have persuaded a number of health occupational groups to seek licensure as a desirable objective. However, the task of these groups is arduous. Each of the fifty states must be approached and effectively lobbied. Resistance by other professions and health care industry groups must be overcome. Other professions have an interest in protecting their territories from erosion. Industry groups tend to resist new licensing because they feel this tends to raise costs that must be passed on to consumers in higher prices for health care services (Begun & Feldman, 1981; Cline, 1985). Also, proposals to reform licensing practices have the potential to negate efforts of anyone occupational group seeking status as a licensed profession.

While large-scale reform in licensing practices is unlikely, reformers have proposed a number of changes in an attempt to make licensure effective and efficient (Faumer, 1984; Rottenberg, 1980; Weisfeld & Falk, 1983). The basic concern is that licensure does not assure quality, and that it is subject to the kinds of criticisms listed by Rottenberg above. Larson suggests that several criteria be used to evaluate the need for licensing a profession:

1. Capacity to harm the public
2. Uniqueness of the discipline
3. Overlapping functions among occupations
4. Availability of *less* restrictive approaches than licensure
5. Availability of nonoccupational regulatory means
6. Economic impact of regulation (Larson, 1980).

Larson's criteria could be consolidated in reforms to existing licensing practices and organization.

Several other reform proposals go further to change the essential character of licensing. One is to enact "sunset laws" that require states to periodically review the need for any given license, with the concept that certain professions should either be deregulated or their scopes of practice modified (Gaumer, 1984; McCready, 1982). A widely discussed reform would be to consolidate all state licensing boards into one superagency, thereby consolidating and augmenting scarce enforcement resources so that compliance with standards would be more consistently and broadly implemented (Cohen, 1979, 1980; Gaumer, 1984; Gross, 1984; Larson, 1980). Other licensing-board reforms include proposals that licensing boards represent consumers and other professionals related to the licensees' scope of practice. The idea is to inject some accountability and consideration of impact on other fields into licensing decisions (Luke & Modrow, 1982; McCready, 1982). Another proposal would be to deregulate all professions (Regulating the professions, 1981; Weisfeld, 1981). That is, eliminate all scope of practice acts as much, and open up opportunities for competitive service delivery. As an example, licensing only professional title is a variation of this reform. Unlicensed practitioners could practice in the same area, but would be restricted from use of a title. Consumers could compare practitioners and make their selections accordingly. Professional services would become more competitive, it is thought. Such deregulation would be accompanied by required information dissemination about practitioners to be made available to the public, state officials and health care institutions, and mandatory informed consent (McCready, 1982; Weisfeld, 1981). Similarly, proposals have been advanced to delegate personnel regulation to health care institutions that, in turn, must be licensed in order to offer services (Frey, 1984; Gray, 1984; Grossman, 1980; Licensing and credentialing, 1983). By investing institutions with personnel regulation authority, the organization would be responsible for monitoring and evaluating personnel the organization has deemed appropriate for the types of services they offer. Reformers would also like to have some assurance that individuals determined to be competent at entry be obligated to demonstrate competence on an ongoing basis. Typically, licensure has focused on entry-level competence and less attention has been paid to continuing competency (Audet & Johnson, 1985; Davy & Peter, 1982). Some states have required continuing education for maintaining a license, but evidence of process and outcome benefits from continuing education has been relatively scarce (Gray, 1984; Quatrano & Conan, 1981). Remarkably, only New York has begun to design actively mandatory relicensure in medicine (Cuomo proposes, 1986), an action that was proposed in 1986.

Some reformers are persuaded that privatization of licensure activities through voluntary certification of individuals would be of benefit (Weisfeld & Falk, 1983). By privatization, states would accrue some significant advantages: They would not need to be involved in studying credentialing issues and developing expertise; they would save time in deliberation, enactment and enforcement; focusing on private mechanisms would subject professional associations and certifying bodies to more public scrutiny; and all professions would be subject to equal employment opportunity, due process, fair trade, and anti-trust regulations that are now largely sheltered (Fox, 1979). In this context, certification avoids some of the major criticisms of occupational licensure already noted. Where it has been criticized, certification has closely emulated licensure: governing boards that are composed of certified practitioners from the same field; certifying agencies sponsored by professional associations; certificates granted for life; and restricted eligibility for certification to those who completed one kind of course of study (Cohen, 1979). Many certifying agencies are attempting to respond to criticism in positive ways. Apparent conflicts of interest among governing boards and professional associations are being met by separating the organization and by following common criteria for evaluating structures, process and outcomes of certifying agencies that have been developed by the NCHCA (NCHCA, 1984).

Breakthroughs in development of criterion-referenced testing have allowed certifying agencies to substantiate the validity and reliability of their assessment tools (Cline, 1985; Goleman, 1981). Application of these criteria raises opportunities for developing alternative educational experiences for certification eligibility, and alternative means for developing and implementing continuing competency tests and skill development programs (Olson & Freeman, 1979; NCHCA, 1980).

Privatization of credentialing enables a variety of legal remedies to be applied to assure accountability (Weisfeld & Falk, 1983). Lawsuits have pursued alleged discriminatory provisions of certain certified health professions (Havighurst & King, 1983a, b; Peterson, 1983). Tests of equal opportunity and potential adverse impact on minority groups have also been attempted (Chesney & Engel, 1983). From a legal perspective, the net effects of private certification can serve to encourage competition not found in licensure, create avenues for competent professionals to acquire certificates, and maintain the accountability of health care providers in health services delivery.

Eligibility for acquiring individual credentials is most often based upon educational attainment in a specialized program or school that has been evaluated by a nongovernmental, nonprofit agency and duly recognized by an authorized accrediting agency (Brodie & Heaney, 1978; Selden, 1971). For many professions, this is the only route that would-be practitioners can pursue to be eligible for needed credentials. However, nonaccreditation does not deter schools and programs from graduating professionals nor them from practicing (Nyre & Riley, 1979). Thus, accreditation only partially contributes to control of professional practice; without individual mechanisms of control it is often necessary but not sufficient. It has been argued that professions attempt to control the supply of practitioners by requiring graduation from accredited programs without the possibility of transferring credits for courses completed or relevant degrees or work experience (Fox, 1979; Orlans, 1980).

Numerous accreditation practices are criticized. Curricula are typically standardized, compromising institutional perogatives, academic freedom, and experimentation. Colleges and universities have an incentive to maintain accreditation for the benefit of their graduates so that they may be eligible to seek an individual credential. Due to increasing specialization among professions, multiple program accreditation standards, procedures, and expenses have accrued to institutions of higher education. Some specialized accrediting agencies have multiple overlapping standards, some of which conflict (Arnstein, 1979; Beckes, 1981; Brodie & Heaney, 1978; Casey & Harris, 1979; Greene, 1984; Horvath, 1983). Nevertheless, educational standards have been recognized as a basic element in the evaluation of a profession.

The importance of developing a systematic means for evaluating educational quality is illustrated by Starr's observation that medicine did not become a profession until it began to control the supply of new professionals entering the field. Even with licensure, medicine could not establish consensus and legitimacy (Starr, 1982). Medical schools adhered to a variety of medical and educational tenets, contributing large numbers of practitioners with little agreement and no public recognition of their special expertise. Licenses were easily obtained with few basic qualifications necessary for eligibility. Once the American Medical Association was formed and its Committee on Medical Education developed, eventually medical curricula became standardized, emphasizing newly emerging science, and resulted in the report of Abraham Flexner in 1910 that accelerated the standardization process. Ironically, the stringent standards for curricula in medical education have resulted in much of the criticism leveled at accreditation: reducing access to entering the profession, rigidity of curricula that reduces the opportunities for educational innovation, growth, and flexibility, and degrees that are self-serving to the credentialed profession (Starr, 1982).

Economic Issues

Another significant issue in credentialing is the observation that health professions use their specialized skills and knowledge for economic and social advantage (Beham & Benham, 1975; Levi, 1980). That is, credentialed health professionals can determine, to a significant degree, the supply of health care services. For example, medicine is defined by licensed physicians. Those wishing to provide medical care must possess a license to do so, with significant legal penalties for those who practice without a license. Medicine is an example of a defined market restricting potential buyers to one type of seller.

Economic markets are made by sellers and buyers seeking each other out to exchange goods and services for something of value. Assumably, both buyers and sellers have equal access to information that will enable economic transactions to take place (Levin, 1980; Stigler, 1961). Information symmetry enables buyers and sellers to search for the most beneficial transaction. In contrast to normal economic assumptions, the market for health services is presumed to have informational asymmetry brought about by the complexities that cannot be adequately evaluated by the consumer and/or that health care services expose consumers to such risks that they must be protected from harm from potentially unscrupulous providers (Benham& Benham, 1975; Hershleifer & Riley, 1979; Rottenberg, 1980). The substitute for market information, then, is the health professional's credentials. Consumers, in this perspective, make decisions to purchase health care services based upon credentials possessed by the practitioner as a substitute for broader and more varied information. As such, this form of economic transaction represents what Freidman calls a "market failure" (Benham & Benham, 1975).

Market failures involve intervention between buyers and sellers by some form of governmental agency, such as licensure. Nevertheless, possession of a license of some sort enables the potential buyer of services to make purchasing decisions. The license serves as an informational device that has certain benefits: the potential buyer has a convenient shortcut to valuable information and reduces the cost of searching for the evaluating information gained. Where services are unique, the efficiency of personal search is low, because the identity of potential sellers is not known (Stigler, 1962). This is often circumvented by advertising, something that has been resisted by health professions.

Interpretation of studies of the effect of professional codes of ethics restricting information available to the public has led to the conclusion that costs are higher for specific services in some states, in contrast to other states that have less restrictive licensing practices (Barney, 1983; Begun & Feldman, 1981; Benham & Benham, 1975). Restrictions on advertising have been criticized for reducing dissemination of information useful for purchasing decisions. On the other hand, it has been held that advertising allows unscrupulous providers to endanger the health and safety of the public (Luke & Modrow, 1982). In this sense, the public is trading higher prices for some assurance of quality. Possession of a license, in economic terms, increases the earnings of the licensee by limiting competition.

Voluntary forms of individual credentialing tend to minimize economic criticisms of occupational licensing practices (Weisfeld, 1981). With certification, typically no one is excluded from the market for selling services even though certified individuals attempt to distinguish the value of the credential from those who do not possess it. Should certified professionals gain regulatory and economic benefits from third party payers, then certification begins to approach licensure restrictions discussed above (Regulating, 1981). How the consumer uses the information supplied by the certificate would determine its economic value. If the credential represents social value, then the individual professional and consumer have benefited from market decisions supported by information conveyed by the certificate.

The demand for services from a particular profession will be affected by a market where there are multiple sources of information, or where there is functional redundancy among several occupational groups (Levi, 1980; Rosse & Rosse, 1981). The consumer can substitute one type of service for another.

Information about health education specialists is not broadly disseminated among the public. A credentialing system would correct this situation partially, but other problems remain (Henderson, 1982). The inability to influence the supply of health educators tends to lower prices, making the market weak for practitioners (Salmon & Culbertson, 1985). There would be economic benefit to the field as a whole in limiting supply, but any effort would have to prevent or minimize the economic criticisms of anticompetitive, costly professions (Hamburg, 1980; Taub, 1980).

Political Issues

Political issues reflect legal, economic, and quality assurance concerns surrounding credentialing. Examples of established health professions have encouraged other health occupations to take on the challenge of developing one or more forms of credentialing. Professional groups that have faced the challenges of developing credentialing systems in response to the issues include occupational therapy, physical therapy, dietetics, environmental health, speech and hearing, physician's assistants, and medical records (Audet & Johnson, 1985; Didier, 1981; Frey, 1984; Gray, 1984; Hofman, 1984; McCready, 1982). Many have been engaged in pursuing licensure, certification and other credentialing mechanisms. The environmental health profession has evaluated performance on its certification examination with professional practice and found substantial, but not perfect, correlation (Cline, 1985). Occupational therapy has been engaged in a national campaign to establish licensure, as previously discussed (Davy & Peters, 1982). Physicians' assistants and speech and hearing professional organizations have uncovered several issues in pursuing credentialing: sunset legislation for licensing boards; consolidation of licensing boards and augmented enforcement of practice standards; consumer representation on licensing boards; proposed deregulation of licensure with required information on performance to consumers, state, and institutions; privatization of credentialing; and institutional licensure (Grossman, 1980; Licensing, 1983). The American Dietetic Association has specified a comprehensive professional development system with quality assurance as its central focus (Report of the task force, 1978).

These groups have determined that the interest of the publics they serve and the sense of identity, purpose and mission of their members are well served by credentialing efforts. For them the information conveyed by a credential has value to policymakers, employers, consumers, other professionals, and the public (Gross, 1984). Despite the numerous issues presented by the various forms of credentialing, the combination of standards for preparation, practice and continuing competence are presumed to provide a consistent system for assuring basic capability. Such systems should not be expected to assure the best job performance, but only to help prevent the worst performance of those entering and staying in the field (Audet & Johnson, 1985; Davy & Peters, 1982). While imperfectly designed and carried out, establishment of a basic level of performance can give identity to a professional field of practice and can give confidence in the value of the services performed by the credentialed practitioner (Starr, 1982).

Once the basic decision has been made to pursue a credentialing system, political forces and strategies have to be evaluated as to how best to achieve this aim. Assets and liabilities of each credentialing mechanism must be weighed. It also needs to be recognized that there is no concerted opposition to a credentialing system. Opposition comes from specific interest groups surrounding a particular credential, such as licensure. There are no states that have designed an interlocking system of credentialing policies to govern any given application for licensure, as an example (Gaumer, 1984). Opposition typically comes from established professions protecting their own territory and health care organizations protecting their market position.

While the health professions credentialing field is already crowded by incumbents and petitioners, changes in society are likely to provide opportunities for new credentialing endeavors. Societal needs change, either from demographic changes and disease patterns or from changing definitions of social values (Cohen, 1979; Larson, 1980; Weisfeld & Falk, 1983). Social change is caused and affected by new knowledge, skills and technology. New or modified forms of service-delivery organizations and financial imperatives necessary to meet socially desirable ends will appear. In turn, health occupations will attempt to stabilize the environment to maintain the identity and continuity of new and existing practitioners, often using credentialing as a balancing force. At present it is unclear whether the need for stabilization using credentialing will maintain a field's integrity or society will change so much as to make the field irrelevant.

PROPOSED CERTIFYING ORGANIZATION

In accordance with the benefits of developing a credentialing system for health educators, it is recommended that an organization be formed to plan, organize and implement a voluntary certification program for health educators. The mission of the organization, to be known as the National Commission for Certifying Health Educators (NCCHE) would be to develop and implement a voluntary certification process for health educators as a means for ensuring the public's access to quality health education services. The purposes of the NCCHE are threefold: (1) to assure quality health education practices; (2) to communicate the roles and functions of certified health educators to constituencies served by health education professionals; and (3) to provide a common standard for preparation, practice and continuing competency of health educators.

To achieve the mission and purposes of the NCCHE, the following objectives must be accomplished:

1. To develop a certifying organization responsive to the needs of health educators and their constituencies for quality health education services.
2. To delineate roles and functions of health educators.
3. To establish criteria for use in certification and recertification procedures.
4. To facilitate opportunities for acquiring essential knowledge and skills for those wishing to become certified.
5. To investigate trends affecting health education practice.
6. To diffuse standards of preparation and practice throughout the health education profession.
7. To provide a means for investigating and disciplining malpractice among certified members.

The accompanying organization chart (Figure 1) depicts the proposed structure of the NCCHE. It is proposed that the NCCHE be formed and that it function in a manner consistent with the criteria for full membership in the NCHCA, meeting the requirements for certifying policies and procedures for NCHCA eligible-member agencies.

It is proposed that NCCHE be incorporated and be legally governed by

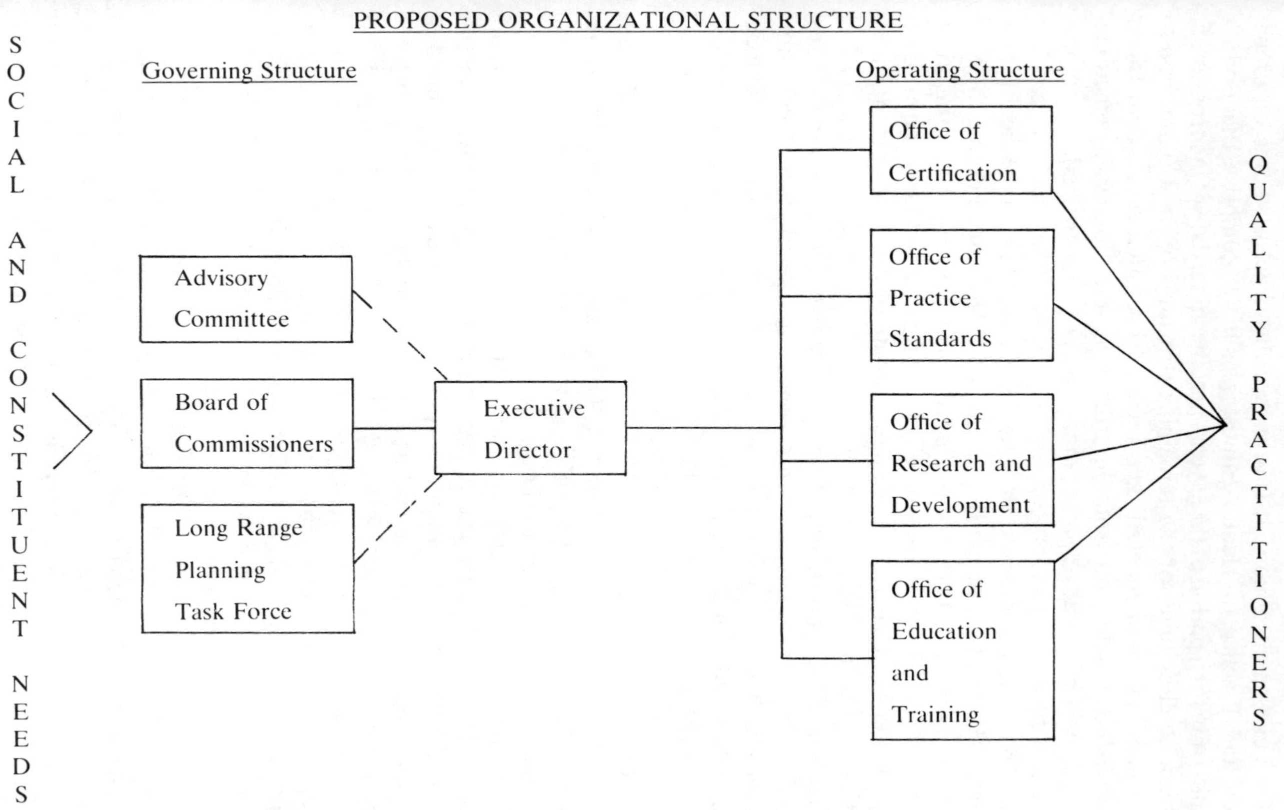

PROPOSED ORGANIZATIONAL STRUCTURE

Governing Structure

Operating Structure

SOCIAL AND CONSTITUENT NEEDS

QUALITY PRACTITIONERS

Advisory Committee

Board of Commissioners

Long Range Planning Task Force

Executive Director

Office of Certification

Office of Practice Standards

Office of Research and Development

Office of Education and Training

Figure 1. National Commission for Certifying Health Educators.

a Board of Commissioners. It is proposed that the Task Force on Preparation and Practice of Health Educators initially comprise the Board's membership for a period of three years past the initial date of incorporation. This could allow time for the remaining structures of the Commission to be planned and implemented. It is recommended that subsequent Board membership include representation from at least the following constituencies: the field of practice, preparation programs in higher education, employers of health educators, consumers of health education services, and professional organizations with a significant membership of health educators. The exact size of the Board should be determined during the term of the initial Board. It is recommended that subsequent Board members be elected for a 3-year term with eligibility for one additional term. Elections should be staggered to assure continuity of the development of the NCCHE's programs and policies.

The Board's functions, aside from considerable start-up responsibilities, would be to examine environmental conditions affecting health educators and the NCCHE, to develop a philosophy for the organization, to set long-range goals and objectives, to develop, review and revise a master plan for the organization, and to establish performance objectives consistent with the long range goals and objectives. The initial Board would be responsible for incorporating the NCCHE, developing by-laws, and achieving tax-exempt status for the corporation. The Board would also recruit, hire, and oversee the actions of the Executive Director. It is anticipated that the Board would meet quarterly.

The Board and Executive Director would be assisted by two groups appointed by the Board. The first is the Advisory Committee. Meeting annually, the Advisory Committee would consist of experts appointed by the Board from the fields of certification, accreditation, public policy and from among senior and distinguished health educators. The Advisory Committee's primary function would be to assist the Board and Executive Director to review and establish the organization's philosophy, environmental assumptions, goals and objectives, and the master plan. To assure a broad and continuing base for input, Advisory Committee members would be appointed for a two-year term.

The second group to assist the Board and Executive Director would be the Long-Range Planning Task Force. This group would be appointed by the Board on an "as-needed basis." Membership on the Task Force would be based on the tasks at hand. The function of the Task Force would be to provide timely direction to the Board and Executive Director as health education, the environment and the Commissions evolve. The Task Force should be able to identify strategic issues that must be faced over an extended period, such as five years.

Staff for the Commission would be headed by an Executive Director, appointed for an indefinite period. Candidates for this position should have experience in working with health professions' organizations, credentialing, managerial and fiscal matters. The Executive Director would be charged with carrying out the mission, purposes, goals and objectives of the Commission reflected in the Board's plans and policies. The Executive Director would report to the Board and act as a staff liaison to the Advisory Committee and Long-Range Planing Task Force. The Executive Director would develop annual operational performance objectives and subsequent policies and procedures necessary for their achievement. Based upon the stated objectives, the Executive Director would conduct periodic evaluations and submission of an annual report on operations and fiscal status for the prior year. Additionally, the Executive Director would be obligated to propose an annual budget and initiate and assist in fund-raising activities on behalf of the Commission.

The Executive Director would be responsible for recruiting, hiring and supervising support and professional staff. Support staff would assist the Executive Director's and professional staff's functions. Professional staff would be responsible for conducting the Commission's functions as described below. The Executive Director would be responsible for disseminating information to constituent groups, individuals and related organizations about the Commission's activities.

To assist the Executive Director to carry out the responsibilities for implementing the Commission's mission and purposes, four specific office functions are suggested. Eventually, each office would be headed by a professional staff member with qualifications appropriate to carry out the delineated functions. First, the Office of Certification would fulfill several responsibilities: reviewing documentation of applicants, proficiency test development and test administration for initial and subsequent certifications, and issuing of certificates to those demonstrating their proficiency. Also, this office would periodically review and evaluate test instuments and administration procedures to assure that the certification process is accurate and up to date. Also, it would work with the National Commission for Health Certifying Agencies to maintain certification standards. Second, the Office of Education and Training would have numerous responsibilities: developing preservice educational standards, reviewing and certifying field training programs for those in the field without formal preparation, collaborating with the Council on Postsecondary Accreditation and constituent agencies, such as the Council on Education for Public Health and the National Commission for Accreditation of Teacher Education, on educational criteria for preparing health educators, developing self-assessment programs for practitioners—including materials and learning modules, and providing consultation to programs and faculty. Third, the Office of Practice Standards would be responsible for working with practitioners and other constituents to achieve the following: reviewing specialty group developments (e.g., patient education), conducting public education, investigating and disciplining deviant certified members, developing practice settings for future placement, and reviewing apprenticeship/internship programs to determine eligibility for certification. Fourth, the Office of Research and Development would assist the Commission's Activities by collecting, analyzing and reporting data essential to certification: collecting data on health education manpower, projecting trends in demand and supply for health education personnel, developing role specifications for advanced-level practitioners, maintaining a research data base on health education services, conducting special projects as needed, and preparing reports and documentation for constituents and related groups.

Each component of the proposed Commission structure should be able to function in a systematic fashion to fulfill the stated mission and purposes while being responsive to the needs of constituents served. Growth of the Commission is envisioned to be evolutionary, as the activities of each Commission advance in complexity.

The Commission will need to encounter and resolve credentialing issues. Initially, the Commission will need to address the means for transforming current health education practitioners from noncertified to certified status and the design of the certification system. The notion of "grandfathering" practitioners, that is allowing some to be credentialed largely due to their existence as active professionals rather than due to demonstrated competency, is problematic. Practitioners who must meet all certification requirements subsequent to the implementation of certification can legitimately cite grandfathering as an issue of fairness. Where jobs are involved, economic discrimination and unfair competition can be cited as consequences of grandfather clauses. Solutions to this issue have been approached on two fronts. First, such clauses have been narrowed in scope and time limits. Second, existing practitioners are required to complete self-assessment and training in areas of weakness to be eligible to participate in the certification process. To the extent that significant numbers of health educators would be certified initially without meeting standards required of those that follow, the value and meaning of the certificate would diminish for consumers of health education services.

Design of the certification program is related to issues surrounding grandfather clauses. Should the definition of eligibility be narrowly drawn to include only those who graduated from a health education program; then those who are or would perform the same functions who do not have a formal health education degree would be excluded from the certification process. Most often, educational requirements are linked with certification when there exists substantial agreement upon the standards for preparation of health educators. No such agreement exists in higher education currently, although efforts are being made. Programs for preparation in health education vary in their scope, content and organization. It would be preferable to design eligilibity criteria to include carefully investigated and described equivalent alternatives for eligibility. Credentialing systems typically consider varying combinations of education, supervised field experience, work experience, recommendations and successful completion of a proficiency examination (DHEW, 1977). These characteristics ought to be used as basic components in a combination supplemented by learning modules to enable those in the field to gain knowledge and skill where needed, in usage similar to a limited grandfather clause. Caution should be exercised in over-reliance upon criterion-referenced examinations in the certification process. Experience insufficient to depend wholly upon the relationship between successful completion of an examination and acceptable professional performance has been reported in the literature. Multiple measures, therefore, are recommended to compensate for deficiencies in individual credentialing components.

A further design question to be considered is the degree of specificity in the credentialing processes. Generally, more rigorous and specific credentialing procedures result in fragmentation of the field, as significant numbers of practitioners may fall outside accepted criteria. In reverse, more general criteria for the credential compromise quality control. Thus, a balance must be sought between the need for quality control and inclusiveness.

Provisions for peer review and disciplinary actions to be taken against substandard professional behavior should be included in the initial system design. To the extent that a profession lacks a rigorous program to accept, investigate and take action on complaints about a certified member, the benefits of the credential to the public are diminished.

To strive to develop a public service demeanor, the proposed Commission should use the information it gathers to educate consumers about health education. Differences between professional and public expectations and values are often due to informational asymmetry (Benham & Benham, 1975). That is, information useful to consumers for making decisions to use particular health care providers is routinely collected by credentialing organizations, but is usually difficult for consumers to collect independently. Lack of efficacy and discrepancies in quality erode public trust of the information disseminated by a profession, and accordingly, confidence in that profession.

While collecting and disseminating information can be useful to constituencies served by health educators, attempts to monopolize information and credentialing can be counterproductive. Constituencies are left with a sole source of information that diminishes competition in the occupational group and can be viewed as self-serving. Furthermore, establishing an information monopoly can result in restricting innovation and impeding professional development in favor of preserving the status quo. The potential for erosion of public confidence in a sole source of information should be considered in the Commission's design.

Each credentialing mechanism has potential for abuse and engendering of public mistrust. Essentially, the fundamental design question to be faced by the proposed Commission will be to anticipate outcomes of the credentialing practices using knowledge of credentialing practice issues. Care must be given to designing the Commission to meet its explicit mission and purposes.

STEPS TOWARD IMPLEMENTING A NATIONAL COMMISSION FOR CERTIFYING HEALTH EDUCATORS

Opportunities for developing a certification program are largely dependent upon the will of the profession's leadership to take the initiative. There is an absence of an acknowledged procedural model to develop the program. Nevertheless, the credentialing issues the Commission must face in conjunction with the recommended organizational structure suggest a progressive series of steps to be taken. Time for implementation could be as short as two years, should adequate funding be secured, or as long as five years with currently available resources.

Initially, the Task Force should convene the leadership of the Society for Public Health Education, the Association for the Advancement of Health Education and other constituent health education groups. Representatives from the National Commission for Health Certifying Agencies, the Council on Postsecondary Accreditation, and the U.S. Public Health Service's Bureau of Health Professions should be included. The purpose of convening leadership and interested parties is to gain consensus on the design and implementation plan for the proposed NCCHE. Development of consensus would help to (1) legitimize the process, and (2) communicate with the profession.

The next step would be to develop an organizational structure for the Commission. Becoming incorporated as a nonprofit corporation and seeking tax-exempt status as an educational institution are the first tasks to be accomplished. These accomplishments will require formulation of the corporation's by-laws by the Task Force, acting as the initial Board of Commissioners (BOC). The BOC should form the Advisory Committee and Long-Range Planning Task Force. The two groups will involve the constituencies served by the Commission for communication and corporate development, plus establish a time table for subsequent development of the Commission's function.

With basic leadership, planning and corporate structure in place, the remaining steps to complete the organizational structure would be to explore the feasibility of contracting with existing health education organizations, to provide staff and institutional support, at least on an interim basis, and to seek an executive director possibly from the same organization sought for interim support. At the same time funding should be sought from foundation or corporate sponsors to begin Commission operations.

As organizational, administrative and fiscal support are secured, a phased implementation of the Commission's activities is projected. Initial work should be concerned with developing the components of the proposed Office of Certification so that an early date to begin certification can be set. Next would come the Office of Education and Training to assure eligibility for those already in practice and to assure professional preparation programs are in possession of standards for preservice education. Subsequently, the Office of Practice Standards would be developed for practice site development, field experience evaluation and public education. Last, the Office of Research and Development would be phased in to provide and evaluate data for the Commission's activities. Functions essential to the Commission's operating would be assumed by existing structures until such time as the volume of activities necessitates functional division into separate offices.

Operationally, the Commission could use the products of Role Delineation Project and materials developed by the Task Force as the foundation for the Commission's work. Distribution of available materials, publicizing the Commission through informal brochures, securing constituent endorsements, and advocating for the Commission to employers and policy-making groups should be undertaken to solidify the Commission's position as a source of reliable information about quality health education practice.

Concurrently, with efforts to position the Commission as a reliable information source, current Task Force efforts to develop networks to strengthen education should be assumed by the Commission, particularly in the area of continuing education. A network for continuing education should be established, beginning with geographic areas with relatively strong health education resources, programs and personnel. Wherever possible, external funding sources to support continuing education should be obtained, including funding for state-of-the-art educational technology. The Commission should encourage health education manpower research by college and university faculty and graduate students. Data would be collected from manpower studies, credentialing results, and professional placement and career advancement information. Systems for credentialing and professional development used by National Commission for Health Certifying Agencies' members, and related organizations such as the American College of Hospital Administrators, should be explored. Collected information and data should be used to help form criteria for certification.

Criteria for certification and recertification should be specified that considers significant issues affecting certification. Provisions for "grandfathering" should be carefully formulated and limited in scope and time. Avenues for eligibility to assure access for qualified candidates using alternative combinations of education, training, experience, supervised field experience, and letters of recommendation should be developed. Eligibility considerations should also consider providing access to training programs for practitioners without formal educational credentials in health education. Certification and recertification procedures should be consistent with National Commission for Health Certifying Agencies criteria. Any proficiency examination developed for certification should be based upon criterion referenced testing principles. Consideration should be given to contracting with a test firm to develop and validate proficiency examinations. Prototype certification should be field tested and modified as necessary before full-scale certification and continuing education; then, the remainder of Commission functions should be able to evolve.

FUNDING

Experience is lacking in health education for funding an organization such as the proposed Commission. Success has been demonstrated from time to time in funding-specific projects with time limits, which suggests two strategies. First, funding should be sought for initial start-up work for the Commission. Second, resources within health education should be developed for continuing and expanding the Commission's credentialing program.

For initial funding, the Board of Commissioners and Executive Director should pursue grants and/or contracts for developing specific components of the Commission. While the current environment for governmental funding is not promising, an effort should be made to explore potential sources. The degree to which initial fund-raising activities are successful to a large extent will determine the scale and pace of the development of the Commission.

Continuing funding should be obtained from a variety of sources. Fees from candidates for certification and recertification should support test development and administration costs. Consideration should be given to enacting an annual maintenance fee for all members and candidates for general support. Accurate manpower estimates as to the number of actively employed health educators and annual figures of the numbers of graduates from baccalaureate and graduate programs should help determine the amount to be assessed, along with an estimated percentage of those who would pursue certification. Materials, learning modules, and programs for continuing education should be priced so that income derived can be applied to general support for the Commission. Consideration should also be given to promoting corporate contributions of annual fees to the Commission. Potential contributors include professional associations, employers, and foundations committed to health education. A consultation-fee schedule for professional staff should be developed. All fees received should accrue to the Commission. Finally, the Commission should pursue grants and contracts from private and public sources for special projects in support of the Commission's functions.

REFERENCES

Anderson, O. W., & Shields, M. C. (1982). Quality measurement and control in physician decision making: State of the art. *Health Services Research, 17*(2), 125–155.

Arnstein, G. (January, 1979). Two cheers for accreditation. *Phi Delta Kappan*, 357–360.

Arrow, K. J. (1951). *Social choice and individual values.* New York: Wiley.

Audet, M. F., & Johnson, D. W. (1985). Credentialing of diagnostic x-ray technologists. A question of public health impact. *American Journal of Public Health, 75*(3), 270–274.

Background statement for credentialing program sponsored by Bureau of Health Professions. (1980, April). Washington, DC, Bureau of Health Professions.

Barney, D. R. (1983). Regulation of health services advertising. *Hospital and Health Services Administration, 28*(3), 85–110.

Baron, C. H. (1983). Licensure of health care professionals: The consumer's case for abolition. *American Journal of Law and Medicine, 9*(3), 335–336.

Bausell, R. B. (1985). Perceived quality of hospital care: Consensus among physicians, nurses, and consumers. *Evaluation and The Health Professions, 8*(4), 401–412.

Bausell, R. B. (Ed.) (1983a). Quality assurance: An overview. *Evaluation and the Health Professions, 6*(2).

Bausell, R. B. (Ed.) (1983b). Quality assurance: Methods. *Evaluation and the Health Professions, 6*(3).

Beckes, S. K. (1981, February). Toward an understanding of accreditation practices. *Nursing and Health Care*, 68–72.

Begun, J. W. (1980). *Professionalism and the public interest: Price and quality in optometry.* Cambridge: MIT Press.

Begun, J., & Feldman, R. (1981, April). *A social and economic analysis of professional regulation in optometry.* DHHS Pub. No. (PHS) 81–3295.

Beinecke, R. H. (1984). The differential effectiveness of oversight mechanisms. *Evaluation and the Health Professions, 7*(3), 341–363.

Benham L., & Benham A. (1975). Regulating through the professions: A perspective on information control. *Journal of Law and Economics, 18*, 421–447.

Blum, A. (1982). Medical activism. In Taylor, R. B., Ureda, J. R., & Denham, J. W. (Eds.),

Health promotion: Principles and clinical applications. Norwalk, CT: Appleton-Century-Crofts.

Brodie, D. C., & Heaney, R. P. (1978) Need for reform in health profession accrediting. *Science (Wash. DC), 201*(18), 589–593.

Brook, R. H., & Lohr, K. N. (1985). Efficacy, effectiveness, variations, and quality. *Medical Care, 23*(5), 710–711.

Brown, L. (1985). How does PE interface with quality assurance? *Patient Education Newsletter, 8*(6), 3–4.

Casey, R. J., & Harris, J. W. (1979). *Accountability in higher education: Forces, counterforces, and the role of institutional accreditation,* Washington, DC: The Council on Postsecondary Accreditation.

Chesney, J. D., & Engel, R. J. (1983). Quantitative analysis of a licensing examination using adverse impact. *Evaluation and the Health Professions, 6*(1), 115–129.

Cleary, H. P. (1986). Policy implications of credentialing health education specialists. *Advances in Health Education and Promotion, 1*(1).

Cline, C. S. (1985). Credentialing and job practice in environmental health: An empirical study. *Public Health Reports, 100*(4), 427–432.

Coates, T. J., & Demuth, N. M. (1984). An analysis of competencies and training needs for psychologists specializing in health enhancement. In Matarazzo J. D., et al. (Eds.): *Behavioral health: A handbook of health enhancement and disease prevention.* New York: Wiley-Interscience.

Cohen, H. S. (1980). On professional power and conflict of interest: State licensing boards on trial. *Journal of Health Politics, Policy and Law, 5*(2), 291–307.

Cohen, H. S. (1979). Public versus private interest in assuring professional competence. *Family and Community Health, 2*(4), 79–85.

Criteria and guidelines for baccalaureate programs in community health education. (1977). *Health Education Monographs, 5*(1), 90–98.

Cuomo proposes to test doctors. (1986, May 29). *The New York Times.*

Davy, J. D., & Peters M. (1982) State licensure for occupational therapists. *American Journal of Occupational Therapy, 36*(7), 429–432.

Didier, E. P. (1981). Licensing in the health occupations (editorial). *Mayo Clinic Proceedings, 56,* 714–715.

Donabedian, A. (1985). Twenty years of research on the quality of medical care: 1964–1984. *Evaluation and the Health Professions, 8*(3), 243–265.

Fallows, J. (1985). The case against credentialism. *The Atlantic Monthly,* 49–67.

Farrington, J. F., Felch, W. C., & Hare, R. L. (1980, July 17). Quality assessment and quality assurance: The performance-review alternative. *New England Journal of Medicine, 3033,* 154–156.

Fifer, W. R. (1984, September). Beyond peer review: The medical staff role in the price-competitive hospital. *Quality Review Bulletin,* 262–268.

Fox, J. G. (1979, November). Public and private credentialing in conflict. *Family and Community Health, 2*(3), 87–97.

Freidson, E. (1970). *Profession of medicine.* New York: Harper & Row.

Frey, W. R. (1984, February). Credentialing nonphysician providers of health care. *Journal of Allied Health,* 70–73.

Gaumer, G. L. (1984). Regulating health professionals: A review of the empirical literature. *Milbank Memorial Fund Quarterly/Health and Society, 62*(3), 380–416.

Goleman, D. (1981, January). The new competency tests: Matching the right people to the right jobs. *Psychology Today,* 35–46.

Gonnella J. S. (1983). Internal versus external quality control: The value of external examination in medical education (editorial). *Journal of Medical Education, 58*(4), 358–359.

Gray, M. S. (1984). Recertification and relicensure in the allied health professions. *Journal of Allied Health, 13*(1), 22–30.

Grebner, F. (1981, June). Role of the profession in credentialing. *Journal of Health, Physical Education, Recreational and Dance*, 58–59.

Green, L. W. (1976). Suggested procedures for moving from programmatic accreditation to peer review under broader institutional accreditation. *Health Education Monographs, 4*(3), 278–284.

Greene, B. R. (1984). The context and social role of specialized accreditation. *Journal of Health Administration Education, 2*(4), 409–418.

Gross, S. J. (1984). *Of foxes and hen houses: Licensing and the health professions*. Westport, CT: Quorum Books.

Grossman, D. B. (1980). Progress and peril: A report on the status of state licensure. *Journal of the American Speech and Hearing Association*, 1004–1009.

Hamburg, M. V. (1980). Concepts and trends in the preparation of health educators in the U.S. *International Journal of Health Education*, 82–86.

Havighurst, C. C., & King, N. M. (1983a). Private credentialing of health care personnel: An anti-trust perspective. Part One. *American Journal of Law and Medicine, 9*(2), 131–201.

Havighurst, C. C., & King, N. M. (1983b). Private credentialing of health care personnel: An anti-trust perspective. Part Two. *American Journal of Law and Medicine, 9*(3), 263–334.

Hemenway D. (1983). Quality assessment from an economic perspective: A taxonomy of approaches with applications to nursing home care. *Evaluation and the Health Professions, 6*(4), 379–396.

Henderson, A. C. (1982). Credentialing: How it applies to school health educators. *Health Values, 6*(1), 54–62.

Hershleifer, J., & Riley, J. G. (1979). The analytics of uncertainties and information—An expository survey. *Journal of Economic Literature, 17*, 1375–1421.

Hofmann, P. B. (1984). Healthcare credentialing issues demand increased attention. *Hospital and Health Services Administration, 29*(3), 86–96.

Horvath, F. L. (1983). Rights and responsibilities in the accreditation process. *Journal of Allied Health, 12*(4), 245–248.

Jung, S. M. (1979). *Accreditation and student consumer protection*. Washington, DC: The Council on Postsecondary Accreditation.

Komaroff, A. L. (1985). Quality assurance in 1984. *Medical Care, 2*(5), 723–734.

LaDuca, A. (1980). The structure of competence in health professions. *Evaluation and the Health Professions, 3*(3), 253–288.

Larson, C. W. (June, 1980). Health occupational credentialing: The challenge for the 1980's. A paper prepared for the New York State Board of Regents.

Levi, M. (1980). Functional redundancy and the process of professionalization: The case of registered nurses in the United States. *Journal of Health Politics, Policy and Law, 5*(2), 333–353.

Levin, H. M. (1980) Teacher certification and the economics of information. *Educational Evaluation and Policy Analysis, 2*(4), 5–18.

Levine, H. G. (1985). Quality of care: Relationship to quality of education. *Evaluation and the Health Professions, 8*(4), 429–437.

Licensing and credentialing health care providers. (1983, March). *Physician Assistant and Health Practitioner*, 24–30.

Lindeman, C. (1984). Nursing and health education, In Matarazzo, J. D. et al. (Eds.), *Behavioral health: A handbook of health enhancement and disease prevention*. New York: Wiley-Interscience.

Luke, R. D., & Modrow, R. E. (1982). Professionalism, accountability, and peer review. *Health Services Research, 17*(2), 113–123.

Matarazzo, J. D. (1984). Behavioral health: A 1990 challenge for the health sciences professions. In Matarazzo, J. D., et al. (Eds.), *Behavioral health: A handbook of health enhancement and disease prevention.* New York: Wiley-Interscience.

Matek, S. J. (September, 1974). *Accountability: Its meaning and its relevance to the health care field.* DHEW Pub. No. (HRA) 77–72.

Mattson, M. R. (1984). Quality assurance: A literature review of a changing field. *Hospital and Community Psychiatry, 35*(6), 605–616.

McCready, L. A. (1982). Emerging health care occupations: The system under siege. *HCM Review, 7*(4), 71–76.

McGinnis, J. M. (1982). Future directions of health promotion. In Taylor, R. B., Ureda, J. R., & Denham, J. W. (Eds.), *Health promotion: Principles and clinical applications,* Norwalk, CT: Appleton-Century-Crofts.

National Commission for Health Certifying Agencies. (April, 1980). *Perspectives on health occupational credentialing.* (DHHS Pub. No. (HRA) 80–39). Washington, DC: U.S. Government Printing Office.

National Commission for Health Certifying Agencies. (1984). *Criteria for approval of certifying agencies.* Washington, DC: National Commission for Health Certifying Agencies.

Nyre, G. F., & Reilly, K. C. (1979). Professional education in the eighties: Challenges and responses. Research Report IM8, Washington, DC: American Association for Higher Education.

Olson, P. A., & Freeman, L. (1979). Defining competence in teacher licensing usage. In Pottinger, P.S. & Goldsmith, J. (Eds.), *Defining and measuring competence.* San Francisco: Jossey-Bass.

Orlans, H. (1980). The end of a monopoly? On accrediting and eligibility. *Change, 2,* 32–87.

Peterson, R. N. (1983, July/August). Legal aspects of health care licensing and credentialing gain prominence. *Cross-Reference on Human Resources,* 4–6.

Quatrano, L. A., & Conant, R. M. (1981). Continuing competency for health professionals: Caveat emptor. *Journal of Environmental Health, 44*(3), 125–130.

Regulating the professions: Is there an ideal way? *ProForum 1–4,* February 1981.

Reid D., & Deane, A. K. (1982, January). Licensure: For whose protection? *Dimensions,* 30–32.

Report of the task force on competencies, council on education preparation, the American Dietetic Association. (1978). *Journal of the American Dietetic Association, 73*(3), 281–284.

Robertson, S. C., & Martin, E. D., Jr. (1981). Continuing education: A quality assurance approach. *American Journal of Occupational Therapy, 35*(5), 312–316.

Rosse, J. G., & Rosse, P. H. (1981). Role conflict and ambiguity: An empirical investigation of nursing personnel. *Evaluation and the Health Professions, 4*(4), 385–405.

Rothman, A. I. (1984). Research approaches in health manpower development: Some alternatives. *Evaluation and the Health Professions, 2*(4), 427–442.

Rottenberg, S. (Ed.) (1980). *Occupational licensure and regulation.* Washington, DC: American Enterprise Institute.

Salmon, M. E., & Culbertson, R. A. (1985). Health manpower oversupply: Implications for physicians, nurse practitioners, and physician assistants. A model. *Hospital and Health Services Administration, 30*(1), 100–115.

Schwartz, R. (1985). Quality assurance, standards and criteria in health education: A review. *Patient Education and Counseling, 7,* 325–335.

Segal, A. (1984). Physician education in clinical prevention. In Matarazzo, J. D. et al. (Eds.),

Behavioral health: A handbook of health enhancement and disease prevention. New York: Wiley-Interscience.

Selden, W. K. (1971). Historical introduction to accreditation of health educational programs. In Selden, W. K. (Ed.), *Study of accreditation of selected health education programs (S.A.S.H.E.P.)*, Washington, DC: Working Papers, Part I: Staff Working Papers.

Simonds, S. K. (1984). Training for Health Promotion: Health education. In Matarazzo, J. D. et al. (Eds.), *Behavioral health: A handbook of health enhancement and disease prevention.* New York: Wiley-Interscience.

Skipper, J. K., Jr., & Hughes, J. R. (1983). Podiatry: A medical care specialty in quest for full professional status and recognition. *Social Science and Medicine, 17*(20), 1541–1548.

Starr, P. (1982). A sovereign profession: The rise of medical authority and the shaping of the medical system. *The social transformation of american medicine.* New York: Basic Books.

Stigler, G. J. (1961). The economics of information. *Journal of Political Economy, 69,* 2313–225.

Stigler, G. J. (1962). Information in the labor market. *Journal of Political Economy, 7* (supplement), 94–105.

Stone, G. C. (1984). Overview: Training for health promotion. In Matarazzo, J. D. et al. (Eds.), *Behavioral health: A handbook of health enhancement and disease prevention.* New York: Wiley-Interscience.

Taub, A. (1980). Health education: A profession? *Health Education, 11*(2), 26–27.

Taylor, R. B., Denham, J. W., & Ureda, J. R. (1982). Health promotion: A perspective. In Taylor R. G., Ureda, J. R., and Denham, J. W. (Eds.), *Health promotion: Principles and clinical applications.* Norwalk, CT: Appleton-Century-Crofts.

U.S. Department of Health, Education, and Welfare. (1977, July). *Credentialing health manpower.* (DHEW Pub. No. (OS) 77–50–057). Washington, DC: U.S. Government Printing Office.

Vaupel, J. W., & Gowan, A. E. (1986). Passage to Methuselah: Some demographic consequences of continued progress against mortality. *American Journal of Public Health, 76*(4), 430–433.

Weisfeld, N. (1981, Spring). An agenda for deregulating health occupations. *New England Journal of Human Services,* 12–19.

Weisfeld, N., & Falk, D. (February, 1983). Professional credentials required: Trends courts enforcement of antitrust laws imply new flexibility. *Hospitals,* 74–79.

Young, K. E. (1976). Accreditation and the office of education. *Educational Record, 60*(2), 212–219.

Young, K. E., Chambers, C. M., & Kells, H. R., et al. (1983). *Understanding accreditation.* San Francisco: Jossey-Bass.

Zufall, D. L. (1981). Credentialing: An ongoing concern in health care. *Health Care Management Review, 6*(2), 71–77.

A MARKETING RESEARCH APPROACH TO HEALTH EDUCATION PLANNING

Rocco De Pietro

INTRODUCTION

The purpose of this article is to provide a conceptual basis for the use of marketing research as a tool for planning health education programs. First, we discuss elements of a marketing approach that distinguish it from a general health education planning approach. Second, we identify the strategic points where a marketing approach fits into a specific health education planning model. Third, we discuss two marketing research methodologies that can be applied to health education planning. Fourth, we discuss a recent application of a marketing approach to health education planning. Finally, we discuss some issues with respect to the use of marketing approaches in the planning of health education programs in the future.

MARKETING AS AN APPROACH TO HEALTH EDUCATION PLANNING

In terms of where health education fits into a general marketing approach, Lovelock (1983) classifies it as an intangible service directed at people's

Advances in Health Education and Promotion, vol. 2, pages 93–118
Copyright © 1987 JAI Press Inc.
All rights of reproduction in any form reserved.
ISBN: 0-89232-617-4

minds; where providers engage in a one-time or continuous delivery of information to clients with whom they ordinarily do not maintain any formal relationship; where there is customer contact and high customization of services; where the supply of the service is constrained by the availability of resources, and where the demand for the service fluctuates over time; and where the modes of service delivery are highly variable (client comes to provider, provider to customer, services delivered at a hand's length through mass media) and there is usually a single outlet for service.

Marketing approaches are not without their limitations. According to some marketing theorists, marketing has a fixation with the brand as the unit of analysis, lacks an interdisciplinary orientation, fails to examine synergy in the design of a marketing program, has a short-run orientation, lacks rigorous competitive analysis, and lacks an integrated orientation (Wind & Robertson, 1983; Webster, 1981). Some authors also criticize its *reactive* posture toward an organization's external environment (Zeithaml & Zeithaml, 1984), and the idea that marketing attempts to understand consumers' preferences not shape them.

As applied to health education planning, marketing is the research-based planning, positioning, promoting, and, in some cases, selling of health information and services to target segments of the organization's external environment. Kotler (1982) has defined marketing as: "The analysis, planning, implementation and control of carefully formulated programs designed to bring about voluntary exchanges of values with target markets for the purpose of achieving organizational objectives." The two definitions do not differ substantially from Kotler's. Embedded in each are the notions of research-based planning, carefully designed programs or products, and the segmentation of target groups. While the management and control aspects of marketing might make it appear source-oriented, its approach is intended to be very much user- or receiver-oriented.

Groups that promote health education, such as hospitals, state governments, large businesses and industry (among employees), or community agencies, have products or services that they develop and wish to exchange with certain members of the public. These products or services include workshops on health topics, publications on health care, telephone dial access systems with tapes on health topics, and counseling services, just to mention a few. Some of these products or services are available to the general public, while others are targeted for specific groups such as teen mothers, company employees, and the elderly. Some are available free of charge or at a nominal fee, while others are available for profit.

A marketing approach assumes that health educators have a program, product or service to offer members of the public. It does not assume that these programs, products or services are appropriate. Instead, the approach treats the fit between a program, product or service and a consumer group as something to be tested or defined by purchase. What is the program, product or service? What are perceived to be its main features? How do these perceived features relate to preferences or benefits sought from such programs, products or services by various target groups? Who are these target groups? How were they identified? These are typical questions that would be part of a market research planning approach.

The need for a marketing approach to health education planning is not self-evident. Health education planners might argue, somewhat justifiably, that many of the elements of a marketing approach are found in health education planning models. However, what distinguishes the marketing approach from a health education approach in many instances is the emphasis placed on certain elements and the extent to which these elements are formally specified in the model.

CHARACTERISTICS OF A HEALTH-MARKETING APPROACH

In this section, we discuss specific elements of a health-marketing approach when applied to health education planning. Rather than present a marketing-planning model (Kotler, 1982; Ray, 1982), we have chosen to focus on the six elements that best discriminate between marketing and health education approaches to planning. While some of these elements might be common to both approaches, they receive different emphasis, development, and formal specification. In his comparison of health care marketing and health education, Hochbaum (1981) found the fields to be "very close relatives." He concluded that both fields have strengths that the other lacks, what the two fields have in common far outweigh their differences, and marketing methods tend to be superior for one-time, or brief, health actions. While we do not disagree with Hochbaum's overall conclusion that the two fields have much in common, we do argue that there are some critical differences in their approach. To some extent, we use a different set of criteria to compare the two fields, so it is reasonable to expect that our conclusions might vary.

Marketing principles have been applied to many other health areas, such as designing new outpatient health services (Neslin, 1983); designing persuasive communication strategies for hospitals (MacStravic, 1984b); planning health care programs (Malhotra & Jain, 1982); integrating a consumer orientation into the planning of HMO programs (Akaah & Becherer, 1983); identifying consumer segments in the ambulatory care pharmacy market (Carroll & Gagon, 1983); understanding the reasons for the demise of an HMO (MacStravic, 1984b); and selecting medical facilities by consumers (Boscarino & Steiber, 1982).

The basic elements of a marketing approach that distinguish it from a general health education approach are its emphasis on research-based planning, its formal treatment of the external environment, and its user-orientation.

Emphasis on Research-Based Planning

One of the primary goals of marketing research is an improved understanding of the users' orientation to a program, product, or service. Market research often goes beyond a simple demographic profile of the user, as is often associated with needs assessment. It seeks to *segment* audiences on behavioral or psychographic orientations. A behavioral orientation might include the volume of use and use occasions or situations; a psychographic one might include life style analysis, benefits sought or problems solved, values, beliefs or perceptions of "truth" in the category of interest, predispositions toward certain products or programs, the readiness of a person to use a product or program (Haley, 1984; Denby, 1974; Wilkie & Cohen, 1977).

Some examples pertinent to health education are: the establishment of points in the life cycle of an infectious disease sufferer when the need for certain types of information changes, e.g., at the discovery stage when the person tends to be overwhelmed with strong emotions such as fear and anger; or "benefit bundles" sought by participants of health education workshops, e.g., in-depth treatment of information, convenient time and location, and provisions for follow-up (Lichter et al., 1986).

Bonaguru and Miaoulis (1983) identified eight market segments of a family planning agency based on the benefits sought by users of the agency's services. These included: (1) the firefighters, who needed an immediate solution to a problem (e.g., pregnancy); (2) desperates, who sought relief from feelings of financial and personal problems; (3) worriers, who sought security in sound health practice; (4) infertiles, who wanted to conceive to have children; (5) married rationales, who wanted freedom, control, and marital and financial stability; (6) married without children, who wanted freedom of choice and financial stability; (7) married with children, who wanted to avoid pregnancy for financial and social reasons; and (8) singles without children, who wanted to avoid pregnancy for independence, financial and social reasons.

In a review of research on preferences for health services, Neslin (1983) distinguishes between research that has focused on program features and others on users' perceptions. He suggests a third stream of research that focuses on the relationship between program features and users' perceptions. For example, the feature-to-preference studies (Parker & Srinivasan, 1976; Malhotra & Jain, 1982) might examine the relationship between preferences and features of an education program such as timing, location, mode of delivery, and duration, but do not answer the question why users prefer certain of these features. On the other hand, perceptions-to-feature studies (Strattman, 1975; Hulka et al., 1975; Hauser & Urban, 1977) might examine the relationship between preferences and perceptions such as quality, personableness and convenience. Neslin's approach is to link all three: actual program features, users' perceptions of features (perceptual attributes) and preferences.

Formal Treatment of the External Environment

The consensus among early marketing theorists was that the external environment of an organization was "uncontrollable" (McCarthy, 1960). They recognized the importance of the consumer, competition, social and economic conditions, and other environmental factors. However, their posture toward them was basically reactive. Organizations took the environment as a given and tried to adopt, or "fit" their products, programs or services to it. Environmental actors such as consumer groups, legislators, competitors, and government regulators, were seen as constraining marketing activities. While a few theorists were talking about creating or stimulating a demand for products, programs and services (Mazur, 1957; Hansen, 1967), the vast majority were in favor of adjusting products, programs and services to a rapidly changing external environment.

Social marketing can also be thought of as a proactive marketing approach directed at influencing factors in the organization's external environment. Kotler and Zaltman (1971) define it as the design, implementation, and control of programs calculated to *influence* the acceptability of social ideas and involving considerations of product planning, pricing, communications and marketing research. Social marketing techniques have been used in Third World countries to encourage people to boil their water, build and use latrines, breastfeed babies, and practice family planning (Fox & Kotler, 1980). Marketing techniques have been used widely in family planning programs (Roberto, 1975; Population Reports, 1980; Schellstede & Ciszewski, 1984; Black & Harvey, 1976; Farley & Leavitt, 1973; Davies & Louis, 1977); and in a well-known heart disease prevention program (Maccoby & Alexander, 1979).

When applied to large-scale social change programs, such as birth control programs, social marketing techniques have not always been successful (Bloom & Novelli, 1981; Population Reports, 1980). Part of the problem is the attempt to reach large audiences without segmenting them; and, in some cases, focusing on segments that are the most resistant to change. For example, in India, a condom distribution scheme, directed at adult males, set an unrealistic goal of selling 200 million condoms in two years. More successful attempts in Sri Lanka and Kenya were based on a more careful segmentation of markets for condoms. For example, in Sri Lanka, the first year target was 1 percent of the estimated number of adult males with discretionary cash (Davies & Louis, 1977); and, in Kenya, the target was to reach 50 percent of males who had discretionary cash (Black & Harvey, 1976).

More recent marketing theorists are proactive in their view of the organization's external environment. Basing their orientation partly on the work of organizational psychologists (Weick, 1976; Pfeffer, 1979), they argue that marketing strategies can be implemented to change the context in which the organization operates (Wind & Shocker, 1983). Through marketing strategies, the organization is able to design the external environment to fit its present structural requirements by managing its competition, promoting regulation to reduce competition, managing symbiotic interdependence, managing uncertainty (both increasing and decreasing it), legitimizing certain organizations, and taking political action (Pfeffer & Salancik, 1978; Mintzberg, 1979; Hedberg, 1981).

The marketing approach also assumes that the external environment of the user is important in understanding the user's behavior. While a user's beliefs are important determinants of health behavior (Rosenstock, 1966; Jantz & Becker, 1984), other factors are also important, such as actual or perceived barriers in the user's immediate environment and the many dimensions of access (Anderson et al., 1983).

The environment becomes a formal variable in the marketing approach. At the macro level, it consists of the economy that can affect people's employment status, health insurance, and general health status; and government policy that can affect entitlements, coverage, and reimbursements for health services. At the micro level, it consists of consumers and the perceived and actual "barriers" to use of a program, product or service; and the competition, or other groups providing programs, products and services. Simon (1978) has identified different consumer groups for medical care facilities including patients and their relatives; physicians and other medical personnel; trustees, employer and union groups; government, including regulatory agencies; and health care administrators.

Micro factors provide some of the most formidable barriers. If the topic is underutilization of clinics by low-income people, the marketing approach might focus on program features that can be modified by clinic management such as access, transportation, convenience and treatment (Anderson et al., 1983; Wan & Gray, 1978; Aday, 1975; Elinson et al., 1976; Aday & Anderson, 1974). Competition among providers is also a barrier of considerable importance. For example, in a study of the utilization of a preventive health service by Medicaid eligibles in Michigan, De Pietro and Rozek (1985) found that health maintenance organizations were actively recruiting enrollees in state-supported preventive health programs and, in some cases, through their aggressive telephone and door-to-door canvassing, causing them to switch services.

The formal recognition of competition among providers of programs or services is an important contribution of a marketing approach. Taking into account the activities of competitors, including their programs and services as well as their marketing strategies, is strategic information that helps organizations to survive in the marketplace. Failing to understand what the competition is doing has been found to be associated with the problems some hospitals have in filling beds and why certain HMOs go out of business (MacStravic, 1982).

MacStravic (1984a) notes several environmental factors that affect clinic utilization. Some of these factors could, likewise, affect the use of health education programs. They include government regulation or reimbursement policy, developments in malpractice that have caused physicians to be more defensive in their approach to the provision of services, and employment levels and patterns. With respect to health education, some government policies permit the reimbursement of clients at clinic sites for transportation (De Pietro, 1985); and high rates of employment in certain states have led to health insurance becoming a topic of much community interest and concern (Lichter et al., 1986).

The environment in which a health education program operates might include other providers, the organization to which the group offering health education belongs, e.g., a large hospital, the health education professionals in the community and elsewhere, other influential professional groups that might not be in complete support of the goals of the health education program, e.g., certain medical groups, and the market segments for which the program is intended. Top managers of the organization providing health education might not consider it a high priority. The health education professionals in the community and elsewhere might not be supportive of the mode of delivery of information, e.g., a health fair. Medical groups in the community might not be convinced of the need for it. Even groups for which the health education program is intended might have more interest in other health topics or not have the means to participate in the particular program being offered.

User Orientation

A user orientation suggests that the people themselves hold the answers to questions about participation in a program, purchase of a product, or use of a service. A source orientation, which relies heavily on the manipulation of persuasive messages (McGuire, 1981; MacStravic, 1984b), is simply insufficient to explain user behavior. The question is not simply:

"What can a source do to make people want to participate in a program, use a service, or buy a product?" The marketing question is: "Why should they bother to do so?" This latter question leads to further queries about users' perceptions of and preferences for program, product or service features; users' real-life situations; and the users' external environment.

In marketing research, there are demographics and psychographics (Denby, 1974; Adams, 1982). The former are researcher defined social categories such as age, sex, residence, income, education that are common descriptors of users in needs-assessment research. The latter are subjective characteristics of populations covering what people know, believe or feel about things, such as their health, health programs or services, or health providers (MacStravic, 1984a). Perceptions of the treatment by providers, such as whether it is helpful, patronizing, or causes embarassment, can affect the use of a program or service.

People have *lifestyles* consisting of specific behaviors or patterns of behaviors descriptive of the way they prefer to live. It might be part of someone's lifestyle to take risks, eat on the run, be attractive to the opposite sex, and so forth. Lifestyle analysis examines how a product, program or service is expressive of a person's self-image or the image they would like to project to others (Adams, 1982; Denby, 1974). Joining an HMO or a fitness club, or attending a health education workshop, might relate to a person's lifestyle of being fit or keeping trim and healthy.

Lifestyle often consists of patterns of related behaviors. Teenagers who smoke are also more likely than others to engage in sexual behavior and drink alcohol (Zabin, 1984). Other studies show that there are patterns in the way people use health information sources, with some people relying primarily on a single source, or on one type of source, while others rely heavily on multiple sources (De Pietro & Clark, 1984). Individual behavior, such as participation in a health education program or use of a preventive health service, is influenced by other behaviors including participation in other health education programs or the use of other services. For example, De Pietro and Rozek (1985) found that in addition to the use of a government-supported preventive health program, Medicaid eligibles were using home remedies, "praying on health," and exploring the use of other preventive health providers such as health maintenance organizations.

The user orientation also focuses on key points in the *life-cycle* of users. These points include life status-changes, such as changing one's residence, getting married or divorced, losing or changing jobs, having someone enter or leave a household, having a first or new child (Andreasen, 1984). These changes have an impact on consumer behavior. This approach suggests that the value of information is not constant, but changes as people's life conditions or situations change. For example, a female adolescent might have the greatest need for birth control information upon deciding to "go steady" or during summer vacation when she spends a lot of time with her boyfriend.

Some market researchers have looked at *usage situations* for understanding people's selection of products, services and programs and the interchangeability of these choices (Srivastava, 1981; Srivastava et al., 1984). Programs, products and services exist in an environment with other related programs, products and services. Over time, people develop sets of programs, products, or services for consideration based on preferences for certain attributes under a variety of real-life situations. People might purchase fresh ingredients for gourmet cooking on the weekend when they have lots of free time and buy gourmet frozen dinners during the week when they are very busy. The same logic applies to the acquisition of health information. For example, a person might join a fitness program because of peer influence at work and also exercise at home for relaxation. Srivastava (1984) sees the consumer, when able to do so, substituting various products, programs or services depending on usage situations. He found that usage situations tend to influence preferences for product benefits and the use of specific products by consumers.

Dervin's work on "sense-making" has provided further valuable insights into the user orientation (Dervin, 1981; Dervin, 1983a; Dervin et al., 1980; Dervin, 1983b). She has theorized that people, in attempting to make sense out of their world, seek information that is helpful to design their next move through time and space. De Pietro and Clark (1984) have extended this perspective to the construction of health information sources. These authors suggest that a source is only a source if it is connected with an individual's need for information, and, more specifically, to information that is needed to facilitate movement in some desirable direction. Information enables people to order and interpret the environment and subsequently to make decisions and take actions (Dervin, 1981).

The perspective that sees sources and information as *constructed* by an information user for purposes of "sense making" suggests that

- an information source is only a source if some user perceives that it is;
- contacts with a potential information source alone are insufficient to account for "effects" of sources;
- people use different sources for different types of information; and
- people use information for a variety of reasons, some of which will be unknown or unanticipated by the information source.

The sense-making approach can be extended also to the use of programs and services. From this perspective, these programs and services only exist in a real sense for users if they help them to answer questions and solve problems. The question is not simply what people need or want (needs assessment) but how a program or service fits in with people's sense of where they are going. An example might be an HMO that is offering clients a wellness package to keep them healthy, fit, and attractive so that they can meet their life goals of good health, physical attractiveness, and energy to do the job at work and home.

Marketing is Behavioral in its Emphasis

Marketing strives to achieve some "level of transaction" or level of behavior on the part of users (Kotler, 1982). With respect to use of a program, product or service, this might be increased use, continued use, the maintenance of a high level of use as during a period when use is customarily low, first-time use, repeated use, a change in use, or some pattern of use. As part of the communication strategy that is part of the overall marketing plan, every input is geared toward how it might affect some predefined level of consumer behavior (Ray, 1973).

A marketing approach also takes into account the relationships among consumer behaviors, intentions, knowledge, and attitudes (Ray, 1973; MacStravic, 1984b). These are largely effect-sequences that result from consumers' exposure to information about a program, product or service from a medium of communication. Marketing literature distinguishes among four effect-sequences based on the degree of consumer involvement, the distinctiveness between the alternatives, and the communication source. Ray's (1973) original model focused on knowledge, attitudes and behavior, whereas MacStravic's model (1984b) formally added intention, perhaps in recognition of Fishbein's contribution to the study of effects (Fishbein & Ajzen, 1975).

Knowledge-Attitude-Intention-Behavior

In this model, there is both high consumer involvement and high distinctiveness among alternatives. Consumers first learn about a program, product or service, develop an attitude about it, make a decision about participating in it or using it, and finally engage in the actual behavior. This model is often referred to as the *learning hierarchy*, since the individual moves through a series of progressive behaviors from simple awareness to behavior (McGuire, 1978). It is the model commonly associated with exposure to some mass media source of information. With respect to health education, the model is applicable for topics in which the consumer is highly involved and the distinction between alternatives is clear. An example might be a choice between a health service that stresses patient education and one that does not. If the consumer is very concerned about health education, he or she is likely to go from learning about the service, developing an attitude about it, deciding whether or not use use it, then actually using it.

Intention-Knowledge-Behavior-Attitude

In this model, consumer involvement is high, but the distinctiveness among alternatives is low. The communication source is also likely to be interpersonal. This might be an emergency situation where consumers feel that they need a service right away and do not see large or meaningful differences among those available to them. De Pietro and Rozek (1985) found that many Medicaid eligibles see themselves as more prone than others to serious medical problems so that when they seek a preventive health service they want a thorough physical exam and test results right away. In terms of marketing theory, Medicaid eligibles select a preventive health service by the I-K-B-A model, not the K-A-I-B model that characterizes the average consumer.

Intention-Behavior-Knowledge-Attitude

In this model, the distinctiveness among alternatives is clear but there is low consumer involvement. The communication source could be mass media or interpersonal. This sequence could happen in a situation where people at a clinic are offered a choice between two different services that they do not have strong feelings about. So they simply try one without thinking very much about it or taking time to examine their feelings about it. In marketing theory, this is referred to as the dissonance-attribution model (Festinger, 1957; Kelley, 1967; Ray, 1973).

Knowledge-Intention-Behavior-Attitude

In this model, both distinctiveness among alternatives and consumer involvement are low. An example of such a situation is a clinic user who is asked to choose between two pamphlets on a topic of marginal interest or concern. This model has been referred to as the low-involvement model (Ray, 1973; Krugman, 1965).

With respect to planning health education programs, it is likely that all models operate at some times, under some conditions for different consumers. The task of the health educator is to be aware of what effects sequences are likely to be triggered by a proposed intervention, whether it involves interpersonal or some other mode of communication.

Positioning and Price

Marketing efforts are often geared toward positioning programs or products so that information about them can be discerned, classified according to receiver categories, processed, and used. Ray (1982) defines positioning as establishing a unique place for a program, product or service in the mental set that a consumer has to deal with in each program, product or service category.

The positioning of programs, products and services can be done intuitively or through the use of research methodologies such as applications of conjoint analysis and metric and nonmetric multidimensional scaling techniques (Green & Srinivasan, 1978; Malhotra & Jain; 1982; Akaah & Becherer, 1983; Green & Rao, 1979). For example, Akaah & Becherer (1983) used conjoint analysis of consumer preferences to design the program of an HMO. Through the use of this methodology, they were able to translate consumer attitudes about products and services into a "bundle of salient attributes." In the above example, the program is positioned so that the features most desired by users are accented by the program.

Pricing refers to both financial and psychological costs incurred in the use of a program, product or service. It can indicate the character of something or its appeal (Ray, 1982). With respect to health education, the emphasis is most likely on reducing perceived psychological costs of participation in a program or in receiving a service. These "costs" can be large and significant, such as perceptions of convenience of the process and treatment by health educators or providers. The health belief model (Rosenstock, 1974) has recognized the perceived costs and benefits of taking action. Engaging in health education may be beneficial to the individual in terms of the usefulness of the information, but the process of taking any health action could be, as Rosenstock describes "inconvenient, unpleasant, painful or upsetting."

Marketing Involves Strategy

Implicit in a research-based marketing approach are the elements of implementation, management, and control (Kotler, 1982). These elements are shared by many other research-based planning models including those used widely in health education (Green et al., 1980). Another element that is often emphasized in a marketing approach is strategy. Sarner (1984) notes that marketing is a management process—the product of strategic planning. The strategy aspect of marketing focuses on the mission of the organization and planning for the future.

Kotler (1982) suggests that a marketing approach helps organizations to adapt to changing conditions in their external task environments, to both threats and opportunities. He defines strategic planning as the managerial process of developing and maintaining a strategic fit between the organization's goals and resources and its changing marketing opportunities. Organizations engage in environmental and resource analysis to help define and adjust their goals, develop strategies, design their information and management systems, and to obtain feedback on their outputs (e.g., programs, products and services). Strategy shapes these offerings so that they are responsive to changing environmental conditions.

Wind and Robertson (1983) note that marketing focuses on the quest for a competitive advantage through empirical assessment of consumers, competitors, and other factors that, when combined with assessments of finances and human resources needs help the organization to arrive at an integrated business strategy. Marketing studies are used to help organizations determine their market share, market growth, market development, product differentiation, performance gaps with close competitors, and consumer responses to strategic options. For example, De Pietro and Rozek (1985) conducted several focus-groups interviews in a low-income community to test the viability of modes of information and education delivery offered by a social service agency. Study data were then used to help select a viable delivery mode.

APPLYING MARKETING TO A HEALTH EDUCATION MODEL

In this section of the article, we will discuss the intersections between marketing and a commonly used model for health education planning, the PRECEDE framework (Green et al., 1980). PRECEDE, which stands for predisposing, reinforcing and enabling causes in educational diagnosis and evaluation, is a systematic planning tool for health educators. It consists of seven phases: (1–2) epidemiological and social diagnosis, including quality of life indicators and health and nonhealth factors; (3-5) behavioral diagnosis, including predisposing factors such as beliefs, attitudes, knowledge, enabling factors such as accessibility and skills, and reinforcing factors such as family members and peers; (6) administrative diagnosis which is the actual development and implementation of a health education program; and (7) evaluation, which occurs as an integral and continuous part of the model.

A marketing approach is particularly relevant to phases 3–6. In the PRECEDE model, as part of phase 3, the behavioral diagnosis, the planner is interested in determining the causes of some health behavior such as utilization, preventive actions, consumption, compliance or self-care. The emphasis might be on certain dimensions of these behaviors such as their earliness, frequency, quality, range or persistence.

A marketing approach might specify from the outset some desirable level of participation in a health education program, and link its diagnosis to those causal factors likely to influence the achievement of that level. At this phase of the planning model, a marketing approach and the PRECEDE model are quite similar. As with the PRECEDE model, the marketing model might ask: "What *is* the present level of some desired behavior?" However, a marketing approach might inquire further: "What effect sequence is likely to follow from exposure to a proposed intervention?"

At phases 4–5, the theoretical contribution of the PRECEDE model is to distinguish among predisposing, enabling and reinforcing factors. Enabling (or disabling) factors, depending on how one views them, are usually categorized by a marketing approach as environmental factors. The marketing approach formally specifies certain enabling factors, such as competitors or providers whose behaviors can enable (or block) the use of programs, products or services.

A marketing approach also offers a refined conceptualization of predisposing factors by linking knowledge and attitudes to the "hierarchy-of-effects" model. As indicated previously, in this model knowledge, attitudes, intensions and behavior are "sequences of mental stages" that people experience after exposure to information from some source (Ray, 1973). In terms of a health-planning model, it would be helpful to know the most likely sequence of relationships among these communication effects for the type of health topic or intervention being contemplated. This information would be helpful in developing behavioral change strategies that are often part of health education programs (Green et al., 1980).

At phase six of PRECEDE, the task according to Green et al. (1980) is for health planners to keep firmly in mind the limitations of their resources, time constraints and abilities, so that the appropriate intervention will "almost be self-evident" from the predisposing, enabling, and reinforcing factors. The authors note that "all that remains is the selection of the right combination of interventions."

A marketing approach differs significantly with this observation by pointing out that a program, product or service is not divorced in a user's mind from the provider that promotes or delivers it. As a result, the marketing approach places considerable emphasis on the analysis of provider factors, e.g., the people who deliver health education, their attitudes, treatment of clients, and professionalism. MacStravic (1982) mentions, in his study of the demise of an HMO, the importance of physician attitudes in clients' perceptions of the quality of services.

In sum, a marketing approach is viewed as a tool to strengthen both conceptual and methodological aspects of health-education planning. It is not offered as an alternative approach, but one that fits in at strategic points. It enables the health-education planner to ask a different set of questions and to give more formal emphasis to certain factors that are important to understanding health behavior.

MARKETING METHODOLOGIES APPLIED TO HEALTH EDUCATION PLANNING

In this section of the article, we examine two commonly used methods in marketing research that can be used for health-education planning. One is a qualitative research method referred to as focus group research. It is used widely by marketing persons to learn about the perceptions of users and nonusers, and their feelings about a range of products and services. The other is a quantitative method, conjoint analysis, that is used in consumer preference studies as a means of segmenting consumer groups (Green & Srinivasan, 1978). While these two research methods are used widely by marketing specialists, a whole "second generation" of techniques, such as canonical correlation and analysis of linear structural relationships are increasingly being applied to marketing problems (Fornell, 1982; Joreskog, 1984).

Focus-Group Research

The focus group is specifically designed to permit in-depth, qualitative exploration of consumer interests, concerns, perceptions, and feelings about programs, products and services (Schearer, 1981; Buggie, 1983; Keown, 1983). The focus group generally functions to permit isolation and exploration of broad underlying components of attitudes and perceptions among the public. It is dynamic in that concepts and ideas emerge from it that were not entirely anticipated beforehand. When done properly, it helps to identify perceptual or attitudinal themes, the most salient of which will be those cited most frequently or most strongly by group members (Allied Research Associates, 1982).

Usually, eight to 12 members are recruited for a focus-group interview from previously existing or newly-created lists, such as health care providers and Medicaid eligibles. Individuals contacted for possible participation in the focus group are selected randomly from these lists, then screened, usually by phone, to determine their eligibility for the group and willingness to participate. As part of the screening, participants are offered a cash amount, usually about $25–35, to cover the cost of their time and effort (Nordhaus Research, 1984). This amount varies considerably depending on the clients for the focus group. Some professionals, such as physicians, might receive as much as a $100 to attend a focus group. The cash amount is not accented to avoid self-selection by people who might be solely motivated by money to attend.

Groups are selected that are relatively homogeneous on some important characteristics, such as male or female users or nonusers of a health program, females with two or more children who are eligible for a health service, community religious leaders interested in sex education, or providers of health services for adolescents.

Focus groups are usually held at special facilities that have rooms with a one-way mirrors, tape-recording devices, reception and waiting rooms for attendees, and storage for light refreshments.

During the focus-group session, certain procedures are followed so that every member feels at ease and has an opportunity to contribute to the group. Every member is on a first-name basis with everyone else, including the moderator. The moderator maintains control of the group by establishing procedures such as "going around the table," asking everyone to comment on a question, or by interrupting any person who has a tendency to dominate the group.

Focus-group research has been used as an adjunct to survey research. In Mexico, a study of adult family-planning knowledge, attitudes and behaviors, found many parallel results between focus-group research and a large statistical survey (Schearer, 1981). In a recent application of focus-group research to health and family-planning education, De Pietro (1985) interviewed different community groups, including providers of services for youth, users of a family-planning clinic, religious leaders, and community leaders to determine their reactions to alternative modes of delivering birth control information and services to adolescents. In a previous focus-group study of users of a health screening service, De Pietro and Rozek (1985) found that many people had strong interest in health education for mothers *and* children as part of the service, and people wanted more opportunities to make suggestions about the design of available services.

The focus-group approach can be viewed as a cost-effective alternative to a community involvement approach that uses many meetings with community leaders, health providers, and the more highly motivated members of the public to determine health needs and interest. Focus-group research can include leaders and providers, but its strength is to go directly to users and nonusers to tap their interests and needs. The results of focus-group studies are often incorporated into more quantitative studies. However, one must take special caution in interpreting focus-group results, because they are based on small, nonrandom samples; also, unless carefully designed, the moderator can easily bias results (Biel, 1978; Holtzman, 1983; Kennedy, 1976).

Conjoint Analysis

Conjoint analysis is a quantitative research methodology that is useful for segmenting consumer groups based on some attributes that they share, such as needs, interests, concerns, preferences, or behaviors (Green & Srinivasan, 1978; Haley, 1984; Green & Shaffer, 1984). It has been described by Green and Srinivasan (1978) as a practical set of methods for predicting consumer preferences for multi-attribute options in a wide variety of product or service contexts. More specifically, the authors consider it "any decompositional method that estimates the structure of a consumer's preference (e.g., part worths, importance weights, ideal points) given an overall evaluation of a set of alternatives that are prespecified in terms of levels of different attributes."

In tracing the historical roots of the methodology in applied research, the authors see conjoint analysis as an alternative to the expectancy-value models (Fishbein & Ajzen, 1975) that have been used widely in attitudinal research. Whereas these models use a "compositional approach," in which the total utility for some multi-attribute object is a weighted sum of the object's perceived attribute levels and associated value ratings judged separately by a respondent, a conjoint analysis approach is based on a "decompositional approach" in which respondents react to profiles consisting of different levels of product or service attributes. The procedure generates a set of *part-worths* for individual attributes, statistics representing respondents' weighting or preferences for attributes given some compositional rule.

Green and Srinivasan (1978) outline steps involved in a conjoint analysis. They include selection of a preference model (e.g., part-worth or ideal-point), data collection model (e.g., two factors at a time or full-profiles), stimulus set construction (e.g., for the full-profile method either a fractional factorial design or random sampling from a distribution), stimulus presentation (e.g., verbal description or multicue card), measurement scales for the dependent variable (e.g., paired comparisons, rank-order rating scales), and estimation methods (e.g., MANOVA, PREFMAP, LINMAP, LOGIT, PROBIT).

In an application of conjoint analysis for planning medical care programs, Malhotra and Jain (1982) analyzed health administrators' perceptions of health care requirements for the elderly. In their study, they first identified nine attributes of health care institutions for the elderly considered important to the administrators. These nine attributes included such items as physician services, recreational services and cost. For each of nine attributes, they developed two or more *levels* of the attribute. For example, for cost there were three levels: (1) $45 per day; (2) $40 per day; and

(3) $35 per day. Administrators had to rank several profiles for health care institutions that combined different levels for each of the nine attributes. The preferences of administrators for various profiles were then analyzed by conjoint analysis techniques to determine the service mix that health administrators believe is desired by the elderly, to assess the relative importance of these services to administrators, to determine how level of care affected perceived relative importance of these services, and to identify the ideal form of the institutional arrangement for providing health care services.

With respect to health education planning, conjoint analysis could be used to help refine notions of target segments for health information programs and different modes of information delivery; features of health education programs that different target-segments seek; and "nests" of related health interests, concerns, or behaviors that distinguish among different groups.

Conjoint analysis has some limitations. First, there is a limit to the number of attributes and levels of attributes that can be presented to a respondent at one time. The greater the number, the more difficult the rating task. Acito and Jain (1980) found that respondents with low levels of education had a tendency to provide poor data during a conjoint analysis interview. Some simple methods for analyzing consumer preferences for program, product or service benefits have been developed to help solve this problem (Green & Shaffer, 1984). Second, the methodology is nearly impossible to implement in telephone surveys, especially when there are many attributes and levels of the attributes. There is simply no way for the respondent to keep everything in mind. Third, some attributes and levels of attributes either do not make sense because no respondent is likely to prefer them, or would obviously be so desirable that including them could affect relative weights assigned to the various attributes. Often the researchers have to rely on their best judgments to make decisions of profiles to exclude from presentation to respondents. This requires compromising the validity of certain factorial designs that are used to identify the attribute profiles. Fourth, while the additive representation of part-worths, or utilities, has the advantage of being conceptually and computationally simple, the validity of such statistics in some cases is questionable (Nygren, 1980).

APPLYING A MARKETING APPROACH TO HEALTH EDUCATION

In this section of the article, we describe an application of a marketing approach to the planning of health education at Oakwood Hospital in

Dearborn, Michigan. What gives the project a distinctive marketing factor is the heavy emphasis on the user and formal treatment of the organization's external environment. In this project, a marketing approach was used in the following ways:

1. to determine community members' concern for certain health topics, their interest in receiving more information about them, and their likelihood of participating in a workshop on them;
2. to select topics for the workshops through a method that took into account the estimated proportion of community residents who expressed concern, a desire for more information about a health topic, and likely participation in a program;
3. to segment potential audiences for workshops by demographics and combined, concern, interest, and participation scores (referred to as CIP scores);
4. to segment potential audiences for other delivery modes of health information by demographics and combined high concern and interest scores, but low scores for participation in the workshops;
5. to use the environment as a formal variable in the design of the health-education program, i.e., by using four conditions of concern for health topics by community members and professionals (e.g., both high in concern, both low, community members high and professionals low, etc.) as a basis for predicting the success of the health education program; and
6. to use the data to plan the marketing strategies for various workshops.

The Oakwood Project (Lichter et al., 1986) was developed as a research-based model for health education. It has a strong user orientation. Users' health concerns, needs for information, and intentions to participate in a health-education workshop were taken into consideration in the identification of workshops that would be likely to have high attendance and useful information. Due to the user orientation adopted by project management, assumptions about workshops as a mode of information delivery were tested. Project management found that while the workshop was likely to be a viable mode for most people, certain groups, such as the elderly, the unemployed, and the handicapped, would not be easily reached by it. For these groups, it was determined that alternative ways of delivering information would have to be found.

Project management also took into account the environment of health education by focusing both on the professionals, many of whom were the planners or providers of health education, and the community members for whom such educational programs were intended. As part of the research design, it was hypothesized that health-education programs had the greatest chance of success when both the professionals and community members were highly concerned with the health topic.

FUTURE USES OF MARKETING FOR HEALTH EDUCATION PLANNING

Whether a marketing research approach to health education planning is used widely in the future depends on several considerations, some of which are conflicts that cannot be resolved easily.

First, is the seemingly inevitable conflict over the goals of marketing and the goals of health education. Hochbaum (1981) states: "In marketing, success is measured, not so much in terms of how many more people are enticed to purchase a product or adopt a new behavior, as it is in terms of a financial or tangible return. In health education, we are judged by how many people carry out a desired action. Thus, what would be considered a success in the commercial field may be considered a failure in health education." The goals of marketing do not need to conflict. A health-education organization can become financially self-supporting without compromising its overall goals. However, it might have to accrue income from some corporate clients that are willing to purchase health-promotion programs so that it can also provide services to people in need who cannot pay. There is nothing inherent in a marketing research approach that suggests that only those people who can afford services are entitled to them.

Here, we place the burden on marketing professionals to demonstrate how their methods can be used to improve services to the poor and underprivileged. Marketing can help to segment target audiences into those who can and cannot afford to pay for services, but it can also be used to segment target audiences into those with the greatest need who can be reached with some modification of delivery systems.

Second, some health-education planners, like some other health professionals, still see marketing as manipulative of the public's interests and needs (Sarner, 1984; Laczniak et al., 1979). This basic problem of the *lack of appreciation* of marketing needs to be overcome before it can be used widely as an approach by health-education planners. This would seem to be a task that schools and professional associations could help to solve.

Third, many health educators do not see much new or different about a marketing research approach to health education planning (Hochbaum, 1981; Bonaguro & Miaoulis, 1983). They argue that, if you take a variety of health education models and compare them with various marketing models, the same factors, albeit with somewhat different names, are present. Some might argue that the models are similar, but that they are implemented differently. This debate needs some resolution. We strongly believe that the differences in the models are real and critical, although there is much overlap as well. The differences appear in what the models develop, formalize, and emphasize.

Fourth, the environment of health-education programs needs to be treated more formally in planning. This is not at the level of macrosocial and economic factors, which are found in many health education models (Green et al., 1980), but at the level of the organization's task environment (Aldrich, 1979). Programs have competition from other providers. The services of other providers might hold the key to why people use or do not use one's programs, products or services. For example, De Pietro (1985) found that one of the reasons adolescents were not widely using the clinic of a family-planning agency was that they could not walk to the clinic, while they could walk to the clinics of two other providers.

Fifth, the user orientation emphasizes that any program, product or service only makes sense to people if it aids their movement through life. There are program use situations (Fennell, 1978) that suggest circumstances in people's lives when health education makes immense sense to them. What are some of these real-life situations? When do they occur? When does health education begin to answer questions people have or help them to achieve some personal goal. Future health-education programs need to be more aware of how they can help people get to where they want to go.

Sixth, market segmentation can help health educators to carefully target their programs, products and services. We disagree with Hochbaum's (1981) analysis of marketing segmentation as those groups most likely to be interested already in purchasing a given product and being able to afford the price. He notes further: "In fact, our primary and most important target populations are, as often as not, exactly those segments that are *least* inclined to listen to us, *least* knowledgeable about health, (and) *least* likely to head our advice." A market could be segmented precisely to segment audiences with the greatest need, such as determining the different program features that might attract Medicaid mothers with large families to preventive health services for children, e.g., short waiting times, all the services under one roof, and all children seen the same day (De Pietro and Rozek, 1985).

Seventh, health educational planners need to pay more attention to the strategy aspect of planning. This is an area to which any organization must pay attention, especially if it offers a program, service, or product in a competitive environment that is changing rapidly. Strategy might involve a complete market analysis, including establishing the mission of the organization, defining one's products and users, analysis of users (e.g., market segmentation approaches), identifying the competition, determining the appropriate niche for one's program in the market, and measuring results such as user satisfaction.

Strategy also includes planning for the future, or attempting to map where the organization is now, where it wants to be, and some ideas of how to get there in the short- and long-term. It also involves plans to shape its own environment as well (Weick, 1976). This latter aspect of strategy might include advocating the upgrading of the health education planning function in various organizations so that health education planners have more decision-making authority in their own organizations; networking with other health professionals so that public policies and programs supported by health education planners have a greater chance of receiving government and private funding, and linking organizational status of health-education planning more closely to the mission or goals of an organization (as is being done with some success with worksite health promotion programs) (O'Donnell & Ainsworth, 1984). This will help to ensure that health-education planning is effective within its own organization and with the markets it intends to serve.

REFERENCES

Acito, F., & Jain, A. K. (1980). Evaluation of conjoint analysis results: A comparison of methods. *Journal of Marketing Research, 17*, 106–112.

Adams, A. J. (1982). Why lifestyle research rarely works. Paper presented at the 13th Annual Attitude Research Conference, American Marketing Association, Chicago, IL.

Aday, L. A. (1975). Economic and noneconomic barriers to the use of needed medical services. *Medical Care, 13*(6), 447–456, 1975,

Aday, L. A., & Anderson, R. (1974). A framework for the study of access to medical care. *Health Services Research, 9*, 208–220.

Akaah, I. P., & Becherer, R. C. (1983). Integrating a consumer orientation into the planning of HMO programs: An application of conjoint segmentation. *Journal of Health Care Marketing, 3*(2), 9–18.

Aldrich, H. (1979). *Organizations and Environments.* Englewood Cliffs, NJ: Prentice-Hall.

Allied Research Associates, Inc. (1982). A report of a focus group study.

Anderson, R., McCutcheon, A., Aday, L. A., Chiu, G. Y., & Bell, R. (1983). Exploring dimensions of access to medical care. *Health Sciences Research, 18*(1), 49–74.

Andreasen, A. R. (1984). Life status changes and changes in consumer preferences and satisfaction. *Journal of Consumer Research, 11*, 784–794.

Biel, A. (1983). Focus groups: the most abused form of research. *Viewpoint,* 6–7.

Black, T. R. L., & Harvey, P. D. (1976). A report on a contraceptive social marketing experiment in rural Kenya. *Studies in Family Planning, 7*(4), 79–88.

Bloom, P. N., & Novelli, W. D. (1981). Problems and challenges in social marketing. *Journal of Marketing, 45*, 79–88.

Bonaguro, J. A., & Miaoulis, G. (1983). Marketing: a tool for health education planning. *Health Education, 23*(2), 6–11.

Boscarino, J., & Steiber, S. R. (1982). Hospital shopping and consumer choice. *Journal of Health Care Marketing, 2*(2), 15–23.

Buggie, F. (1983). Focus groups: The most abused form of research. *Viewpoint, 72*, 39–41.

Carroll, N. V., & Gagon, J. P. (1983). Identifying consumer segments in health services markets: an application of conjoint and cluster analyses to the ambulatory care pharmacy market. *Journal of Health Care Marketing, 3*(3), 22–34.

Davies, J., & Louis, T. D. J. (1977). Measuring the effectiveness of contraceptive marketing programs: Preethi in Sri Lanka. *Studies in Family Planning, 8*(4), 82–90.

Denby, E. (1974). Psychographics and from whence it came. In *Life style and psychographics*. Chicago: American Marketing Association.

De Pietro, R., & Clark, N. (1984). A sense-making approach to understanding adolescents' selection of health information sources. *Health Education Quarterly, 11*(4).

De Pietro, R., & Rozek, D. (1985). *The utilization of EPSDT services by medicaid eligibles.* A report to the Michigan Department of Public Health.

De Pietro, R. (1985). *The utilization of health and birth control information sources and services by low income youth.* A report to Planned Parenthood of Mid-Michigan.

Dervin, B. (1983, May). An overview of sense-making research: Concepts, methods, and results to date. A paper presented at the annual meeting of the International Communication Association, Dallas.

Dervin, B. (1981). Mass communicating: Changing conceptions of the audience. In Rice, R. E., & Paisley, W. J. (Eds.), *Public communication campaigns*. Beverley Hills: Sage.

Dervin B., Harlook, S., Atwood R., & Garzone, C. (1980). The human side of information: An exploration in health communication context. In Nimmo, D. (Ed.), *Communication Yearbook 4*. New Brunswick, NJ: Transactions.

Dervin, B. (1983). Information as a user construct: The relevance of perceived information needs to synthesis and interpretation. In Ward, S. A., & Reed, L. J. (Eds.), *Knowledge structure and use: Implications for synthesis and interpretation*. Philadelphia: University Press. 153–183.

Elinson J., Henshaw, S. K., & Cohen, S. D. (1976). Response by low income population to a multiphasic screening program: A sociological analysis. *Preventive Medicine, 5*, 414–424.

Fennell, G. G. (1978). Perceptions of the product-use situation, *Journal of Marketing, 42*, 39–47.

Festinger, L. (1957). *A theory of cognitive dissonance*. Stanford: Stanford University Press.

Fishbein, M., & Ajzen, I. (1975). *Belief, attitude, intention and behavior: An introduction to theory and research*. Boston: Addison-Wesley.

Fornell, C. (1982). A second generation of multivariate analysis: An overview. In Fornell, C. (Ed.), *A second generation of multivariate analysis*. Vol. 1. New York: Prager. 1–21.

Fox, F. A., & Kotler, P. (1980). The marketing of social causes: The first 10 years. *Journal of Marketing, 44*, 24–33.

Green, L. W., Kreuter, M. W., Deeds, S. G., & Partridge, K. B. (1980). *Health education planning: A diagnostic approach*. Palo Alto, CA: Mayfield.

Green, P. E., & Rao, V. R. (1979). *Applied multidimensional scaling*. New York: Holt, Rinehart and Winston, Inc.

Green, P. E., & Schaffer, C. M. (1984). A simple method for analysing consumer preferences for product benefits. *Journal of the Market Research Society, 26*(1), 51–61.

Green, P. E., and Srinivasan, V. (1978). Conjoint analysis in consumer research: Issues and outlook. *Journal of Consumer Research, 5*, 103–123.

Haley, R. I. (1984). Benefit segmentation—20 years later. *The Journal of Consumer Marketing, 2*(1), 5–13.

Hansen, H. (1967). *Marketing-text techniques and cases*. Homewood, IL: Irwin.

Hauser, J. R., & Urban, G. L. (1977). A normative methodology for modeling consumer response to innovation. *Operations Research, 25*, 579-719.

Hedberg, B. (1981). How organizations learn and unlearn. In Nystrom, P. C. & Starbuck, W. (Eds.), *The handbook of organizational design*. Vol. 1. New York: Oxford University Press. 3-27.

Hochbaum, G. M. (1981). Application of marketing principles to health education. A paper presented at the workshop of the Texas Society for Public Health Education and the Texas Public Health Association, Austin, Texas, August 13-14.

Holtzman, E. (1983). Focus group moderators should be well-versed in interpretative skills. *Marketing News, 17*(23), February 18.

Hulka, B. S., Kupper, L. L., Daley, M. B., Cassel, J. C., and Schoen, F. (1975). Correlates of satisfaction and dissatisfaction with medical care: A community approach. *Medical Care, 13*, 648-658.

Jantz, N. K., & Becker, M. H. (1984). The health belief model: A decade later. *Health Education Quarterly, 11*(1), 1-47.

Joreskog, K. G., & Sorbom, D. (1984). *Lisrel V, analysis of linear structural relationships by the method of maximum likelihood*. Chicago, IL: National Educational Resources, Inc.

Kelley, H. H. (1967). Attribution theory in social psychology. In Levine, D. (Ed.), *Nebraska symposium on motivation*. Lincoln: University of Nebraska Press. 1967, 192-238.

Kennedy, F. (1976). The focused group interview and moderator bias. *Marketing Review, 31*, 19-21.

Keown, C. (1983). Focus group research: tool for the retailer. *Journal of Small Business Management, 21*, 59-65.

Kotler, P. (1982). *Marketing for nonprofit organizations*. 2nd Ed. Englewood Cliffs, NJ: Prentice-Hall, Inc.

Kotler, P. (1979). Strategies for introducing marketing into non-profit organizations. *Journal of Marketing, 43*, 37-44.

Kotler, P., & Zaltman, G. (1971). Social marketing: an approach to planned social change. *Journal of Marketing, 35*, 3-12.

Krugman, H. E. (1965). The impact of television advertising: Learning without involvement. *Public Opinion Quarterly, 29*, 349-365.

Laczniak, G. R., Lusch, R. F., & Murphy, P. E. (1979). Social marketing: Its ethical dimensions. *Journal of Marketing, 43*, 29-36.

Lazer, W., & Kelley, E. J. (1973). *Social marketing: Perspectives and viewpoints*. Homewood, IL: Richard D. Irwin, Inc.

Lichter, M. (1984). An internal report of the Oakwood Project, Dearborn, MI.

Lovelock, C. H. (1983). Classifying services to gain strategic marketing insights. *Journal of Marketing, 47*, 9-20.

Maccoby, N., & Alexander, J. (1979). Field experimentation. In Munoz R. F., Snowden, L. R., & Kelly, J. G. (Eds.), *Research in social contexts: Bringing about change*. San Francisco: Jossey-Bass.

MacStravic, R. (1982). The demise of an HMO: A marketing perspective. *Journal of Health Care Marketing, 2*(4), 9-16.

MacStravic, R. (1984a). *The forecasting of health care services*. Rockville, MD: Aspen Systems Corporation.

MacStravic, R. (1984b). Persuasive communication strategies for hospitals. *Health Care Management Review*, Spring, 69-75.

Malhotra, N. K., & Jain, A. K. (1982). A conjoint analysis approach to health care marketing and planning. *Journal of Health Care Marketing, 2*(2), 35-44.

Mazur, P. (1953). *The standards we raise*. New York: Harper.

McCarthy, E. J. (1960). *Basic marketing.* Homewood, IL: Irwin.

McGuire, W. J. (1978). An information processing model of advertising effectiveness. In Davis, H. L., & Silk, A. J. (Eds.), *Behavioral and management sciences in marketing.* New York: Ronald (Wiley). 156–180.

McGuire, W. J. (1981). Theoretical foundations of campaigns. In Rice R. E., and Paisley, W. J. (Eds.) *Public communication campaigns.* Beverley Hills, CA: Sage Publications.

Mintzberg, H. (1979). *The structuring of organizations.* New York: McGraw-Hill.

Neslin, S. A. (1983). Designing new outpatient health services: Linking service features to subjective consumer perceptions. *Journal of Health Care Marketing, 3*(3), 8–21.

Nordhaus Research Inc. (1985). A focus group research proposal.

Nygren, T. E. (1980). Limitations of additive conjoint scaling procedures: Detecting non-additivity when additivity is known to be violated. *Applied Psychological Measurement, 4*(3), 367–383.

O'Donnell, M. F., and Ainsworth, T. H. (Eds.), (1984). *Health promotion in the workplace.* New York: Wiley Medical Publications.

Parker, B., & Srinivasan, V. (19 A consumer preference approach to planning rural primary health care facilities. *Operations Research, 24,* 991–1025.

Pfeffer, J. (1978). *Organizational design.* Arlington Heights, IL: AHM Publishing Co.

Pfeffer, J., & Salancik, G. (1978). *The external control of organizations.* New York: Harper.

Population information program: Social marketing, does it work? *Population Reports,* (1980). Family Planning Programs, Series J, Number 21, The Johns Hopkins University.

Prottas, J. M. (1983). Encouraging altruism: Public attitudes and the marketing of organ donation. *Milbank Memorial Fund Quarterly (Health and Society), 61*(2), 278–306.

Ray, M. L. (1982). *Advertising and communication management.* Englewood Cliffs, NJ: Prentice-Hall, Inc.

Ray, M. L. (1973). Marketing communications and the hierarchy of effects. In Clarke, P. (Ed.), *New models for mass communication research.* Beverly Hills, CA: Sage Publications.

Roberto, E. (1975). *Strategic decision-making in a social program: the case of family planning diffusion.* Lexington, MA: Lexington Books.

Rosenstock, I. M. (1974). The health belief model and preventative health behavior. *Health Education Monographs, 2,* 354–385.

Rosenstock, I. M. (1966). Why people use health services. *Milbank Memorial Fund Quarterly, 44*(3), 94–127.

Rothschild, M. (1979). Marketing communication in non-business situations. *Journal of Marketing, 43,* 11–20.

Sarner M. (1984). Marketing health to Canadians. *Health Education, 23*(2), 2–9.

Schearer, S. (1981). Special issue: Focus group research, *Studies in Family Planning, 12*(12).

Schellstede, W. P., & Ciszewski, R. L. (1984). Social marketing of contraceptives in Bangladesh. *Studies in Family Planning, 15*(1), 35–39.

Simon, J. K. (1978). Marketing the community hospital: A tool for the beleaguered administrator. *Health Care Management Review, 3,* 11–23.

Srivastava, R. K. (1981). Usage-situational influences on perceptions of product markets: Theoretical and empirical issues. In Monroe, K. (Ed.), *Advances in Consumer Research,* 8. Chicago, IL: Association for Consumer Research. 106–111.

Srivastava R. K., Alpert M. I., & Shocker, A. D. (1984). A customer-oriented approach for determining market structures. *Journal of Marketing, 48,* 32–45.

Strattman, W. C. (1975). A study of consumer attitudes about health care: The delivery of ambulatory services. *Medical Care, 13,* 537–548.

Urban, G. L., & Hauser, J. R. (1980). Market definition. In *Design of new products and services.* Chapter 5. Englewood Cliffs, NJ: Prentice-Hall.

Wan, T. T. H., & Gray, L. C. (1978). Differential access to preventive services for young children in low-income urban areas. *Journal of Health and Social Behavior, 19*, 312–324.

Webster, F. E. (1981). Top management's concern about marketing: Issues for the 1980's. *Journal of Marketing, 45*, 9–16.

Weick, K. (1976). Educational organizations as loosely coupled systems. *Administrative Science Quarterly, 21*, 1–19.

Wilkie, W. L. & Cohen, J. B. (1977, June). An overview of market segmentation: Behavioral concepts and research approaches. Marketing Science Institute working paper.

Wind, Y., & Robertson, T. S. (1983). Marketing strategy: new directions for theory and research. *Journal of Marketing, 47*, 12–25.

Zabin, L. (1984). The association between smoking and sexual behavior among teens in US contraceptive clinics. *American Journal of Public Health, 74*(3), 261–263.

Zeithaml, C. P., & Zeithaml, V. A. (1984). Environmental management: Revising the marketing perspective. *Journal of Marketing, 48*, 46–53.

SECTION II:

RESEARCH AND EVALUATION

INTRODUCTION TO RESEARCH AND EVALUATION

Patricia D. Mullen

Research and evaluation occupy an increasingly important position in the design of programs and policies and in decisions about their impact. Allocation of one of three of the sections of *Advances* to research and evaluation is an indication of this importance. In Volume 1 (B) of *Advances*, Dr. Jane Zapka included a mix of papers—reviews of the intervention literature in two settings, in two age groups, and in two methodological chapters. The section reflected not only the tenets of traditional experimental and quasi-experimental design, but also many of the advances in evaluation methods that have emerged from the diverse disciplines now interested in evaluation. The chapters included also reflected the growing experience and special issues of health education and promotion research and evaluation.

This volume was planned to follow this model and to address complementary topics. Only half of the papers originally solicited were completed in time for publication. Happily, however, the mix was maintained. As a result it was possible to include an unusually long paper by Flay in its entirety, and your section editor and co-author were, therefore, able to treat information synthesis and meta-analysis in more depth. Each of the

Advances in Health Education and Promotion, vol. 2, pages 119–120
Copyright © 1987 JAI Press Inc.
ISBN: 0-89232-617-4

three chapters that comprise the research and evaluation section can be read both for substantive and methodological reasons, although they focus primarily on one or the other area.

The first chapter on school-based smoking prevention programs is a model narrative review, and it provides substantial methodological information and guidelines for readers wishing to evaluate such research efforts or to conduct research themselves. The "social influences" and "life/social skills" approaches described and critiqued by Flay have been widely heralded for advancing health-education practice. The evolution in quality of such research is demonstrated by the fact that the results from two of the evaluations he reviews were published simultaneously in the *American Journal of Public Health* in 1980. The chapter's description of the interrelationships among the four generations of smoking-prevention projects offers insight into the cumulative and simultaneous development of knowledge.

Social learning theory has captured the attention of health education and promotion practitioners and academicians, and the self-efficacy construct, in particular, is a frequently measured application of this theory. Yalow and Collins deepen our understanding of the measurement of self-efficacy by clarifying the construct in relation to similar constructs, such as behavioral intention, and by reviewing selected studies and pointing out the strengths and weaknesses of measures of self-efficacy of each of these studies. This critique assists readers interested in "state of the art" measurement approaches, and it offers a basis on which to evaluate the claim that a given investigation has, indeed, adequately operationalized the self-efficacy construct. Bandura reviewed this chapter, and several interesting notations indicate differences of opinion between him and the chapter authors.

The third chapter in the section, by Mullen and Ramirez, describes methods for synthesizing the results of multiple studies. This topic seemed particularly appropriate for readers of *Advances* who understand well the cumulative nature of scientific advance. As the chapter points out, reviews of literature often fail to describe the search procedures and study limitations, explain criteria for inclusion of primary studies, distinguish between primary and secondary sources, or report study characteristics uniformly. Reviews often use "vote-counting" methods or tallies of significant and nonsignificant findings, an approach that can be misleading because of the influence of sample size in determining statistical significance. Mullen and Ramirez describe these and other issues related to the synthesizing of studies, bolstered by examples from public health and health education and promotion. They devote much of the chapter to quantitative techniques of meta-analysis. Guidelines for conducting (and evaluating) syntheses are presented that hopefully will influence contributions to subsequent volumes of *Advances*.

SOCIAL PSYCHOLOGICAL APPROACHES TO SMOKING PREVENTION:

REVIEW AND RECOMMENDATIONS

Brian R. Flay

INTRODUCTION

Twenty-six school-based studies of psychosocial approaches to smoking prevention are reviewed. Two major approaches are represented: the "social influences" approach, and the broader "life/social skills" approaches. The research studies are considered in four "generations:" (I) the seminal work by Richard Evans and colleagues at the University of Houston; (II) seven "pilot" studies of improved programs at Stanford, Minnesota, New York and Washington, with one school or classroom per experimental condition; (III) eleven improved "prototype" studies by these four groups and others, with two or three units randomly assigned to conditions; and (IV) six studies where maximizing internal validity was of prime concern. Reported results from the pilot and prototype studies were fairly consistent, with each tested program seeming to reduce smoking onset by about 50 percent. Considered alone, however, none of these studies provided interpretable results. Thus, the major contribution of the pilot and prototype studies was improved programs and methods. The findings from the fourth

Advances in Health Education and Promotion, vol. 2, pages 121–180
Copyright © 1987 JAI Press Inc.
All rights of reproduction in any form reserved.
ISBN: 0-89232-617-4

generation of studies are more easily interpreted, though only two of them are interpretable with high confidence. It seems that psychosocial approaches to smoking prevention, particularly the social influences approach (the broader life/social skills approaches have yet to be subjected to fourth generation tests), are effective, but at this time we know very little about why, for whom, or under what conditions. Suggestions are provided for improved future research.

BACKGROUND

The U.S. Surgeon General has documented the wide-ranging influence of smoking on health (U.S. Public Health Service, 1964, 1979, 1980, 1981, 1982, 1983). The limited efficacy of smoking-cessation programs, particularly in the long-term, is also well documented (Bernstein, 1969; Bernstein & McAlister, 1979; Best & Bloch, 1979; Glasgow & Bernstein, 1981; Lichtenstein & Danaher, 1976; Pechacek, 1979; Schwartz, 1969). Preventing young people from becoming regular smokers might be a logical alternative to smoking cessation. The major purpose of this paper is to review the social psychological research on smoking prevention of the last decade. First, however, a brief review of the process of becoming a smoker is provided, for it is only through an understanding of that process that the most successful approaches to smoking prevention will be, or have been, formulated.

Becoming a Smoker

The process of becoming a smoker is not yet totally understood. Few well-designed prospective studies of the factors promoting cigarette smoking have yet been completed (Chassin et al., 1981a, b; Cherry & Kiernan, 1976; Downey & O'Rourke, 1976; Jessor & Jessor, 1977; Kandel, 1975, 1978). Evidence about why people start to smoke must, therefore, be gathered from many different types of studies, including hundreds of cross-sectional and retrospective studies. Many past studies have methodological shortcomings, and different reviewers have different standards for the acceptability of evidence from them. Despite these differences, various investigators and reviewers have suggested rather similar processes to describe the onset of smoking (Botvin & McAlister, 1982; Dunn, 1973; Flay et al., 1983a; Horn, 1976; Leventhal & Cleary, 1980; McAlister, et al., 1979; Salber et al., 1968).

Peer and family influences have been shown with greater certainty than any other factors to be primary antecedents of the onset of smoking among adolescents. Media influences are also thought to be important, although this has not yet been established clearly. Personal skills of self-management and/or self-esteem are also thought to be related to smoking among adolescents, though empirical evidence for this has been ambiguous (Botvin & McAlister, 1982; Evans & Raines, 1982; Flay et al., 1983a; Murray & Perry, 1985; Williams, 1971). The evidence concerning the relationship between having general social competence and starting to smoke is also mixed, with some recent work even suggesting that those adolescents with better general social skills might be more likely to try cigarette smoking (Wills, in press).

Becoming a regular cigarette smoker is thought to be a developmental process involving three to five discrete stages, with the importance of the above factors changing across stages (see Flay et al., 1983a). During a "preparation" or "anticipation" stage (Leventhal & Cleary, 1980), a knowledge and attitude base is formed. Family attitudes and behavior are probably the most important determinants of an individual's early knowledge and attitudes about cigarette smoking, although other social influences obviously play some role. Preparation will sometimes lead to trying the first cigarette, or "initiation." At this point, peer influence is thought to be of major importance; the first few cigarettes are almost invariably taken with others. Social reinforcements and personality factors are likely determinants of whether or not the "tryer" will continue to "experiment" with smoking. The next stage is where the individual starts to smoke alone and on a more "regular" basis, though this may still be only once or a few times per week or month. At this stage, physiological gratification and social reinforcement probably determine whether or not the individual makes the transition to becoming a "habitual" or "adult" smoker.

The developmental process summarized above occurs from elementary school through high school, and sometimes beyond. The first cigarette may be tried early in elementary school, but for most people the event is likely to occur during late elementary school or middle school. The greatest onset into regular smoking occurs during middle school and early high school years. Hence, most smoking-prevention research has been conducted with these groups.

Conventional Smoking Education Programs

Many antismoking education programs have been developed and implemented over the years by schools, voluntary health agencies, and other educators and researchers. Unfortunately, most of them have not been investigated with scientific rigor, and so their efficacy is not easily judged. Most past programs have been based on the premise that if children know why cigarette smoking is bad for them, they should choose to not start smoking. Of those conventional smoking education programs evaluated, many have succeeded in changing students' knowledge, some their beliefs and attitudes, but very few have consistently reduced the onset of smoking behavior (Green, 1979; Thompson, 1978).

The failure of informational or fear programs to change behavior comes as no surprise to psychologists (Leventhal & Cleary, 1980). Information can be preventive at the "preparation/anticipation" stage, but not beyond. Other factors, particularly social influences and associated social skills, are more potent determinants of behavior as children mature into young adolescents and beyond. The recognition of these issues led to the developments in prevention, and research on educational programs based on those developments, to be reviewed here.

Psychosocial Prevention Approaches

The failure of conventional smoking-education programs to consider the social and psychological processes that lead to the adoption of smoking often has been blamed for their lack of success. The empirical literature on adolescent smoking suggests that onset is not caused by any single factor or event; rather, a combination of factors—including social, psychological, and environmental factors—interact to influence onset (Botvin & Mc-Alister, 1982; Chassin et al., 1981a, b; Dunn, 1973; Evans & Raines, 1982; Flay et al., 1983a; Horn, 1976; Jessor & Jessor, 1977; Krohn et al., 1983; Leventhal & Cleary, 1980; McAlister, et al., 1979; Murray & Perry, 1985; Salber et al., 1968; Williams, 1971). The last decade has seen more effort to consider the complexities of the psychosocial processes involved in becoming a cigarette smoker, and to incorporate such complexities in the design of prevention interventions. While most of the recent programs include material on the long-term health consequences of cigarette smoking, they also include information on (a) the immediate physiological and social consequences of smoking, and (b) the prevalence of smoking. In addition, psychosocial smoking-prevention programs focus on one or more of (c) correcting students' perceptions of social norms regarding smoking, (d) teaching students about the social influences to smoke, (e) providing them with behavioral skills to resist those influences, (f) enhancing their personal skills and/or self-esteem, and (g) providing them with general social competence skills. Programs that focus only, or mostly, on social influences (i.e., items c–e) are referred to as the "social influences" approach. Programs that include all, or most, of the above components, or emphasize the latter components (f and g), are referred to as the broader "life/social skills" approaches.

For this review, experimental tests of the psychosocial approaches to smoking prevention have been divided into four generations (see listing in Table 1). Richard Evans and his colleagues at the University of Houston

Table 1. Four Generations of Psychosocial Smoking Prevention Studies

Generation	Study	References	Start Date
I	HOUSTON I	Evans et al., 1978	75
	HOUSTON II	Evans et al., 1981	76
II	CLASP (Stanford)	McAlister et al., 1979, 1980; Perry et al., 1980a; Telch et al., 1982	77
	RASP (Minnesota I)	Hurd et al., 1980; Luepker et al., 1983	77
	WASHINGTON I	Schinke & Blythe, 1981.	77
	WASHINGTON II	Gilchrist, Schinke, & Blythe, 1979; Schinke & Gilchrest, 1983	78
	NEW YORK I	Botvin & Eng, 1980; Botvin et al., 1980	78
	NEW YORK II	Botvin & Eng, 1982	79
	NEW YORK III	Spitzhoff et al., 1981; Wills, 1985	81
III	PCSC (Minnesota II)	Arkin et al., 1981; Murray et al., 1980, 1984	79
	NEW YORK IV	Botvin et al., 1984	80
	NEW YORK V	Botvin et al., 1983	81
	WASHINGTON III	Gilchrist & Schinke, 1984; Schinke & Gilchrist, 1984	81
	TENNESSEE	Pentz, 1982, 1983, 1985	81
	HIGH SCHOOL STUDIES		
	STANFORD HIGH I	Perry et al., 1980	78
	STANFORD HIGH II	Perry et al., 1983a	80
	HASP (USC I)	Johnson et al., 1986	81
	COMMUNITY STUDIES		
	NORTH KARELIA	Vartiainen et al., 1983	78
	OSLO	Tell et al., 1984	79
	CURRENT MINNESOTA	Perry et al., 1983b	81
IV	WATERLOO	Best et al., 1984; Flay et al., 1983a, 1985	79
	STANFORD/ HARVARD	McAlister, 1983; McAlister et al., 1982	79
	AUSTRALIA	Fisher et al., 1983	81
	MICHIGAN	Dielman et al., 1984, 1985	81
	OREGON	Biglan et al., in press; Hops et al., 1986	82
	TVSP (USC II)	Flay et al., 1982, 1983b, c	82

(Evans, 1976; Evans et al., 1978, 1981) derived the basis for the social influences approach, and the first tests of it are regarded as the first generation in this review. All subsequent generations of research were influenced to varying extents by the first Houston study, with the researchers of the social influences approach perhaps being influenced more directly than researchers of the more general life/social skills approaches.

The seminal study (Evans et al., 1978) relied heavily on McGuire's (1964) social inoculation theory. Social inoculation is analogous to biological inoculation, whereby a person is exposed to a small dose of an infectious agent to develop antibodies, thereby reducing susceptibility to subsequent exposure. This model applied to smoking posits that resistance to persuasion will be greater if one has developed arguments with which to counter social pressure to smoke (Evans, 1976). According to the theory, the development of counter-arguments should inoculate one against social influences in real-life situations in a manner analogous to biological inoculation increasing resistance to the disease inoculated against. Two studies by the Houston group (Evans et al., 1978, 1981) were based on this theoretical approach, with added theoretical bolstering from attitude change (persuasive communications) theory (McGuire, 1969) and social learning theory (Bandura, 1977). Their programs used same-age peers on film to impart information about the three major social influences to smoke and focused on immediate rather than long-term consequences of smoking.

The second generation of studies on psychosocial approaches to smoking prevention placed greater emphasis on elements derived from theories of social learning (Bandura, 1977), attribution (Jones et al., 1972), commitment (Kiesler, 1971), problem behavior (Jessor & Jessor, 1977), decision-making (Janis & Mann, 1977), cognitive-behavior therapy (Pentz & Tolan, in press), and peer teaching (Hartup & Louge, 1975; Vriend, 1969). While the first studies by Evans et al. included films showing students being exposed to peer pressure and ways of resisting it, learning those skills does not appear to have been a primary objective of the program. The second generation of studies, particularly those at Stanford and Minnesota, provided students opportunities to role-play and receive feedback on their performance of behavioral skills. Some of the second generation of studies, particularly those in New York and Washington, also added general, personal and social competence skills training.

The first attempts to test (a) the various components of the programs, and (b) the differential effectiveness of different program providers or facilitators were made in the second generation of studies. These studies were, however, of limited value in this respect because they all involved only one unit (school or classroom) per experimental condition. The third generation of studies reduced this problem somewhat by including two or three units per condition, usually with some attempt at randomization.

Questions of major interest in the third generation of studies concerned (a) the construct validity of the treatment (i.e., does a particular program component have the direct effects expected of it?), (b) program dissemination (e.g., is the approach more or less effective when delivered or facilitated by different types of people?), and (c) the generalizability of the treatment (e.g., do the approaches work for high school students as well as junior high school students or in different settings?).

As this review will suggest, the so-called second and third generations of studies of psychosocial approaches to smoking prevention can be considered now as no more than pilot and prototypical studies of promising approaches. They each had serious methodological flaws that made the interpretation of their results difficult, particularly any results regarding the construct validity, dissemination, or generalizability of the treatment. However, the consistency of results in terms of overall program effects encouraged further exploration of the approaches. Smoking-prevention research is a young field and early results, as in any new science, need to be considered only as suggestive, not definitive. Much-improved fourth generation studies were made possible by the experiences and lessons of the early second and third generation studies. The fourth generation of studies has included mostly large-scale randomized trials that have attempted to maximize internal validity to demonstrate the overall effectiveness of the psychosocial approaches.

Twenty-six school-based studies of psychosocial approaches to smoking prevention were located (Table 1). Figure 1 shows the developmental relationships between the generations—influence from one project to another has been most direct where one or more of the same investigators has been involved (lines with arrows). In other cases, there has been direct influence from one project to another when new research teams learned directly from previous investigators (lines without arrows). The Houston, Stanford, and Minnesota teams have been most influential in this way. No doubt there has been influence to varying degrees between every pair of studies where no lines are shown, but it appears that such influence has been less direct than others, such as through the literature.

The studies are reviewed in rough chronological order within the four groups (generations) described above (see Table 1). For each study, the program(s) tested are described in terms of the grade(s) of intervention, number of sessions, total duration of the program, the primary provider, the types of peer leaders used, and other salient factors. Methodological characteristics of each study are also described, including the experimental comparisons attempted, the number of units assigned to each condition, what those units were, whether or not they were randomly assigned, whether or not pretest differences were reported, the time of longest follow-up, whether or not individual stu-

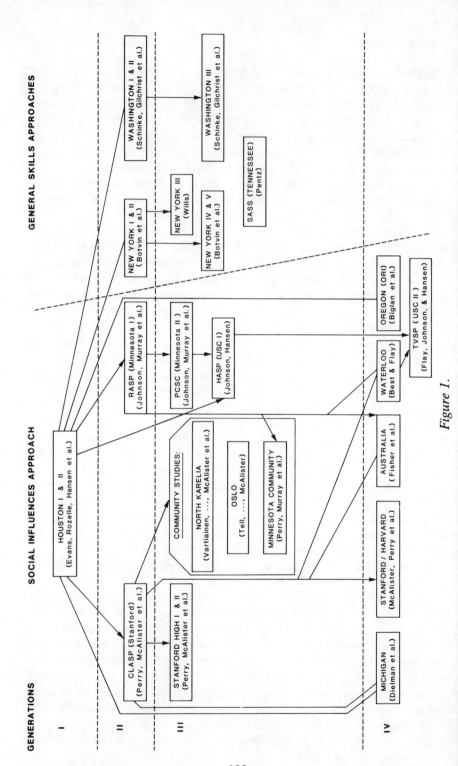

Figure 1.

dents could be tracked over time, the extent of attrition, and whether or not there was biological validation of self reports of smoking and its nature. For each study, the reported results are also described, with comments on any plausible alternative interpretations. Finally, the extent of our knowledge from all reviewed studies is synthesized, and recommendations are provided for future research.

THE HOUSTON STUDIES (THE FIRST GENERATION)

Richard Evans and his colleagues (1978, 1981) at the University of Houston developed and tested the first of the social influences programs for smoking prevention. Their program used nonsmoking peers on film to impart information about the three major social influences to start smoking. The presentation of each film was followed by "knowledge tests" that emphasized immediate rather than long-term consequences of smoking, small group discussions of resistance to persuasion, and the provision of posters to be placed around the school to serve as continuing reminders.

An experimental test compared students in schools that received this program over four consecutive days, a group that received both the program and feedback about the smoking rates among their classmates at the three post-tests (at 1, 5 and 10 weeks), a repeated testing group that was exposed only to the pretest and three post-tests, and a minimal-testing control group that was exposed only to the pretest and the final post-test. A total of 750 students in 10 junior high schools were included in the study. Two schools were assigned to each of the four conditions (procedure unknown) and in two other schools, students were assigned randomly to the four conditions. Reported results did not separate the between-school and within-school conditions. This was the first prevention study to include a collection of samples of saliva to enhance the honesty of self-reports of smoking (Evans, Hansen, & Mittlemark, 1977) by using a variation of the bogus pipeline technique (Jones & Sigall, 1971).

Results at the 10-week post-test indicated that the proportion of pretest nonsmokers in the program conditions who reported smoking at least one cigarette in the last month (10.0 percent in the program condition and 8.6 percent in the program plus feedback condition) was approximately half that of the minimal-testing group (18.3 percent). However, there were no significant differences between the program groups and the repeated testing group (10.3 percent). Note too, that any subjects who reported having tried smoking at the pretest (31 percent of the total sample) were excluded from the analysis of program effects.

Evans and colleagues (1981) reported long-term results of the Houston program. A total of thirteen schools was assigned (nonrandomly) to one of three experimental or four control conditions during the course of the study. Initially, however, a six-group design, three experimental and three control groups, was set up in seven of the schools. Aspects of the program (up to eight films presenting various messages) were provided to a cohort in each of the experimental schools during each of three years, grades 7 through 9. The control schools varied from a repeated measurement condition (12 measures during the study that included saliva thiocyanate testing) to an additional set of schools that was added at the end of the study as post-test-only controls. Due to administrative and other difficulties, groups were successively combined during the course of the study so that only three conditions remained by grade 9. Subjects were not identified across time, so that only cross-sectional analyses were possible rather than more appropriate longitudinal analyses.

The reported cross-sectional analyses are difficult to interpret because the extent to which the composition of the sample changed over time is not known (sample sizes ranged from 1,352 to 3,296). It is clear that there were no program effects by the end of grade 7; indeed, there may have been a significant reverse effect. The authors claim significant program effects in subsequent years on the basis of approximately 9.5 percent of program students versus 11–14 percent of controls reporting smoking two or more cigarettes per day by the end of grade 9. Evans et al. also reported superior knowledge by the program groups and a correlation between knowledge and smoking behavior. The inability to conduct longitudinal analyses, however, means that such data cannot be interpreted to show that changes in knowledge caused changes in behavior. Overall, it must be concluded that (a) this study did not replicate the earlier results at the end of the grade of intervention (grade 7), and (b) the claimed program effects at three-year follow-up are small and difficult to attribute to the program.

THE SECOND-GENERATION STUDIES

Despite the inconclusive results of the Houston studies, the theoretical derivations seemed firm enough to encourage other researchers to strengthen and test the approach. The second generation of studies on the psychosocial approaches to smoking prevention are characterized in three ways. First, they expanded upon the basic inoculation-with-communication model by enhancing the role of social learning theory, considering attribution and commitment theories and, in some cases, more general personal and social competence skills. Second, they were all small-scale studies, as far as school-based studies go, with one classroom or school per condition, sometimes with noncomparability at pretest even when random assignment was attempted. Third, some of them attempted to test the relative contribution of the various components of their more complex interventions and/or the importance of those who provided the programs.

The second-generation studies can be divided conveniently into two further groups. Two of the studies (CLASP and RASP) provide tests of the basic "social influences" approach to smoking prevention. In these studies, the focus is confined to making students aware of social influences, correcting their normative expectations, and providing them with the skills to resist social influences. The other five studies in the second generation expand upon the social influences approach by adding a concern with more general personal and social skills. That is, these studies attempted to improve personal skills (and, therefore, it is argued, self-esteem) and general social competence skills such as assertiveness. It has been argued that (a) personal skills and/or improvement in self-esteem will enable better use of the social resistance skills and (b) more general social skills will be applied in many settings in everyday life, not only to resist social influences to smoke.

Project CLASP (Stanford)

Investigators at Stanford (Perry et al., 1980a; McAlister et al., 1980; Telch et al., 1982; see also McAlister et al., 1979) expanded upon the basic "social inoculation with persuasive communication" model. Project CLASP (Counseling Leadership Against Smoking Pressures) included the same features as the Evans et al. program with three important theory-based innovations. First, high school students were used as "peer" teachers for seventh graders; second, a session was introduced to increase social commitment not to smoke; and third, behavioral learning techniques (Bandura, 1977) were introduced in the form of role playing, where students acted out situations requiring resistance to social influences. The program consisted of three sessions on consecutive days, with four booster sessions spaced over the remainder of the grade-7 school year. The program was tested in one school that had been identified as having a high rate of smoking among older students, and where administrators were seeking a solution to the smoking problem. Two "roughly matched" schools were used as nonrandom controls. Breath samples were collected from all subjects in an attempt to increase the honesty of self-reports of smoking behavior. Individual subjects could not be followed, so analyses were limited to cross-sectional comparisons. At the end of grade 7, students in the treatment school reported significantly less smoking in the past week (5.3 percent) than students in the control schools (11 percent). At the end of grade 8, 5.6 percent of students in the program school reported smoking in the last week compared to 16.2 percent in one of the control schools

(McAlister et al., 1980—one control school was dropped from the analyses because of problematic pretest differences). At the end of grade 9, 5.2 percent of students in the program school reported smoking in the last week, compared to 15.1 percent in the remaining control school (Telch et al., 1982).

This is the first study to have reported large preventive effects of the social influences approach, with the program group smoking weekly at only one third the level of the control group. This is also one of the few social influences smoking-prevention programs for which prevention of alcohol and marijuana use has also been reported (McAlister et al., 1980). Unfortunately, the encouraging results cannot be attributed with total confidence to the program because of the methodological problems noted above. The authors of the study are well aware of the shortcomings, labeling the study as a pilot project and pointing out some of the possible alternative interpretations; "It is possible that these results are biased by natural differences between the students in the two schools, by statistical regression, or by 'pseudo-regression' caused by deliberately choosing a population with reportedly acute problems as the experimental group and one with fewer reported problems as the control group" (McAlister et al., 1980, pp. 720–721).

The First Minnesota Study (RASP)

The Robbinsdale Anti-Smoking Project (RASP) was initiated in the fall of 1977. Data have been reported for the end of the intervention year (Hurd et al., 1980) and for one- and two-year follow-ups (Luepker et al., 1983). Project RASP was the first study to attempt to test the value of (a) peer leaders and (b) a public commitment procedure. The initial design involved four schools and five experimental conditions. The five experimental conditions were (a) controls with questionnaire and saliva-sample monitoring, (b) minimally measured controls (later dropped from the study because saliva samples were not collected at pretest), (c) a social influences curriculum, (d) a social influences curriculum with peer leaders (personalization), and (e) a social influences curriculum with peer leaders and a commitment procedure. The tested social influences curriculum consisted of a combination of video/film presentations (some of them modifications of the Evans et al. materials) and discussion groups. The group discussions covered the social consequences of smoking, ways of saying no, correcting misperceptions of the proportions of people who smoke, and media pressures. Students were provided with opportunities to develop counterarguments, to role-play, and to practice resistance skills. In the peer-led condition, selected peers appeared in some of the video materials and led the group discussions. In the commitment procedure, students were recorded making a statement of why they were not going to smoke, and the recordings played back to the class. The basic curriculum was four sessions long, with the commitment procedure adding a fifth period; the sessions were spread fairly evenly across the grade-7 school year, and were delivered or supervised by trained pharmacy students.

Classrooms within one school were assigned randomly to whether or not they received the commitment procedure. The four schools were assigned to the remaining four conditions so that one lower SES and one higher SES school were assigned to program conditions and one pair was assigned to control conditions. All students (except those in the dropped minimal measurement conditions) were measured at pretest, between the second and third sessions of the curriculum, at the end of the school year, and at one- and two-year follow-ups. A distinct improvement over previous studies was that individual students were tracked through the study.

At each measurement point, data were collected from approximately 80 percent of those present at the previous measurement point; 53 percent of the original students completed the two-year follow-up. At the end of the intervention year, both the social influences programs seem to have reduced the amount of ever smoking, though not to a statistically significant degree; only the social influences curriculum without peer leaders (but still with films) seems to have reduced experimental smoking; and only the peer-led social influences curriculum seems to have prevented an increase in regular (usually weekly) smoking. The commitment procedure did not add significantly to the peer-led program. By the one-year follow-up, the only significant effect was a greater number of never smokers remaining in the peer-led condition school. By the two-year follow-up, even that difference seems to have decayed somewhat, though when a continuous index of smoking is created that includes a measure of quantity as well as frequency, the peer-led curriculum still appears to be superior to a significant degree.

This study made some innovative advances. However, methodological problems make the reported results very difficult to interpret. The major difficulty is that SES and other social-risk factors for smoking (e.g., parental, sibling, and friends smoking) were perfectly confounded with the expected strength of the experimental condition. That is, the control school was the lowest on SES and the highest on all the social-risk factors, the school that received the social influences curriculum with peer leaders was the highest on SES and the lowest on all social-risk factors, and the school that received the social influences curriculum from pharmacy students was in between (see detailed pretest data reported by Hurd et al., 1980). Thus, without any program, the highest rates of smoking would be expected in the control school, and the lowest rates in the peer-led program school. Large pretest differences in smoking rates add to the difficulties of interpretation—at the final post-test, the rank-ordering of the three conditions remaining at that time in terms of level of smoking (experimental plus regular) is exactly the same as at pretest. Even the finding that peer leadership was superior is difficult to interpret, in that the selected peers also appeared in some of the film materials—that is, peer leadership was perfectly confounded with the familiarity of actors in the media materials.

The First Two Washington Studies

Schinke and his colleagues at the University of Washington have conducted three tests of their "cognitive-behavioral" approach to smoking prevention. Two of them are second-generation studies, and one belongs in the third generation. The intervention strategy is derived from extensive research on pregnancy prevention (Schinke, 1982; Gilchrist & Schinke, 1984). The components of their program seem to be very similar to those of other programs, though with more emphasis on (a) problem solving and decision making designed to help individuals avoid peer pressure situations without alienating friends, and (b) self-instructional techniques designed to help individuals exercise self control over their behavior. Training methods also seem to be similar to other programs, involving Socratic teaching, role play, feedback, reinforcement, and coaching. Extended practice via homework is used to increase the likelihood that the skills will be learned, utilized, and generalized to various life situations. The program is delivered to grade 6 students in eight, semiweekly, one-hour sessions by two graduate interns.

In the first Washington Study (Schinke & Blythe, 1981), twenty-eight students in one school were included in two classrooms randomly assigned to program or control conditions. All students were assessed by questionnaire at pretest, immediate post-test and six-month follow-up. Saliva samples were collected only at the six-month measure. Measures included presumed mediating variables that were hypothesized to be changed by the program, such as "perspective taking," "means-end thinking," and "anticipation of consequences." In addition, students were videotaped as they resisted eight different offers or pressure to smoke from a same-age confederate. Results indicated that the students in the treatment group had significantly greater increases in knowledge, problem solving, decision-making skills, and interpersonal skills. By six-month post-test, program students had better attitudes toward nonsmoking, fewer intentions to smoke, more refusals of cigarettes, and less smoking in the past week or month (these apparently were not assessed at the immediate posttest).

In a second test of the Washington program (Gilchrist et al., 1979; Schinke & Gilchrist, 1983), four classrooms in two schools were assigned to the four conditions of a Solomon four group design (Solomon, 1949). A sample of students from each classroom (14 per condition) was included in the study. Students were post-tested after two months, and follow-up data were collected after six months, using the same type of measures as in the first Washington study. Again, students in the intervention group were more knowledgeable, more skilled in decision making and problem solving, and performed more actively in interpersonal situations requiring a consistent antismoking stance. At the six-month follow-up, program students reported more instances of refusing cigarettes, having smoked fewer cigarettes, and having fewer intentions of ever smoking. Pretesting was not found to make any significant difference.

The intensive measurement of process variables and presumed mediators is impressive in these studies, and these are the first studies reviewed to have demonstrated significant improvements in behavioral skills. The studies are limited, however, because contamination of conditions is a distinct possibility when two classrooms in the same school are in different experimental conditions. The attempt to establish whether or not pretesting is reactive was also marred by small sample sizes. The expected effects of pretesting are smaller than program effects, so would require much larger samples to detect.

The First Two New York Studies

Gil Botvin and his colleagues, first at the American Health Foundation and now at Cornell University Medical College, have developed and tested a broad psychosocial approach to smoking prevention that they call "Life Skills Training" (LST). Botvin's approach is distinguished from those reviewed so far by a greater emphasis on underlying individual difference variables. LST programs include components that (a) are designed to modify the presumed underlying core of intrapersonal cognitive and personality factors, and (b) provide general life skills thought to be related to smoking onset, as well as (c) sometimes focusing on specific skills with which to resist social influences to smoke. In a series of four studies, the LST program has ranged from 10 to 20 sessions, and incorporated techniques such as cognitive strategies for enhancing self-esteem, techniques for resisting persuasive appeals, techniques for coping with anxiety, verbal and nonverbal communication skills, and a variety of social skills. A combination of instruction, modeling, rehearsal, feedback and reinforcement, and extended practice through homework are used to develop these skills. Botvin and Wills (1985) and Glasgow and McCaul (1985) provide comprehensive analyses of the differences between the basic social influences approach and the life skills approach.

In the first study of the life skills training approach, Botvin and colleagues (Botvin & Eng, 1980; Botvin, Eng, & Williams, 1980) tested a 10-session program with grade 8, 9, and 10 students. The 10 sessions were delivered by professional health educators on a weekly basis. Two suburban New York schools of comparable SES and baseline smoking rates were randomly assigned to program and control conditions. Smoking status and presumed mediating variables were assessed by questionnaire, without biological validation, at pretest, immediate posttest, and three-month follow-up. Twenty-three percent of the immediate posttest sample were not surveyed at three-month follow-up.

By the immediate posttest, significantly fewer pretest nonsmokers in the experimental school had tried smoking (4 percent) than in the control school (16 percent). By the three-month follow-up, these rates were 6 and 18 percent, respectively. Significant differences between the experimental and control groups were also reported for changes in knowledge, social anxiety (for males only), need for group acceptance (grades 8 and 9 only), and peer identification (females only), all of which decayed somewhat by the three-month follow-up.

In a second study, Botvin and Eng (1982) tested a 12-session LST program delivered to grade 7 students by older (grade 11 and 12) peer leaders. Two suburban New York schools of comparable SES and baseline smoking rates were randomly assigned to program and control conditions. Students were followed for one year after the intervention, and saliva samples supplemented self-report measures of smoking. As with the first study, analysis of program effects was confined to those students who had never tried smoking by pretest. Complete data were collected on 84 percent of the total sample.

By the immediate posttest, 8 percent of pretest nonsmokers had smoked (in the previous month) in the program school versus 19 percent in the control school. These results were corroborated by saliva thiocyanate analysis. Significant differences were also reported for changes in smoking knowledge, psychosocial knowledge, advertising knowledge, social anxiety, and influenceability, but not locus of control nor self-esteem. These changes in presumed mediators of smoking were also found to differentiate subsequent regular smokers from others. At one-year follow-up, the difference in the proportion of pretest nonsmokers smoking in the previous month was no longer significant (24 percent vs. 32 percent); however, there were significant differences between groups on more regular (weekly) smoking (11 percent vs. 25 percent).

The results of these two New York studies are impressive, but their interpretability is limited by a number of factors. As Botvin and colleagues have noted, "demand characteristics" of the testing situation may have biased self-report results, particularly in the first study because no biological samples were collected. Furthermore, as with other second generation studies, the use of only one school per experimental condition, and serious attrition impose serious constraints on the interpretability of results. As with the first Evans et al. (1978) study, students who had already tried smoking before pretest were eliminated from further analysis. As with the Washington studies, the reported program effects on presumed mediating variables are also impressive, though their interpretability is also limited by the factors noted above.

The Third New York Study (Wills)

Wills (1985) and his colleagues (Spitzhoff, Ramirez, & Wills, 1980) have tested a variation of the LST approach, called the Decision Skills Curriculum (DSC). This variation emphasizes the potential role of stress and coping in the etiology of cigarette smoking by adolescents. The program consisted of eight sessions delivered over two weeks to grade 7 students and five booster sessions delivered to the same students in grade 8 by professional health educators while the regular classroom teachers observed and assisted where necessary with exercises and activities. Three New York City schools, closely matched on baseline smoking prevalence, were assigned, two to the treatment and one to control conditions. Students were tested with questionnaires and saliva samples at the beginning and end of grades 7 and 8.

The overall effect of the program, moderated by school differences, was only marginal. The intervention was effective in one treatment school, affecting both presumed mediating variables and smoking behavior (42 percent less experimental smoking and 39 percent less regular smoking than in the control school), but not in the other school. The authors suggest that the "atmosphere" in the second program school, which was not very conducive to smooth program implementation, is to blame for the lack of program effects there. Such results emphasize the necessity of having multiple schools per condition in school-based studies, in that results can be markedly affected by school-level variables even when they are matched on baseline smoking prevalence.

Summary of Second Generation Studies

The seven studies reviewed in this section have all provided encouraging results. While the consistency of findings across studies is impressive, results from none of the studies were interpretable in their own right because of methodological problems. Table 2 summarizes findings from the second-generation studies and their plausible alternative interpretations.

With only one school per condition, often nonrandomly assigned, many studies had noncomparable pretest levels of smoking behavior and/or social risk values (i.e., numbers of peers, parents, or siblings who smoke, and SES). Attrition was also a very serious problem for most of these studies,

Table 2. Reported Results and Plausible Alternative Interpretations of
Second Generation Studies

Study	Reported Results	Alternative Interpretations
CLASP (Stanford)	Program cut smoking prevalence by two thirds.	Possible pretest differences (program provided in "problem" school). Inability to track students. Incomplete data reported.
Minnesota I (RASP)	Social programs reduced onset of ever smoking in short-term; but only peer-led social program effective at one year, with some decay by two years.	Pretest differences in social risk factors perfectly confounded with hypothesized treatment strength. Pretest differences in smoking prevalence. Peer leadership confounded with familiarity of actors in media materials. Serious attrition.
Washington I	Significant program effects by six months on smoking. Also significant effects on mediators, including skills.	Class selection Short follow-up
Washington II	Significant program effects by six months on smoking (8% vs. 37.5%; i.e., 79% reduction). Significant effects on mediators, including skills. No significant effects of pretesting.	Class selection Short follow-up Inadequate power for test of pretesting effect.
New York I	Program cut new triers by 75% at immediate posttest, and 67% by 3 months. Significant changes in various presumed mediators that decayed by 3 months.	Demand characteristics (no biological sample) Incomplete data reported School selection
New York II	Program cut new triers by 58% at immediate posttest, and cut regular smoking (among pretest nonsmokers) by 56% at 1 year follow-up. Significant changes in various presumed mediators. Significant differences in SCN.	Incomplete data reported School selection
New York III	Marginal effects moderated by school-level differences	Incomplete data reported School selection

ranging from 10 percent after six months to 47 percent after two years. Attrition can be a threat to internal validity if it differs across conditions. This does not appear to have been the case in any of these studies. External validity is always threatened by attrition, however; for example, if students who have a high risk of becoming smokers are more likely to be absent from measurement, this would decrease the possible program effect that could be observed.

Review of many of these studies was often difficult because of inadequate reporting of data. Some did not provide pretest data, and most provided inadequate data about smoking behavior at post-tests. To judge fairly the practical significance of findings and make comparisons across studies, results for all categories of smoking behavior for all pretest categories need to be reported, not just selected significant findings (Flay et al., 1985).

THE THIRD GENERATION STUDIES

The third generation studies all involved two or three units (schools or classrooms) per experimental condition, with some attempt to yoke pairs so that the resulting conditions would be comparable. As far as school-based research is concerned, these studies were still relatively small, though they were considered large in their time. Tests of program components were more prevalent; three of the studies tested the social influences approach with high school students; and three other studies tested them in the context of broader community programs.

The Second Minnesota Study (PCSC)

The second Minnesota study (Arkin et al., 1981; Murray et al., 1980, 1985) overcame many of the methodological problems of Project RASP, and also attempted to make other advances in our knowledge of prevention. In two studies, three versions of a "social influences" curriculum were compared with a "long-term influences" (health) curriculum. The type of leader (adult health educator vs. peer), the use vs. nonuse of media (films), and the public-commitment procedure were also tested. In sequential replications of the study, type of provider/facilitator (research staff health educator vs. regular classroom teacher) was tested. All curricula consisted of five class sessions for grade 7 students spread throughout the school year. Eight schools were split at the median for pretest smoking rates, and then one from each group assigned randomly to the four conditions. Within all eight schools, half the classrooms were randomly assigned to the commitment procedure. Two of the eight schools in Project RASP, and historical control data from them were used as the only control for the first study (research staff delivered). For the second study (teacher delivered), two additional schools, nonrandomized, served as a nonequivalent control group. Students were assessed by questionnaire and saliva samples were collected at pretest (beginning of grade 7, in 1979 for the first study and in 1980 for the second study), immediate post-test at the end of grade 7, and one year follow-up (for the first study only) at the end of grade 8. Most results were reported in terms of an index of weekly smoking formed by averaging three self-report measures of smoking. Results are reported only for pretest nonsmokers and experimental smokers. The few students who were regular smokers (i.e., monthly) at pretest were not included in analyses of program effects.

Data reported by Arkin et al. (1981) suggest that in the short term, the health consequences program was most successful in reducing the proportion of nonsmokers who tried smoking by the immediate post-test (15 percent), and the social influences programs next most successful (18–21 percent), when compared with the historical control (31 percent). The analyses presented by Murray et al. (1985), based on a composite index measure of smoking and covarying for pretest differences in social risks to smoke (i.e., parental, peer, and sibling smoking and socioeconomic status), did not show differences among the four program conditions, but did suggest that all four programs were better than controls. By one year follow-up of the first study, however, the peer-led conditions appeared to be more successful for pretest nonsmokers. When pretest experimental smokers are considered, there were no differences between conditions when health educators delivered all programs (Study I), but when programs were delivered by teachers (Study II), the addition of peer leaders had a significant effect, at least by the immediate post-test. However, the pretest experimenters in the control group had the lowest level of smoking by the immediate post-test, making it difficult to interpret any other program differences. The pattern of differences found among the four program conditions at the immediate post-test for Study II was replicated at one year follow-up in Study I. That is, by one year follow-up, pretest experimental smokers were smoking at significantly higher rates when they received the social influences program without peer leaders than when they received either the social influences program with peer leaders or the health program from health educators. At no point in time, in either study, were there differences due to the use of films or the commitment procedure.

These results are difficult to interpret for several reasons. First, despite the use of an improved procedure of random assignment after matching, baseline smoking experience in Study I was lower for the two peer-led conditions (average proportion never smoked = 50 percent) than for all other conditions (average of 64 percent for the other program conditions, and 56 percent for the historical controls) (Arkin et al., 1981). Second, although no baseline smoking level data were reported for Study II, the existence of large differences in the same schools in Study I would lead one to expect such differences in Study II unless otherwise reported. Third, pretest differences in smoking levels were not adjusted out, even though the acknowledged (but unreported) baseline differences in social-risk factors were covaried out in all but the Arkin et al. (1981) paper. Fourth, the use of historical and nonequivalent control groups is questionable, and no baseline data were reported for one of them.

To summarize, these studies attempted to overcome many of the problems of Project RASP, and found (a) no significant overall differences between programs at the immediate posttest, (b) a suggestion that social influences programs were more effective when peer leaders were used, (c) that peer-led social influences programs were more effective than adult-led social influences or health programs at preventing pretest nonsmokers from starting to smoke, and (d) no significant program effects on pretest experimental smokers. However, despite the methodological improvements, the meaning of any of these findings is unclear because of serious methodological problems that remained.

The Fourth New York Study (LST)

Botvin et al. (1984) provided a test of the LST approach when delivered to grade 7 students by specially trained regular classroom teachers. For this study, the tested program consisted of 15 sessions delivered over 4–6 weeks (the intensive format) or 15 weeks (the less intensive format). Seven suburban New York schools were randomly assigned to three conditions, two to each of the program conditions, and three to the control condition. One of the intensive program schools subsequently received eight booster sessions during the following school year, between the immediate posttest, and the one-year follow-up. Students were assessed by both questionnaire and saliva sample at pretest, immediate posttest, and one-year follow-up.

By the immediate posttest, 6 percent of pretest nonsmokers in the combined program groups had started smoking vs. 13 percent in the control conditions, with no differences between the two program format conditions. By the one-year follow-up, 15 percent of pretest nonsmokers were smoking monthly in the combined program conditions vs. 22 percent in the control condition; for weekly smoking, results were 8 vs. 15 percent and for daily smoking, 6 vs. 11 percent. By the one-year follow-up, the more intensive program was more effective than the less intensive program; 10 vs. 19 percent onset of monthly smoking. Indeed, the less intensive program was no longer significantly different from the control condition— 19 vs. 22 percent onset rates. These patterns of results were the same for weekly and daily measures of smoking. Students who received the booster sessions were reported to have started smoking at lower rates than other students, but these results were not significant because of small sample sizes. Program effects were also reported on pretest smokers, but sample sizes were also too small for any of those effects to be significant. Treatment effects were also reported for several of the presumed mediators of cigarette smoking, though they tended to decay almost completely by one-year follow-up, especially in the less intensive condition and the intensive condition without boosters.

These results are somewhat ambiguous for a number of reasons. Because the less intensive program apparently was not effective after one year, and so did not replicate findings from other studies, it cannot be concluded with any confidence that more intensive programming is superior. The addition of booster sessions to the intensive program had no detectable effect on smoking behavior, but did appear to lead to more lasting changes in at least some presumed mediating variables. However, as Botvin et al. correctly point out, the test of boosters is difficult to interpret because of a confounding with school effects as in the second generation of studies. Furthermore, the finding that some mediating variables were still changed significantly in the intensive plus booster condition, but not in the intensive without booster condition, while behavior did not change differentially in those same conditions, raises questions about the relationship between changes in mediators and changes in behavior. Botvin et al. also correctly point out that whatever results were found could have been partly due to demand characteristics, because most program students were pretested in the first program class, and the immediate posttest for the intensive program students also took place during program hours.

The Fifth New York Study (LST)

A fourth study of the LST approach by Botvin and his colleagues (Botvin et al., 1983) was designed to compare teacher-led vs. older peer-led (teams of 4–5) delivery, the addition of booster sessions, and the effectiveness of the approach in preventing alcohol and marijuana use as well as cigarette smoking. A 20-session version of the program was delivered over four months to grade 7 students. Ten suburban New York schools of comparable SES and baseline smoking rates were randomly assigned to four program (teacher-led vs. peer-led crossed by boosters or not) plus control conditions. Students were assessed by questionnaire and saliva sample at pretest and immediate post-test (the study is ongoing, and results regarding the effectiveness of boosters are not yet available). Attrition was 10 percent by the immediate post-test.

Self-reported cigarette smoking and marijuana use were analyzed using a general linear model (GLM) approach to categorical data (Overall, 1980) to compare posttest response frequencies for each of the three experimental conditions (teacher-led vs. peer-led vs. control) using pretest response frequencies as covariates and partialling out individual school-level effects. Adjusted posttest response frequencies indicated significant program effects for the monthly measure of cigarette smoking, the monthly and weekly measures of marijuana use, and the amount of alcohol consumed per drinking occasion for the peer-led program only. Fifteen percent of students in the peer-led condition reported smoking in the last month compared to 21 percent in the control condition and 22 percent in the teacher-led condition. No significant effects were observed for the teacher-led program, nor for the weekly or daily measure of cigarette smoking. The peer-led program also produced significant improvements in smoking, drinking, and marijuana knowledge and attitudes, locus of control and smoking influenceability (plus improved self-esteem for males only); the teacher-led program produced such effects only for smoking and marijuana knowledge and social anxiety.

The major limitation to this study at this date is the lack of longer-term follow-up data. As the results of the previous LST study demonstrate, results at immediate posttest are not always a good indication of the pattern of results at longer-term follow-ups. The surprise from this study was the failure to replicate the effectiveness of the teacher-led program. The investigators suggest that this may have been due to less than adequate implementation, in that the teachers were not monitored intensively as in the previous study or as the peer leaders were in this study. Final evaluation of this study obviously must await reports of follow-up data.

The Third Washington Study

In a third study of their "cognitive-behavioral" approach, Schinke & Gilchrist (1984; Gilchrist & Schinke, 1984), randomly assigned six schools to three conditions: program, "placebo" (instruction without training of skills), and control. All students were assessed, using questionnaire and saliva samples, at pretest, immediate posttest, three-month follow-up and 15-month follow-up.

At immediate posttest, both the program and placebo groups had improved their knowledge compared to the control group, but only the program group had improved on measures of communication, self reward, and problem-solving skills. By three-month follow-up, the proportion of program students who had tried smoking had not increased at all over baseline, while the placebo group increased 18.75 percent, and the control group increased 29 percent. By the 15-month follow-up, the proportion of program students who had tried smoking had increased 3.6 percent compared to 31.7 percent for the placebo group and 41.7 percent for the control group.

This replication demonstrates the importance of the skills training component of the intervention. The use of two schools per condition reduces concerns of program effects being confounded with school characteristics, though N's of two are still too low to provide complete confidence about this.

The Tennessee Study (Project SASS)

Pentz (1982, 1983, 1985) tested an intervention based on a social competence approach to substance abuse that derives from both social learning and problem behavior theories. The Socializing and Social Skills (SASS) program focused on the enhancement of general social skills and self efficacy through the use of modeling, rehearsal, feedback with social reinforcement, and extended practice. It seems to differ from other programs reviewed here mainly in not addressing the issue of cigarette or other substance use directly. The program consisted of nine 55-minute sessions provided to grade 6 through 9 students by trained teachers assisted by project assistants and facilitated by peers working in groups of four in the classroom.

Eighteen classrooms per grade level in eight schools, approximately half urban and half rural, were randomly assigned to three experimental conditions. The three experimental conditions were full intervention (instruction plus modeling), instruction only (three sessions), and control. Analyses were blocked on urban/rural and pretest level of assertiveness. Students were assessed by questionnaire only every six months over two years, with the program being provided between the first two waves. Assessment included extensive measures of self-efficacy, social skills (from a role-play measure), drug use (cigarettes, alcohol, and marijuana combined), and drug-related attitudes. Each student was also rated on level of assertiveness by three or four teachers. Several items relevant to school behavior were derived from school records as well as self reports. Attrition amounted to 20 percent over the two-year period.

Results indicated that the social skills program had no effects on cigarette smoking, but did increase self-efficacy, social skills, grade-point average, and decreased alcohol use significantly more than the instruction-only program or controls. The greatest effects occurred for those students who were most aggressive at baseline. The program effects were greatest for grade 6 and 9 students, and this is thought to be because they were "transition" years, i.e., where students had just changed schools. In rural areas drug use was primarily related to social competence, whereas in urban areas drug use was affected by a broader range of variables. Results for the social competence measures were maintained at six-month and one-year follow-ups, but the effects on alcohol use were not maintained.

Like the New York and Washington investigations of the more general social skills approaches to smoking prevention, Pentz paid careful attention to measurement of presumed mediating variables and potential covariates. Given the maintained program effects on presumed mediators of drug use, however, the decay of effects on actual drug use, and the lack of effects on cigarette smoking, are difficult to explain—it suggests that other mediators have not been measured or affected.

Three High School Studies

Three studies (two at Stanford and one at USC) have tested the social influence approach with high school students. The broader social skills approaches have not yet been tested with high school students.

The Stanford group (Perry et al., 1980b) tested a program that emphasized the short-term physiological effects of smoking and the social pressures influencing adoption of the smoking habit. For the short-term physiological effects component, measures taken from smoking and non-smoking students were compared. Students were also introduced to several smoking-cessation procedures. Regular health teachers were trained to deliver the program on four consecutive days. All five high schools in one school district near Stanford University were matched on SES and then assigned randomly to experimental or control conditions. All students in three schools received the program, and students in the other two schools received the traditional tenth-grade health material emphasizing the harmful long-term effects of smoking. Students were assessed by questionnaire and physiological measures at pretest (September, 1978) and post-test (February, 1979). At posttest, fewer students in the program condition than in the control condition were smoking (in the past day, the past week, or the past month). These results appear to be statistically significant, and they were paralleled by changes in biochemical indicators (carbon monoxide) and knowledge. This is the first study to demonstrate that the social influences approach can be effective for high school students. Unfortunately, separate results were not reported for those students who were smokers at pretest, and no long-term data are available.

In a second high school study, Perry et al. (1983a) used a 2 × 3 factorial design to compare the relative effectiveness of teachers and college-age peer leaders in delivering health vs. social influences vs. physiological effects programs. Twenty classrooms from four high schools were randomly assigned to the three levels of programs; then the four schools were randomly assigned to teacher or college student delivery. Each program consisted of three one-hour sessions. Students were pretested immediately before the programs (February, 1980) and post-tested about two months after the programs (May, 1980). Assessments consisted of questionnaires and carbon monoxide samples. Staff members observed the implementation of the programs in all classrooms. All programs were implemented equally well. Of all students who reported weekly smoking at pretest (N = 82), 23 percent reported not smoking during the week before post-test. Differences between conditions were not statistically significant because of small sample sizes and there certainly were no significant changes in the overall rates of weekly smoking. (The apparent effects observed, however, suggested that teachers may have been better than college students at delivering health information, but college students may have been better than teachers at delivering the social influences program—this pattern was also observed in the Second Minnesota study [PCSC]).

The High School Anti-Smoking Project (HASP) at the University of Southern California (Johnson et al., 1986) compared the relative effectiveness of social influences and health programs with grade 10 students. The value of peer leaders, and the differential contribution made by having familiar peers as actors in the media material were also tested. The tested social influences program included material on media influences, social influences and skills for resisting them, values clarification/decision making, and a public-commitment procedure. The health program included materials on lifestyles and health, the long-term effects of smoking, the short-term physiological effects of smoking, and the public commitment procedure. Both programs included four sessions delivered by project staff (health educators) over a three-month period.

On the basis of pretest data, nine high schools were stratified and eight of them formed into pairs such that one high- and one low-smoking school were yoked together. The four yoked pairs were then randomly assigned to four experimental conditions created by crossing the two program types (social vs. health) with whether peers in media material were familiar or unfamiliar. The one remaining unyoked school, which was ranked in the middle for smoking level, was assigned to be the control. Within each program school, the program was delivered to only that half of the student body who were in health classes during the semester of intervention. The other half acted as within-school controls. One half of the classes that received the program were randomly assigned to a peer-leader condition. The other half received the program without the use of peer leaders. Students were assessed via questionnaire and saliva samples at pretest (Jan/Feb, 1981), immediate post-test (May/June, 1981), and at one- and two-year follow-ups (May, 1982, 1983). All data collection was conducted by trained data collectors who visited the schools on predetermined, but unannounced, days. In most cases, the classes in which data were collected were not the same classes in which the program was or had been delivered. Attrition rates were very high—65 percent by the end of the study, with no differences in rates between conditions (Hansen et al., 1985). Three sets of main-effect comparisons were made—social vs. health program, peer leaders or not, and familiar vs. unfamiliar actors in media material. Possible interactions were ignored because of limited sample size. Comparisons were made for four possible transitions in smoking behavior: no smoking to any smoking, experimental use (monthly or less) to heavier use, regular use (a pack or less a week) to heavy use (more than a pack a week), and current smoking (regular or heavy use) to nonsmoking (quit) status.

Attrition was lowest for pretest never smokers (20 percent by the final post-test). Pretest never-smokers were marginally less likely to become users if they were exposed to the health program than if they were exposed to the social influences program or were controls. Significant differences were observed only at the one-year follow-up, where 46 percent of the health program students had tried smoking vs. 59 percent of the social program students and 58 percent of controls. Although not significant, the same general pattern held at the two-year follow-up (60 vs. 68 vs. 68 percent, and 65 percent for the within-health-school controls). Of all experimental smokers at pretest, only 51 percent were present at the immediate posttest, 36 percent at the one-year follow-up, and 31 percent at the two-year follow-up. Using these samples, significant differences in the onset of regular smoking were observed, with the social program holding the onset rate to approximately half that observed for the health program and control students (4 percent at immediate post-test, to 6 percent at one year, to 7 percent at two years for social program students, vs. 8–9 percent to 9 percent to 13–14 percent for both health program and control students). When the one- and two-year follow-up waves were combined, attrition was significantly less than when considering either wave on its own (59 percent of subjects had data at pretest and at least one of these follow-ups). The above pattern of results was replicated using these pooled data, possibly reducing, to a small extent, the concern raised by high levels of attrition. Attrition by pretest regular smokers was very high (87 percent by the two year follow-up), and no significant program effects were detectable using the remaining sample. Neither peer leadership nor familiarity of actors in media materials made any significant difference to the pattern of any of the results. The reported results are obviously compromised to an unknown extent by (a) severe attrition, and (b) possible ceiling effects, where only a small proportion of the total sample had never tried smoking even at pretest.

Three Community Studies

Three studies (North Karelia, Oslo, and Minnesota) have tested the social influences approach within the context of broader, community-based intervention programs. The broader social skills approaches have not yet been tested in such settings.

The North Karelia Youth Project (Vartiainen, Pallonen, McAlister, Koskela, & Puska, 1983) consisted of community- and school-based interventions to influence behaviors that are risk factors for cardiovascular disease. A portion of the comprehensive program was a school-based smoking prevention curriculum that was based on the CLASP (Perry et al., 1980a) model. Two selected schools in North Karelia comprised an intensive intervention condition in which project staff provided a ten-session curriculum; two matched schools in North Karelia represented a County-wide condition, in which regular teachers provided a five-session version of the curriculum; and two matched schools in another county comprised a control condition. Grade 7 students were surveyed by questionnaire and serum samples were collected at pretest (Fall, 1978), immediately after the two-year intervention (Fall, 1980), and after a further six months (Spring, 1981). Of all students participating in the pretest, 95 percent participated in the immediate posttest two years later, and 88 percent in the final follow-up six months later. At the first follow-up, 21 percent were students in the intensive intervention condition of those who reported smoking monthly; 19 percent in the county-wide intervention schools; and 29 percent in the reference schools. By the final posttest, these percentages had increased to 24, 22, and 34 percent, respectively. This pattern of results was repeated for proportions of students smoking daily as well. Analyses by gender found that the significant program effects were confined to boys.

In the Oslo Youth Study, Tell, Klepp, Vellar, and McAlister (1984) provided a test of a social influences smoking prevention program delivered as a component of a comprehensive health education curriculum. A ten-session program was delivered to grade 5, 6, and 7 (age 11–14 years) students partly by older peer leaders and partly by project staff. Six schools were formed into matched pairs. One school from each of two pairs was randomly assigned to receive the program, while the third program school was assigned due to an existing relationship between that school and project staff. Signed consent for participation was obtained from 82 percent of parents. Students were pretested via questionnaire, saliva samples, and other health measures at pretest (early 1979), and two years later (early 1981). The intervention took place over the two years between surveys. Sixty-eight percent of the initial sample of students completed both questionnaires. Attrition was greater in control schools (40 percent) than program schools (25 percent). Overall results indicated program effects on those students who had never tried smoking prior to pretest. Of all pretested never smokers, 16.5 percent of the program group and 26.9 percent of the control group reported smoking by the posttest. In a step-wise discriminant analysis, the program entered after pretest measures of "acceptability of smoking," parental concern with the student's health, gender, and availability of discretionary funds. Pretest measures of friends' smoking and smoking knowledge also entered at significant levels after the effect of the program. Significant program effects were also reported for smoking knowledge and intentions. Changes were also observed in other health-related behaviors as a result of the complete program—the program group improved significantly more than the control group in terms of exercise, and reduced alcohol consumption. The results of the Oslo study are similar to others, with the pretest nonsmokers from the program group smoking at 39 percent less than the control group by the final post-test.

As part of a large-scale, community-based heart disease prevention project in Minnesota (Blackburn, Carleton, & Farquhar, 1984), several approaches to smoking prevention are being tested (Perry et al., 1983b). One of these was a social influences program. A six-session version of the "Keep It Clean I" program was tested in three schools (N of students $= 397$) within one of the program communities in 1981–82. Two schools in the outskirts of Minneapolis were matched on size, socioeconomic status, and grade 7 smoking prevalence, and used as controls ($N = 325$). The program was taught one day each month during the school year. Teachers and same-age peer leaders received special training from project staff. Students were assessed with questionnaires and saliva samples at the beginning and end of the school year. Equal numbers of students reported smoking in the week before pretest (4.7 percent) in the program and control schools. At post-test, more control than program students reported smoking in the previous week (8 vs. 5 percent); this difference was marginally significant. When all grade 7 and 8 students in both sets of schools were assessed, it was found that 8.1 percent of the program school students reported smoking in the previous week compared to 11.8 percent of control school students. This suggests that some or all of the observed effect could have been due to the other antismoking activities being conducted in the communities of the program schools.

The reported findings of the three community-based tests of the social influences approach to smoking prevention are very encouraging. However, they must be accepted with caution, because in every case it is impossible to separate the effects of the smoking prevention curriculum from effects of the broader community or school intervention within which it was embedded.

Summary of Third Generation Studies

Eleven studies assigned two or three schools or classrooms to experimental conditions to test the efficacy of various psychosocial approaches to smoking prevention. Five of the studies tested different programmatic approaches (social influences, Life Skills Training, cognitive-behavioral, and social competence) on sixth through ninth graders; three studies tested the social influences approach with high school students (grade 10); and three of the studies tested the social influences approach with fifth through seventh graders within the context of broader classroom or community interventions. The tested programs varied greatly in many respects, including their content, length (from three to 20 sessions over three days to two years), and who provided them. The third generation studies were also characterized by many attempts to test planned variations of programs—the variables tested included provider (project staff, regular classroom teachers, social workers, peer leaders), the age of peer leaders, social vs. health oriented programs, duration of the program (5 vs. 15 weeks), use of media, and use of boosters.

The third generation of studies is also characterized by improved methodology. In addition to assigning at least two units (schools or classrooms) to experimental conditions, in all but two of the studies, assignment involved some level of randomization. In all but one study, biological samples were collected to enhance the validity of self-reports of smoking; and in all studies students could be tracked over time. Like the nine first- and second-generation studies, the eleven third-generation studies also provided encouraging results. Despite the many methodological improvements, however, results from no one of these studies were interpretable by themselves because other serious methodological problems remained. Table 3 summarizes the findings reported by the third generation studies and their plausible alternative interpretations.

With only two schools or classrooms per condition, but with all statistical analyses having been done using the individual (inappropriately) as the unit of analysis, the chances are still high that school-level differences can explain many of the observed effects. Attrition was still a serious problem in third generation studies.

Reported results across these eleven studies were not as consistent in their exact nature as in their magnitude. The PCSC, fourth New York, Oslo, Stanford High I, and the HASP health program were reported as reducing the onset of smoking by pretest nonsmokers. The fifth New York, North Karelia, Current Minnesota, and the HASP social program, on the other hand, were reported as reducing the prevalence of regular smoking and/or the transition from experimental to regular smoking status. In most instances, the results for the other type of change were not reported.

All of the third generation studies are also susceptible to two other alternative interpretations of any observed effects:

1. a testing by treatment interaction, because in most instances the program and data collection activities would have been perceived by students as related; and

Table 3.   Reported Results and Plausible Alternative Interpretations of
Third Generation Studies

Study	Reported Finding	Plausible Interpretation
Minnesota II	Significant effects at immediate posttest. Social program more effective when peer leaders used. Peer-led social program most effective at preventing onset by pretest nonsmokers. No significant effects on pretest smokers.	Pretest differences in smoking prevalence (peer-led group different from others). No pretest data reported for Study II. Historical and non-equivalent controls used. Serious attrition. Incomplete data reported.
New York IV	Program cut new regular smoking by 50%. Intensive format significantly better. Boosters improved impact. Significant effects on mediators.	Incomplete data reported. School selection.
New York V	Significant effects on tobacco, alcohol & marijuana use.	Incomplete data reported. School selection.
Washington III	Significant changes in smoking only for program group compared to "placebo" and control. Decrease in smoking by 78% by fifteen months. Significant changes in knowledge in both program and placebo.	Small N; class selection
Tennessee	No significant effects on cigarette smoking. Significant effects on "Substance use" (tobacco & alcohol use combined)—decayed by six months. Significant effects on mediators, including skills, that were maintained for six months.	Lack of biological validation of self-reports. Possible contamination of conditions within schools.
High School Studies Stanford High I	Program effects on pretest non-smokers at four months.	(No long term data.)
Stanford High II	No significant differences between social, health, and physiological programs. (Teachers better with health programs; college students better with social program.)	Inadequate data reported.

Table 3.   Continued

Study	Reported Finding	Plausible Interpretation
USC I (HASP)	Health program marginally superior at preventing transition from never smoked to smoked. Social program cut transition from experimental to regular smoking by about 50%	Severe attrition Inadequate data reported (as yet).
Community Studies North Karelia	Program cut prevalence in regular smoking by 30% (boys only). No difference between intensive and county-wide conditions.	Program was small component of a more intensive intervention in North Karelia. School selection.
Oslo	Program cut nonsmoking to smoking transition by 39%.	Program was small component of a more comprehensive curriculum.
Minnesota	Cut prevalence of smoking in the last week by 38%.	Program was component of an intensive community-based intervention. Inadequate data reported (as yet).

2.   a Hawthorne effect, in that in almost all studies program students received more special attention than controls.

Much enthusiasm about the efficacy of psychosocial approaches to smoking prevention was generated by the earlier reports from some of the first three generations of studies. For example, E. Fisher (1980) concluded that "It now seems well established that these interventions work, at least to an appreciable if not totally satisfactory extent" (p. 678). While these studies, taken together, provided some encouragement for examining the psychosocial approaches to smoking prevention further, the numerous methodological problems with most of these studies when considered alone, and the fact that some of the problems were common to all studies, suggested a need for fourth generation studies designed to establish whether or not the social influences approach to smoking prevention is efficacious when tested under more rigorous methodological conditions.

THE FOURTH GENERATION STUDIES

Despite the many weaknesses of the second- and third-generation studies, the consistency of reported results provided the impetus for improved studies. The fourth generation of studies of psychosocial approaches to smoking prevention placed a primary value on enhanced internal validity. They may be characterized as large-scale field trials, with five or more (half with 11 or more) units randomly assigned to each condition. Most may also be characterized as demonstration projects or summative evaluations, in that they compared only program and control conditions, without attempting to test components or providers. All six of the fourth-generation studies tested the social influences approach—no fourth-generation test of the broader life/social skills approaches is yet available. The studies reviewed in this section varied, however, in the success with which the tested programs were implemented, the exact nature and length of the program tested, the grade level it was tested on, and the type of peer leaders who provided it. The latter variable was explicitly tested in one of the studies.

The Waterloo Study

The Waterloo Smoking Prevention Program (Best, et al., 1984; Flay et al., 1983a, 1985) followed the basic principles of the social influences approach as improved at Stanford and Minnesota but added a component on decision making that was tailored to the smoking decision. The program was tested on grade 6 students. Six, one-hour, weekly sessions were delivered by health educators near the beginning of the grade 6 school year (October/November 1979), two maintenance sessions were delivered near the end of grade 6, and three booster sessions were provided, two at the beginning of grade 7 and one at the beginning of grade 8. Evans' films were reproduced for the Canadian context using student actors from the local theater group who were one or two years older than the grade 6 students. Same-age leaders were not used in the classroom, but the health educators were Master's students who deliberately "underdressed" and encouraged students to call them by their first names. Thus, they were similar to the college-age peer leaders used in the Houston studies, Project RASP, and the second New York study.

Twenty-two schools in two school districts in Southern Ontario volunteered to participate in the study, and were assigned, mostly randomly, 11 to each of experimental and control conditions. Pretest differences were minimal, and were not observed for smoking behavior. Study students were in the same schools for the duration of the project, grades 6 through 8. Students were tested with questionnaire and saliva samples at pretest

(T1), immediate posttest (T2), the end of grade 6 (T3), the beginning and end of grade 7 (T4 and T5), and the end of grade 8 (T6—30 months after the core program). The health educators were present at pretest and immediate post-test data collection in both program and control schools, but new project staff collected data at all other follow-ups. Total attrition plus absenteeism was less than 10 percent per year, and 67 percent of students provided data at all six data points. The low rates of attrition are attributed to the stability and homogeneity of the Southern Ontario population.

Program results were analyzed according to the pretest status of subjects, and considerable complexity was found in the pattern of changes over time. For students who had never tried smoking before pretest, the program was marginally effective in preventing trying—by the end of grade 8, 53 percent of the control students who were never smokers at pretest had tried smoking while only 40 percent of the program students had done so. For students who had tried smoking but classified themselves as quitters at pretest, 69.2 percent of the program group and 50 percent of the control group remained quitters at the end of grade 7, but this difference had reduced to 50 vs. 46 percent, respectively, by the end of grade 8. For those students who had tried smoking only once before pretest, by the end of grade 8 almost equal proportions of the program and control students had tried smoking again (64 vs. 63 percent) but significantly more program than control students had decided to never smoke again (43 vs. 25 percent), and only 5 percent of the program group vs. 13 percent of the control group had become regular smokers (usually every week). For students classified as experimenters (tried more than once, but smoke less than weekly) at pretest, the results varied more across time. Almost all of the control students in this category (95 percent) reported smoking on at least one of the five posttests compared to less than three quarters (74 percent) of program students. A high proportion of program group experimenters quit immediately after the program, and this effect held to the end of grade 7, when 63 percent of this group were still quitters compared with 28 percent of the control group experimenters. By the end of grade 8, however, so many more of the control group experimenters had also quit that the difference was no longer significant (58 percent of program group vs. 50 percent of control group). (Note that we must expect many experimental smokers to quit eventually because many more adolescents experiment with smoking than ever become regular smokers.) The small number of pretest regular smokers (five in the program and 8 in the control conditions) precluded any statistical analysis of program impact on this group. In summary, program effects varied over time, having greatest immediate effects on those experienced with smoking and later effects on those with no or little smoking experience at pretest.

The Waterloo investigators also analyzed the effects of their program on those students assumed to be at high risk of becoming smokers for social influence reasons. The program was found to have its major effect on those students who had parents, siblings and friends who smoke. For example, among high-risk students who had never tried smoking before pretest, by the end of grade 8, 67 percent of those in the program group vs. 22 percent of controls were still never smokers, 6 percent of the program group vs. 39 percent of controls were experimental smokers, and none of the program students vs. 6 percent of controls were regular smokers (Best et al., 1984). Such results provide some validation for the theoretical rationale for the social influences approach to smoking prevention.

The Waterloo study successfully overcame many of the methodological problems of earlier studies, so that the reported results are more readily interpreted as being due to the program. However, while pretest comparability was maximized, attrition minimized, and more detailed analyses reported, there remain several alternative plausible explanations of at least some of the reported program effects. First, a measurement by treatment interaction is possible. This is especially likely at the first posttest where the health educators also collected the data, although the collection of saliva samples should have minimized it, and the lack of any significant program effects at that point suggest that this interpretation of subsequent effects is not very plausible. Second, as in all other studies to date, a Hawthorne effect may be operating; the program students received a great deal of attention from outsiders, and their subjective evaluations tell us that they liked the health educators a great deal. Third, there was large variability between schools (not yet reported in detail), and program effects were apparent in only some of the program schools—was there something special about them that caused some or all of the observed effects? Despite these limitations, however, the Waterloo study represents one of the more rigorous tests to date of the social influences approach to smoking prevention; and the demonstration of strong program effects on those students most at risk provides strong support for the approach.

The Stanford/Harvard Study

McAlister et al. (1982) tested a twelve-session, two-year version of the CLASP curriculum delivered to grade 7 and 8 students by high school students under the supervision of research staff. Junior high or middle schools were randomly assigned to program or control conditions from five matched pairs in Massachusetts and California. The program was not implemented in full in two of the program schools because of administrative difficulties. Saliva samples and questionnaire data were collected from students on four occasions (October, 1979; May, 1980; October, 1980; and May, 1981). School districts insisted that individual students not be identified, so students generated their own identification codes. Analyses indicate some problems with inconsistent use of codes (McAlister, 1983). School administrators estimated that between the first and last survey periods approximately 30 percent of the students transferred to other schools. Approximately 15 percent of parents excluded their children from measurement, with no differences between conditions within sites. Overall, only about one third of the original students could be included in the longitudinal (cohort) analyses.

Overall results suggest that the program only marginally reduced the rates of weekly or monthly smoking, regardless of whether cross-sectional (using all responses at each time point) or longitudinal (using only those students who responded and could be matched across all measurement periods) analyses are considered. Wide school variations were observed, however, and the authors attempt to provide reasons for significant program effects in two pairs of schools and not others. Unfortunately, in the two pairs of schools where significant program effects were observed, the program schools had over 60 percent higher rates of smoking before the program than the control schools. While the pattern of effects looks promising, with the proportion of smokers actually decreasing in the program schools and increasing in the control schools, it is difficult to interpret; it could be due to expected patterns of quitting by early starters as observed by grade 8 in the Waterloo study. In those schools where pretest levels were more nearly equal, no significant program effects were observed. Significant program effects on marijuana use were reported for only one school pair, where there was a large pretest difference.

The Australian Study

Fisher, Armstrong and de Klerk (1983) have tested the social influences approach to smoking prevention in Western Australia. The Minnesota program (Arkin et al., 1981) was modified only slightly, including the remaking of film materials for the Australian context and idiom. The program was delivered to grade 7 students, one session every month over the last five months of the Australian academic year (August to December, 1981). The study compared teacher vs. peer-led programs and controls. Both teachers and peer leaders received special training for the program.

A total of 45 elementary schools were randomly assigned to the three conditions after stratification on school size, geographical location, and SES. Students were assessed with questionnaires and saliva samples immediately before the program, and one year after the end of the program (November, 1982). The data collectors were blind to the experimental condition of the students. By careful tracking, 82 percent of the initial sample were posttested, even though students had made the transition from elementary to dispersed high schools during the intervening year.

One-year follow-up results indicate that teacher- and peer-led programs both reduced the onset of smoking among girls (26 percent of pretest nonsmokers had smoked during the twelve months before posttest in the two program groups compared to 35 percent for the control group, i.e., a 26-percent reduction in onset), but the effect was only marginally significant for the peer-led curriculum after adjustment for the effect of social-risk factors. Only the teacher-led program was effective for boys (19 percent in the teacher-led condition, compared to 36 percent in the peer-led condition and 31 percent of controls, i.e., 39 percent reduction in onset). No program effects were observed for students who had smoked during the 12 months before the program.

This study demonstrates that a social-influences classroom curriculum can, by itself, be effective in countries other than the United States and Canada, at least in reducing onset by previous nonsmokers, This study does, however, raise questions about the superiority of peer leaders over adult leaders; it appears that the use of peer leaders may sometimes not be beneficial. Of course, cultural differences could explain this finding— Australian adolescents may not identify as closely with their peers as Americans. It also seems that the peer leaders had a greater responsibility for the entire program than peer leaders have had in most other studies, and one must wonder how well they were able to implement the program. Small pretest differences between conditions in smoking prevalence (nonsignificant) cannot explain the observed effects of the teacher-led programs, and a multiple logistic regression analysis demonstrates that social-risk predictors of smoking (e.g., number of friends who smoke, response to cigarette advertising, intentions) do not explain them either.

The Michigan Study

Dielman et al. (1984, 1985) tested the social influences approach to smoking prevention on grade 5 and 6 students. The program consisted of four sessions delivered by research staff health educators. In addition, grade 5 students also received a three-session booster in grade 6. Ten urban schools in Michigan were formed into matched pairs on achievement scores, ethnic distribution, and SES, and then randomly assigned to program, control, or "mixed" conditions. In the mixed condition (two schools) classrooms were randomly assigned to program or control conditions. Signed consent was provided by 83 percent of the parents of program students and 75 percent of parents of control students. Students were assessed via questionnaire only (no biological samples were collected nor bogus pipeline procedures used), at pretest (March, 1981), immediate posttest (June, 1981), four-month follow-up at the beginning of the following academic year (October, 1981), and at one-year follow-up (June, 1982). The health educators who delivered the program were usually present at data collection in both program and control schools. Approximately 80 percent of students were present at all four measures. By the second and fourth posttests, significant effects were observed on recent smoking for both males and females. Reports of smoking in the last month increased from 1 percent at pretest to 7 percent by the four-month follow-up to 15 percent by the one-year follow-up for control students, vs. 4 to 1 to 8 percent by program students. No effects were observed on intentions to smoke in the future, or on the numbers of students who had ever tried smoking cigarettes (increase from 30 percent at pretest to 50 percent at one-year follow-up for both groups). Alcohol and marijuana intentions and behavior were also measured but no program effects were observed.

The lack of any biological sampling, plus the presence of the health educators in the classroom during data collection makes interpretation of these data somewhat precarious, because both of these factors can serve to increase the demands on program students to underreport their smoking. However, the lack of any program effects on either intentions or trying smoking suggests that these alternative explanations of the reported findings may not be entirely plausible. Because of the young age of the subjects, final evaluation of this study requires longer-term follow-up data.

The Oregon Study

At the Oregon Research Institute, Biglan et al. (in press) tested a social influences program delivered/facilitated by classroom teachers. The tested program consisted of three sessions delivered on consecutive days with one booster session delivered about two weeks later. Grade 7 and 9 classes of volunteer teachers in six middle schools and three high schools were randomly assigned to program ($N = 41$) or control ($N = 45$) (traditional health education) conditions. Students were assessed by questionnaire and saliva sample at pretest, six-month posttest, and 12-month posttest. Seventy-seven percent of the initial students were present at the six-month assessment and 68 percent at the 12-month assessment. The questionnaire included innovative measures of the proportion of cigarette offers refused during the week prior to measurement. In addition, refusal skills were assessed directly for a sample of students (Hops et al., in press).

Despite random assignment, control students were significantly more likely to have smoked before pretest. Accordingly, analysis of covariance procedures were used in tests of program effects. At the first posttest there were fewer regular smokers (at least weekly) among the program than the control students (10 vs. 14 percent). By the one-year follow-up, however, this marginally significant difference had disappeared (10 vs. 11 percent). When only those students who were smokers before pretest were considered, there was still a significant program effect at one-year post-test, but only for relatively heavy daily smoking (more than 10 cigarettes every day). Program effects were evident on both the questionnaire and behavioral measures of use of refusal skills.

As others have reported, students present at pretest, but not at subsequent tests, were more likely to be smokers and to have parents who smoke. They also scored significantly higher on a scale of deviant behaviors involving alcohol and marijuana use, had lower educational aspirations, and less-educated parents.

The small magnitude of effects on behavior in this study is somewhat intriguing given the demonstrated effects on presumed intervening constructs. The assignment of classrooms could have reduced the difference between treatment and control conditions, in that one of the presumed effects of social influences programs is thought to be alteration of the norms for complete social environments. The demonstrated differences between groups in the use of social resistance skills reduce the plausibility of this interpretation, but do not remove it entirely. Other data that might throw light on this issue have not yet been reported. The fairly serious attrition rate also raises questions in that those students who were most likely to become smokers were less likely to be present for follow-up measurement, thus reducing the probability of finding program effects that might be present. On the other hand, the reported pretest differences would lead one to expect the observed posttest differences even without an intervention.

The USC Television Smoking Project (TVSP)

At the University of Southern California, Flay and colleagues (1983b, c) tested the social influences approach to smoking prevention when implemented in a widespread way. Widespread implementation was attained by the development of a series of television segments that was coordinated with a five-day classroom program. In addition, parents were involved via homework activities; and a television smoking-cessation program was provided for smoking parents the week after the prevention program. The prevention program consisted of lessons on social influences to smoke, including peer pressure, family modeling, and media influences; role playing and practice of social skills with which to resist those pressures; immediate physiological and social consequences of smoking; and decision-making skills and a commitment procedure. Teachers received a detailed curriculum guide; all students received personal copies of an activities booklet, the second half of which included self-help smoking cessation materials for their parents; and peer leaders were provided with their own special guide on group leadership skills.

This study was different from other fourth-generation studies in that it included quasi-experimental tests of teacher training and "curriculum milieu" (whether all or half the students within a school received the program). Four months before the program, and on the basis of very little information, program schools self-selected themselves to provide the program. Within each school district where not all schools had requested the program, comparable schools were selected and asked to participate as control schools in the evaluation. Students in the 28 selected grade 7 control schools were at a marginally greater risk of becoming smokers than students in the 28 grade 7 program schools at pretest. The program schools self-selected themselves further to provide the program to all or half of their grade 7 students (this variable has been called "curriculum milieu"). This selection was based on school-district policy regarding whether students are provided with one or two semesters of health education. All program schools were further randomly assigned from matched pairs (on SES, school size, geographical location, and the curriculum milieu variable) to receive or not receive special training for the teachers who were to implement the program. Once schools were selected for teacher training, school principals selected one to three teachers to be trained. Implementation evaluation data show that teachers selected for training were different from teachers who implemented the program in other schools: they were more likely to be science, rather than health, teachers. Classes taught by these trained teachers were also found to be different—more likely to be smokers, and to have parents and friends who smoke—from classes taught by untrained teachers. These differences were evidently caused by principals in those schools offered teacher training selecting more "problematic" classes than principals in schools not offered teacher training. Students from three to six classrooms in each program and control school were assessed by saliva sample and questionnaire at pretest (Jan, 1982), immediate post-test (Mar/April, 1982), and one-year follow-up (April, 1983).

Implementation evaluation results (Flay et al., 1983c) showed that trained teachers implemented the program more diligently and more enthusiastically than untrained teachers. Students who received the classroom program were much more likely to view the TV segments (65 percent) than control students (10 percent), and participation by parents was high (70 percent for program students). The program produced significant immediate effects on student knowledge, attitudes, and social normative beliefs. However, many of the effects had partially decayed by a one-year follow-up. Only small program effects on behavior were observed. Experimental smokers who viewed the TV segments and whose parents participated in program activities were more likely to quit smoking than control students (approximately 59 vs. 40 percent in preliminary analyses). Non-smokers who viewed the TV segments and whose parents participated in program activities were less likely to start smoking than control students (approximately 15 vs. 27 percent). These effects, however, had also decayed somewhat by one-year follow-up. Teacher training made a significant difference in the amount of change in the above variables in the short term. Perhaps the largest effects on behavior were observed for smoking parents. Of smoking parents of viewing students, approximately 45 percent viewed the cessation programming, 30 percent attempted to quit or reduce, and 15 percent were not smoking at both one-month and one-year follow-up.

This study constitutes the first "effectiveness trial" of the social influences approach to smoking prevention. An approach thought to be efficacious was taken and implemented under real-world conditions, that is, without strict monitoring to ensure even implementation, so that issues of availability of the program to the target audience, and acceptance of it by them, become important, as well as program effectiveness (cf., Flay, 1986, c). Results for students are not particularly encouraging and, like the second-generation studies, the primary lessons concern hints for the improvement of future programming and ways to test them effectively. That is, this study might be considered as no more than a prototype of future "fifth-generation" dissemination studies.

Summary of Fourth Generation Studies

The six fourth-generation studies were mostly methodologically superior to the second- and third-generation studies. The use of simpler and more rigorous designs provided for greater internal validity and more interpretable findings. Nevertheless, certain methodological problems remained, and every one of these studies is still susceptible to one or more plausible alternative interpretations (see Table 4). Some of the methodological problems, such as difficulties in achieving complete random assignment, problems with program implementation, and serious attrition rates serve to remind us of the difficulties of large-scale, school-based research.

Four of these studies (Stanford/Harvard, Michigan, Oregon, and TVSP) suffer from more serious methodological problems than the others. Ironically, they also reported less promising results in many ways. The most rigorous studies, Waterloo and Australia, on the other hand, provided the most encouraging results to date. The Waterloo study reported the most comprehensive results, demonstrating effects for students with different pretest experience and for different transitions over time. Long-term results suggest reasonably good maintenance of effects, though not total. The finding that the program was most effective for students at high risk seems particularly important, as it provides some validation for the theory un-

Table 4.   Reported Findings and Plausible Alternative Interpretations
of Fourth Generation Studies

Study	Reported Finding	Plausible Interpretation
Waterloo	Significant effects on knowledge. Significant effects on cross-sectional prevalence of never smoking, quitters, tried oncers, and experimenters (e.g., cut experimental smoking by 43% at grade 8). Significant effects on transitions from nonsmoking to trying, tried once to quit or experimenting, and experimenting to quit. Even greater effects on students at high social risk (e.g., reduced never smoker transitions to trying by 58%, to experimental smoking by 85%, and to regular smoking by 100%.	Not total randomization. Measurement by treatment interaction* Hawthorne effect**
Stanford/ Harvard	No significant effects on prevalence of regular smoking. (Significant effects in two pairs of schools only.)	Large pretest differences in the two pairs of schools where program effects were observed. Serious attrition. Inadequate data reported (as yet).
Australia	Both teacher- and peer-led programs reduced nonsmoker to smoker transition by 26% for girls. Only teacher-led program cut same transition for boys (39%). Effects still significant after adjustments for pretest number of friends smoking, responses to cigarette ads, and intentions.	Hawthorne effect** (No long-term data yet.)
Michigan	Cut prevalence of experimental smoking by 47%. No effects on ever smoked or intentions.	Measurement by treatment interaction* Lack of biological validation of self-reports. No report of results from "mixed" schools. (No long-term data yet.)

Table 4. Continued

Study	Reported Finding	Plausible Interpretation
Oregon	Temporary cut in prevalence of smoking (29%). No significant effects for pretest nonsmokers by one year. For pretest smokers, significant cut in transition to daily smoking. Significant effects on questionnaire and behavioral measures of use of social resistance skills.	Serious attrition. Assignment of classrooms within schools (possible contamination). Inadequate data reported (as yet).
USC II (TVSP)	Important implementation evaluation data. Significant, but temporary changes in knowledge, attitudes, social normative beliefs. Minimal effects on student behavior. Large effects on parental smoking.	Serious attrition. Differential implementation. Nonrandom assignment. No validation of parent behavior. Inadequate data reported (as yet).

Notes:
  *Most studies are susceptible to measurement by treatment interactions in that students often know of the association between program and testing activities. This alternative is clearly minimized only in the Australian study.
  **All studies that have reported effects to date are susceptible to this alternative interpretation. The only studies to guard against the Hawthorne effect (e.g. Stanford High II) found no differences between programs.

derlying the whole social influences approach to smoking prevention. The Australian study, on the other hand, found program effects only for students who had not smoked at all during the 12 months before pretest. The differences in the patterns of outcomes provided by the two most rigorous studies have no obvious explanation. Major differences between the programs that might explain the differences in findings include

1. the length and duration of the programs, with the Waterloo program consisting of more sessions spread over a longer time,
2. the structure of the school systems, where the Waterloo students have not yet made a transition from elementary to high school, while the Australian students did so between the program and the one-year posttest,

3. program providers, with the Waterloo program using college-age teachers/"peer leaders" and the successful Australian program using teachers, and
4. length of follow-up, with the Australian study yet to report long-term data.

On the basis of existing theory and assumptions, some of these differences could be expected to lead to the observed differences between the studies in their magnitude of impact. Differences in the type of effect are less easily explained.

The Australian finding that the teacher-led program was most effective is intriguing because the use of peer leaders has become almost "institutionalized" among major prevention efforts (Flay et al., 1983a; McAlister et al., 1979; McCaul & Glasgow, 1984). Also, both of the U.S.A. studies that relied on classroom teachers to implement the program (Oregon and TVSP) found much smaller program effects on behavior. They each also reported effects on intermediate presumed mediating variables, however, such as knowledge, attitudes, beliefs, social perceptions of norms, and intentions. The Oregon study was even able to demonstrate improved social resistance skills and increased use of those skills. Both of these programs were very short, however, with the Oregon program being only four sessions over three weeks and TVSP being only five sessions over one week. It is possible that the training of sustained behavioral skills requires a program of longer duration if not more actual program time (the Australian program was also only five sessions, but they were spread over five months).

Overall, the findings from the most rigorous studies to date suggest that the social influences approach to smoking prevention can be effective some of the time. However, this conclusion seems to be somewhat fragile, given the considerable differences between studies in the patterns of reported results. Also, at least two plausible alternative interpretations of the reported effects remain—namely, effects of testing (or screening), and the Hawthorne effect. It may be that students who are tested and/or who receive special attention in the classroom will be influenced to alter their behavior or their reports of it. The likelihood of these processes causing the observed effects is small, however, especially when one considers that many tests of other approaches to smoking prevention have not reported significant effects.

While the results of the fourth-generation studies support the suggestion of second- and third-generation studies that the social influences approach to smoking prevention is an efficacious approach, much further research is needed on the conditions under which the social influences programs are effective, for whom they are effective, and why they work. This theme will be taken up in the next section.

DISCUSSION

What Have We Learned From Past Studies?

Twenty-six school-based studies of psychosocial approaches to smoking prevention have been reviewed. They were divided into four "generations" of studies. The first generation consisted of the two seminal studies of the Houston group. While the results from these studies were not very encouraging, their theoretical justification seemed compelling enough to encourage other researchers to improve upon the approach and conduct further tests.

The second- and third-generation of studies either improved upon the approach, provided additional tests of these improved programs, or provided tests of alternative (more general skills development) approaches. At this time, however, all of the second- and third-generation studies can be considered as no more than pilot or prototypical studies, although most of them, particularly those of the third generation, were undoubtedly designed with much loftier goals in mind. Our knowledge of whether or not psychosocial approaches to smoking prevention are effective, or the conditions under which they might be effective, was not advanced by any one of these studies considered alone. Taken together, however, fairly consistent results across studies, at least in the reported magnitude of effects, provided encouragement that the approaches can be efficacious. However, the greatest contribution of these studies was to improve knowledge of program development and methodological issues in school-based prevention research, though this was in subtle and largely undocumented ways until recently. For example, approaches to random assignment of large, aggregated units (schools) to conditions (Graham et al., 1984a), informed consent procedures (Severson & Ary, 1983), tracking of individuals over time, minimizing and analyzing attrition (Hansen et al., 1985), and measurement (Graham et al., 1984b; Pechacek et al., 1984) have been developed, tested, and improved during the course of these studies. Indeed, without these pilot and prototypical studies, the better controlled, large-scale studies of the fourth generation probably would not have been attempted.

The first three generations of studies had too many methodological shortcomings, some of them common across studies, and there were too few fourth-generation studies to make a meta-analytic approach (Cook & Leviton, 1980; Strube & Hartmann, 1983; Mullen & Ramirez, this volume) to this review worthwhile. In addition, while the fourth-generation studies were more successful at maximizing internal validity, certain methodological problems remain to be solved. Some of the more serious methodological issues concern unit of assignment to experimental conditions, integrity and strength of the treatment as delivered, unit of analysis, attrition, measurement by treatment interactions, and possible Hawthorne effects. Biglan and Ary (1985) and Cook (1985) provide detailed discussions of many of the above methodological issues, and Flay (1985b) provides a discussion of the theoretical implications of some of these methodological issues. Future fourth- (or fifth-) generation studies will surely learn from these commentaries as well as the experiences from the studies to date.

What is it that is effective? The fourth-generation research produced slightly more interpretable findings than the earlier research. Even in the fourth generation, however, findings were mixed, and there seems to be a certain fragility to them, with different studies reporting different types of effects. While programmatic and methodological differences between studies might explain their different findings, the crucial differences are not readily ascertained from the descriptions provided in publications. The social influences programs tested in the two most rigorous studies (Australia and Waterloo) had certain elements in common that might inform us of crucial programmatic components. They both included

1. media material, with similar-age peers, derived from the original Houston program,
2. information on immediate physiological effects of smoking,
3. correction of misperceptions about the prevalence of smoking,
4. discussion of family and media influences on smoking, and ways of dealing with them,
5. role playing and explicit learning of behavioral skills,
6. a public commitment procedure, and
7. extended duration.

While this list of common elements is suggestive, we really know very little at this time, either from these studies or others, about which of these program components are necessary for program effectiveness, or how other components (e.g., health information) or methods (e.g., use of peer leaders) might or might not add to program effectiveness. Johnson (1982) and McCaul & Glasgow (1985) have reached similar conclusions.

It was appropriate, however, for fourth-generation studies to be concerned with determining whether or not an approach works at all before exploring further the who, why, how, what and when questions. Indeed, the early attempts to explore some of these questions in the second- and third-generation studies now seem somewhat premature, though it is as well to remember that at that time they would have seemed most appropriate to psychological researchers who had little experience with large-scale field trials and all the methodological traps they entail (see Biglan & Ary, 1985; Flay et al., 1983a).

We also know very little from all the studies reviewed about the generalizability of their findings. The most rigorous studies were conducted on white, middle-class populations, in countries with slightly more "authoritarian" childrearing norms than the United States. We still do not know for sure, then, whether or not the approach is effective in the United States for various SES and ethnic groups. Two of the fourth generation studies (Waterloo and Stanford/Harvard), and a number of others, hinted at large between-school variations, but we know nothing as yet about the types of schools in which these programs will be more or less effective. (Studies now underway are also investigating these issues.)

We also know relatively little as yet about the types of students for whom the psychosocial approaches are most effective. Most studies have not performed separate analyses by sex, grade, or other characteristics of the study participants. Where such analyses have been done, differences have sometimes been found. Results from the Australian study suggest that males and females are equally influenced by a teacher-led program, but that they may be differentially influenced by a peer-led program. The Waterloo investigators analyzed program effects by both pretest experience with smoking and the social risk of becoming smokers. The results suggested that (a) the program had its initial effects on those experienced with smoking, influencing pretest never smokers only in the longer term, and (b) the approach is most effective for those students at greatest risk of becoming smokers because of social factors. These findings need replicating, and we also need to investigate the effectiveness of this approach for students who may be at risk for other reasons (cf., Leventhal & Cleary, 1980; Flay et al., 1983a).

Another area that past research has not yet addressed sufficiently concerns broader issues of program dissemination. Once we have an efficacious program, how will it be disseminated broadly? Should regular teachers be trained? Trained how? Or would some other group, such as school nurses, or health agency volunteers, be more effective? What is the potential role of media, both small and mass? All such questions remain for future research to answer.

To summarize, the fourth generation studies have confirmed the suggestion by second- and third-generation studies that the social influences approach to smoking prevention can be effective. We know very little at this point, however, about the construct validity or generalizability of the treatment.

Implications for Future Research

Having established from four generations of research that the social influences approach to smoking prevention can be effective on some adolescents some of the time, what is the most appropriate next step? Should we immediately go out and implement the approach in a wide-spread way? This seems unwise, because we know so little about what works, why, when, how, and for whom. Large-scale implementation would, therefore, run the risk of failure. Not every school district implements a new curriculum exactly as recommended, and without knowledge of the crucial components and conditions, any changes could result in failure. Widespread failure could devastate the prevention research field. Knowledge of the crucial components and conditions would allow variations that would be less likely to fail. Therefore, the focus for the fifth generation of research should be on the construct validity and generalizability of the treatment, that is, on the who, what, when, where, how, and why questions alluded to above.

Obviously, however, focusing on issues of the construct validity and generalizability of the treatment cannot be at the neglect of internal validity. Indeed, internal validity is desirable for answers to construct validity questions to be interpretable (this is the reason that the complex designs of some of the second generation studies produced uninterpretable results). Even generalizability questions are more easily interpreted when internal validity has been maximized, although high external validity is also required.

Construct validity of the treatment concerns the questions of whether or not the various components of a program have the immediate effects expected of them, and whether or not any immediate effects on presumed mediating variables are related to subsequent smoking behavior. Few of the reviewed studies even reported program effects on presumed mediating variables (see review by McCaul & Glasgow, 1985), and even fewer made any attempt to link any such changes to subsequent smoking behavior. It is interesting to note that investigators of the more general life and/or social skills approaches have been more diligent, including assessment of presumed mediating variables. An analysis by Glasgow and McCaul (1985) demonstrates, however, a great deal of inconsistency across studies in those mediating variables affected, even by the same or very similar programs tested by the same researchers.

Three major approaches to research on the construct validity of smoking prevention programs are available. They are as follows:

(A) Extensive process evaluation of large-scale studies like those of the third generation, where data are collected on program effects on presumed mediating variables: Each component of a program is designed to produce a particular effect, and it is the combination of all those effects that should prevent smoking. As noted above, too few of the studies reviewed have even collected data on intervening variables, and none of them has linked changes in those variables to subsequent smoking behavior in a satisfactory way. The nine studies of broader social and personal skills approaches have been more diligent in this regard to date. Future large-scale studies need to include measures of as many of these immediate and mediating effects as possible in addition to measuring the final behavioral outcomes.

(B)   Small-scale, tightly controlled experimental studies of the short-term effects of program components: These would preferably be with children from the target group, but analogue laboratory studies may sometimes be worthwhile. Only a few small-scale experimental studies, namely those by students of the Houston group (e.g., Hansen, 1978; Hill, 1979; Mittlemark, 1978) and the North Dakota group (Glasgow et al., 1981; McCaul et al., 1983; O'Neill et al., 1983) have tested some of the components of social influences smoking-prevention programs as to their effects on presumed mediating variables. These types of studies could be of value in establishing that program components produce their hypothesized effects on variables presumed to mediate smoking intentions and behavior; however, results from the two groups of studies conducted to date have not been very promising.

(C)   Experimental comparisons of programs derived from competing theoretical positions in large-scale field trials that include measurement of target population acceptance and characteristics, and program effects on mediating variables: Successful smoking prevention programs have now been, or soon will be, developed from competing theoretical perspectives. This is a healthy sign for a science of prevention. Programs developed from competing theoretical perspectives will need to be pitted against one another, not as tests of the competing theories, but with an eye to determining which approaches, or which combination of approaches, are most effective for which types of people, under what conditions.

Generalizability concerns the transferability of an effective program—for whom it is effective and under what conditions of implementation/dissemination? Such questions can be addressed in studies of types (A) and (C) above as well as two other approaches:

(D)   Experimental studies of approaches to program dissemination: Most studies of the efficacy of the social influences approach to smoking prevention have involved the program being provided or facilitated by research project staff. Such arrangements obviously will not be possible under most real-world conditions. So questions of who should provide the program (teachers, school nurses, health agency volunteers, other public health personnel), how they should be trained, the role of media (both small and mass), and the role of auxiliary programming (e.g., other interventions on the school environment, such as changes in regulations or disciplinary procedures regarding smoking, smoking-cessation programs for teachers and/or parents), will all need to be investigated. The TVSP project from USC provides one early example of this type of study. Others are already in progress.

(E) Evaluations of large-scale demonstration projects that include measurement of population characteristics as well as program effects on presumed mediating variables: Once efficacious approaches to smoking prevention are implemented on a wide scale, evaluation needs to include assessment of availability to the target population (or program implementation), acceptance of the program by the target audience (or involvement in program activities), characteristics of the treated population, and program effects on presumed mediating variables, as well as outcomes.

How do we choose between the five types of research suggested above? Should we conduct further large-scale research or should we confine ourselves to tightly controlled, small-scale, laboratory-style studies to answer questions of treatment construct validity?

Tightly controlled, small-scale studies can inform about whether or not program components have the desired effects on presumed mediating variables, why or how the programs have the effects they do, and the program components that are most crucial. Such knowledge is necessary, and small-scale studies are less costly, more easily controlled, and of short duration. However, they are of low external validity, can miss important complex interactions (McGuire, 1973, 1983), and the end-point dependent variable usually cannot be smoking behavior. In addition, the small-scale, components analysis approach has not proven to be very useful so far, just as it has not in educational or smoking cessation research (Lando, 1981).

Large-scale studies, on the other hand, can be of long duration, costly, and entail certain methodological problems (see Biglan & Ary, 1985). However, the methodological problems are rapidly being reduced (see Cook, 1985), smoking behavior is the end-point, and such studies are necessary for assessing generalizability, determining whether program components still have their presumed effects on mediating variables in real-world settings, testing variations in dissemination variables, and comparing different programs derived from competing theoretical perspectives. Large-scale studies are also necessary for testing components by removing them one-by-one from an efficacious combination—an approach to components-testing with more promise than small-scale studies of one component at a time. Large-scale studies also allow for the investigation of multivariate interactions. Even extremely large-scale studies, like evaluations of state-wide or national models, can provide valuable information on which models work best under which conditions.

The results of four generations of studies on the social influences approach to smoking prevention are consistent enough to suggest that large-scale studies be employed to answer questions of the construct validity and generalizability of the approach. In addition, given that the review or synthesis, rather than the individual study, is the unit of advancement of knowledge, the sooner a large number of studies are accumulated the more certain will be our knowledge. For the broader life and/or social skills approaches, fourth-generation studies are still needed.

The conclusions reached above have several implications for future research. First, future studies need to be of the highest level of internal validity, including random assignment of whole schools (or, in some cases, classrooms) to experimental conditions, tracking of individuals over time, minimally reactive measures and measurement procedures, and employing rising "placebo" control groups. The fourth-generation studies have demonstrated that we now have the capability of conducting large-scale studies of high internal validity, though not without great difficulty. Without high internal validity, however, answers to questions of treatment construct validity will be uninterpretable.

Second, future large-scale studies need to include assessments of program implementation (including characteristics of the provider) and availability to the presumed target audience. Many current studies are already doing this, but much further work will be needed to develop rigorous methods. Such assessment is needed to determine the integrity and strength of a program as actually delivered (Sechrest et al., 1979). Without such information, variations in the level of program impact reported by different studies will not be interpretable: they could be due to variations in delivery and we would never know it.

Third, all future studies need to include comprehensive assessment of presumed mediating variables. Most ongoing studies are already improving the process evaluation component. Much further attention will need to be paid to the selection and development of high-quality measures of presumed mediating variables, though we can learn much from the investigation of the life/social skills approaches. Without highly valid measures of the presumed mediating variables such as social normative beliefs, self-efficacy, resistance skills, and intentions, as well as outcome variables such as smoking behavior, results from future research, particularly negative or no difference results, will be uninterpretable. Without such information, questions about program components cannot be answered. With such information, recently developed analytic approaches (e.g., Dwyer, 1983; Judd & Kenny, 1981) can be used to investigate causal linkages between the presumed mediating variables and subsequent smoking behavior.

Fourth, future large-scale studies need also to include comprehensive measurement of target-audience involvement (or acceptance), characteristics of the treated audience (i.e., individual differences), and properties of the social environment (family, classroom, school, community) inhabited by the target audience. With such information, questions about generalizability cannot be answered. Effort needs to be spent, therefore, in developing measures of audience and social environment characteristics with good psychometric properties and high construct validity.

CONCLUSION

Four generations of research on psychosocial approaches to smoking prevention have been conducted within less than one half of a human generation (indeed, less than one decade). Given this, progress has been remarkable. The tested programs have been improved and strengthened dramatically; difficult research design issues have been resolved or their seriousness reduced, and recent findings provide some confidence that psychosocial approaches to smoking prevention may be worthwhile. In particular, the so-called social influences approach has been effective in those fourth-generation studies of highest internal validity. Nevertheless, certain plausible alternative interpretations of these findings remain to be ruled out. While second- and third-generation research suggests that some of the more general life/social skills training approaches might also be effective, fourth-generation research on these approaches is still needed. Whether it is better to target skills specific to a behavior, as was done in the social influences approach, or more generally, as was done in other approaches, remains for future empirical tests.

This review has identified promising directions for future research as well as the problems of past and current research. Hopefully, future research will focus on the promising directions suggested, and not recreate or bemoan past problems. To summarize, future research needs to move from focusing on whether or not psychosocial approaches to smoking prevention can be effective to

1. determining those program components that are important for program efficacy,
2. establishing the conditions under which programs are most effective,
3. determining for whom the programs are most helpful,
4. investigating alternative approaches to disseminating successful programs, and
5. comparing programs derived from competing theoretical perspectives (with careful assessment of mediating variables presumed to be differentially affected by different treatments).

These research objectives will be accomplished best by the use of five types of large-scale field trials. The five types of studies go hand-in-hand, with results from each type (re)validating findings from the others. All future large-scale studies need to:

1. be of the highest internal validity,
2. include comprehensive measures of presumed mediating variables, and
3. include comprehensive measures of (i) program implementation, (ii) involvement by the target audience, and (iii) population characteristics.

Meeting these conditions will lead to the development of a true science of prevention and maximize the probability of developing effective prevention programs.

ACKNOWLEDGMENTS

Portions of this material have previously been presented at a Research Analysis and Utilization System (RAUS) Review at the National Institute on Drug Abuse in April of 1984 (Flay, 1985a), and a summary review has appeared in *Health Psychology* (Flay, 1985b).

NOTES

1. This paper was prepared with support from the National Institute on Drug Abuse (Grant #'s DA03046 and DA03468) and the National Cancer Institute (Grant # CA34622).
2. I am grateful to Tony Biglan, Gil Botvin, Ted Dielman, Bill Hansen, Andy Johnson, Al McAlister, David Murray, Mary Ann Pentz, Cheryl Perry, Steve Schinke, and Greta Tell for draft reports and/or personal communications about details of their studies. The quality of this paper was also improved greatly by comments and feedback from all of the above plus Catherine Bell, Allan Best, Bill Bukoski, Tom Cook, Dick Evans, Jonathan Fielding, Russ Glasgow, Nancy Gordon, Larry Gruder, Harry Lando, Howard Leventhal, and Bill McCarthy.

REFERENCES

Arkin, R. M., Roemhild, H. F., Johnson, C. A., Luepker, R. V., & Murray, D. M. (November, 1981). The Minnesota smoking prevention program: A seventh-grade health curriculum supplement. *Journal of School Health*, 611–616.

Bandura, A. (1977). *Social learning theory*. Englewood Cliffs, NJ: Prentice-Hall.

Bernstein, D. A. (1969). Modification of smoking behavior: An evaluative review. *Psychological Bulletin, 71*, 418–440.

Bernstein, D. A., & McAlister, A (1976). The modification of smoking behavior: Progress and problems. *Addictive Behaviors, 1*, 89–102.

Best, J. A., & Bloch, M. (1976). Compliance in the control of cigarette smoking. In Haynes, R. B., Taylor, D. W., & Sackett, D. L. (Eds.), *Compliance with therapeutic and preventive regimen*. Baltimore: Johns Hopkins University Press.

Best, J. A., Flay, B. R., Towson, S. M. J., Ryan K. B., Perry, C. L., Brown, K. S., Kersell, M. W., & d'Avernas, J. R. (1984). Smoking prevention and the concept of risk. *Journal of Applied Social Psychology, 14*(3), 257–273.

Biglan, A., Severson, H. H., Ary, D. V., Faller, C., Gallison, C., Thompson, R., Glasgow, R., Lichtenstein, E. (in press). Do smoking prevention programs really work?: Attrition and the internal and external validity of an evaluation of a refusal skills program. *Journal of Behavioral Medicine*.

Biglan, A., & Ary, D. V. (1985). Current methodological issues in research on smoking prevention. In Bell, C., & Battjes, R. (Eds.), *Prevention research: Deterring drug abuse among children and adolescents*. Washington, DC: NIDA Research Monographs #63.

Blackburn, H., Carleton, R., & Farquhar, J. (1984). The Minnesota heart health program: A research and demonstration program in cardiovascular heart disease prevention. In Matarazzo, J. D., Weiss, S. M., Herd, J. A., Miller, N. E., & Weiss, S. M. (Eds.), *Behavioral health: A handbook of health enhancement and disease prevention*. New York: Wiley.

Botvin, G. J., Baker, E., Renick, N., Filazzola, A. D., & Botvin, E. M. (1984). A cognitive-behavioral approach to substance abuse prevention. *Addictive Behaviors, 9*, 137–147.

Botvin, G. J., & Eng, A (1980). A comprehensive school-based smoking prevention program. *Journal of School Health, 50*, 209–213.

Botvin, G. J., & Eng, A. (1982). The efficacy of a multicomponent approach to the prevention of cigarette smoking. *Preventive Medicine, 11*, 199–211.

Botvin, G. J., Eng, A., & Williams, C. L. (1980). Preventing the onset of cigarette smoking through life skills training. *Preventive Medicine, 9*, 135–143.

Botvin, G. J., & McAlister, A. (1982). Cigarette smoking among children and adolescents: Causes and prevention. In Arnold, C.B. (Ed.), *Annual review of disease prevention*. New York: Springer.

Botvin, G. J., Renick, N., & Baker, E. (1983). The effects of scheduling format and booster sessions on a broad-spectrum psychosocial approach to smoking prevention. *Journal of Behavioral Medicine, 6*(4), 359–379.

Botvin, G. J., & Wills, T. A. (1985). Personal and social skills training: Cognitive-behavioral approaches to substance abuse prevention. In Bell, C., & Battjes, R. (Eds.), *Prevention research: Deterring drug abuse among children and adolescents*. Washington, DC: NIDA Research Monograph #63.

Chassin, L., Corty, E., Presson, C. C., Olshavsky, R. W. Bensanberg, M., & Sherman, S. J. (1981). Predicting adolescents intentions to smoke cigarettes. *Journal of Health and Social Behavior, 22*, 445–455.

Chassin, L., Presson, C. C., Sherman, S. J., Corty, E., & Olshavsy, R. W. (1981). Self-images and cigarette smoking in adolescence. *Personality and Social Psychology Bulletin, 7*(4), 670–676.

Cherry, N., & Kernan, K. (1976). Personality scores and smoking behavior: A longitudinal study. *British Journal of Preventive and Social Medicine, 30*, 123–131.

Cook, T. D., & Campbell, D. T. (1979). *Quasi-experimentation: Design and analysis issues for field settings*. Chicago: Rand McNally.

Cook, T. D. (1985). Priorities in research on smoking prevention. In Bell, C., Battjes, R.

(Eds.), *Prevention research: Deterring drug abuse among children and adolescents*. Washington, DC: NIDA Research Monograph.

Cook, T. D., & Leviton, L. C. (1980). Reviewing the literature: A comparison of traditional methods with meta-analysis. *Journal of Personality, 48*, 449–472.

Dielman, T. E., Leach, S. L., Lyons, A. C., Lorenger, A. T., Klos, D. M. & Horvath, W. J. (1985). Resisting pressures to smoke: Fifteen-month follow-up results of an elementary school based smoking prevention project. *HYGIE: International Journal of Health Education, 4*, 28–35.

Dielman, T. E., Horvath, W. J., Leach, S. L., & Lorenger, A. L. (1984). *Peer pressure in recruitment to smoking*. University of Michigan, Report to NIDA.

Downey, A. M., & O'Rourke, T. W. (1976). The utilization of attitudes and beliefs as indicators of future smoking behavior. *Journal of Drug Education, 6*, 283–295.

Dunn, W. L., Jr. (Ed.). (1973). *Smoking behavior: Motives and incentives*. Washington, DC: Winston.

Evans, R. I. (1976). Smoking in children: Developing a social psychological strategy of deterrence. *Preventive Medicine, 5*, 122–127.

Evans, R. I., Hansen, W. B., & Mittelmark, M. (1977). Increasing the validity of self-reports of behavior in a smoking in children investigation. *Journal of Applied Psychology, 62*(4), 521–523.

Evans, R. I., & Raines, B. E. (1982). Control and prevention of smoking in adolescents: A psychological perspective. In Coates, T. J., Peterson, A. D., & Perry, C. (Eds.), *Promoting adolescent health: A dialog on research and practice*. New York: Academic Press.

Evans, R. I., Rozelle, R. M., Mittelmark, M., Hansen, W. B., Bane, A., & Havis, J. (1978). Deterring the onset of smoking in children: Knowledge of immediate physiological effects and coping with peer pressure, media pressure, and parent modeling. *Journal of Applied Social Psychology, 8*(2), 126–135.

Evans, R. I., Rozelle, R. M., Maxwell, S. E., Raines, B. E., Dill, C. A., Guthrie, T. J., Henderson, A. H., & Hill, P. C. (1981). Social modeling films to deter smoking in adolescents: Results of a three-year field investigation. *Journal of Applied Psychology, 66*, 399–414.

Fisher, D. A., Armstrong, B. K., & de Klerk, N. H. (1983, July). *A randomized-controlled trial of education for prevention of smoking in 12 year-old children*. Presented at 5th World Conference on Smoking and Health, Winnipeg, Canada.

Fisher, E. B. (1980). Progress in reducing smoking behavior. *American Journal of Public Health, 70*, 678–679.

Flay, B. R. (1985a). What do we know about the social influences approach to smoking prevention? Review and recommendations. In Bell, C., & Battjes, R. (Eds.), *Prevention research: Deterring drug abuse among children and adolescents*. Washington, DC: NIDA Research Monograph #63.

Flay, B. R. (1985b). Psychosocial approaches to smoking prevention: A review of findings. *Health Psychology, 4*(5), 449–488.

Flay, B. R. (1986). Efficacy and effectiveness of health promotion programs. *Prevention Medicine, 15*, 451–474.

Flay, B. R., d'Avernas, J. R., Best, J. A., Kersell, M. W. & Ryan, K. B. (1983a). Cigarette smoking: Why young people do it and ways of preventing it. In McGrath, P., & Firestone, P. (Eds.), *Pediatric and adolescent behavioral medicine*. New York: Springer-Verlag.

Flay, B. R., Hansen, W. B., Johnson, C. A., & Sobel, J. L. (1983b July/August). *Involvement of children in motivating smoking parents to quit smoking with a television program*. Presented at the 5th World Conference on Smoking and Health, Winnipeg, Canada, and the 91st annual meetings of the American Psychological Association, Anaheim, CA.

Flay, B. R., Johnson, C. A., Hansen, W. B., Grossman, L. M., Sobel, J., & Collins, L. M.

(1983c, October). *Evaluation of a school-based, family-oriented, television-enhanced smoking prevention and cessation program: The importance of implementation evaluation.* Presented at the Joint Meeting of Evaluation Network and the Evaluation Research Society, Chicago.

Flay, B. R., Ryan, K. B., Best, J. A., Brown, K. S., Kersell, M. W., d'Avernas, J. R., & Zanna, M. P. (1985). Are social psychological smoking prevention programs effective? The Waterloo study. *Journal of Behavioral Medicine, 8*(1), 37–59.

Gilchrist, L. D., Schinke, S. P. (1984). Self-control skills for smoking prevention. In Engstrom, P. F., & Anderson, P. N., & Mortenson, L. E. (Eds.), *Advances in cancer control.* New York: Liss. 125–130.

Gilchrist, L. D., Schinke, S. P., & Blythe, B. J. (1979). Primary prevention services for children and youth. *Children and Youth Services Review, 1*, 379–391.

Glasgow, R. E., & Bernstein, D. A. (1981). Behavioral treatment of smoking behavior. In Prokop, C. K., & Bradley, L. A. (Eds.), *Medical psychology: Contributions to behavioral medicine.* New York: Academic Press.

Glasgow, R. E., & McCaul, K. D. (1985). Life skills training programs for smoking prevention: Critique and directions for future research. In Bell, C., & Battjes, R. (Eds), *Prevention research: Deterring drug abuse among children and adolescents.* Washington, DC: NIDA Research Monograph #63.

Glasgow, R. E., McCaul, K. D., Freeborn, V. B., & O'Neill, H. K. (1981). Immediate and long-term health consequences information in the prevention of adolescent smoking. *The Behavior Therapist, 4*, 15–16.

Graham, J. W., Flay, B. R., Johnson, C. A., & Hansen, W. B., & Collins, L. M. (1984a). Group comparability: A multiattribute utility approach to the use of random assignment with small numbers of aggregated units. *Evaluation Review, 8*(2), 247–260.

Graham, J. W., Flay, B. R., Johnson, C. A., Hansen, W. B., Grossman, L. M., & Sobel, J. L. (1984b). Reliability of self-report measures of drug use in prevention research: Evaluation of the project SMART questionnaire via the test-retest reliability matrix. *Journal of Drug Education, 14*(2), 175–193.

Green, D. E. (1979). Youth education. In *Smoking and Health: A Report of the Surgeon General.* Washington, DC: Department of Health, Education, and Welfare, U.S. Public Health Service.

Hansen, W. B. (1978). *Monitoring carbon monoxide in conjunction with immediate, delayed, withheld, or vicarious feedback as a means of deterring smoking in children.* Unpublished doctoral dissertation, University of Houston.

Hansen, W. B., Collins, L. M., Malotte, C. K., Johnson, C. A., & Fielding, J. E. (1985). Attrition in prevention research. *Journal of Behavioral Medicine, 8*, 261–275.

Hartup, W., & Louge, R. (1979). Peers as models. *School Psychology Digest, 4*, 11–21.

Hill, P. C. (1979). *The impact of immediate physiological consequences versus long-term health consequences on the smoking beliefs, intentions, and behavior in adolescents.* Unpublished doctoral dissertation, University of Houston.

Hops, H., Weissman, W., Biglan, A., Thompson, R., Faller, C., & Severson, H. H. (1986). A taped situation test of cigarette refusal skill among adolescents. *Behavioral Assessment 8*, 145–154.

Horn, D. (1976). A model of personal choice health behavior. *International Journal of Health Education, 19*(2), 89–98.

Hurd, P. D., Johnson, C. A., Pechacek, T., Bast, L. P., Jacobs, D. R., & Luepker, R. V. (1980). Prevention of cigarette smoking in seventh grade students. *Journal of Behavioral Medicine, 3*(1), 15–28.

Jessor, R., & Jessor, S. L. (1977). *Problem behavior and psychosocial development: A longitudinal study of youth.* New York: Academic Press.

Johnson, C. A. (1982). Untested and erroneous assumptions underlying anti-smoking programs. In Coates, T., Peterson, A., & Perry, C. (Eds.), *Promoting adolescent health: A dialog on research and practice.* New York: Academic Press.

Johnson, C. A., Hansen, W. B., Collins, L. M., & Graham, J. W. (1986). High-school smoking prevention: Results of a longitudinal study. *Journal of Behavioral Medicine, 3*(1), 15–28.

Jones, E. E., Kanouse, D. E., Kelley, H. H., Nisbell, R. E., Valins, S., & Weiner, B. (1972). *Attribution: Perceiving the causes of behavior.* Morristown, NJ: General Learning Press.

Jones, E. E., & Sigall, H. (1971). The bogus pipeline: A new paradigm for measuring affect and attitude. *Psychological Bulletin, 76,* 349–364.

Judd, C. G., & Kenney, D. A. (1981). Process analysis: Estimating mediation in treatment evaluations. *Evaluation Review, 5,* 602–619.

Kandel, D. B. (1975). Stages in adolescent involvement in drug use. *Science (Wash. DC), 190,* 912–914.

Kiesler, C. A. (1971). *The psychology of commitment: Experiments linking behavior to beliefs.* New York: Academic Press.

Lando, H. (1981). Behavior treatments in the modification of smoking. In Daitzman, R. J., (Ed.), *Clinical behavior therapy and behavior modification.* New York: Garland.

Leventhal, H., & Cleary, P. D. (1980). The smoking problem: A review of research and theory in behavioral risk modification. *Psychological Bulletin, 88,* 370–405.

Lichtenstein, E., & Danaher, B. G. (1976). Modification of smoking behavior: A critical analysis of theory, research and practise. In Hersen, M., Eisler, R. M., & Miller, P. M. (Eds.), *Progress in behavior modification.* Volume 3. New York: Academic Press.

Luepker, R. V., Pechacek, T. F. Murray, D. M., Johnson, C. A., Hund, F., & Jacobs, D. R. (1981). Saliva thiocyanate: A chemical indicator of cigarette smoking in adolescents. *American Journal of Public Health, 71*(2), 1320–1324.

Luepker, R. V., Johnson, C. A., Murray, D. M., & Pechacek, T. F. (1983). Prevention of cigarette smoking: Three-year follow-up of an education program for youth. *Journal of Behavioral Medicine, 6*(1), 53–62.

McAlister, A. L. (1983). *Randomized study of tobacco and marijuana smoking prevention.* University of Texas, NIDA Contract Report.

McAlister, A. L., Perry, C., Killen, J., Slinkard, L. A., & Maccoby, N. (1980). Pilot study of smoking, alcohol, and drug abuse prevention. *American Journal of Public Health, 70,* 719–721.

McAlister, A. L., Gordon, N. P., Krosnick, J., & Milburn, M. (1982, March). Experimental and correlational tests of a theoretical model for smoking prevention. Presented at the meeting for the Society for Behavioral Medicine, Chicago, IL.

McAlister, A. L., Perry, C., & Maccoby, N. (1979). Adolescent smoking: Onset and prevention. *Pediatrics, 63,* 650–658.

McCaul, K. D., Glasgow, R. E., Schafer, L., & O'Neill, H. K. (1983). Commitment and the prevention of adolescent smoking. *Health Psychology, 2,* 353–365.

McCaul, K. D., & Glasgow, R. E. (1985). Preventing adolescent smoking: What have we learned about treatment construct validity? *Health Psychology, 4*(4), 361–387.

McGuire, W. J. (1964). Inducing resistance to persuasion. In Berkowitz, L. (Ed.). *Advances in experimental social psychology.* Volume 1. New York: Academic Press.

McGuire, W. J. (1969). The nature of attitude and attitude change. In Lindzay, G., & Aronson, E. (Eds.), *Handbook of social psychology,* Second Edition, Volume 3. Reading, MA: Addison-Wesley.

McGuire, W. J. (1973). The yin and yang of progress in social psychology: Seven koan. *Journal of Personality and Social Psychology, 26,* 446–456.

McGuire, W. J. (1983). A contextual theory of knowledge: Its implications for innovation and reform in psychological research. In Berkowitz, L. (Ed.), *Advances in experimental social psychology.* Volume 16. New York: Academic Press.

Mittlemark, M. B. (1978). *Information of imminent versus long-term health consequences: Impact on children's smoking behavior, intentions, and knowledge.* Unpublished doctoral dissertation, University of Houston.

Murray, D. M., Johnson, C. A., Luepker, R. V., & Mittelmark, M. B. (1984). The prevention of cigarette smoking in children: A comparison of four strategies. *Journal of Applied Social Psychology, 14*(3), 274–288.

Murray, D. M., Luepker, R. V., Pechacek, T. F., Jacobs, D. R., & Johnson, C. A. (1980, September). Issues in smoking prevention research. Presented at the 88th annual meetings of the American Psychological Association, Montreal, Quebec.

Murray, D. M., & Perry, C. (1985). The prevention of adolescent drug abuse: Implications from etiological, developmental, behavioral models. In Jones, C. L., Battjes, R. J. (Eds.), *Etiology of drug abuse: Implications for prevention,* Washington, DC: *NIDA Research Monograph # 56.*

O'Neill, H. K., Glasgow, R. E., & McCaul, K. D. (1983). Component analysis in smoking prevention research: Effects of social consequences information. *Addictive Behaviors, 8,* 419–423.

Overall, J. E. (1980). Calculation of adjusted response frequencies using least squares regression methods. *Applied Psychological Measurement, 4,* 65–78.

Pechacek, T. (1979). Modification of smoking behavior. In *Surgeon general's report: Smoking and health.* Washington, DC: U.S. Department of Health, Education and Welfare.

Pechacek, T., Murray, D. M., Luepker, R. V., Mittelmark, M. B., Johnson, C. A., & Schultz, J. M. (1984). Measurement of adolescent smoking behavior: Rationale and methods. *Journal of Behavioral Medicine, 7*(1), 123–140.

Pentz, M. A. (1982, August), Social skills training: A preventive intervention for drug use in adolescents. Presented at the 90th annual meetings of the American Psychological Association, Washington, DC.

Pentz, M. A. (1983). Prevention of adolescent substance abuse through social skill development. In Glynn, T. J., Leukefeld, C. G., & Ludford, J. P. (Eds.), *Preventing adolescent drug abuse: Intervention strategies.* Washington, DC: NIDA Research Monograph #47.

Pentz, M. A. (1985). Social competence skills and self-efficacy as determinants of substance use in adolescence. In Shiffman, S., Wills, T. A. (Eds.), *Coping and substance use.* New York: Academic Press.

Pentz, M. A., & Tolan, P. (in press). Adolescent social skills training: A critical review of time trends, dimensions and outcomes. *Psychological Bulletin.*

Perry C., Killen, J., Slinkard, L. A., & McAlister, A. L. (1980). Peer teaching and smoking prevention among junior high students. *Adolescence, 15*(58), 277–281.

Perry, C., Killen, J., Telch, M., Slinkard, L. A., & Danaher, B. G. (1980). Modifying smoking behavior of teenagers: A school-based intervention. *American Journal of Public Health, 70*(7), 722–725.

Perry, C. L., Telch, M. J., Killen, J., Dass, R., & Maccoby, N. (1983a). High school smoking prevention: The relative efficacy of varied treatments and instructions. *Adolescence, 18*(71).

Perry, C. L., Murray, D. M., Pechacek, T. F., & Pirie, P. L. (1983b). *Community-based smoking prevention: The Minnesota Heart Health Program.* Unpublished manuscript, University of Minnesota.

Puska, P., Vartiainen, E., Pallonen, U., Sallonen, J. T., Polyhia, P., Koskela, K., & McAlister, A. L. (1981a). The North Karelia youth Project: A community-based intervention study on CVD risk factors among 13- to 15-year-old children: Study design and preliminary findings. *Preventive Medicine, 10,* 133–148.

Puska, P., Tuomilehto, J., Salonen, J., Nissinen, A., Virtamo, J., Bjorkqvist, S., Koskela, K., Neittaanmaki, L., Takalo, T., Kottke, T. E., Maki, J., Sipila, P., & Varvikko, P. (1981b). *Community control of cardiovascular diseases: The North Karelia project.* World Health Organization Regional Office of Europe, Copenhagen.

Salber, E. L., Freeman, H. E., & Albalin, T. (1968). Needed research on smoking: Lessons from the Newton study. In Borgatta, E. F., Evans, R. R. (Eds.), *Smoking, health and behavior.* Chicago: Aldine.

Schinke, S. P. (1982). A school-based model for teenage pregnancy prevention. *Social Work in Education, 4,* 34–42.

Schinke, S. P., & Blythe, B. J. (1982). Cognitive-behavioral prevention of children's smoking. *Child Behavior Therapy, 3,* 25–42.

Schinke, S. P., & Gilchrist, L. D. (1983). Primary prevention of tobacco smoking. *Journal of School Health. 53,* 416–419.

Schinke, S. P., & Gilchrist, L. D. (1984). Preventing cigarette smoking with youth. *Journal of Primary Prevention, 5*(1), 48–56.

Schwartz, J. L. (1969). A critical review and evaluation of smoking control methods. *Public Health Reports, 84,* 483–506.

Sechrest, L., West, S. B., Phillips, M. A., Redner, R., & Yeaton, W. (1979). Some neglected problems in evaluation research: Strength and integrity of treatments. In Sechrest, L., West, S. B., Phillips, M. A., Redner, R., & Yeaton, W. (Eds.), *Evaluation Studies Review Annual,* (Volume 4). Beverly Hills: Sage.

Severson, H., Ary, D. (1983). Sampling bias due to consent procedures with adolescents. *Addictive Behaviors, 53*(7), 416–419.

Spitzhoff, D., Ramirez, S., & Wills, T. A. (1980). The decision skills curriculum: A program for primary prevention of substance use. Unpublished manuscript, American Health Foundation.

Strube, M. J., & Hartmann, D. P. (1983). Meta-analysis: Techniques, applications, and functions. *Journal of Consulting and Clinical Psychology, 51,* 14–27.

Telch, M. J., Killen, J. C., McAlister, A. L., Perry, C. L., & Maccoby, N. (1982). Long-term follow-up of a pilot project on smoking prevention with adolescents. *Journal of Behavioral Medicine, 5*(1), 1–8.

Tell, G. S., Klepp, K., Vellar, O. D., & McAlister, A. (1984). Preventing cigarette smoking in Norwegian adolescents: The Oslo youth study. *Preventive Medicine, 13,* 256–275.

Thompson, E. L. (1978). Smoking education programs, 1960–1976. *American Journal of Public Health, 68,* 250–257.

U.S. Public Health Service. (1964). *Smoking and health: Report of the advisory committee to the surgeon general.* Washington, DC: U.S. Department of Health, Education, and Welfare.

U.S. Public Health Service. (1976). *Teenage smoking: National patterns of cigarette smoking, ages 12 through 18, in 1972 and 1974.* (NIH Pub. No. 76–931.) Washington, DC: U.S. Department of Health, Education, and Welfare.

U.S. Public Health Service. (1976). *Smoking and health: A report of the surgeon general,* Washington, DC: U.S. Department of Health, Education, and Welfare.

U.S. Public Health Service. (1980). *The health consequences of smoking for women: A report of the surgeon general.* Washington, DC: U.S. Department of Health and Human Services.

U.S. Public Health Service. (1981). *The health consequences of smoking: The changing cigarette. A report of the surgeon general.* Washington, DC: U.S. Department of Health and Human Services.

U.S. Public Health Service. (1983). *The health consequences of smoking for cardiovascular disease: A report of the surgeon general.* Washington, DC: U.S. Department of Health and Human Services.

Vartiainen, E., Pallonen, U., McAlister, A., Koskela, K., & Puska, P. (1983). Effect of two years of educational intervention in adolescent smoking (The North Karelia youth project). *Bulletin of the World Health Organization, 61*(3), 529–532.

Vriend, T. (1969). High-performing inner-city adolescents assist low-performing peers in counseling groups. *Personnel Guidance, 48*, 897–904.

Williams, T. (1971). *Summary and implications of review of literature related to adolescent smoking.* Bethesda, MD: National Clearinghouse for Smoking and Health.

Wills, T. A. (1985). Stress, coping, and substance use in early adolescence. In Shiffman, S., & Wills, T. A. (Eds.), *Coping and substance use.* New York: Academic Press.

SELF-EFFICACY IN HEALTH BEHAVIOR CHANGE:
ISSUES IN MEASUREMENT AND RESEARCH DESIGN

Elanna S. Yalow and Janet L. Collins

INTRODUCTION

As medical and scientific research establish new links between behavior and health, many practitioners remain frustrated by individuals' unwillingness to adopt behaviors likely to reduce morbidity and mortality. One promising line of investigation into health behavior change has explored the relationship between self-efficacy and behavior. Perceived self-efficacy is defined as an estimate of one's capability for coping successfully with a particular situation or task. First hypothesized by Bandura (1977a), these self-appraisals have been shown to predict behaviors such as effort expenditure, persistence, initiation, and avoidance in a variety of domains. Since Bandura first described the self-efficacy construct, a considerable amount of research has been conducted, particularly in the area of clinical behavior change (e.g., phobias).

Currently there is an upsurge of self-efficacy research in the area of health behavior change. In light of this trend, this paper was written to assist health educators in their roles as consumers and designers of such

Advances in Health Education and Promotion, vol. 2, pages 181–199
Copyright © 1987 JAI Press Inc.
All rights of reproduction in any form reserved.
ISBN: 0-89232-617-4

research. We illuminate a variety of weaknesses in the design of research on self-efficacy in health. Solutions to these problems and exemplary research designs are also described. The studies reviewed here are not comprehensive. Rather, they were selected to represent the health contexts in which self-efficacy has been applied and to highlight the strengths and weaknesses of various research designs.

SELF-EFFICACY: DEFINITION AND MODEL

Self-efficacy focuses on individuals' assessments of their capability for successfully completing a task as determinants of behavior (Bandura, 1977a, 1978a, 1982a, 1982b). Individuals are unlikely to initiate or persist in tasks for which they perceive themselves lacking in the requisite skills. Unlike generalized self-concept notions, an individual can have high efficacy for performing one task, but low efficacy for a task requiring a different set of skills. Bandura (1977a) hypothesized that self-efficacy develops through individuals' cognitive processing of information from a variety of sources. These sources include current and past performance accomplishments, as well as vicarious and persuasive information. Thus, for example, viewing a peer's success or failure on a task can contribute to one's sense of efficacy, as can assurances from acquaintances of one's ability to succeed. However, it is not the information gained from these sources that determines self-efficacy, but how the information is appraised by the individual.

A single piece of contradictory information, such as failing when success is expected, may not influence efficacy dramatically, if at all. However, efficacy does change over time. To illustrate, the efficacy of a new driver is likely to be far less than the efficacy of an individual who has driven successfully for many years. Note that there are likely to be actual differences in skill, as well as differences in perceived self-efficacy.

Clearly, individuals who know they have the requisite skills for an action do not always act. Self-efficacy alone does not fully explain behavior. Rather, the self-efficacy construct falls within a broader theory of motivation based on social learning theory (Bandura 1977b, 1978b). As shown in Figure 1, additional variables clearly come into play. One such variable is outcome expectations, that is, judgments about whether a given behavior will lead to a particular outcome. In a health context, this factor might be manifest as the belief that refraining from smoking will result in a longer or healthier life. Presumably, individuals who believe that refraining from smoking is likely to lead to a healthier life are, in fact, more likely to refrain. Another variable that must be considered in explaining behavior is incentive value, that is, the extent to which an expected outcome resulting from behavior is valued by an individual.

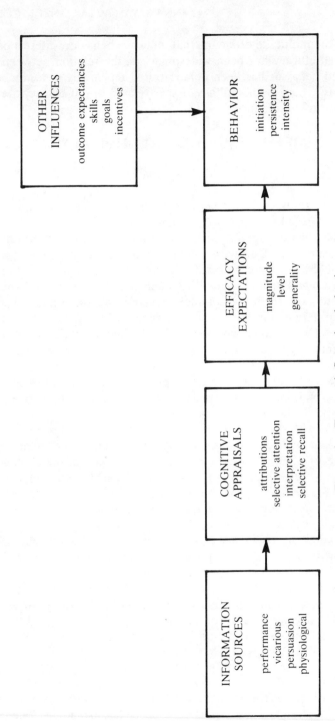

Figure 1. Factors influencing behavior.

Despite the multitude of factors that influence behavior, interest particularly in self-efficacy has been widespread, as the relation between self-efficacy and behavior has been demonstrated repeatedly in a number of health areas. Thus, methodological issues related to self-efficacy are particularly worthy of attention.

MEASUREMENT OF SELF-EFFICACY

Traditional Approaches

In research studies, self-efficacy has traditionally been operationalized by paper-and-pencil responses to questions about how confident individuals are that they can engage in particular behaviors, such as "refrain from smoking at a party." During initial work with phobics, the behaviors (or threats) could be ordered hierarchically from, for example, standing in a room with a caged snake to actually handling a snake. Hierarchies may be less likely to exist for more complex behaviors such as smoking, where individual differences in the perceived strength of the provocative stimuli vary greatly. One advantage of hierarchies is that individuals can be placed on a continuum to assess their progress. Where generic hierarchies are inappropriate, individualized hierarchies can be developed for treatment purposes, but typically they are not appropriate for research. Regardless of whether a hierarchy is developed or not, the statements to be rated must represent specific behavioral responses.

Consistent with the original mode of self-efficacy, ratings for each behavior are first made on the basis of magnitude, that is, an estimate by the respondents of whether they can perform the behavior or not. Individuals who respond "yes," indicating that they could perform the behavior are then asked to rate the strength of this belief. Individuals who respond "no" go on to the next item without rating the strength of their belief. The strength rating is, therefore, only used to get an indication of an individual's confidence that the task can be performed. Confidence ratings typically range from 10 (little confidence) to 100 (a great deal of confidence) in 10-point intervals. Correlations between subsequent performance and the strength measure have been consistently higher than correlations between subsequent performance and magnitude. These differential correlations are probably due to the greater variability in efficacy assessed by a 10-point scale as compared to a 2-point scale.

Alternative Approaches to the Measurement of Self-efficacy

Not surprisingly, as the research tradition in self-efficacy has progressed, the variety of strategies used to assess efficacy has expanded. One of the earliest departures from the original conceptualization of the measurement of self-efficacy was the abandonment of the magnitude/strength dichotomy. Hence, as will be noted in subsequent studies to be reviewed, many (although certainly not all) researchers ask respondents to provide their efficacy ratings on an expanded strength scale, ranging from no confidence to high confidence. The initial magnitude rating has been dropped, simplifying the response process, so that individuals are no longer required to use a two-part procedure.

This shift has resulted in more than a cosmetic change in the measurement of self-efficacy. Previously, only those individuals who believed that they *could* engage in the target behavior (e.g., refrain from smoking at a party) went on to rate the strength of their efficacy. Thus, efficacy ratings as low as 10 to 30 points indicated some confidence in the ability to display the behavior. All variability in strength was associated with positive self-efficacy. In contrast, when the magnitude rating is incorporated into the strength rating, the lower points on the scale (e.g., 10, 20, 30) are used to indicate the relative strength of the *lack* of self-efficacy (e.g., definitely not, probably not, possibly not). It is not clear whether respondents to a traditional self-efficacy scale would have answered "no" to the magnitude portion of the scale and, therefore, never indicated the strength of their efficacy, or if they would have responded "yes" to the magnitude question and provided a low strength estimate. Regardless, the current modification ensures assessment of variability in very low levels of self-efficacy.

It appears that the magnitude ratings are of little utility in the assessment of self-efficacy, and that they add an unnecessary complexity for respondents (by requiring a two-step response procedure). It must be recognized, however, that scaling differences may have an impact on the comparability of efficacy estimates across studies.

Another approach to the assessment of self-efficacy was a more traditional Likert scale (typically of either five or seven points), rather than the 10-point confidence (strength) scale. High and low points on the Likert scale usually correspond to respective values on the confidence scale. Magnitude estimates usually are not employed when the Likert scale is used. This strategy is directly comparable to the confidence scale without magnitude estimates, insofar as similar labels are attached to corresponding positions (particularly the extremes).

Examples of the use of these assessment strategies, as well as others, will be described throughout the remainder of this review. Additional concerns regarding the measurement of self-efficacy are presented by Eastman and Marzillier (1984). However operationalized, it is essential for an assessment of self-efficacy to retain a clear focus on perceptions of *ability*. Questions asking respondents to indicate whether they "will" engage in specified behaviors, or "intend" to engage in specified behaviors, are clearly different constructs—constructs that may be more or less predictive of behavior than self-efficacy, depending on the circumstances. But without a clear operationalization of the efficacy construct, investigations into its impact on behavior change are likely to yield confusing results. This clarity is far more important than the particular assessment strategy selected.

SELF-EFFICACY RESEARCH IN HEALTH CONTEXTS

Given the apparent importance of self-efficacy as a predictive construct, it is not surprising that many health researchers are examining its role in explaining health behavior. The range of health behaviors to which self-efficacy has been applied is quite extensive, as are the varieties of ways in which the construct has been operationalized (O'Leary, 1985; Schunk & Carbonari, 1984). The following review of selected studies is intended to highlight problems in the application of efficacy theory to the health arena, and to suggest fruitful approaches for future investigations.

Smoking Behavior

More often than in any other health area, the role of self-efficacy has been considered in relation to smoking behavior. Typically, these studies focus on the self-efficacy of individuals who are successful or unsuccessful in their attempts to quit. For example, DiClemente (1981) conducted a study of recent quitters from three different types of smoking cessation programs. Self-efficacy was assessed using a seven-point Likert scale in which participants were required to rate their degree of certainty that they could refrain from smoking in 12 situations (e.g., "with friends at a party"). Self-efficacy scores within one month after quitting were correlated with smoking behavior approximately four months later. Successful abstainers had significantly higher self-efficacy scores than recidivists. The author noted, however, that the extent to which the self-efficacy scale incorporated an individual's expectation of success was not clear. That is, when individuals are asked whether they "can avoid smoking" it is not clear how they interpret the question. Do they interpret it as the researcher intended, namely, "Do I have the skills that would permit me to refrain?" Or is the question interpreted as, "Do I think I might smoke a cigarette in a situation like this in the future?" Predictions about future behavior are based, in part, on self-efficacy, but also include considerations such as incentives (e.g., pressure from doctor or family to quit) and beliefs (e.g., belief in the adverse effects of smoking). Without an attempt to measure these other attitudinal dimensions in addition to self-efficacy, it is likely that such constructs will be incorporated into respondents' self-efficacy ratings.

As discussed previously, this problem becomes even more pronounced when researchers specifically ask respondents about their likely future behavior, then interpret the responses in terms of self-efficacy. DiClemente & Prochaska (1981) reported asking respondents to rate how confident they were that they *would* not smoke in a variety of smoking-related situations. The responses were indeed related to an individual's likelihood of moving from one smoking stage, such as recent quitter, to another smoking stage, such as relapser or long-term quitter. Based on this study, however, such changes should be attributed to individuals' predictions about their likely behavior, not their self-efficacy.

Another methodological problem common to the investigation of self-efficacy in health behavior change is found in a study by Prochaska et al. (1982). In this study, prior smokers who had maintained nonsmoking status for at least six months were compared to smokers who had quit for at least 24 hours, but subsequently resumed smoking. Individuals were asked to rate how certain they were that they *could* resist smoking in each of 35 potential smoking situations. Not surprisingly, the two groups differed significantly on their efficacy to refrain from smoking. The authors concluded that the self-efficacy data suggest that maintainers are more confident of their abilities to cope in difficult situations without resorting to smoking. In other words, the study merely demonstrated that nonsmokers have more confidence in their ability to refrain from smoking than do smokers. Because behavior and self-efficacy are confounded, it is not possible to determine whether self-efficacy contributed to a particular smoking status, or was simply the result of that status. Baer & Lichtenstein (in press) highlight this problem and argue that, for self-efficacy to be truly useful, it must demonstrate predictive power beyond that accounted for by current behavior.

McIntyre et al. (1983, p. 633) also pointed out that the "critical test of self-efficacy requires a control for smoking status." In their study, pretreatment, quit-date, and end-of-treatment efficacy were measured by asking participants in a smoking cessation program to rate, on a scale of 0–100, their confidence that they *would* be able to resist the urge to smoke in 46 different situations. A total efficacy score was obtained by averaging a participant's responses across the situations. Pretreatment efficacy did not relate to smoking status at any assessment point. Analyzing the results for only those individuals who were abstinent at the end of treatment, the correlation between efficacy and three-month follow-up was significant. However, the six-month and one-year correlations were not. The authors concluded that, consistent with Bandura's theory, efficacy ratings are better predictors of proximal than distal outcomes. However, when all individuals were considered, "end-of-treatment smoking status was a better predictor of follow-up than self-efficacy" (p. 633). Regardless of the particular findings, however, the critical point is that the effects of smoking status must be controlled to examine appropriately the role of self-efficacy.

In a study by Condiotte and Lichtenstein (1981), pretreatment, post-treatment, and follow-up assessments were made of smoking behavior and self-efficacy for participants in one of two smoking-cessation programs. Efficacy was assessed by asking individuals to estimate the probability that they will be able to resist the urge to smoke in 48 different smoking-related situations. Results indicated that self-efficacy was enhanced during treatment for participants who benefitted from the intervention, that is, quit smoking. Thus, efficacy for refraining from smoking was higher for those individuals who were able to abstain. This increase in self-efficacy, however, cannot be presumed to affect behavior, but may merely increase as a function of skill development that leads to both increased efficacy and smoking abstinence. Although the authors noted that self-efficacy is expected to be determined, in part, by actual performance, the importance of the confounding was possibly understated. Had efficacy completely covaried with performance, the efficacy construct would have been unnecessary. Thus, it is essential that studies be designed so that the independent effects of efficacy can be assessed.

As was used by McIntyre et al. (1983), an appropriate design for examining the effects of efficacy would be to compare levels of posttreatment efficacy for abstainers in an attempt to predict recidivism. The Condiotte and Lichtenstein (1981) study included an examination of post-treatment efficacy and later-smoking status. Unfortunately, all clients, not just abstainers, were included in this analysis, again confounding behavioral status with self-efficacy.

In a unique approach to examining the relationship between efficacy and later behavior, Condiotte & Lichtenstein (1981) employed an adapted version of microanalysis (Bandura, 1977a). The analysis involved examining the degree of correspondence between factor-analytic clusters of smoking situations in which individuals reported low self-efficacy and the cluster of situations in which they reported relapse. A high degree of correspondence would strengthen the case for a causal link between self-efficacy and behavior because of the direct correspondence between self-efficacy and specific behaviors. A reanalysis of the data by Baer and Lichtenstein (in press) revealed that the clusters were no more effective in predicting relapse situations than was the assumption that all relapses occurred in the most frequent relapse cluster, namely, negative affect (e.g., feeling nervous or tense). Thus, the ability to predict the specific relapse situation from knowledge of situation-specific efficacy has yet to be demonstrated.

In addition to the reanalysis, Baer and Lichtenstein reported new data regarding the relationship of self-efficacy during post-program maintenance to later smoking status. In a study of successful quitters, self-efficacy was assessed by telephone at one, two, and three months post-treatment. Smoking status was similarly assessed at two-, three-, and six-month intervals. Correlations between average efficacy at one month and later smoking status were low but significant (− .23 to − .25). Correlations between average efficacy at two or three months and later smoking status were considerably higher (− .51 to − .56). To apply these findings to program planning, Baer and Lichtenstein recommend setting a cut-score to identify individuals at risk for relapse. Clients with extremely high efficacy at two months post-program are at very low risk of resuming smoking; clients with relatively lower efficacy may be excellent candidates for a "booster intervention."

Colletti et al. (1981) examined the relationship of self-efficacy to recidivism after smoking treatment. Efficacy was assessed with the traditional magnitude rating followed by a strength scale. Results showed that efficacy for 17 smoking situations was correlated significantly with treatment outcome, even after success in the treatment program was partialed out. Intrasubject analyses revealed a relationship between smoking status and (1) changes in self-efficacy from post-treatment to maintenance, and (2) the strength of self-efficacy immediately after treatment. Although the sample size was small, the study was carefully designed and permitted an assessment of the independent contribution of efficacy to behavior. Careful consideration was also given to the development and validation of the efficacy scale.

The final study to be reviewed linking self-efficacy to smoking behavior (Brod & Hall, 1984) compared joiners of a treatment program to non-joiners on a variety of measures related to self-efficacy. In general, joiners showed higher self-efficacy than non-joiners, as assessed by a scale that required respondents to both indicate important characteristics perceived to be necessary for quitting, and then rank the extent to which they possessed each characteristic ("The Quality Possession Scale"). No differences between joiners and non-joiners were found on an additional scale that measured general perceptions of ability to succeed rather than smoking-specific self-efficacy ("Self-Efficacy Assessment").

The "Quality Possession Scale" is a unique way to measure self-efficacy because it provides information about what skills individuals consider to be relevant, as well as their efficacy for those skills. Because this study did not include a more traditional measure of self-efficacy, it is unclear whether the new approach is more or less useful in predicting behavior. Asking individuals to determine (1) relevant skills for a task, and (2) their status on each, would appear to serve some diagnostic needs. For example, interventions might alter an individual's perception of which skills are actually requisite, then enhance those skills for which an individual has low self-efficacy. The other measure, the "Self-Efficacy Assessment," is a generalized measure of perceived ability to succeed. It is not a "true" efficacy measurement in that efficacy must be assessed in relation to a specific behavioral task. Thus, this assessment device might be better labeled as a measure of self-concept than self-efficacy.

Physical Performance

Leg Extension

An attempt has been made to assess the effects of efficacy expectations in a variety of studies of physical performance. In one series of studies (Weinberg et al., 1979, 1980, 1981) the impact of existing and manipulated self-efficacy on a competitive leg-extension task was explored. In these studies, participants were asked to extend their legs against resistance into a horizontal position and to maintain the extension for as long as possible. In each case, the participant was required to compete against a confederate who reported either strained ligaments (thus instilling high efficacy in the participant) or involvement in weight training (thus instilling low efficacy in the participant). The dependent variable in these studies was the amount of time the participant maintained a horizontal leg extension after being outperformed by the confederate on one trial. Although different experimental variables were manipulated in each of these studies (e.g., face-to-face or back-to-back competition), the high self-efficacy group consistently maintained leg extension longer than the low self-efficacy group.

These studies are among the few in the health field in which attempts have been made to experimentally alter levels of self-efficacy. Furthermore, the investigations are exemplary in that efficacy was assessed after the manipulation to verify that the two groups differed in efficacy. In the third study (Weinberg et al., 1981), the effects on performance of pre-existing efficacy levels were assessed in addition to the effects of manipulated self-efficacy. Students with existing high self-efficacy were found to extend their legs longer than low self-efficacy students. However, because there was no control for actual skill level, this difference may be due to differences in strength rather than differences in self-efficacy. That is, given that efficacy is based, in part, on performance attainments, these pre-existing efficacy differences are likely to be related to actual ability differences.

This potential confounding of ability with self-efficacy highlights the advantages of a randomly assigned, experimentally induced efficacy procedure. In many areas of study, such as children's efficacy for achievement, self-efficacy cannot ethically be lowered. However, when a manipulation can be used, the researcher can either assume, due to random assignment, that actual ability differences are equivalent across groups or can demonstrate equivalence following assignment.

The Weinberg et al. line of research provides a good example of the experimental approach to examining efficacy. Despite some interesting anomalies, for example, a lack of efficacy effects for females on performance (Weinberg et al., 1980), the studies support the notion that self-efficacy influences effort and persistence.

Competitive Performance

Barling and Abel (1983) investigated the role of self-efficacy in tennis performance. This study provided a great deal of conceptual clarity to the assessment of self-efficacy. Not only was self-efficacy assessed (e.g., "I can play most of my shots correctly"), but response-outcome ("Improving my strokes will win me more points") and incentives ("Winning more points is very important to me") were also assessed in order to isolate the unique effects of each type of belief. The self-ratings were correlated with the average ratings of two professional coaches on 12 behavioral measures. The results indicated that self-efficacy was significantly related to all 12 behavioral criteria. Only two of the criteria were related to response-outcome expectations, and two criteria were related to incentive beliefs. Although the measurement of self-efficacy was well conceived, the study did not avoid another common pitfall in efficacy research, namely, the potential confounding of efficacy beliefs and ability differences. Specifically, the relationship between tennis performance and efficacy may have been explicable solely on the basis of differences in skill level.

Postmyocardial Infarction Patients

Ewart et al. (1983) examined the role of self-efficacy on the physical activity of postmyocardial infarction patients. In this study, self-efficacy was assessed using an 11-point scale in which patients reported their degree of confidence in performing increasingly more demanding activities such as walking, running, stair climbing, sexual activity, and lifting. Efficacy was measured before and after a treadmill test, but before an explanation of the treadmill results. Self-efficacy judgments predicted performance on the treadmill test and were, in turn, modified by the treadmill performance. These modified judgments were shown to be more accurate predictors of duration and intensity of physical activity in the home environment than were the patients' treadmill performances. This study not only measured self-efficacy appropriately, it also demonstrated a relationship between efficacy and subsequent behavior in addition to differences in skill level (treadmill performance). Thus, the study serves as an example of well-designed research on self-efficacy and also lends considerable support to the utility of the efficacy construct in predicting health behavior.

Pain Control

Both manipulated and naturally occurring self-efficacy have also been linked to individuals' tolerance for pain. Neufeld and Thomas (1977) examined pain tolerance and endurance in a task requiring individuals to submerge their hands in very cold water. Efficacy was manipulated by encouraging individuals to use relaxation, and by giving them false information about the effects of the relaxation. Individuals in the high-efficacy condition were led to believe that their relaxation efforts were successful in helping them cope with the pain. These participants displayed more pain tolerance than other participants. It should be noted that self-efficacy was invoked to explain the results, but was never actually measured.

An interim report is available from a study of self-efficacy for patients with chronic arthritis (Shoor, 1983). Self-efficacy was assessed by requiring patients to indicate how certain they were that they could engage in specific behaviors using a confidence scale from 10 (very uncertain) to 100 (very certain). The study explored the independent contribution of self-efficacy to the prediction of future self-reported pain. The effects of self-efficacy were explored after controlling for initial reports of pain and disability. Results indicated that that self-efficacy is not simply a surrogate measure for self-reported disability. Scores for initial disability did not correlate with future pain reports, whereas self-efficacy did. Even with initial pain held constant, self-efficacy correlated with reports of pain four weeks later.

Weight Control

The role of self-efficacy has been investigated in individuals with specific health-related conditions. Chambliss and Murray (1979b) examined the relationships among self-efficacy, locus of control, and weight loss in overweight females. Self-efficacy was manipulated via feedback regarding a placebo medication for weight control, but was not independently assessed. Successful participants in the high self-efficacy group were informed that the medication they were given was a placebo. Hence, it was anticipated that attributions for weight loss during a previous two-week period were transferred from the placebo to the individuals themselves. These individuals were compared to individuals who continued in a placebo condition. Internal individuals in the self-efficacy condition lost significantly more weight in a subsequent two-week period than did individuals in other conditions. The self-efficacy manipulation did not yield differential results for externals. This study replicated findings for individuals in a smoking cessation program (Chambliss & Murray, 1979a). The interaction between locus of control and behavior change may occur because self-efficacy was not enhanced in the external group. However, without a measure of self-efficacy, this hypothesis cannot be tested. A measure of self-efficacy could also strengthen the authors' contention that self-efficacy is the appropriate explanatory construct for these results.

Dental Behavior

In a study that examined the effects of persuasive communications on self-reported behavior change, dental patients viewed one of two tapes designed to influence their beliefs regarding the severity of periodontal disease and their susceptibility to it (Beck & Lund, 1981). Self-efficacy was assessed via three items, one each regarding the patients' ability to floss, brush properly, and disclose. Responses were made (on a 10-point scale from "not at all' to "extremely") to the question, "How effective do you think you will be in (target behavior)?" In addition to personal efficacy, measures of response efficacy (a judgment about the effectiveness of each procedure) and intention (a judgment about likely behavior on a regular basis) were administered. Results indicated that reported efficacy was related to self-reported behavior only in the area of flossing.

Although the efficacy question asked about what individuals were likely to do ("will") not what they were capable of doing ("can"), the addition of both the response efficacy and intention measures probably helped clarify the unique meaning of the efficacy question. Including measures of efficacy, outcome expectation, and intention in the same study is an excellent model for future research. However, the appropriateness of measuring adults' efficacy for a behavior such as brushing teeth seems somewhat questionable. The vast majority of adults, when given visual instruction in proper dental care (as these participants were), would be *capable* of executing the behaviors. Thus, variability in adults' efficacy for tooth brushing would not be expected. Without variability in the efficacy measure, a relationship with behavior cannot be established. The finding that only self-efficacy for flossing is related to self-reported behavior may indicate that this was the only area in which participants did vary in their perceptions of capability.

Bandura (personal communication, 1985) argues that this interpretation of the study is based on a view of self-efficacy that is too narrow. According to Bandura, the issue is not whether individuals can brush their teeth, but their judged capability to perform such routines repeatedly. In contrast, it is the current authors' view that incorporating expectations about one's capability for repeated performance goes beyond self-efficacy to a broader concept of motivation. Such a judgment would be based, in part, on self-efficacy, but also on factors that are typically separate from the efficacy construct, such as incentives and outcome expectations.

IMPLICATIONS OF SELF-EFFICACY FOR HEALTH PROMOTION RESEARCH

Given the array of studies linking self-efficacy to behavior, particularly health behavior, substantial evidence suggests that self-efficacy plays an important role in influencing behavior. Unfortunately, several methodological and conceptual problems highlighted in this review frequently mar such research. These problems and possible solutions stemming from the research literature are below.

Assessment of Self-efficacy

Scaling

It is clear from the range of studies reviewed here that a variety of approaches can be used to assess self-efficacy. Some researchers have obtained both magnitude and strength estimates; others have only assessed strength. Some have used a confidence scale from 0 (or 10) to 100; others have used modified Likert scales. There is no empirical evidence to suggest that any of these approaches yields considerable advantages over the other. In investigations conducted by the current authors (IOX Assessment Associates, 1983), respondents found a single response scale easier to use than the more cumbersome magnitude and strength estimates. In addition, the use of a single response scale eliminates the possibility (and, in our investigations, the likelihood) that some individuals will indicate the strength of their lack of self-efficacy after indicating that they did *not* believe that they could engage in specified behaviors. Although such confusions can certainly be corrected in the coding and analysis of data, they do suggest a lack of understanding by some respondents when a two-part response scale is used.

Specificity of Construct

As initially proposed by Bandura (1977a), self-efficacy relates to individuals' beliefs in their abilities to engage in specific behaviors. It is distinct from more general constructs such as locus of control or generalized self-concept. It is precisely because of this specificity that self-efficacy seems to offer promise, not just of explaining behavior, but also of modifying it. That is, beliefs regarding one's ability to engage in specified behaviors may be relatively amenable to change by, for example, providing new information through successful experiences. This potential for change can be contrasted with concepts such as self-worth, locus of control, or Type A behavior patterns that have been established throughout a lifetime. Modifications of these broader constructs could require a total reorganization of an individual's beliefs and lifestyle, thus accounting for the relative intransigence of such constructs.

With few exceptions (e.g., the "Self-Efficacy Assessment," Brod & Hall, 1984), the studies reviewed did maintain specificity in the operationalization of self-efficacy. Variants of the standard procedures for self-efficacy assessment, such as the "Quality Possession Scale" also used by Brod & Hall (1984), provide an interesting new approach to the measurement of self-efficacy, while maintaining the requisite specificity. As was pointed out previously, however, it might be desirable also to use more standard approaches to measuring self-efficacy when these newer approaches are used, to permit an examination of the relative utility of the newer procedures in assessing self-efficacy.

An Ability Focus

Assessment of affective constructs is notoriously difficult. Participants are usually required to report on internal states, feelings, and emotions that they have not categorized with the same conceptual clarity that researchers employ when modeling human behavior. Self-efficacy, intentions, and expectations about future behavior can all be isolated on a flowchart. It is far more difficult to disentangle them in the human mind.

Self-efficacy focuses on perceptions of one's ability to engage in specified behaviors. For researchers to be able to assess its independent contribution to behavior, it is important that they state, with clarity, that it is the ability component on which they want respondents to focus, not on other related constructs. Although, by and large, researchers did maintain this clarity, certain investigators (e.g., DiClemente & Prochaska, 1981) required respondents to estimate the likelihood of specified future behaviors. Such estimates involve a multitude of beliefs, of which self-efficacy is just one. Thus, the interpretation of the findings of such studies cannot directly link self-efficacy to behavior.

Confounding of Skill and Self-efficacy Differences

Parsimony is often touted when psychological investigations proceed. If a given behavior can be explained by a limited number of constructs, additional overlapping constructs become superfluous. There is no doubt that earlier behaviors influence and help predict future behaviors, and that skill and self-efficacy are not independent. Skillful performance can, indeed, enhance self-efficacy. Self-efficacy, in turn, can enhance persistence and effort, thereby improving skill. Thus, these two factors are clearly intertwined. Nonetheless, a considerable amount of evidence is now available to suggest that self-efficacy has an influence on behavior beyond that explained by prior behavior or by actual ability differences. Much of this evidence comes from research outside the field of health. Path analysis, in particular, has been used to establish the independent contribution of self-efficacy to behavior (Covington & Omelich, 1979). However, path-analytic studies in the area of health are not yet available for review.

In every investigation of self-efficacy, it is important to ensure that actual skill differences are not confounded when comparing high- and low-efficacy participants. This can be accomplished by, for example, (1) experimentally altering efficacy levels of randomly formed groups, (2) comparing individuals with high and low efficacy matched on skill level, or (3) using procedures such as multiple regression or path analysis to partial out the variance in outcome accounted for by skill differences before examining the role of self-efficacy. In studies where the potential confounding of ability and efficacy was noted, the importance of self-efficacy in explaining the results could be seriously questioned.

Attribution to Self-efficacy

The majority of studies presented in this review used some procedure to assess directly the existing efficacy level of participants in the study. However, an interesting approach to an examination of self-efficacy was also provided in studies in which self-efficacy was experimentally manipulated (e.g., Weinberg et al., 1979, 1980, 1981; Neufeld & Thomas, 1977; Chambliss & Murray, 1979a, b). This experimental approach can help provide compelling evidence that self-efficacy has a causal relationship to behavioral change. However, such assertions can only be made in light of evidence that differences in self-efficacy were, in fact, induced. The assessment of self-efficacy is necessary to confirm the effectiveness of an efficacy manipulation. Without such an assessment it is not clear whether the manipulation actually altered efficacy levels. It also provides a mechanism for determining each participant's level of efficacy, not merely a dichotomous distinction of high vs. low self-efficacy.

Limitations of the Self-efficacy Construct

As was emphasized throughout this chapter, self-efficacy is an appropriate construct to consider only when a target behavior involves a perceived ability component. This distinction has implications beyond that of devising or selecting the particular assessment instrument to be used. It imposes a restriction on the types of behaviors for which self-efficacy should be considered as an explanatory construct. The discussion of the Beck &

Lund (1981) study highlighted this point. When the target behaviors are such that, for most respondents, the ability dimension is not at issue, variance in self-efficacy is not expected. This, in turn, will attenuate relationships between self-efficacy and behavior. Where variance is noted, respondents may be describing differences in their expectations for engaging in the behavior. This problem was noted in a pilot study conducted in our research efforts requiring efficacy ratings by healthy respondents regarding their ability to exercise in a variety of situations (IOX Assessment Associates, 1983). In a debriefing interview with respondents after completing the efficacy questionnaire, they indicated a confusion in answering such questions because they knew that they *could* exercise in the variety of situations, but might well choose not to. Thus, they either consistently indicated yes, with high confidence, or provided an estimate of what they were likely to do. Such piloting of measurement instruments may be essential in ensuring that respondents interpret self-efficacy questionnaires as researchers intend.

SUMMARY AND CONCLUSIONS

An appraisal of the data currently at hand suggests that self-efficacy may, indeed, be a potent construct for health promotion. However, the purpose of this review was not to judge the value of self-efficacy in the health arena; such a judgment would probably be premature. The purpose was to highlight the pitfalls that confront researchers who attempt to study self-efficacy. For each study to contribute to a true test of the usefulness of self-efficacy in predicting health behavior, such pitfalls must be avoided. Striving for clarity in the measurement of self-efficacy and designing studies as stringent tests of the efficacy construct are essential to the advancement of knowledge in the critically important field of health behavior change.

ACKNOWLEDGMENTS

The authors appreciate the assistance of Robin Harte, Robin Matas, and Timothy Jones, of IOX Assessment Associates, in the preparation of this manuscript.

REFERENCES

Baer, J. S., & Lichtenstein, E. (in press). Cognitive assessment in smoking cessation. In Donovan, D. M. & Marlatt, G. A. (Eds.), *Assessment of addictive behaviors*. New York: Guilford Press.

Bandura, A. (1977a). Self-efficacy: Toward a unifying theory of behavioral change. *Psychological Review, 84*, 191–215.

Bandura, A. (1977b). *Social learning theory*. Englewood Cliffs, NJ: Prentice-Hall.

Bandura, A. (1978a). Reflections on self-efficacy. In Rachman, S. (Ed.), *Advances in behaviour research and therapy*. Volume 1. Oxford: Pergamon Press.

Bandura, A. (1978b). The self system in reciprocal determinism. *American Psychologist, 33*, 344–358.

Bandura, A. (1982a). Self-efficacy mechanism in human agency. *American Psychologist, 37*, 122–147.

Bandura, A. (1982b). The self and mechanisms of agency. In Suls, J. (Ed.), *Psychological perspectives on the self*. Volume 1. Hillsdale, NJ: Erlbaum.

Barling, J., & Abel, M. (1983). Self-efficacy and tennis performance. *Cognitive Therapy and Research, 7*, 265–272.

Beck, K., & Lund, A. K. (1981). The effects of health threat seriousness and personal efficacy upon intentions and behavior. *Journal of Applied Social Psychology, 11*, 401–415.

Brod, M. I., & Hall, S. M. (1984). Joiners and non-joiners in smoking treatment: A comparison of psychological variables. *Addictive Behaviors, 9*, 217–221.

Chambliss, C. A., & Murray, E. J. (1979a). Cognitive procedures for smoking reduction: Symptom attribution versus efficacy attribution. *Cognitive Therapy and Research, 3*, 91–95.

Chambliss, C. A., & Murray, E. J. (1979b). Efficacy attribution, locus of control, and weight loss. *Cognitive Therapy and Research, 3*, 349–353.

Colletti, G., Supnick, J. A., & Rizzo, A. A. (1981). *Part I. An analysis of relapse determinants for treated smokers. Part II. Measurement of self-efficacy in high risk smoking situations*. Paper presented at the meeting of the American Psychological Association, Los Angeles.

Condiotte, M. M., & Lichtenstein, E. (1981). Self-efficacy and relapse in smoking cessation programs. *Journal of Consulting and Clinical Psychology, 49*, 648–658.

Covington, M. V., & Omelich, C. L. (1979). Are causal attributions causal? A path analysis of the cognitive model of achievement motivation. *Journal of Personality and Social Psychology, 37*, 1487–1504.

DiClemente, C. C. (1981). Self-efficacy and smoking cessation maintenance: A preliminary report. *Cognitive Therapy and Research, 5*, 175–187.

DiClemente, C. C., & Prochaska, J. O. (1981). *Self-efficacy and the stages of self-change of smoking*. Paper presented at the meeting of the American Psychological Association, Los Angeles.

Eastman, C., & Marzillier, J. S. (1984). Theoretical and methodological difficulties in Bandura's self-efficacy theory. *Cognitive Therapy and Research, 8*, 213–229.

Ewart, C. K., Taylor, C. B., Reese, L. B., & DeBusk, R. F. (1983). Effects of early post-myocardial infarction exercise testing on self-perception and subsequent physical activity. *American Journal of Cardiology, 51*, 1076–1080.

IOX Assessment Associates. (1983). Program evaluation handbooks for health education programs (in seven fields). Culver City, CA.

McIntyre, K. O., Lichtenstein, E., Mermelstein, R. J. (1983). Self-efficacy and relapse on smoking cessation: A replication and extension. *Journal of Consulting and Clinical Psychology, 51*, 632–633.

Neufeld, R. W. J., & Thomas, P. (1977). Effects of perceived efficacy of a prophylactic controlling mechanism on self-control under pain stimulation. *Canadian Journal of Behavioral Science, 9*, 224–232.

O'Leary, A. (1985). Self-efficacy and health. *Behavior Research and Therapy, 23*, 437–451.

Prochaska, J. O., Crimi, P., Lapsanski, D., Martel, L., & Reid, P. (1982). Self-change processes, self-efficacy and self-concept in relapse and maintenance of cessation of smoking. *Psychological Reports, 51*, 983–990.

Schunk, D. H., & Carbonari, J. P. (1984). Self-efficacy models. In Matarazzo, J. D., Herd, J. A., Miller, N. E., & Weiss, S. M., (Eds.), *Behavioral health: A handbook of health enhancement and disease prevention.* (pp. 230–247). New York: Wiley.

Shoor, S. M. (1983). *Psychological contributors to outcome of chronic arthritis.* Unpublished manuscript, Stanford University, Stanford Arthritis Center, Palo Alto, CA.

Weinberg, R. S., Gould, D., & Jackson, A. (1979). Expectations and performance: An empirical test of Bandura's self-efficacy theory. *Journal of Sport Psychology, 1,* 320–331.

Weinberg, R. S., Yukelson, D., & Jackson, A. (1980). Effect of public and private efficacy expectations on competitive performance. *Journal of Sport Psychology, 2,* 340–349.

Weinberg, R. S., Gould, D., Yukelson, D., & Jackson, A. (1981). The effect of preexisting and manipulated self-efficacy on a competitive muscular endurance test. *Journal of Sport Psychology, 4,* 345–354.

INFORMATION SYNTHESIS AND META-ANALYSIS

Patricia D. Mullen and Gilbert Ramirez

Being able to say what is known (and as yet unknown) about the nature of a public health problem, the effectiveness of alternative policies and programs, and the most productive directions and methods for future studies is widely understood to be important to practitioners and researchers alike. The growing number of "annual review" volumes such as this publication attests to the need to accumulate and interpret findings from the burgeoning literature of health promotion and public health. And yet, numerous observers (Glass, 1976; Jackson, 1980; Goldschmidt, 1984; Light & Pillemer, 1984) note the low status of reviews (as compared to the conduct of new studies) and the lack of application of reliable and valid techniques for retrieving, evaluating, and integrating past research studies.

The introduction to a recent textbook on techniques for synthesizing study results entitled *Summing Up*, (Light & Pillemer, 1984, p. 2) recounts a hypothetical encounter between a graduate student and a faculty adviser in which the student has asked how a research review should be conducted.

It is easy to imagine the student being slightly embarrassed to ask these questions, and the adviser feeling mild annoyance. Reviewing the literature is something a com-

Advances in Health Education and Promotion, vol. 2, pages 201–239
Copyright © 1987 JAI Press Inc.
All rights of reproduction in any form reserved.
ISBN: 0-89232-617-4

petent young scholar should know how to do.... Go to the library. Use the social science abstracts. Thumb through current journals. Identify relevant articles. Briefly summarize them and draw some coherent overall conclusions.

Yet if the faculty member is pressed to give explicit guidelines, her annoyance may turn to frustration. How can relevant articles be identified? Which of tens or hundreds of studies . . . should a summary present? How should conflicting findings from different studies be resolved?

Several books and papers are now available to guide syntheses. Light and Pillemer (1984), Cooper (1984), and Goldschmidt (1984) provide discussions and recommendations on steps preceding the analysis phase. Rosenthal (1984), Hunter et al. (1982), Hedges and Olkin (1985), and Wolf (1986) focus primarily on quantitative analytic techniques. (Several of these books were recently critiqued by Hedges & Olkin, in press.) Mullen and Rosenthal (1985) published a series of BASIC programs for use in quantitative syntheses. Light and Pillemer (1984) dedicate a chapter on the merits of combining "numbers and narrative," although they do not offer explicit recommendations for qualitative analysis. Entire monographs in several evaluation series are devoted to methodological articles and examples of syntheses (Light, 1983a; Yeaton & Wortman, 1984).

Syntheses using quantitative techniques have appeared in the public health literature on such topics as psycho-educational interventions with patients who are about to undergo surgical and other procedures (Mumford et al., 1982; Devine & Cook, 1983a, b), education for people afflicted by long-term chronic conditions (Posavac, 1980; Mazzuca, 1982; Mullen et al., 1985), education for patients with various medical regimens (Posavac et al., 1985), nutrition education (Levy et al., 1980; Johnson & Johnson, 1985), weight loss as a treatment for hypertension (Hovell, 1982), and programs to prevent adolescent pregnancy (Iverson & Levy, 1982). Several of these studies are summarized in a review of meta-analyses in the 1985 *Annual Review of Public Health* (Louis et al., 1985). This activity and numerous examples from the related fields of education, psychology, and epidemiology suggest a heightened interest in the review and in the application of more rigorous procedures and methods for information synthesis.

The goal of this chapter is to provide an overview of synthesis issues and methods for readers interested in improving their own "reviews of the literature" and for those with a specific interest in quantitative techniques popularly known as "meta-analysis." We begin with a review of the terms being used to describe information synthesis. To provide the larger statistical and epidemiological context for "meta-analysis," we trace the history of synthesis techniques. We then discuss the criticisms of the traditional literature review that have been offered by advocates of synthesis and meta-analytic methods, and we describe the advantages of systematic, usually quantitative, syntheses. In the last half of the chapter, we describe seven considerations in conducting a synthesis, and we highlight related issues (and give examples of syntheses that employed the various techniques).

Our focus is quantitative syntheses. We use the term "meta-analysis" to describe statistical techniques developed under that rubric as well as traditional techniques that are appropriate for synthesizing study results. Nevertheless, several of the sections below should also benefit the reader who wishes to learn more about the conduct of qualitative syntheses.

TERMINOLOGY

Writing about information synthesis is characterized by widely ranging nomenclature and a surprising lack of cross referencing among authors. An array of overlapping terms such as "meta-evaluation," "meta-analysis," and "research synthesis" used within the behavioral sciences is virtually unknown among biostatisticians who employ similar techniques to "combine or pool results across studies."

In comparing terms, it is useful to keep in mind two major dimensions: type of analytical approach and type of primary study. Analytic techniques for synthesizing study results range from the purely quantitative to the purely qualitative, although most syntheses use a combination of the two. The terms "information synthesis" (Goldschmidt, 1984) and "meta-evaluation" (Scriven, 1969; Stufflebeam, 1974) refer to such combinations or at least do not exclude one or the other type of analysis. Terms that usually refer to quantitative techniques include "meta-analysis" (Glass, 1976), "data synthesis" (Pillemer & Light, 1980), "quantitative research integration" (Walberg & Haertel, 1980), "quantitative synthesis" (Cordray & Orwin, 1983), "quantitative review" (Green & Hall, 1984), "combining results" (Rosenthal, 1978), "combining data" (Light & Smith, 1971), and "vote-counting" (Light & Smith, 1971). Similarly, "qualitative synthesis" and "qualitative review" represent integration efforts employing qualitative techniques. Reference to the "traditional review" usually implies qualitative analysis, although vote-counting techniques are often used.

Synthesis terminology varies with regard to the types of primary studies used. "Meta-evaluation" (Scriven, 1969; Stufflebeam, 1974) and "evaluation synthesis" (Chelimsky & Morra, 1984) represent the most restrictive terms, in that primary studies are limited to those conducted for purposes of evaluation. These terms have led some readers to overlook the possibility of applying synthesis techniques to correlational studies, epidemiological studies, and descriptive studies.

To summarize, the integration of findings across studies may be accomplished via qualitative and/or quantitative methods; the type of study is unrestricted. Several terms have been suggested that are consistent with the views presented in this review. We favor "information synthesis" to describe this larger enterprise. It has been defined as

> [the result of] the systematic gathering of research findings on a defined topic for use by a specific audience for a given purpose; the systematic assessment of their validity; and the presentation of valid findings in a form useful to the intended audience, including a discussion of critical information gaps that should be the subject of subsequent research (Goldschmidt, 1984, p. 2).

(We take the reference to specificity of audience and purpose to mean simply that the questions or hypotheses being addressed should be clear.) Synonymous terms are "research integration" (Walberg & Haertel, 1980), "integrative research review" (Cooper, 1984) and "research synthesis" (Light & Pillemer, 1984).

We use the term meta-analysis to refer to the subset of syntheses that emphasizes quantitative methods. As stated earlier, "meta-analysis," as used by the present authors and by methodologists such as Rosenthal (1984) and Hedges and Olkin (1985), includes all appropriate quantitative techniques for combining studies and not just to those associated with the metaanalytic approach of Glass et al. (1981).

HISTORY

Synthesizing information from independent studies has a long history. One of the earliest examples is a paper entitled "Equality of Males and Females" by the physician John Arbuthnot in 1710 (cited by Pearson, 1978). Arbuthnot's intent was to demonstrate that sex ratio at birth was not the "Effect of Chance but Divine Providence working for a good end." To accomplish his objective, Arbuthnot synthesized christening data in London for the previous 82 years, using the binomial. Much later, Fisher (1916) and Gosset (1914) in consultation with Pearson (1914, cited in Fisher, 1916) also suggested that data from independent studies could be combined. Fisher (1921) and Cochran (1937) applied the concept to the practical needs of agricultural research, where data were synthesized not only over several years but also over research centers and agricultural plots. Agricultural studies were logical candidates for early syntheses owing to the homogeneity of study conditions, research methods, and outcome measures.

We view the evolution of information synthesis in the context of three distinct, although chronologically overlapping eras. The first era, as implied above, is characterized by the developing of basic statistical methods with application in the context of homogeneous samples (agricultural plots). Contributors in this era were Tippett (1931), Fisher (1932), Pearson (1933), and Cochran (1937), Yates (Yates & Cochran, 1938), and Snedecor (1946). At least one application of quantitative methods of synthesis in educational psychology appeared during this period (Thorndike, 1933). (Rosenthal, 1984, and Hedges & Olkin, 1985, present in greater detail the contributions of several of the statisticians mentioned above.) Hedges and Olkin (1985) note two distinct subthemes in early synthesis methods: (1) concern for omnibus or nonparametric tests, and (2) concern for testing magnitude of effect. The sophistication of methods employed during this era did not progress beyond testing to assure that the study findings all represented the same underlying population of findings (homogeneity testing). Multivariate techniques were not relevant, given the characteristics of agricultural experiments with virtually identical measures and designs.

During the first era, the concept of information synthesis was also employed in epidemiology. The simplest form of epidemiological synthesis involves methods for combining information across strata (of multiple fourfold tables) resulting in a summary measure of effect. Summarization across age strata, for example, is concerned not only with how to arrive at a summary measure, but also with whether or not the data should be summarized. This latter concern is the objective of homogeneity testing. The Cochran-Mantel-Haenszel procedure (Fleiss, 1981) is the principal technique for combining data across strata and for testing homogeneity of strata. This method has also been extended to the combination of data from multiple epidemiological studies, each study represented as data in a fourfold table. (These procedures will be elaborated in more detail in a later section.)

In the second era, primarily within the field of education, Scriven (1969), Stufflebeam (1974, 1979), Cook and Gruder (1978), and Glass (1976) contributed to the conceptualization and popularity of meta-evaluation and meta-analysis as approaches to inquiry. Glass (1976; Glass et al., 1981) and colleagues alone specify methods for meta-analysis, although they draw explicitly from the statistical contributions of the first era.

We note the work of Glass (1976) and Rosenthal (1963, 1964 cited in Rosenthal, 1984) during the second era. Testing magnitude of effect was popularized by Glass (1976) when he coined the term "meta-analysis." Rosenthal (1963, 1964 cited in Rosenthal, 1984) and Glass (1976) addressed the analysis of factors associated with variations in effect size estimates, using conventional statistical procedures (t-tests, analysis of variance, multiple regression analysis). This suggested the importance of examining the impact of other study characteristics on study findings.

Glass and Rosenthal sparked a resurgence of interest by social scientists in synthesis methods. Of even greater importance, however, is the criticism that emerged during this period, criticism that ultimately launched information synthesis into the current, or third era. Criticism of meta-analysis by statisticians centered on the use of conventional statistical methods for the analysis of effect size estimates. Another group of statisticians, those primarily associated with the fields of education and psychology, have applied statistical theory to meta-analysis (Rosenthal & Rubin, 1982; Hedges, 1984; Hedges & Olkin, 1985). Most importantly, during this current era, Hedges (1984; Hedges & Olkin, 1985) developed analogues to analysis of variance and multiple regression. Hedges and Olkin's treatise (1985) on statistical methods for meta-analysis is the most complete to date.

WEAKNESSES OF TRADITIONAL REVIEWS

Several criticisms of traditional narrative reviews have been advanced by advocates of "new," usually quantitative, syntheses (Cooper & Rosenthal, 1980; Jackson, 1980; Glass et al., 1981). Critics charge that conventional reviews are highly subject to the biases of the particular reviewer, fail to report methods of locating and selecting primary studies, neglect large amounts of information contained in primary research reports, imprecisely weight their conclusions with respect to the data from the primary studies, and often fail to detect statistical interactions.

Cook and Leviton (1980) argue that these criticisms are merely reflective of poor practices and not the broad type of synthesis. We concur. Each of the considerations discussed below is germane to qualitative and quantitative syntheses.

One valid criticism of narrative reviews is their frequent reliance on tests of significance in a procedure that has been dubbed "vote-counting" (Light & Smith, 1971). This familiar method of integrating studies involves assigning a positive, negative, or nonsignificant label to each of the relationships measured in the primary studies and tallying the number in each category. If a plurality falls into any one of these categories, the modal category is assumed to represent the best estimate of the true relationship between the variables under study. At least one synthesis in the health education and promotion literature has employed a variation of vote-counting, the "significance ratio," in which the number of studies with significant (and positive) results was divided by the total number of studies reporting significance levels (Janz & Becker, 1984).

The major problem with vote-counting (whatever the cutoff criterion) is that it disregards sample size (Light & Smith, 1971; Rosenthal, 1984; Hedges & Olkin 1985), and statistical significance is, of course, a function of both sample size and effect size. Consider a study where the effect size is constant and the sample size is allowed to increase. The algebraic manipulation of the t-test equation below highlights the direct relationship between sample size and level of significance, that is, holding effect size constant, increasing sample size will increase the level of significance (Rosenthal, 1984).

$$t = (X_E - X_C)/S_X,$$
$$\text{where } X_E = \text{experimental group mean}$$
$$X_C = \text{control group mean}$$
$$S_X = \text{standard error of the mean difference}$$
$$= (2S^2/n)^{.5}$$
$$\text{and } S^2 = \text{a pooled variance}$$
$$t = (X_E - X_C)/(2S^2/n)^{.5}$$
$$t = (X_E - X_C)/S[(2/n)^{.5}]$$
$$t = (X_E - X_C)/S \times (n/2)^{.5}$$
$$t = \text{effect size} \times \text{function of sample size.}$$

Studies with large sample sizes are more likely to produce statistically significant results than are those with small sample sizes. This problem can occur when, for example, nine of ten studies to be integrated have small sample sizes and report nonsignificant results, and when the tenth study has a large sample size and a significant result (Glass et al., 1981). Using the vote-counting method, we would conclude that there is no relationship between the variables of interest, whereas the true situation might be inadequate power in the nine small studies to detect a significant difference. Conversely, the plurality of studies can demonstrate statistical significance as a result of large sample sizes but not the practical significance of the effect under examination. Cook and Leviton (1980) express the hope that all reviewers will show greater sensitivity to the problems of significance tests just mentioned, and they point out examples of qualitative syntheses that avoid relying on significance tests in favor of effect sizes. Investigators conducting reviews should at least make a practice of estimating the sample sizes necessary to detect an effect and commenting on the relationship of the sample sizes of the primary studies to that estimate (e.g., Windsor & Orleans, 1986).

Another fallacy of conventional vote-counting is that it may more often lead to an incorrect conclusion as the number of studies increases (Hedges & Olkin, 1980; Glass et al., 1981; Hedges & Olkin, 1985). Hedges and Olkin (1980, 1985) present a detailed statistical explanation of how this occurs. Basically, it involves the average power of the studies to detect a nonzero effect. When the average power is less than the preset cutoff criterion, the probability that a vote-count results in a correct conclusion tends toward zero as the number of studies increases. This phenomenon occurs particularly when effect sizes are moderate to small (less than 0.5), which is typical of the social sciences research (Light & Pillemer, 1984).

Two widely cited critiques of vote-counting (Light & Smith, 1971; Glass et al., 1981) introduce data pooling techniques as improvements over vote-counting. And yet, pooling data across independent studies is not a preferred synthesis technique. Recommended methods for representing study results, including an improved technique for vote-counting, are presented below.

SOME ADVANTAGES OF SYNTHESES

In the debate over methods for combining the results of completed studies, the synthesis enterprise itself has received increased attention. Advocates of synthesis point to contributions to knowledge made by syntheses over individual studies. Light (1984) delineates several research tasks or questions resolved better by synthesis than by a single study, highlighting the usefulness of syntheses in identifying the specificity of effects, that is, when a social, medical or educational program works, not just whether it works on average. In single studies, it is expensive to plan to study interaction and risky to do so later. Syntheses, with several independent investigators and variation in constructs, methods, settings, time, and population, are often better suited to expose interactions.

Treatment-type and recipient-type interaction is one concern addressed by syntheses. Light (1984) cites the large and influential Westinghouse Head Start study conducted in the late 1960s as an example of failure to detect such an interaction in a single study. The Westinghouse researchers found little effect for the one-year Head Start Program. Indeed, a synthesis of early childhood education programs (Bissell, 1970 cited in Light, 1984) found small main effects. Instead, Bissell found a significant interaction of program and participant type. Directive, highly structured preschool programs tended to be more effective with the more disadvantaged poor children whereas nondirective, less structured programs tended to be more effective with less disadvantaged poor children. Most of the programs studied by Westinghouse had open and permissive styles, with comparatively little formal cognitive work.

Synthesis is better suited to explain which features of a treatment matter most, because the components of the treatment are likely to vary over several studies, thereby offering a better opportunity for assessing their impact. A synthesis of information and education programs for patients with chronic conditions being treated with drugs (Mullen et al., 1985) found no significant difference among seven major types of educational approaches (e.g., one-to-one education, group education, and written and other audio-visual materials) in terms of their effects on adherence to the regimen. A multivariate analysis of the influence of study and intervention characteristics on effect size estimates, however, produced a well-specified equation that accounted for 84 percent of the variance in study findings. The best-fitting variable was rating of educational quality. The five major components of this rating scale were reinforcement, feedback, individualization, facilitation, and relevance. Thus the results of this synthesis are suggestive of specific qualities of educational interventions that promote adherence.

Syntheses can help explain conflicting results from primary studies. Light and Pillemer (1984, p. 159) refer to the "myth of the single decisive study," which claims that despite dozens of past research efforts with disparate findings, just one new "really good" study would settle the issue. Light and Pillemer (1984) believe the evidence supports the opposite conclusion, and diversity among studies provides an interpretive context not available in any one study. An example is found in Raudenbush's (1983) synthesis of teacher-expectancy studies that helped to resolve more than a decade of controversy beginning in 1968 with the publication of *Pygmalion in the Classroom* (Rosenthal & Jacobson, 1968). The "Pygmalion study" had sparked both controversy and hundreds of research studies with its conclusion that children's rates of intellectual growth depend in part on the rates their teachers expect them to grow. Raudenbush (1983) scrutinized the original study, critiques, replications, and other reviews to develop hypotheses for the synthesis, including one pertaining to the timing of the expectancy induction. He reasoned that if teachers were given the expectancy-inducing information after they knew the students well, the information may be unpersuasive. He found an overall .49 negative correlation between prior contact and I.Q. effects, and this relationship was independent of numerous potential confounding variables. Timing of teacher "treatment" was thus advanced to explain the conflicting findings.

A fourth advantage presented by Light (1984) is the ability of syntheses to determine the importance of intermediate outcomes in achieving a social and health impact. Does, for example, the child know how to count better, and does the child who knows how to count better get higher marks in school? In health promotion, a likely pair would be adherence to a therapeutic regimen for hypertension and blood pressure control. Light contends that a well-conducted synthesis would look at the primary studies in both ways. That is, it could examine the correlation across study sites between the percentage of people adhering to the regimen and the percentage under control.

Synthesis alone, however, cannot establish a causal linkage, as in the above example, between adherence and blood pressure control unless the primary analyses examined these relationships. Did the patient who adheres to the therapeutic regimen also achieve better blood pressure control? Correlations based on data from individuals are required to answer this question. If available, these correlations could then be integrated across the studies. If the primary studies do not report such correlations (and the raw data cannot be obtained), it would be unwise to correlate the summary measures (mean adherence score and mean blood pressure reading) across the studies to estimate the relationships for individuals.

Syntheses can assess the importance of research design and measurement approaches, and several syntheses have investigated these interactions. Although there is widespread belief that stronger designs find smaller effects, the evidence appears to be mixed. A casual search found syntheses showing an effect for design (Smith & Glass, 1980; Hoaglin et al., 1982; Hovell, 1982; White, 1982; Wortman & Yeaton, 1983) as well as those that did not (Glass, 1978; Mazzuca, 1982; Devine & Cook, 1983a; Stock et al., 1983; Mullen et al., 1985). The magnitude of difference can be substantial, as, for example, an estimate of the sample statistic (mean mortality data) of 4.4 (SD = 5.5) for randomized controlled trials vs. 13.8 (SD = 16.9) for quasi-experiments in a study of coronary artery bypass graft surgery (Wortman & Yeaton, 1983). The indices of methodological quality and categories of design varied greatly within the studies cited above, and it would be prudent to analyze the studies for possible effects of design if the range of acceptable studies is great. Other hypotheses have also been advanced to explain a design effect in health education studies. Green (1977) notes that strong interventions, such as community health education projects, are not readily susceptible to random assignment and that strong designs may ironically be associated with weaker interventions.

Measures also can make a difference. Mullen et al. (1985) found that less objective measures of adherence to prescription drug regimens showed larger effects for patient education than did more objective measures such as physiologic tests for presence of the drug. In a synthesis of studies of socioeconomic status and school achievement, White (1982) found that as the number of items in the measure of SES increases, indicating increased reliability due to more adequate sampling of the SES construct, the magnitude of the correlations increased. It is not uncommon, however, to assess the validity of less objective measures within studies, and the attenuation problem also could have been observed in a single study.

The last advantage pointed out by Light (1984) is that syntheses can better assess the stability of treatment effectiveness in light of varying approaches to the implementation of study constructs, settings, methods, populations, and the like. This is the other side of the interaction coin. Donaldson and Billy (1984) synthesized studies of the impact of prenatal visits on birth weight in an international data set from six countries at varying stages of development. Data from women having single births and whose pregnancies went to term indicate that a dose-response relationship of number of prenatal visits with birth weight for term babies persists even when the analysis takes into account numerous variables known to influence birth weight and the variations in setting and population represented by the six countries.

An advantage of syntheses noted by several methodologists (e.g., Fisher, 1932; Glass et al., 1981; Rosenthal, 1984) is the possibility of detecting small but persistent effects in studies with low power (small *n*'s). Fisher argued

> When a number of quite independent tests of significance have been made, it sometimes happens that although few or none can be claimed individually as significant, yet the aggregate gives an impression that the probabilities are on the whole lower than would often have been obtained by chance. It is sometimes desired, taking account only of these probabilities, and not of the detailed composition of the data from which they are derived, which may be of very different kinds, to obtain a single test of the significance of the aggregate, based on the product of the probabilities individually observed.

Collins and Langman (1985) synthesized 27 small randomized controlled trials of the effect of histamine (H_2) antagonists in treating acute upper gastrointestinal hemorrhage. No single study provided reliable evidence of a benefit for the important end points of surgery and death, and, in fact, only one study produced conventionally significant results. Collins and Langman found a protective effect of H_2 antagonists for the end points of surgery and death when data were examined for bleeding from all sites.

The example just cited suggested to us another advantage of synthesis. This is that syntheses can shed light on the consistency of relationships observed in individual studies where multiple tests were conducted, and where there is an increased probability of finding a significant relationship by chance alone (Type I errors). We believe, therefore, that Collins and Langman are overly cautious in their interpretation of the site-specific synthesis results when they state that the data for these analyses resulted from dredging for significant results on the part of the primary studies. Our position is supported by Mantel & Haenszel (1959, p. 724) who point out that the problem of multiple comparisons

> does not exist when several retrospective and other type studies are at hand, since the inferences will be based on a collation of evidence, the degree of agreement and reproducibility among studies, and their consistency with other types of available evidence, and not on the findings of a single study.

CONSIDERATIONS IN CONDUCTING A SYNTHESIS

Generic considerations in conducting a synthesis (see numbered list, below) and the methods and research bearing on each of them are discussed below together with examples from syntheses conducted with health education and promotion literature.

Considerations in Conducting a Synthesis
1. Formulating synthesis questions,
2. Determining selection criteria for studies,
3. Assembling relevant and acceptable studies,
4. Coding primary studies for methodologic and other characteristics,
5. Representing study outcomes with an appropriate metric,
6. Integrating the findings of primary studies, and
7. Analyzing between-group differences and the influence of study characteristics on outcomes.

Formulating Synthesis Question(s)

As with other research studies, syntheses and reviews are best organized to answer specific questions. Cooper (1984) used another research term for this step—formulation of the problem. Several authors have pointed out the widespread absence of well-defined questions (or problem statements) in reviews (Waxman & Walberg, 1982; Goldschmidt, 1984; Light & Pillemer, 1984). Prime types of questions for syntheses are

- What is the average effect of the treatment across studies?
- Where and with whom is the treatment effective (ineffective)?
- Will it work here?
- What is the norm for the occurrence of a condition or characteristic?
- What is the relationship of a condition or characteristic to another variable on average?
- Does the relationship vary with specific populations and settings?

The first three questions were delineated by Light and Pillemer (1984), together with examples of syntheses organized to answer each of them. Traditional reviews often address questions about average effects or relationships, "Does patient education improve adherence to therapeutic regimens?" at the risk of obscuring important interactions. As pointed out above in the discussion of advantages of synthesis, however, the interaction questions are also well-suited to syntheses.

Only one example could be found of a synthesis that addressed a question regarding norms (Lehman & Zastowny, 1983). In this case, the specific topic was average norms for patient satisfaction with mental health services and the differential norms for various groups of patients. Examples of syntheses organized around correlational studies are provided by Cooper and his colleagues on locus of control and academic achievement (Findley & Cooper, 1983) and social-class and ethnic-group differences in achievement motivation (Cooper & Tom, 1984). Other examples of well-specified questions or hypotheses are contained in syntheses by the U.S. Government Accounting Office (1983), Raudenbush (1983), Stock et al. (1983), Devine and Cook (1983a, b), and the National Institutes of Health (1984).

Determining Selection Criteria for Studies

Replicable methods imply precise selection criteria for studies to be included in a synthesis. The problem of fuzzy criteria is illustrated in examples such as those cited by Waxman and Walberg (1982, p. 587), "We have summarized the studies we could locate on the relation between . . . " Several authors have addressed the selection issue (Bryant & Wortman, 1984; Cooper, 1984; Haynes et al., 1984; Light & Pillemer, 1984), but perhaps the clearest and most useful approach to developing selection criteria is presented by Bryant and Wortman (1984) in their case study of a synthesis of the impact of school integration on the achievement of minority children. These investigators use Cook and Campbell's (1979) typology of validity to conceptualize criteria of relevance and acceptability.

Criteria of Relevance

The first task is to decide which studies are relevant to the questions or hypotheses being investigated. This may be viewed as a function of construct and external validity, where construct validity is concerned with the degree to which treatment and outcome measures accurately represent underlying constructs and external validity is concerned with the degree to which the settings, populations, or time periods involved in a particular study are relevant to the problem being examined in the synthesis.

In a synthesis by Mullen and Green (1984; Mullen et al., 1985), for example, it was necessary to define "patient drug information and education." Should special pill containers or calendar reminders be considered information? In this case, a broad definition was selected, and specific qualities of patient education interventions were coded and analyzed. It was also necessary to decide what outcomes would best represent the impact of patient information and education. Although knowledge, beliefs and attitudes, intentions, behavior, and clinical outcomes are typical measures for such studies, only knowledge, behavior and clinical outcomes (as indirect indicators of behavior in the absence of direct indicators and as indicators of multiple behavioral changes) were selected. Attitudes were deemed to represent too many constructs and, on the whole, to be poorly measured. Behavior was accepted, whether it was measured by self-report alone, or via pill counts, or via tracer substances. The measurement techniques were coded and analyzed for any tendency for less objective measures to inflate estimates of study effects (they did). Effects of patient education on knowledge and on behavior were assessed separately, because they do not represent the same construct.

Mazzuca (1982), on the other hand, accepted only studies measuring behavior, physiologic progress, and/or long-range health outcome. He then looked at the differential effects of two broad classes of patient education (counseling vs. behavior modification) on types of study outcomes.

Bryant and Wortman (1984) included studies with standardized tests of math, reading, or general achievement to measure student achievement and excluded studies that used only I.Q. scores, grade-point averages, and unstandardized tests. In each of the last three examples, the investigators retained a certain amount of breadth within constructs, but they wisely avoided the admixture of constructs that frequently characterizes meta-analyses conducted during the second era (e.g., Posavac, 1980).

Restricting studies on the basis of external validity is especially important for syntheses that ask the question, "Will the program work here?" External validity is, however, a question that might be investigated in syntheses that are searching for average effects. Devine and Cook (1983a, b) conducted a synthesis of the impact on length of hospital stay of psychoeducational interventions with patients about to undergo surgery and other procedures. They noted that another synthesis conducted concurrently, but published earlier (Mumford et al., 1982), had not looked for trends over time, even though several of the older primary studies registered much longer lengths of stay in the control groups than more recent studies. Devine and Cook (1983a, b) tested the hypothesis that smaller effects have been observed in more recent studies, because of the overall decrease in length of stay over time (the hypothesis was confirmed, although the number of recent studies was small).

Criteria of Acceptability

Once studies have been screened for their relevance, the next question is whether they are acceptable. Acceptability is a function of statistical conclusion validity and internal validity, where statistical conclusion validity is concerned with the degree to which valid inferences can be drawn from the statistical analyses performed in a particular study and internal validity is concerned with the degree to which valid causal inferences can be drawn from the design. Although authors writing on this subject agree on the importance of resisting any temptation to believe that all information is equally valid, the degree of restriction based on methodological considerations is a matter of debate. Although Glass (1978, p. 3) has declared that "It's bad advice to eliminate virtually any studies on strictly methodological grounds;" other authors have eliminated from consideration all but randomized controlled studies (Mazzuca, 1982; Haynes et al., 1984; Collins & Langman, 1985).

The answer depends, in part, on the literature in a given substantive or theoretical area, and in part, on the procedures for coding and analysis that are to be used. The estimated degree of the potential bias is another important consideration. Criteria of acceptability present particularly difficult issues, in light of the uneven quality of the research in public health (e.g., Shadish, 1982), conflicting evidence regarding the effect of design on study findings (see above), and the possibility—at least in health education and promotion—that more rigorous designs have been applied to weaker interventions (Green, 1977).

The issue of statistical conclusion validity is largely a question of whether to eliminate studies with insufficient data on which to calculate estimates of effect sizes. Bryant and Wortman (1984) have recommended eliminating studies without sufficient information for calculating an effect size on the grounds that requests to the investigators for additional data are unlikely to be successful. Several syntheses have even eliminated studies that had insufficient data for a specific effect size calculation (e.g., Mumford et al., 1982; Levy et al., 1980, which used standardized mean differences). Although some authors express pessimism about obtaining additional data from primary study investigators (Bryant & Wortman, 1984), at least one report of such correspondence found a good return (12 out of 15) (Mullen et al., 1985).

Evidence that methodological qualities of studies create biases in estimating effect sizes is reasonably compelling, as was discussed earlier. Some syntheses report separately the results of subgroups of studies (for example, according to the strength of their measures or whether randomization or matching was employed in the design) (Smith & Glass, 1980; Mazzuca, 1982; Devine & Cook, 1983a, b; Wortman & Yeaton, 1983). Others use multivariate analyses to assess the influence of design characteristics (Smith & Glass, 1980; Mullen et al., 1985).

Effects of Using Criteria of Relevance and Acceptability

In any review, a great many studies must be retrieved to extract relevant and acceptable material. The gross numbers and exact citations of discarded studies are rarely documented, however. This was done in Bryant and Wortman's (1984) synthesis of desegregation studies, with the following results: 71 percent of the studies they retrieved were deemed relevant, and only 28 percent of these (20 percent of all retrieved studies) met their criteria of acceptability. In another example, Mazzuca (1982) identified approximately 320 articles in his preliminary literature searches (he does not give the number actually retrieved), and determined that 63 articles were relevant and of these, 30 were acceptable. In one literature search, Shadish (1982) determined that none of the 38 relevant studies of preventive services that he inspected closely (from the 150 retrieved) was acceptable!

Because the searching process, particularly one that makes use of automated databases, yields many irrelevant and unacceptable citations, Goldschmidt (1984) recommends titrating false negatives and false positives and reporting the proportion of relevant and acceptable studies from a sample of studies that were not retrieved initially (false negatives) in addition to reporting the proportion of irrelevant studies among those that were retrieved (false positives).

Assembling Relevant and Acceptable Studies

Selection bias and efficiency in various citation bases and publication bias constitute major issues in assembling studies (Glass et al., 1981; Goldschmidt, 1984; Light & Pillemer, 1984). Manual searches, automated data bases, "pearling" and other methods based on citations taken from other studies and reviews of the literature, and panels of experts are all discussed in the references cited above. The usefulness of a given strategy always depends on the objectives of the synthesis and the subject matter. Health education and promotion topics often present special problems, because the literature is produced in disparate disciplines and is consequently indexed in separate (and not necessarily overlapping) databases. Several guides can acquaint novice searchers with the automated databases and with methods for searching them (Gilreath, 1984; Hansen, 1984). Recording the marginal return for each data base (e.g., Glass et al., 1981) is helpful to other investigators. Given a large number of potentially relevant and acceptable studies and limited resources, sampling strategies may need to be developed. Alternative approaches are weighed by Light and Pillemer (1984.)

One alternative for conserving search resources is selecting only published studies, but mounting evidence suggests that there is indeed a selection bias favoring significant, positive results in journals (Greenwald, 1975, cited in Light & Pillemer, 1984; Smith et al., 1980; Smith & Glass, 1980; White, 1982; Devine and Cook, 1983a). In their synthesis of psychotherapy studies, for example, Smith et al. (1980) compared published and unpublished studies. Dissertations found lower effects on average than published studies, although the relatively few unpublished papers found larger effects. Devine and Cook (1983a) found only a small difference between dissertations or theses and published studies, but smaller effects were found in the unpublished works.

"Fail-safe" numbers have been developed to estimate the number of new or unretrieved studies averaging null results that would be required to "undo" the results of a meta-analysis (Rosenthal, 1979). Fail-safe numbers are estimated based on the values obtained from the studies that were retrieved. Thus, if the retrieved studies do not represent the population of studies relevant to the synthesis, then the fail-safe number should be viewed with particular caution. Rosenthal's formula is based on the z scores from the individual studies. Another formula, based on average effect size estimate from the individual studies and using an effect size criterion rather than a probability criterion such as $p = .05$ is given by Orwin (1983 cited in Wolf, 1986). Olkin (personal communication, May 1986) is at work on an alternative fail-safe n. Interpretation of the strength of study results is best done using confidence intervals and significance testing, however (see below).

Coding Studies for Methodologic and Other Characteristics

Coding schema are often employed in tabular presentation of studies. Studies typically are classified according to population, design, measure, and nature of the exposure or intervention. One methodologic coding scheme developed by Sackett and Haynes (1976) for patient education studies encompasses components of internal and external validity and measurement quality, and it has been used in several reviews and syntheses (Haynes et al., 1979; Mullen et al., 1985; Windsor & Orleans, 1986). Hovell (1982) presented rating criteria for study methods and for blood pressure and weight measures. The U.S. Preventive Services Task Force is using a rating scheme based on one employed earlier by the Canadian Task Force on Periodic Health Examination (1979) to assess the quality of evidence from various studies (Mickalide, 1985).

Smith et al. (1980) developed rating systems for study design and measures, client characteristics, and types of psychotherapeutic interventions. A scoring scheme for educational interventions developed by Mullen & Green (1984; Mullen et al., 1985) based on earlier work (Neufeld, 1976) showed good predictive validity for knowledge and behavioral outcomes of studies of patient education and information for prescription drugs.

The elegance of rating schema often exceeds the availability of information reported in the primary studies. It is sometimes difficult to ascertain from study methods, as for example, whether randomization was compromised by differential attrition from study and control groups or whether study measures possess certain psychometric characteristics. It is often difficult to ascertain qualities of educational interventions. In patient education studies it may be impossible to discern not only critical qualities of the interaction but also the duration and frequency of contact (Green et al., 1978; Mullen & Green, 1984; Mullen et al., 1985). One important characteristic of Sackett and Haynes' (1976) coding scheme, therefore, is that it encompasses the problem of missing information in the scores related to external validity. An example of the codes for the specification of the illness or condition in patient education studies is presented below (Sackett & Haynes, 1976, p. 195):

Points

3 = replicable diagnostic criteria stated with inclusion/exclusion criteria;

2 = diagnostic criteria stated;

1 = diagnoses only;

0 = no diagnoses or where diagnosis can only be inferred (e.g., visiting the dentist);

1 bonus = for all categories—if a comorbidity is described.

Whatever the coding schema that are applied, it is important to assure the reliability of their application, through rater training and monitoring and assessment of interrater reliability.

Representing Study Outcomes with a Common Metric

Direction of Effect

Traditional vote-counting techniques are not recommended for syntheses because of the relationship between statistical significance and sample size. One way to avoid the influence of sample size and to take advantage of the simplicity offered by vote-counting procedures is to represent each study by its direction of effect (positive or negative) rather than whether or not it has reached statistical significance. The studies can then be synthesized either by simple tally or by testing the null hypothesis that the proportion of studies demonstrating a positive (or negative) direction of effect is equal to one-half. For example, consider the following group of studies:

	Difference		
	+	−	*Total*
Number of Studies	27	13	40

From a tally, the majority of studies demonstrate a positive effect. The statistical significance of this observation is shown below, using a sign test corrected for continuity (Snedecor & Cochran, 1980):

$$Z_C = (|2r - n| - 1)/(n)^{.5}$$

where r = the number of studies with a positive effect, and
n = the total number of studies.

$$Z_C = (|(2)(27) - 40| - 1)/(40)^{.5} = 2.06.$$

From a table of normal distribution, Z_C (2.06) is equal to a p-value of .04 (two-tailed test). The sign test is easy to use and although it does not provide an estimate of magnitude of effect, it can be very useful in a preliminary analysis where the number of primary studies is moderate to large.

Effect Size

Definition of Effect Size.   Effect size, the summary statistic employed in meta-analysis, has been defined as an estimate of the magnitude of the relationship between two variables (Rosenthal, 1984). It has been popularized as a standardized mean difference by Glass (1976) and Rosenthal (1978) who described it as "Cohen's d." In principle, the relationship is not restricted to standardized mean differences but may also be based on other types of data and study types, including descriptive and correlational studies. "Effect magnitude" has been introduced as a more inclusive term (Hedges & Olkin, 1985). As described by Cohen (1962), however, the term "effect size" refers to all magnitude of effect measures, and it is used in the present discussion.

Methods for Estimating Effect Sizes

Standardized Mean Difference.   Effect sizes may be estimated as the standardized mean difference that is expressed by the following formula as the difference between the mean scores of the experimental and control groups divided by the standard deviation of the control group.

$$ES = (X_E - X_C)/SD_C.$$

The following example traces the computational steps for one of the studies included in the meta-analysis by Mullen et al. (1985). The study measured the effect of group discussions on mothers of children with seizure disorders in terms of the mothers' knowledge of the medication regimen and their adherence to it over an 11-week period (Shope, 1980). The post-test means of the knowledge test for the experimental and control groups were 9.2 and 7.4, respectively. The standard deviation of the control group at post-test was 3.06. The *ES* value is estimated as

$ES = (9.2 - 7.4) / 3.06$
$= 0.59$ (standard deviation units).

(The interpretation of effect size estimates is discussed below.)

There has been debate about the appropriate divisor in the preceding formula. Glass et al. (1981) recommend using the standard deviation of the control group for situations with multiple experimental groups, and they make no recommendation for studies with a single experimental group. More recent thought on this subject suggests that the pooled standard deviation has desirable statistical properties such as small sampling error (Hedges, 1984; Rosenthal, 1984). Also, a pooled standard deviation is often all that is available when effect sizes must be estimated from test statistics. The control-group standard deviation is preferred, however, when the within-group variances differ because the variance of the experimental group may have been affected by the treatment (Glass, 1981; Hedges, 1984; Rosenthal, 1984).

As previously stated, effect size estimates are often derived from test statistics. When the result of a study is reported as a t statistic, effect size may be estimated using the following relationship:

$$ES = t\,[(1/N_E) + (1/N_C)]^{.5},$$

where $t = t$ statistic, $N_E = $ sample size of experimental group, and $N_C = $ sample size of control group. For example, suppose a t statistic of 3.52 is reported for a comparison where the sample sizes of the experimental and control groups are 25 and 30, respectively. The estimate of effect size using the above formula is

$$ES = 3.52\,[(1/25) + (1/30)]^{.5} = 0.95.$$

This and other formulae for estimating effect sizes from statistical tests are provided by Glass et al. (1981) and Rosenthal (1984).

Correlations.   Cohen (1977) suggests using as an estimate of effect size, the difference between two correlation coefficients. The primary estimate of effect size in the text by Rosenthal (1984) is based on the correlation coefficient; this publication is an excellent reference for syntheses of studies that report correlation coefficients. The product-moment correlation coefficient is also discussed by Hedges & Olkin (1985) as a scale-free index of effect magnitude. They point out, however, that with small sample sizes, the correlation coefficient tends to underestimate the absolute magnitude of the population correlation. An unbiased estimate of the population correlation for such cases is given as $G(r)$, where

$$G(r) = r + [r(1 - r^2) / 2\,(n - 3)] \text{ (p. 225)}.$$

From the table below, it is evident that the bias is more pronounced as sample size decreases.

	G(r)		
	n = 5	*n = 10*	*n = 50*
r = .2	.248	.214	.202
r = .5	.594	.527	.504

Proportions. Researchers often report study findings as proportionate data, e.g., the proportion of patients whose blood pressure is under control, the proportion of people with a disease. When synthesizing proportionate data, an important consideration is the existence of an underlying metric. In the case of blood pressure there is an underlying metric, and the researcher could have reported mean blood pressure readings. Instead, a value (C_x) has been prescribed to delineate success and failure. In the disease example, however, no underlying metric exists. Synthesis of truly nominal data is presented below in the context of an epidemiological model.

When integrating studies based on an underlying metric, it is possible to include studies that report proportionate data. One method for estimating effect sizes from proportionate data is probit transformation (Glass et al., 1981) where the estimation of effect size is calculated as

$$ES = PB_C - PB_E,$$

where PB_C = the probit equivalent of the proportion of control subjects not achieving success, and, PB_E = the probit equivalent of the proportion of experimental subjects not achieving success. The probit is simply the normal equivalent deviate of a proportion increased by 5 (Finney, 1971). Finney has facilitated probit transformation by providing an extensive table of probit-proportion equivalents.

Glass et al. (1981) have shown that effect size estimates based on a probit transformation are equal to estimates based on the standardized mean differences when the underlying probability distribution is normal. Suppose the experimental and control groups have mean outcome scores of 13.7 and 6.7, respectively, with standard deviations equal to 7.5 (assumption of homogeneous variance). The effect size estimate as a standardized mean difference is expressed as

$$ES = (13.7 - 6.7)/7.5 = 0.93.$$

A probit is a function of the area under the standard normal curve. This area corresponds to the proportion of subjects not achieving successes, and is expressed as the probability of a value less than Z, where

$Z_E = [(C_X - X_E)/ SD_X]$ and
$Z_C = [(C_X - X_C)/SD_X]$,

where C_X is an assumed cutoff point, below which subjects are judged not to have achieved success.

For $C_X = 5$, $X_E = 13.7$, $X_C = 6.7$, and $SD_X = 7.5$, the following are obtained:

$Z_E = [(5 - 13.7)/7.5] = -1.16$
$Z_C = [(5 - 6.7)/7.5] = -0.23$.

The probability of a value less than Z may be found in a table of the cumulative normal distribution. This probability p is the area under the standard normal curve from minus infinity to Z.

For $Z_E = -1.16$, $p_E = .123$
     $Z_C = -0.23$, $p_C = .409$.

Therefore, the corresponding probit equivalents for P_E and P_C are 3.8399 and 4.7699, respectively (Finney, 1977). The estimate of effect size is then calculated as

$ES = PB_C - PB_E$
   $= 4.7699 - 3.8399$
   $= 0.93$,

which is identical to the estimate of effect size calculated as a standardized mean difference.

In this example, the value of the cutoff criterion C_X was known. In practice, this information is not required. The effect size can be estimated via probit transformation as long as both proportions have been reported (or can be derived) and one is assured that the same cutoff criterion was applied to both groups.

In cases where the underlying probability distribution cannot be presumed to be normal, and where the probit approach would tend to inflate the effect size estimates, it may be necessary to consider other methods of transformation. Some methods that have been suggested include an arcsin transformation (Cohen, 1977) and the logit transformation (Glass et al., 1981). Hedges and Olkin (1985) offer nonparametric estimators of effect size. Where studies report extreme proportions (0 or 1), Glass et al. (1981) recommend a Bayesian estimate of p.

Techniques for integrating studies that are closely related are found in the field of epidemiology. These techniques are of interest in that they typically involve proportionate data, and the underlying probability distribution is frequently not normal. Several techniques have been suggested

(Fleiss, 1981) which are all based on some variation of the difference between proportions.

The technique that appears frequently in the epidemiological literature is that credited to Mantel and Haenszel (1959) (as cited in Collins & Langman, 1985; Yusuf et al., 1985). The measure of effect (or association) is a summary odds ratio, which is expressed as

$$OR = \exp (GT/VT),$$

where GT = the sum of (Observed − Expected) events, and VT = the sum of the variances of $(O - E)$.

Dichotomous data in the field of epidemiology are typically presented as a fourfold table such as

Factor A	Factor B		Total
	Present	*Absent*	
Present	A	B	n_1
Absent	C	D	n_2
Total	m_1	m_2	N

where $n_1 = A + B$; $n_2 = C + D$; $m_1 = A + C$; $m_2 = B + D$; and $N = n_1 + n_2 = m_1 + m_2$.

When A is the observed number of events that are of interest to the researcher, the expected number of events are estimated as

$$E = (n_1) (m_1)/N$$
with $VAR(O- E) = E(n_2) (1 - m_1/N)/(N - 1)$.

Consider the following example of patients diagnosed as schizophrenic by a cooperative team of psychiatrists in New York and London (Cooper et al., 1972; as cited by Fleiss, 1981).

		Diagnosis of Schizophrenia		
		Yes	*No*	*Total*
Study 1	New York	81	24	105
	London	34	71	105
	Total	115	95	210
Study 2	New York	118	74	192
	London	69	105	174
	Total	187	179	366
Study 3	New York	82	63	145
	London	52	93	145
	Total	134	156	290

From the equations provided above, the following table can be generated:

Study	O	E	$(O - E)$	$VAR\ (O - E)$
1	81	57.5	23.5	13.07
2	118	98.1	19.9	22.87
3	82	67.0	15.0	18.08
Total			58.4	54.02

The summary odds ratio across the three studies is calculated as

$$OR = \exp\ (GT/VT)$$
$$= \exp\ (58.4/54.02)$$
$$= \exp\ (1.08)$$
$$= 2.95.$$

A technique described by Fleiss (1981) that is also credited to Mantel-Haenszel is the weighted average of the separate odds ratios (the importance of weighting will be discussed in a later section) and is calculated as

$$OR = \{\Sigma\ [(n_{i1}\ n_{i2}/N_i)\ p_{i1}\ (1 - p_{i2})]\}/$$
$$\{\Sigma\ [(n_{i1}n_{i2}/N_i)\ p_{i2}\ (1 - p_{i1})]\},$$

where p_{i1} = the proportion of the first sample having the studied characteristic = A_i/n_{i1}, p_{i2} = the proportion of the second sample having the studied characteristic = C_i/n_{i2}, $N_i = n_{i1} + n_{i2}$ for studies i to g. The chi-square test for the significance of the overall degree of association is in fact based on a weighted average of the g differences between proportions, d, where

$$d = \{\Sigma\ [(n_{i1}n_{i2}/N_i)\ (p_{i1} - p_{i2})]\}/$$
$$\{\Sigma\ [n_{i1}n_{i2}/N_i]\}.$$

The weighted average of the separate odds ratios from the g studies as calculated by this approach in fact yields the same result as the Mantel-Haenszel $(O - E)$ approach, as Mantel has indicated they should (personal communication to the authors, March 1986). Using the schizophrenia data described previously, the weighted average of the separate odds ratios from the three studies is estimated based on the following table:

Study	$n_1 n_2/N$	p_1	$(1 - p_1)$	p_2	$(1 - p_2)$
1	52.5	.77	.23	.32	.68
2	91.3	.61	.39	.40	.60
3	72.5	.57	.43	.36	.64

$OR = \{[(52.5) \ (.77) \ (.68)] + [(91.3) \ (.61) \ (.6)] + [(72.5) \ (.57) \ (.64)]\} / \{[(52.5) \ (.32) \ (.23)] + [(91.3) \ (.40) \ (.39)] + [(72.5) \ (.36) \ (.43)]\}$
$= [87.3/29.3]$
$= 2.97.$

The same summary odds ratio was calculated for both procedures, with the first procedure $(O - E)$ being simpler to use. This measure of effect was also used by Donaldson and Billy (1984) differing slightly in that it was employed in a log-linear model.

"Improved Vote-Counting." Authors of primary studies often do not report effect sizes, nor do they always provide sufficient information that would allow for their reconstruction. Hedges & Olkin (1985) present an "improved vote-counting" technique that includes statistical methods for the analysis of vote-count data that provide explicit estimates of effect size parameters such as the correlation coefficient or standardized mean difference. The method is relatively simple to use when experimental and control groups have equal sample sizes, which, in most research circles, would be considered a limitation of this method. Another limitation is that it requires a relatively large number of studies to obtain accurate estimates.

Hedges' Adjustment. Hedges (1984) identifies a tendency toward overestimation of effect size, where sample sizes are small and recommends adjusting individual estimates before they are combined into an overall estimate. The adjustment procedure involves multiplying each effect size estimate by a constant (c) that is dependent upon the experimental and control-group sample sizes (n_1 and n_2, respectively) and is given by the following formula:

$$c = 1 - \{3/[4(n_1) + 4(n_2) - 9]\}.$$

This constant is almost always very close to 1, except in cases of very small sample sizes. The minimum value this constant can have is 0.57 when the experimental and control group each have a sample size of 2. The constant quickly approaches 1 when, for example, each group has a sample size equal to 7 (constant = 0.936) (Ramirez & Mullen, 1985). The adjustment factor will never exceed 1, and therefore it only penalizes those studies with very small sample sizes. Syntheses that involve only studies with large sample sizes may exclude this adjustment factor without any noticeable difference in outcome. Reporting study n's enables the reader to judge the effects of not adjusting.

Interpreting Effect Sizes.   Following Cohen (1962), several authors writing about synthesis techniques use his rules of thumb for categorizing effect size estimates (Light, 1983b): A 0.2 effect size is "small," a 0.5 effect size is "medium," and a 0.8 effect size is "large." Glass et al. (1981) and Sechrest and Yeaton (1981) all argue that use of absolute values to interpret effect sizes is inappropriate because some small effects may be important, while some large effects may be trivial, that is, the question of "clinical significance." Sechrest and Yeaton (1981) describe two ways of classifying an effect-size estimate, the "judgmental" and "normative" approaches. The judgmental approach involves assessment by an expert or experts, as for example, the method employed in the consensus development activities of the National Institutes of Health (e.g., NIH, 1984). The normative approach uses a comparative standard derived from previous studies.

Effect-size estimates can be expressed in units other than standard deviations. If an investigator can assume that the control group has a distribution of scores approximating normal, he or she can consult a standard normal table and determine the percentile rank of the average person in the treated group over the average person in the control group. Thus, a mean decrease in drug errors of 0.37 standard deviation units in studies of patient education would be interpreted as meaning that the average number of the experimental group would be better off than 64 percent of the control group. Stated differently, the person who would score at the fiftieth percentile of the control group—the expected average score—$F(c) = .50$ could expect to rise to the sixty-fourth percentile $F(z) = .64$ after receiving drug information. Thus, the calculation of percent improvement is then

$$[F(z) - F(c)]/F(c),$$

or in the example: $[0.64 - (0.50)]/(0.50) = 28\%$ (Mullen & Green, 1984). All of these methods of representing effect size estimates can also be applied to average estimates across studies.

Where possible, authors should provide a meaningful interpretation of their synthesis findings. For example, in a patient education synthesis, Mazzuca (1982) derived a clinical interpretation of statistical estimates of change by imposing these numbers on normative data from a clinical site. Mazzuca applied his findings of a .74 median improvement for therapeutic progress to a diabetes research center that was following the clinical course of about 500 patients. The mean fasting blood glucose level in the group was 233 mg/dl with a standard deviation of 101 mg/dl. With a .74 median improvement, a program of behavioral instruction for these patients could be expected to lower their mean fasting blood glucose level to

$$233 - [(0.74)(101)] = 158 \text{ mg/dl.}$$

Using the upper limit of normal for diagnosed diabetics, 140 mg/dl, as a cutoff criterion, the proportion of patients "under control" (less than or equal to 140 mg/dl) is calculated as

$$Z = (158 - 140)/101 = 0.178,$$

which translates from a normal distribution table to 43 percent under control. Practitioners can readily compare this figure (percentage under control) to that expected under routine care, 18 percent.

Integrating Effect Sizes Across Studies

Weighted Average

Estimates of effect size from individual studies can be combined to form an overall estimate of the magnitude of the relationship. One way they have been combined is by simple averaging (Glass et al., 1981). This method does not utilize fully the information available from each study, however. A more precise method is based on a weighted average (Hedges, 1984; Hedges & Olkin, 1985) where the weighting procedure is based on the precision (variance) of the individual effect size estimates. The variance of an effect size is calculated as

$$v = [(n_1 + n_2)/n_1 n_2] + \{d^2/[2(n_1 + n_2)]\},$$

where d = the adjusted effect size.

The weight (w) is the inverse of the effect size variance ($1/v$). The weighted average effect size is calculated as

$$D = [\Sigma (w_i d_i)]/[\Sigma w_i].$$

These formulae are provided by Hedges and Olkin (1985) as are similar formulae for correlation data.

To illustrate the importance of weighting, consider the following example:

Study	Effect Size (d)	Weight		
		Variance	w	wd
1	.25	.08	12.5	3.13
2	.30	.11	9.1	2.73
3	.23	.05	20.0	4.60
4	.27	.07	14.3	3.86
5	.86	.38	2.6	2.24
Total	1.91		58.5	16.56

The overall estimate of effect size determined as a simple average (1.91/ 5) is equal to .382. This value is greatly influenced by the fifth study, with its large estimate of effect size and large variance (less precision). The weighted average effect size for these data is

$$D = [\Sigma \ (w_i d_i)]/[\Sigma \ w_i]$$
$$= 16.56/58.5$$
$$= .283.$$

The weighted average effect size is considerably smaller than the simple average and is closer to that reported by the more precise studies. Where the individual variances of effect sizes exhibit a wide range, the weighted average effect size is clearly a better estimate. The effect of weighting is minimal, however, where individual estimates of effect size or their variances are fairly equal. So that readers may judge the precision of individual effect size estimates, authors should report the individual variances or standard deviations.

Test of Significance and Confidence Intervals

If the integrated studies share a common population effect size, the weighted average is approximately normally distributed with population variance V (Hedges & Olkin, 1985). The population variance is estimated as

$$V = 1/[\Sigma \ w_i].$$

A test of the hypothesis that the population effect size is equal to zero can be rejected at significance level .05 when

$$|D/(V^{.5})| > 1.96.$$

Similarly, a 95-percent confidence interval for the population effect size is given by

$$D \pm 1.96(V^{.5}).$$

Using the data provided in the previous section, the following is obtained:

$$V = 1/58.5$$
$$= .017$$
$$|D/(V^{.5})| = |.283/(.017^{.5})|$$
$$= 2.17$$
$$D \pm 1.96(V^{.5}) = .283 \pm 1.96 \ (.017^{.5})$$
$$= .283 \pm .256$$
$$= .027 \ \text{to} \ .539.$$

Test of Homogeneity

Another issue that must be addressed is whether all studies should be combined. One test is, of course, for construct validity; the other is statistical. Individual effect size estimates should be combined only when they share a common population effect size. This can be examined via a test of homogeneity, that is, a test of treatment by study interactions using a chi-square distribution with $n-1$ degrees of freedom, where n is equal to the number of studies (Hedges, 1984; Hedges & Olkin, 1985).

When the outcome of the homogeneity test is significant, indicating heterogeneity, several diagnostic procedures can be used to identify outlier studies (Hedges & Olkin, 1985). In addition to the homogeneity statistic, such procedures include methods based on graphical representation of effect sizes and one based on residuals. The graphic method is a plot of individual effect sizes and their 95-percent confidence intervals. Those studies whose effect sizes are included in none or in only a small number of the confidence intervals of the other studies would be suspect. The graphic procedure is crude, but quick. Examination of residuals provides the same results as those based on the homogeneity statistic. This method requires more calculations but is easily set up on an electronic spreadsheet (Green et al., 1985; Ramirez & Mullen, 1985).

A meta-analysis of six randomized, placebo-controlled clinical trials of aspirin in postmyocardial infarction (Canner, 1983) illustrates the usefulness of homogeneity analysis in identifying and understanding the source(s) of conflicting findings. Five of the studies showed modest positive results, and one, a slightly negative effect. A statistical test of the homogeneity of the study findings suggested that one study did not represent the same underlying population of findings as the others. Canner (1983) then inspected the studies closely for variations in design and operating features that might explain the different mortality rates. In the outlier study (which, ironically, was to have been the "decisive study") he noted imbalances between treatment and control groups in certain baseline factors that appeared to favor the control group. He then reanalyzed the original data from that study to adjust for these factors, and the adjusted analysis also indicated a modest positive effect for aspirin. Light & Pillemer (1984) stress the importance of "outlier" studies and conflicting results in generating hypotheses regarding the impact of different programs, populations, settings, and times.

Multiple Measures and Multiple Experimental Groups Within Studies

Evaluation studies often employ multiple measures and may include more than one treatment group. Integration of studies that exhibit these characteristics risks violating the assumption of stochastic independence of effect size estimates. This problem has been recognized by several methodologists (Glass et al., 1981; Hunter et al., 1982; Rosenthal, 1984; Cooper, 1984; Hedges & Olkin, 1985).

Multiple Measures. Several examples appear in the literature (Smith & Glass, 1977; Smith & Glass, 1980; Mumford et al., 1982; Posavac, 1980) that treat multiple measures as if they were independent. Posavac's synthesis of patient education studies, for example, also mixed constructs, grouping together 104 measures of knowledge, attitudes, behavior, and physiologic change from 23 studies to obtain an average effect for "patient education."

Other syntheses have treated separate constructs in separate analyses (Johnson and Johnson, 1985; Mullen et al., 1985; Devine & Cook, 1986). Thus, for example, Mullen and associates segregated knowledge effects from drug adherence, and Devine and Cook treated patient satisfaction separately from measures of psychological well-being.

Confronting the problem of multiple measures of a construct from the same study, Johnson and Johnson (1985) weighted them as suggested by Cooper (1984) by the number of distinct measures within the study. Mullen et al. (1985) selected a single measure to represent a construct, in this case, the most direct and objective measure of adherence from the longest follow-up. Devine and Cook (1986) used an unweighted average to represent constructs with multiple measures and/or constructs that applied the same measure on multiple occasions. They also conducted an analysis using multiple measures (unaveraged). (In general, Devine and Cook found similar average effect size estimates with both procedures.) This dual-analysis approach thus allows the investigator to examine the degree of difference that stochastic dependence of estimates makes in the analysis. It does not, however, resolve situations in which results from the two procedures differ.

We read Hedges and Olkin (1985) as recommending the representation of constructs with a single measure in most cases. Pooling the measures adds little when the measures are highly correlated; measures that have a low correlation may represent different constructs, and therefore probably should not be pooled. For situations with moderate correlations, pooling may be desirable, yet the pooling techniques (Hedges & Olkin, 1985) require knowledge of the intercorrelation, and this information is not often available.

Multiple-Treatment Groups. Multiple-treatment groups from the same study also present the problem of stochastic dependence, and various investigators doing syntheses have dealt with the problem in ways that are similar to their handling of multiple measures. That is, examples can be found in which multiple-treatment groups are (incorrectly) treated as if they were independent (Smith & Glass, 1977, 1980; Mumford et al., 1982; Posavac, 1980). Others select a single-treatment group, as for example, on the basis of the primary study author's hypothesis regarding the "strongest" intervention (Devine & Cook, 1983a, b, 1986; Mullen & Green, 1984;

Mullen et al., 1985). Devine and Cook present analyses for all treatment groups and for one treatment group per study, and they find few differences.

The issue of multiple-treatment groups differs from that of multiple measures in two ways, however. First, the loss of information is more serious, in that useful comparisons may be lost. Secondly, there are as yet no published techniques for handling multiple treatment groups. However, Hedges & Olkin (personal communication, May, 1986) are currently addressing this important gap in meta-analysis.

Analyzing Between-Group Differences and the Influence of Study Characteristics on Study Outcomes

One-Way Analysis of Variance Analogue

A statistical procedure for testing the significance of variations between groups of studies has been introduced by Hedges (1982, 1984). He referred to this procedure as an analogue to analysis of variance for effect sizes. After studies have been grouped according to some characteristic(s) that can influence effect size, the analytical approach is to partition the homogeneity statistic into two homogeneity statistics—one that reflects between-group homogeneity and one that reflects within-group homogeneity.

The ANOVA analogue can be employed in cases where the homogeneity hypothesis is not confirmed, and where the synthesis investigator can form *a priori* subgroups based on a theoretical framework (Hedges, 1984; Hedges & Olkin, 1985). There may also be situations where treatment or effect constructs are believed to differ. The homogeneity of a multitreatment or multi-effect group of studies would not, therefore, be tested immediately. Instead, the *a priori* groups would be formed and tested for within-group homogeneity. Confirmation of the distinction between the groups could be accomplished with the ANOVA analogue (e.g., Mullen et al., 1985).

Regression Analogue

Investigation of the relationship between methodology, population, and other study variables and variations in effect size has been accomplished using conventional multiple regression analysis (Smith & Glass, 1977; Glass & Smith, 1979). Hedges (1984) argues, however, that conventional types of analyses do not apply to effect sizes. As an alternative, an analogue-to-multiple-regression analysis for effect sizes that is based on weighted least squares has been provided (Hedges, 1984; Hedges & Olkin, 1985). The weight is the inverse of the variance for each effect size.[1]

CONCLUSIONS

Techniques for information synthesis have received increasing attention and, despite limitations, they appear to be helpful in making the best use of prior studies for policy decisions, for guidance of professional practice, and for planning future research. Such techniques also appear to be helpful in investigating issues that cannot as easily be explored in single studies. Sound statistical practices have been brought into the synthesis enterprise, and new advances are being made to cure questionable practices that had been used in meta-analyses conducted in the last decade. Most importantly, the whole review/synthesis process has come to be taken more seriously and the methods subject to healthy debate, so that the process of inquiry is, indeed, systematic and cumulative.

GUIDELINES

The following guidelines are intended to improve both qualitative and quantitative syntheses, and they may also be used to evaluate an existing synthesis. They are consistent with guidelines and evaluation criteria given by other synthesis methodologists (Cooper, 1984; Goldschmidt, 1984; Light & Pillemer, 1984; Mullen & Rosenthal, 1985; Wolf, 1986).

1. Define study questions or hypotheses, and consider questions other than ones that focus only on average effects.
2. Specify and report criteria for inclusion, including criteria of relevance and acceptability.
3. Describe your strategy for locating relevant studies, and search for unpublished studies as a check on the possibility of publication bias (Type I error). It is also helpful to give the yields of the respective sources.
4. Develop and describe coding categories for substantive, methodological, and descriptive characteristics of the studies—for example, the type, frequency, and duration of the intervention; the study design, measurement quality, and attrition rates; and the sample, setting, and time of the study. Specify codes carefully to increase reliability of coding, and check on inter-rater reliability in applying codes.
5. Represent each study finding with a common metric, avoiding overreliance on tests of statistical significance. Adjust effect sizes

for sample size, if some studies have very small sample sizes. Always report sample sizes.

6. Examine conceptually distinct dependent variables separately. If there would still be multiple measures from the same study within these groups, do two analyses—one with only one measure per study and one with multiple measures. Consider the former to be the more conservative estimate of the effect.

7. Be sensitive to the problem of using multiple experimental groups from the same intervention study in your analyses. Do at least one analysis with single representations of each study. Watch the meta-analysis literature for statistical procedures for dealing with this important limitation of current procedures.

8. Look closely at the study findings in graphic as well as numerical presentations. Test for homogeneity of results, and examine outliers closely for characteristics that give rise to new hypotheses.

9. When computing average effect size estimates, weight the individual effect size estimates according to their precision (variance). Report the variances of individual studies.

10. Inspect the study outcomes for interaction as well as main effects.

11. Combine quantitative with qualitative analyses. Use the numeric data as an aid to thought and not as an end in itself or a substitute.

12. Describe the limitations of your synthesis, and offer guidance for research and practice.

ACKNOWLEDGMENTS

We are grateful to Larry Hedges, Gary S. Persinger, and Ralph Frankowski for advancing our knowledge of statistical procedures for information synthesis. Rhonda B. Friedman, Lawrence W. Green, Donald C. Iverson, Virginia C. Kennedy, Ronald J. Lorimor, Carl H. Slater, William B. Ward, and Alisa Wilson raised insightful questions and provided valuable comments. Andrea Biddle prepared the manuscript.

NOTES

1. Packaged programs for computing estimates of regression coefficients and the test for model misspecification such as SAS are recommended for this analysis. SPSS does not estimate a weighted least-squares equation directly, and does not produce the inverse matrix necessary for estimates of the variance of regression coefficients. However, supplementary programs to assist SPSS/PC users are available (Persinger, 1985).

REFERENCES

Arbuthnot, J. (1710). Equality of males and females, an argument for the society of London, *27*, 186–190. In Pearson, E. S. (Ed.), *Lectures by Karl Pearson given at University College London during the academic sessions 1921–1933*, 1978. New York: MacMillan.

Bissell, J. W. (1970). *The effects of preschool programs for disadvantaged children*. Unpublished doctoral dissertation, Harvard University.

Bryant, F. B., & Wortman, F. B. (1984). Methodological issues in the meta-analysis of quasi-experiments. *New Directions in Program Evaluation*, *24*, 25–42.

Canadian Task Force on the Periodic Health Examination. (1979). The periodic health examination. *Canadian Medical Association Journal*, *121*, 3–45.

Canner, P. L. (1983). Aspirin in coronary heart disease: Comparison of six clinical trials. *Israel Journal of Medicine*, *19*, 413–423.

Chelimsky, E., & Morra, L. G. (1984). Evaluation synthesis for the legislative user, issues in data synthesis. *New Directions for Program Evaluation*, *24*, 75–89.

Cochran, W. G. (1935). A note on the influence of rainfall on the yield of cereals in relation to manurial treatment. *Journal of Agricultural Science*, *25*, 510–522.

Cochran, W. G. (1937). Problems arising in the analysis of a series of similar experiments. *Journal of the Royal Statistical Society*, *4(Suppl.)*, 102–118.

Cochran, W. G. (1954). Some methods of strengthening the common chi-square tests. *Biometrics*, *10*, 417–451.

Cohen, J. (1962). The statistical power of abnormal-social psychological research: A review. *Journal of Abnormal and Social Psychology*, *65*, 145–153.

Cohen, J. (1977). *Statistical power analysis for the behavioral sciences* (rev. ed.). New York: Academic Press.

Collins, R., & Langman, M. (1985). Treatment with histamine H_2 antagonists in acute upper gastrointestinal hemmorhage. *The New England Journal of Medicine*, *313*, 660–666.

Cook, T. D., & Campbell, D. T. (1979). *Quasi-experimentation: Design and analysis issues for field settings*. Boston: Houghton Mifflin.

Cook, T. D., & Gruder, C. (1979). Metaevaluation research. In Light, R. J. (Ed.), *Evaluation studies review annual*. Volume 4, pp. 469–515. Beverly Hills: Sage.

Cook, T. D., & Leviton, L. C. (1980). Reviewing the literature: A comparison of traditional methods with meta-analysis. *Journal of Personality*, *48*, 449–472.

Cooper, H. M. (1984). *The integrative research review: A systematic approach*. In Bickman, L., & Rog, D. (Eds.), *Applied social research methods series* Volume 2. Beverly Hills: Sage.

Cooper, H. M., & Rosenthal, R. (1980). Statistical versus traditional procedures for summarizing research findings. *Psychological Bulletin*, *87*, 442–449.

Cooper, H., & Tom, M. (1984). Social class and ethnic group differences in achievement motivation. In Ames, R., & Ames C. (Eds.), *Research on motivation in education* Volume 1. New York: Academic Press.

Cordray, D. S., & Orwin, R. C. (1983). Improving the quality of evidence: Interconnections among primary evaluation, secondary analysis, and quantitative synthesis. In Light, R. J. (Ed.), *Evaluation studies review annual*, Volume 8, pp. 91–119. Beverly Hills: Sage.

Devine, E. C., & Cook, T. D. (1983a). A meta-analytic analysis of effects of psychoeducational interventions on length of postsurgical hospital stay. *Nursing Research*, *32*, 267–274.

Devine, E. C., & Cook, T. D. (1983b). Effects of psycho-educational intervention on length of hospital stay: A meta-analytic review of 34 studies. In Light, R. J. (Ed.), *evaluation Studies Review Annual*, Volume 8, pp. 417–432. Beverly Hills: Sage.

Devine, E. C., & Cook, T. D. (1986). Clinical and cost-savings effects of psychoeducational interventions with surgical patients: A meta-analysis. *Research in Nursing and Health*, 9, 89–105.

Donaldson, P. J., & Billy, J. O. G. (1984). The impact of prenatal care on birth weight: Evidence from an international data set. *Medical Care*, 22, 177–188.

Findley, M., & Cooper, H. (1983). Locus of control and academic achievement: A literature review. *Journal of Personality and Social Psychology*, 44, 419–427.

Finney, D. J. (1971). *Probit Analysis* (3rd ed.). Cambridge: Cambridge University Press.

Fisher, R. A. (1916). Biometrika. *Eugenics Review*, 8, 62–64. In Bennett, J. H. (1971). *Collected papers of R. A. Fisher* (Volume 1, 1912–1924). South Australia: The University of Adelaide.

Fisher, R. A. (1921). Studies in crop variation. I. An examination of the yield of dressed grain from Broadbalk. *Journal of Agricultural Science*, 11, 107–35. In Bennett, J. H. (1971). *Collected Papers of R. A. Fisher* (Volume 1, 1912–1924). South Australia: The University of Adelaide.

Fisher, R. A. (1932). *Statistical methods for research workers* (4th ed.). London: Oliver & Boyd.

Fleiss, J. L. (1981). *Statistical methods for rates and proportions* (2nd ed.). New York: Wiley.

Gilreath, C. L. (1984). *Computerized literature searching*. Boulder: Westview Press.

Glass, G. V. (1976). Primary, secondary, and meta-analysis of research. *Educational Researcher*, 5, 3–8.

Glass, G. V. (1978). Integrating findings: The meta-analysis of research. *Review of Research in Education*, 5, 351–379.

Glass, G. V., McGraw B., & Smith, M. L. (1981). *Meta-analysis in social research*. Beverly Hills: Sage.

Glass, G. V., & Smith, M. L. (1979). Consequences of failure to meet assumptions underlying the fixed effects analyses of variance and covariance. *Review of Educational Research*, 42, 237–288.

Goldschmidt, P. (1984). *Information synthesis: A practical guide*. (HSR&D Document RES # 29–07–110). Washington, DC: Veterans Administration.

Gosset, W. H. (student) (1914). The elimination of spurious correlation due to position in time and space. *Biometrika*, 10, 179.

Green, B. F., & Hall, J. A. (1984). Quantitative methods for literature reviews. *Annual Review of Psychology*, 35, 37–53.

Green, L. W. (1977). Evaluation and measurement: Some dilemmas for health education. *American Journal of Public Health*, 67, 155–161.

Green, L. W., Ramirez, G., Mains, D., & Mullen, P. D. (1985). Lotus 1–2–3 template for combining effect sizes and testing for homogeneity [Computer Program]. Houston, TX: Center for Health Promotion Research and Development, The University of Texas Health Science Center at Houston, P.O. Box 20186, Houston, TX 77225.

Green, L. W., Rimer, B., & Bertera, R. (1978). How cost-effective are smoking cessation strategies? *World Smoking Health*, 3, 33–40.

Greenwald, A. G. (1975). Consequences of prejudice against the null hypothesis. *Psychological Bulletin*, 82, 1–20.

Hansen, C. (1984). *The microcomputer user's guide to information online*. Hasbrouck Heights, NJ: Hayden Book Co.

Haynes, R. B., Davis, D. A., McKibbon, A., & Tugwell, P. (1984). A critical appraisal of the efficacy of continuing medical education. *Journal of the American Medical Association*, 251, 61–64.

Haynes, R. B., Taylor, D. W., Snow, J. C., & Sackett, D. L. (1979). Annotated and indexed bibliography on compliance with therapeutic and preventive regimens. In Haynes, R.

B., Taylor, D. W., & Sackett, D. L. (Eds.), *Compliance in health care* (Appendix I). Baltimore: The Johns Hopkins University Press.

Hedges, L. V. (1984). Advances in statistical methods for meta-analysis. *New Directions in Program Evaluation, 24,* 25–42.

Hedges, L. V., & Olkin, I. (1980). Vote-counting methods in research synthesis. *Psychological Bulletin, 88,* 359–369.

Hedges, L. V., & Olkin, I. (1985). *Statistical methods for meta-analysis.* New York: Academic Press.

Hedges, L. V., & Olkin, I. (in press). Meta-analysis: A review, a new view, and a preview. *Educational Researcher.*

Hoaglin, D. R., Light, R., McPeek, B., Mosteller, & Stoto, M. (1982). *Data for Decisions.* Cambridge, MA: ABT Books.

Hovell, M. F. (1982). The experimental evidence for weight-loss treatment of essential hypertension: A critical review. *American Journal of Public Health, 72,* 359–368.

Hunter, J. E., Schmidt, F. L., & Jackson, G. B. (1982). *Meta-analysis: Cumulating research findings across studies.* Beverly Hills: Sage.

Iverson, B. K., & Levy, S. R. (1982). Using meta analysis in health education research. *Journal of School Health, 52,* 234–239.

Jackson, G. B. (1980). Methods for integrative reviews. *Review of Educational Research, 50,* 438–460.

Janz, N. K., & Becker, M. H. (1984). The health belief model: A decade later. *Health Education Quarterly, 11,* 1–47.

Johnson, D. W., & Johnson, R. T. (1985). Nutrition education: A model for effectiveness: A synthesis of research. *Journal of Nutrition Education, 17(Suppl.),* S1–S44.

Lehman, A. F., & Zastowny, T. R. (1983). Patient satisfaction with mental health services: A meta-analysis to establish norms. *Evaluation and Program Planning, 6,* 265–274.

Levy, S. R., Iverson, B. K., & Walberg, H. J. (1980). Nutrition education research: An interdisciplinary evaluation and review. *Health Education Quarterly, 7,* 107–116.

Light, R. J. (Ed.) (1983a). *Evaluation Studies Review Annual* Volume 8. Beverly Hills: Sage.

Light, R. J. (1983b). Introduction. In Light, R. J. (Ed.), *Evaluation Studies Review Annual* Volume 8. Beverly Hills: Sage.

Light, R. J. (1984). Six evaluation issues that synthesis can resolve better than single studies. In Yeaton, W. H., & Wortman, P. M. (Eds.), *Issues in Data Synthesis* (pp. 57–73). New Directions for Program Evaluation. San Francisco: Jossey-Bass.

Light, R. J., & Pillemer, D. B. (1984). *Summing up: The science of reviewing research.* Cambridge: Harvard University Press.

Light, R. J., & Smith, P. V. (1971). Accumulating evidence: Procedures for resolving contradictions among different research studies. *Harvard Educational Review, 41,* 429–471.

Louis, T. A., Fineberg, H. V., & Mosteller, F. (1985). Findings for public health from meta-analyses. In Breslow, L., Fielding, J. E., & Lave, L. B. (Eds.), *Annual review of public health* (pp. 1–20). Palo Alto: Annual Reviews.

Mantel, N., & Haenszel, W. (1959). Statistical aspects of the analysis of data from retrospective studies of disease. *Journal of the National Cancer Institute, 22,* 719–748.

Mazzuca, S. A. (1982). Does patient education on chronic disease have therapeutic value? *Journal of Chronic Disease, 35,* 521–529.

Mickalide, A. D. (1985, November). *U. S. Preventive Services Task Force: Issues in Financing and Cost Containment.* Paper presented at the American Public Health Association, Washington, DC.

Mullen, B., & Rosenthal, R. (1985). *BASIC meta-analysis: Procedures and programs.* Hillsdale, NJ: Lawrence Earlbaum Associates.

Mullen, P. D., & Green, L. W. (1984). *Measuring patient drug information transfer: An assessment of the literature*. Washington, DC: Pharmaceutical Manufacturers Association 1100 15th St., NW, Washington, DC 20005.

Mullen, P. D., Green, L. W., & Persinger, G. (1985). Clinical trials of patient education for chronic conditions: A comparative meta-analysis of intervention types. *Preventive Medicine, 14*, 753–781.

Mumford, E., Schlesinger, H. J., & Glass, G. V. (1982). The effect of psychological intervention on recovery from surgery and heart attacks: An analysis of the literature. *American Journal of Public Health, 72*, 141–151.

National Institutes of Health. (1984). Health implications of obesity. *Consensus development conference statement* (Volume 5). Washington, DC: U.S. Government Printing Office.

Neufeld, V. R. (1976). Patient education: A critique. In Sackett, D. L., & Haynes, R. B. (Eds.), *Compliance with therapeutic regimens* (pp. 83–92). Baltimore: The Johns Hopkins University Press.

Orwin, R. G. (1983). A fail-safe *N* for effect size. *Journal of Educational Statistics, 8*, 157–159.

Pearson, E. S. (Ed.) (1978). *Lectures by Karl Pearson given at University College London during the academic sessions 1921–1933*. New York: MacMillan.

Pearson, K. (1933). On a method of determining whether a sample of given size *n* supposed to have been drawn from a parent population having a known probability, integral has probably been drawn at random. *Biometrika, 25*, 379–410.

Persinger, G. S. (1985). Weighted least-squares matrix rotation program for SPSS/PC (Computer program). Washington, DC: Pharmaceutical Manufacturers Association, 1100 15th St., NW, Washington, DC 20005.

Pillemer, D. B., & Light, R. J. (1980). Synthesizing outcomes: How to use research evidence from many studies. *Harvard Educational Review, 50*, 176–195.

Posavac, E. J. (1980). Evaluations of patient education programs: A meta-analysis. *Evaluation and the Health Professions, 3*, 47–62.

Posavac, E. J., Sinacore, J. M., Brotherton, S. E., Helford, M. C., & Turpin, R. S. (1985). Increasing compliance to medical treatment regimens: A meta-analysis of program evaluation. *Evaluation and the Health Professions, 8*, 7–22.

Ramirez, G., & Mullen, P. D. (1985). Everything you always wanted to know about effect sizes. Unpublished manuscript, The University of Texas Health Science Center at Houston, Center for Health Promotion Research and Development, P.O. Box 20186, Houston, TX 77225.

Raudenbush, S. W. (1983). Utilizing controversy as a source of hypotheses for meta-analysis: The case of teacher expectancy's effects on pupil IQ. In Light, R. J. (Ed.), *Evaluation Studies Review Annual*, Volume 2, pp. 303–325. Beverly Hills: Sage.

Rosenthal, R. (1963). On the social psychology of the psychological experiment: The experimenter's hypothesis as unintended determinant of experimental results. *American Scientist, 51*, 268–283.

Rosenthal, R. (1964). Effects of the experimenter on the results of psychological research. In Maher, B. A. (Ed.), *Progress in Experimental Personality Research*, Volume 1, pp. 79–114. New York: Academic Press.

Rosenthal, R. (1978). Combining results of independent studies. *Psychological Bulletin, 85*, 185–193.

Rosenthal, R. (1979). The "file drawer problem" and tolerance for null results. *Psychological Bulletin, 86*, 638–641.

Rosenthal, R. (1984). Meta-analytic procedures for social research. In Bickman, L., & Rog, D. (Eds.), *Applied Social Research Methods Series*, Volume 6. Beverly Hills: Sage.

Rosenthal, R., & Jacobson, L. (1968). *Pygmalion in the Classroom*. New York: Holt, Rinehart, & Winston.

Rosenthal, R., & Rubin, D. B. (1982). Comparing effect sizes of independent studies. *Psychological Bulletin*, 92, 500–504.

Sackett, D. L., & Haynes, R. B. (Eds.) (1976). *Compliance with Therapeutic Regimens*. Baltimore: The Johns Hopkins University Press.

Scriven, M. (1969). An introduction to meta-evaluation. *Educational Product Report*, 2(Suppl. 5), 36–38.

Sechrest, L., & Yeaton, W. (1981). Empirical basis for estimating effect size. In Boruch, R. F., Wortman, P. M., & Cordray, D. S. (Eds.), *Renalayzing Program Evaluations*. San Francisco: Jossey-Bass.

Shadish, W. R., Jr. (1982). A review and critique of controlled studies of the effectiveness of preventive child health care. *Health Policy Quarterly*, 2, 24–52.

Shope, J. T. (1980). Intervention to improve compliance with pediatric anticonvulsant therapy. *Patient Counseling and Health Education*, 2, 135–141.

Smith, M. L., & Glass, G. V. (1977). Meta-analysis of psychotherapy outcome studies. *American Psychologist*, 32, 752–760.

Smith, M. L., & Glass, G. V. (1980). Meta-analysis of research on class size and its relationship to attitudes and instruction. *American Educational Research Journal*, 17, 419–433.

Smith, M. L., Glass, G. V., & Miller, T. I. (1980). *The benefits of psychotherapy*. Baltimore: The Johns Hopkins University Press.

Snedecor, G. W. (1946). *Statistical Methods* (4th ed.). Ames, IA: Iowa State College Press.

Snedecor, G. W., & Cochran, W. G. (1980). *Statistical methods* (7th ed.), pp. 138–140. Ames, IA: The Iowa State University Press.

Stock, W. A., Okun, M. A., Haring, M. J., & Witter, R. A. (1983). *Age differences in subjective well-being: A meta-analysis*. Beverly Hills: Sage.

Strube, M. J., & Hartmann, D. P. (1983). Meta-analysis: Techniques, applications, and functions. *Journal of Consulting and Clinical Psychology*, 51, 14–27.

Stufflebeam, D. L. (1974). *Meta-evaluation* (Paper #3 in Occasional Paper Series). Kalamazoo, MI: Western Michigan University, College of Education.

Stufflebeam, D. L. (1979). *Meta-evaluation: A topic of professional and public interest*. Kalamazoo, MI: Western Michigan University, College of Education.

Suen, H. K. (1984). A bayesian aggregate meta-analytic evaluation approach. *Evaluation and the Health Professions*, 4, 461–470.

Thorndike, R. L. (1983). The effect of the interval between test and restest on the constancy of the IQ. *Journal of Educational Psychology*, 24, 543–549.

Tippett, L. H. C. (1931). *The method of statistics*. London: Williams, & Norgate.

U.S. General Accounting Office. (1983). Lessons learned from past block grants: Implications for congressional oversight. In Light, R. J. (Ed.), *Evaluation Studies Review Annual*, Volume 3, pp. 552–583. Beverly Hills: Sage.

Walberg, H. J., & Haertel, E. H. (1980). Research integration: An introduction and overview. *Evaluation in Education*, 4, 5–10.

Waxman, H. C., & Walberg, H. J. (1982). The relation of teaching and learning: A review of reviews of process-product research. *Contemporary Education Review*, 1, 103–120.

White, K. R. (1982). The relation between socioeconomic status and academic achievement. *Psychological Bulletin*, 91, 461–481.

Windsor, R. A., & Orleans, C. T. (1986). Guidelines and methodological standards for smoking cessation intervention research among pregnant women: Improving the science and art. *Health Education Quarterly*, 13, 131–161.

Wolf, F. M. (1986). *Meta-analysis: Quantitative methods for research synthesis*. Beverly Hills: Sage.

Wortman, P. M., & Yeaton, W. H. (1983). *Synthesis of results in controlled trials of coronary artery bypass graft surgery*. Beverly Hills: Sage.

Yates, F., & Cochran, W. G. (1938). The analysis of group experiments. *Journal of Agricultural Science, 28*, 556–580. In Cochran, B. I. M. (Ed.), *Contributions to statistics*. New York: Wiley.

Yeaton, W. H., & Wortman, P. M. (Eds.) (1984). *Issues in data synthesis*. New Directions for Program Evaluation. San Francisco: Jossey-Bass.

Yusuf, S., Peto, R., Lewis, J., Collins, R., & Sleight, P. (1985). Beta blockade during and after myocardial infarction: An overview of the randomized trials. *Progress in Cardiovascular Diseases, 27*, 335–371.

SECTION III:

THEORETICAL FOUNDATION OF HEALTH EDUCATION AND PROMOTION

INTRODUCTION TO THEORY IN HEALTH EDUCATION

Marshall H. Becker

Health education approaches and strategies abound—but relatively few have been developed from established educational or social science traditions. Thus, many attempts at intervention lack the presumption of efficacy that a clear association with theoretical formulations and relevant empirical evidence would provide (Beery, Schoenbach, & Wagner, 1986). Fortunately, the past two decades have witnessed a renaissance of interest in the potential application of behavioral-science principles to health education efforts; some examples of major concepts might include: Social Learning Theory (Parcel & Baranowski, 1981); self-efficacy (Strecher et al., 1986); adoption and diffusion of innovation (Green, 1975); cognitive models of health-related behavior (Cummings, Becker, & Maile, 1980); behavioral-intention models (Fishbein & Ajzen, 1975); locus of control (Wallston & Wallston, 1982); behavior modification (McAlister et al., 1976); threatening messages (or "fear arousal") (Sutton, 1982); and social networks/social support (Gottlieb, 1985).

Conceptualizations and research findings in several of these important theoretical areas are reviewed and updated in the papers that follow.

Advances in Health Education and Promotion, vol. 2, pages 241–243
Copyright © 1987 JAI Press Inc.
All rights of reproduction in any form reserved.
ISBN: 0-89232-617-4

Becker and Rosenstock compare social family theory with the Health Belief Model. Clark traces Social Learning Theory from Bandura's original construct, distinguishes it from other theories of learning, and employs the central principles of self-regulation and reinforcement, cognitive restructuring, and emotional coping as a rubric for organizing a critical review of extant research.

Starting from the generally-accepted premise of broad agreement in favor of the patient's right to personal control, Lewis offers a new "typology of control" that attempts to integrate "processual control," "contingency control," "cognitive control," "behavioral control," and "existential control," each of which is related to the determinants of health and to health outcomes in various and complex ways. On the basis of her review of the control literature, it is interesting to speculate on the degree to which health educators and health-education activities act to increase or decrease clients' perceptions and/or actual levels of control.

Theory and evidence from the fast-growing literature on social networks and social support suggest new and highly-promising implications for health education practice. Israel and Rounds have dealt with the difficulties of deriving themes and principles from the mass of relevant papers and books in a most ingenious fashion: they have created a "review of reviews," extracting and summarizing relevant information from recent reviews so as to provide "a synthesis for health educators." The article discusses the major concepts (and confusions) in this area, documents relationships between social networks/support and both health behavior and health status, and describes how these concepts have been (and can be) applied in different kinds of practice situations.

Finally, Ottoson and Green bring sociological, political, philosophical, and organizational theories to bear upon the many problems faced by health educators trying to translate concepts and policies into actual programs and practices. The authors review four critical influences on policy implementation: components of the policy itself; the implementing organization's structure, technical capacity, and employee characteristics; the political milieu (i.e., power and control, at both the intra- and interorganizational level); and environmental factors (i.e., the social, cultural, political, and economic conditions that can affect, or be affected by, implementation of the policy). By carefully applying this litany of considerations to any policy-implementation request, the practitioner can do much to avoid the pitfalls that usually lead to lack of program success.

REFERENCES

Berry, W., Schoenbach, V. J., & Wagner, E. H. (1986). Health risk appraisal: Methods and programs, with annotated bibliography. Washington DC: U.S. Government Printing Office, DHHS Pub. No. (PHS) 86–3396.

Cummings, K. M., Becker, M. H., & Maile, M. C. (1980). Bringing the models together: An empirical approach to combining variables used to explain health actions. *Journal of Behavioral Medicine, 3*, 123–145.

Fishbein, M., & Ajzen, I. (1975). Belief, attitude, intention and behavior. Reading, MA: Addison-Wesley.

Gottlieb, B. H. (1985). Social networks and social support: An overview of research, practice, and policy implications. *Health Education Quarterly, 12*, 5–22.

Green, L. W. (1975). Diffusion and adoption of innovations related to cardiovascular risk behavior in the public. In Enelow, A. J., & Henderson, J. B. (Eds.), *Applying behavioral science to cardiovascular risk: Proceedings of a conference*. American Heart Association, pp. 84–108.

McAlister, A., Farquhar, J., Thoreen, C., & Maccoby, N. (1976). Behavioral sciences applied to cardiovascular health: Progress and research needs in the modification of risk-taking habits in adult populations. *Health Education Monographs, 4*, 45–74.

Parcel, G. S., & Baranowski, T. (1981). Social learning theory and health education. *Health Education, 12*, 14–18.

Strecher, V. J., DeVellis, B. McE., Becker, M. H., & Rosenstock, I. M. (1986). The role of self-efficacy in achieving health behavior change. *Health Education Quarterly, 13*, 73–92.

Sutton, S. R. (1982). Fear-arousing communications: A critical examination of theory and research. In Eiser, J. R. (Ed.). *Social psychology and behavioral medicine*. (pp. 303–337) New York: Wiley.

Wallston, K., & Wallston, B. (1982). Who is responsible for your health? The construct of Health Locus of Control. In Sanders, G., & Suls, J. (Eds.), *Social Psychology of Health and Illness*. (pp. 65–95) Hillsdale, NJ: Lawrence Erlbaum, Associates.

COMPARING SOCIAL LEARNING THEORY AND THE HEALTH BELIEF MODEL

Marshall H. Becker and Irwin M. Rosenstock

Several theoretical models of health-related behavior commonly discussed and employed in health education programs (e.g., the Health Belief Model and the PRECEDE Framework) have recently been the subjects of extensive published reviews (cf. Janz & Becker, 1984; Green et al., 1980). However, we have observed that, despite a substantial history of research and analysis focused on the Health Belief Model, on Social Learning Theory (including self-efficacy), and on generalized expectancies for control of reinforcements (or "locus of control"), there remains some conceptual confusion about the interrelationships among these explanatory schemes. Therefore, we will attempt to clarify some of these relationships.

Social Learning Theory as developed by Bandura (1977a, b) holds that behavior is determined by expectancies and incentives.

1. Expectancies: For heuristic purposes, these may be divided into three types:
   a. Expectancies about environmental cues (i.e., beliefs about how events are connected—what leads to what);

Advances in Health Education and Promotion, vol. 2, pages 245–249
Copyright © 1987 JAI Press Inc.
All rights of reproduction in any form reserved.
ISBN: 0-89232-617-4

    b. Expectancies about the consequences of personal action (i.e., opinions about how behavior is likely to influence outcomes); this is termed "outcome expectation"; and

    c. Expectancies about one's own competence to perform the behavior needed to influence outcomes; this is termed "self-efficacy."

2. Incentive: Incentive (or reinforcement) is defined as the significance or importance of a particular object or outcome. Behavior is regulated by its consequences (reinforcements); but *only as those consequences are interpreted and understood by the individual.*

Thus, for example, individuals with *incentives* to change lifestyles (smoking, drinking, etc.) will attempt to change if they believe that (a) their current lifestyles pose *threats* to them; (b) that particular behavioral *changes will reduce the threats*; and (c) that they are personally *capable of adopting* the new behaviors.

The Health Belief Model (Rosenstock, 1966; Becker, 1974; Janz & Becker, 1984) emphasizes quite similar concepts. According to that model, health-related action depends on the simultaneous occurrence of three classes of factors

1. The existence of sufficient *motivation*, or health concern, to make health issues salient or relevant;

2. The belief that one is *susceptible* or vulnerable to a *serious* problem, or to sequelae of that health problem; this is often termed "perceived *threat*"; and

3. The belief that following a particular health recommendation would be *beneficial* in reducing the perceived threat at subjectively acceptable *cost*, where "cost" refers to perceived *barriers* to following the health recommendation; it includes (but is not restricted to) financial outlays.

The similarity of the Health Belief Model and Bandura's social learning concepts may be illustrated in the concepts diagram at the top of the facing page.

Social Learning Theory has made a number of contributions to explanations of health-related behavior that were not included in the Health Belief Model. The most important of these is the explicit introduction of the concept of self-efficacy, or "efficacy expectation" (as distinct from "outcome expectation") (Strecher et al., 1986). An outcome expectation (defined as a person's estimate that a given behavior will lead to certain outcomes) is quite similar to the Health Belief Model's concept of "perceived benefits." An efficacy expectation, on the other hand, is defined as

CONCEPTS

Social Learning Theory	Health Belief Model
Expectancies about environmental cues— what leads to what.	Perceived threat, including perceived susceptibility to and severiy of illness or its sequelae.
Expectations about outcomes (Social Learning Theory does not explicitly include barriers or costs).	Perceived benefits of following a recommendation minus perceived costs or barriers to action.
Expectations about self-efficacy.	Not explicitly included in Health Belief Model but implied in "perceived barriers."
Incentive.	Health motive: value of reduction of perceived threats to health.

the personal conviction that one can successfully execute the behavior required to produce the outcomes. The distinction between outcome and efficacy expectations is important because both are required for behavior. The following diagram (from Bandura, 1977) illustrates the relationship:

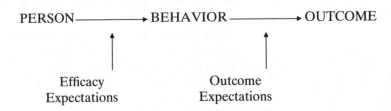

$$\text{PERSON} \longrightarrow \text{BEHAVIOR} \longrightarrow \text{OUTCOME}$$

Efficacy   Outcome
Expectations   Expectations

For example, for a woman (Person) to quit smoking (Behavior) for health reasons (Outcome), she must believe both that cessation will benefit her health (Outcome Expectation) and *that she is capable of quitting* (Efficacy Expectation).

According to Bandura (1977) locus of control (Rotter, 1966) is not the same as self-efficacy, since it is a generalized concept about the self, while self-efficacy is situation specific—focused on beliefs about one's personal abilities in specific settings. Moreover, locus of control relates more to outcome expectations than to efficacy expectations. In this view, internality reflects the opinion that individual behavior would influence outcomes, but disregards the question of whether one is capable of performing that behavior.

Bandura (1977, 204) puts it this way " . . . convictions that outcomes are determined by one's own actions can have any number of effects on self-efficacy and behavior. People who regard outcomes as personally determined but who lack the requisite skills would experience low self-efficacy and view activities with a sense of futility." One might consider how different combinations of internality-externality and self-efficacy might influence compliance with a medical regimen (assuming optimal levels of perceived threat):

		Locus of Control	
		Internal	*External*
Self-Efficacy	*High*	A	B
	Low	C	D

In this simple 2 × 2 classification, persons in cell A (Internal control and High self-efficacy) would be most likely to comply, while persons in cell D (External control and Low self-efficacy) would be least likely to comply. Those in cell B believe themselves capable of compliance but will not comply because they are not convinced that compliance would attain some desired effect. People in cell C are those described in the quote from Bandura—they believe outcomes are personally determined but that they lack the skills to execute the action.

This analysis reveals that both locus of control (or outcome expectation) and efficacy expectation are necessary for a given behavior to occur. When we turn from this overly-simplified model of dichotomous expectations to the more realistic world of continuously-distributed expectations, the joint effects of the two dimensions become very complex indeed, and it is not surprising therefore that the multitude of studies on locus of control that disregard self-efficacy and perceived threat have yielded inconsistent findings.

It is useful to turn the argument around and question whether self-efficacy, in the absence of satisfactory expectations about outcomes, can predict behavior. Both theory and data make clear the necessity of proper outcome expectations as well as efficacy expectations. People may feel quite confident in their ability, for example, to quit smoking, but will not do so in the absence of incentive.

The reader may wonder about the similarity of social learning and Health Belief Model concepts. It needs to be pointed out that both derive from the seminal work of Kurt Lewin (1944). This brief overview cannot deal with the many issues suggested by the foregoing analysis. That topic will be addressed in a subsequent publication.

REFERENCES

Bandura, A. (1977a). *Social learning theory*. Englewood Cliffs, NJ: Prentice-Hall.

Bandura, A. (1977b). Self-efficacy: Toward a unifying theory of behavioral change. *Psychological Review, 84*, 191–215.

Becker, M. H. (Ed.), (1974). *The health belief model and personal health behavior*. Thorofare, NJ: Slack.

Beery, W., Schoenbach, V. J., & Wagner, E. H. (1986). *Health risk appraisal: Methods and programs, with annotated bibliography*. Washington, DC: U.S. Government Printing Office, DHHS Pub. No. (PHS) 86–3396.

Cummings, K. M., Becker, M. H., & Maile, M. C. (1980). Bringing the models together: An empirical approach to combining variables used to explain health actions. *Journal of Behavioral Medicine, 3*, 123–145.

Fishbein, M., & Ajzen, I. (1975). *Belief, attitude, intention and behavior*. Reading, MA: Addison-Wesley.

Gottlieb, B. H. (1985). Social networks and social support: An overview of research, practice, and policy implications. *Health Education Quarterly, 12*, 5–22.

Green, L. W. (1975). Diffusion and adoption of innovations related to cardiovascular risk behavior in the public. In Enelow, A. J., & Henderson, J. B., (Eds.), *Applying behavioral science to cardiovascular risk: Proceedings of a conference*. American Heart Association, pp. 84–108.

Green, L. W., Kreuter, M. W., Deeds, S. G., & Partridge, K. B. (1980). *Health education planning: A diagnostic approach*. Palo Alto: Mayfield.

Janz, N. K., & Becker, M. H. (1984). The health belief model: A decade later. *Health Education Quarterly, 11*, 1–47.

Lewin, K., Dembo, T., Festinger, L., & Sears, P. S. Level of asperation. In Hunt, J. McV. (Ed.), (1944). *Personality and the behavior disorders*. (pp. 333–378) New York: Ronald.

McAlister, A., Farquhar, J., Thoresen, C., & Maccoby, N. (1976). Behavioral sciences applied to cardiovascular health: Progress and research needs in the modification of risk-taking habits in adult populations. *Health Education Monographs, 4*, 45–74.

Parcel, G. S., & Baranowski, T. (1981). Social learning theory and health education. *Health Education, 12*, 14–18.

Rosenstock, I. M. (1966). Why people use health services. *Milbank Memorial Fund Quarterly, 44*, 94–124.

Rotter, J. B. (1966). Generalized expectancies for internal versus external control of reinforcement. *Psychological Monographs, 80*, 1–28.

Strecher, V. J., DeVellis, B. McE., Becker, M. H., & Rosenstock, I. M. (1986). The role of self-efficacy in achieving health behavior change. *Health Education Quarterly, 13*, 73–92.

Sutton, S. R. (1982). Fear-arousing communications: A critical examination of theory and research. In Eiser, J. R. (Ed.), *Social psychology and behavioral medicine*. (pp. 303–337) New York: Wiley.

Wallston, K., & Wallston, B. (1982). Who is responsible for your health? The construct of Health Locus of Control. In Sanders, G., & Suls, J. (Eds.), *Social Psychology of Health and Illness*. (pp. 65–95) Hillsdale, NJ: Lawrence Erlbaum, Associates.

SOCIAL LEARNING THEORY IN CURRENT HEALTH EDUCATION PRACTICE

Noreen M. Clark

Social learning theory[1] as discussed by Bandura (1977a, b, 1982, 1986) has received increasing attention as a basis for health education efforts. The theory is useful to health educators primarily because it attempts to describe how individual behavior is changed. Several theories have been shown to predict health behavior effectively. For example, the Health Belief Model (Rosenstock, 1974; Becker, 1974; Janz & Becker, 1984) suggests that if certain conditions are fulfilled, individuals can be expected to behave in certain ways regarding their health. Bandura's social learning theory predicts behavior only in the sense of describing what influences it. The theory focuses on explaining the mechanisms by which one learns, consciously or unconsciously, to behave in a given way. These are explained in such a fashion to enable the design of interventions, educational and other, likely to elicit new behavior. For example, while the Health Belief Model suggests that if one believes he is susceptible to an illness he is more likely to follow a preventive regimen, the theory does not claim to describe how one comes to see himself as susceptible. Social learning theory, on the other hand, does not predict a particular behavior. Rather, it describes the factors that

Advances in Health Education and Promotion, vol. 2, pages 251–275
Copyright © 1987 JAI Press Inc.
All rights of reproduction in any form reserved.
ISBN: 0-89232-617-4

operate, in this case, to cause one to believe himself susceptible. The theory attempts to explain the processes that create and hold beliefs and behaviors in place. By consciously activating these processes, individuals (often assisted by someone else—for example, a health educator) can bring about changes in their own behavior.

ELEMENTS OF BANDURA'S SOCIAL LEARNING THEORY

Before considering how social learning theory has been evident in several recent health education programs and before examining the effects of these programs on health behavior, it is useful to consider the major elements of the theory. *Reciprocal determinism* is an important concept. While other learning theories see behavior as a function of a person's environment or as a function of the interaction of a person and the environment, social learning theory proffers that behavior, personal factors and the environment all operate as mutually interacting determinants of each other. Learning is dynamic and multidirectional in the sense that different factors are influential in different situations.

The theory also diverges from radical behavioristic interpretations of learning in that it places great importance on cognitive events. Behaviorists who subscribe to operant theories ascribe cognition to the effect of external events. Emotions, as well, are therefore the byproducts of behavior. As described by Parcel and Baranowski (1981), social learning theory expands on the focus of operant theory by introducing mediating constructs. Operant conditioning looks at learning as mechanical associations among stimulus, response and reinforcement, and behaviorists such as Skinner (1976) disregard cognitions as determinants of behavior. Social learning theorists on the other hand, and particularly Bandura, believe that cognitive aids are used in learning. Cognition has a causal influence on behavior. For example, according to Skinner's theory, when people act to avoid an aversive experience when stimuli are presented, it is the stimuli that have become aversive. There is no judgment by the person that intervenes to control behavior. The stimulus elicits the behavior. Social learning theory teaches that when people act protectively when presented with stimuli previously associated with painful experience, it is the person's knowledge of his environment that leads him to expect another painful experience. Therefore, if a word foreshadows pain, the word has come to hold predictive significance for the person. Expectancy is a cognitive function. Bandura's social learning theory differs from strict behaviorist interpretations of learning in another way. An important rule of operant theory is that behavior is controlled by the immediate consequence of behavior.

However, intermittent reinforcement has proven to be more effective in shaping behavior than has continuous reinforcement (Skinner, 1976; Nye, 1979; Bandura, 1977). According to social learning theory, intermittent reinforcement works because the individual integrates data regarding the consequences of his behavior over time and regulates behavior based on aggregate consequences (Bandura, 1977). Integration and regulation are functions of cognitive processes.

Several concepts are fundamental to social learning theory:

Vicarious learning. While no social learning theorist would deny the importance of one's own overt behavior in learning, it is clear that much of how we behave results from observing the experience of others not only (as operant theory suggests) from the direct consequences of our own behavior. The capacity to learn by observation allows people to acquire large, integrated patterns of behavior without having to form them gradually by trial and error. The observation of models of behavior is a primary way by which vicarious learning occurs.

Symbols. Social learning theory teaches that the capacity to use symbols is a powerful means to handle the environment. Through verbal and visual symbols, people process and preserve experiences in representational form. These representations serve as guides to future behavior and lead individuals to expect certain outcomes. Symbols enable people to solve problems (cognitively) rather than having to enact all the possible alternatives and solutions. Interpreting symbols entails reflective thought.

Self-regulation. People exercise control over their own behavior by arranging environmental inducements, generating cognitive supports or aids to learning, and producing consequences for their own actions. Self-regulation can be created and supported by external influences but self-influence plays a part in determining which actions one performs. According to Bandura, human nature is characterized by a vast potentiality that within biological limits can be shaped by direct and vicarious experience into a variety of forms. The level of psychological and physiological development restricts what an individual can achieve at any given time.

Reinforcement. Social learning theory posits that reinforcement is fundamental to learning. To be reinforcing, a consequence of behavior must be apparent to a person, that is, one must be aware of what is being rewarded. Learning without such awareness is slow and difficult. There are three systems that serve as reinforcement. External reinforcement is the consequence that occurs in the environment that is experienced as rewarding. Vicarious reinforcements are those consequences that one observes have been positive and rewarding for others. Self-reinforcement is the process by which people set standards for their own behavior and act in a self-rewarding or self-punishing way. Individuals expect, judge, reward or punish their own behavior. The standards one sets for oneself are a result of direct experience, and/or the behavior of others that has served as a model.

Expectations and Expectancies. Learning and change in social learning theory are mediated through cognitive processes. Cognitive events are induced and altered most readily by experiences of mastery arising from successful performance. As a result, one's efficacy expectations and outcome expectations are important. Efficacy expectation is the person's conviction that he can perform those behaviors needed to produce certain outcomes and this expectation determines whether or not he will even attempt to cope with a situation. The stronger the efficacy or mastery expectations, the more active the efforts of an individual will be. Outcome expectation is the belief that a certain behavior or occurrence will produce a certain outcome; one's expectancy that the action will produce the consequence. Self-efficacy or the internal state that one experiences as being competent to perform certain tasks can be influenced by one's own performance, by vicarious experience, by verbal persuasion and by emotions such as anxiety.

Emotional coping. A person deals with emotions, particularly fear and anxiety, through emotional coping mechanisms. One devises ways to handle strong feelings so that one is able to reduce anxiety and perform desired behaviors.

THE REVIEW AT HAND

The purpose of this paper is to describe health education programs in which concepts from Bandura's social learning theory have been utilized. Emphasis in this review is placed first on describing the learning activities that constituted the health education. The second emphasis is on description of program effectiveness so that the value of the theory in practice can be determined, that is, whether programs based on theoretical assumptions have yielded behavior change, psychosocial change, or change in health status. In some instances, the program planners of work reviewed here have intentionally set about to use social learning theory in their program designs. In other cases, planners have utilized techniques that reflect the theoretical principles without explicit reference to the theory.

The intention of this discussion is to be illustrative, not exhaustive, in reviewing recent educational efforts. Only programs that involved a reasonable number of participants and attempted to use experimental or quasi-experimental designs to evaluate the effect of education on health beliefs and behaviors are included in this review. Three principles of Bandura's social learning theory will serve as a framework for this discussion: self-regulation and reinforcement, cognitive restructuring, and emotional coping.

Self-regulation and self-reinforcement are defined by Bandura as the processes by which individuals arrange environmental inducements, generate cognitive supports, and produce consequences for their own actions. The capacity to do these things gives people some measure of control over their own behavior.

Cognitive restructuring refers to the capacity to use verbal and imagined symbols to process and preserve experiences in representational forms, to manipulate symbols to deduce causal relationships, and to use this understanding as a guide to future behavior.

Emotional coping refers to the idea that thoughts acquire emotion-activating potential through rewarding and punishing experiences. One can learn to foresee events from predictive stimuli and summon up appropriate anticipatory reactions.

It is, of course, somewhat artificial to separate out a few theoretical principles from an entire body of theory, especially one as eclectic as social learning theory. To date, however, no comprehensive social learning-based health education program has been undertaken. Therefore, for purposes of this review and ease of discussion, these three notions which have, to a degree, been used in health education programs will be treated separately, and the single aspect of a program that best illustrates a principle will receive attention.

SELF-REGULATION AND REINFORCEMENT

While external factors exert a powerful influence on behavior, according to Bandura, people exert control by activating and creating environments for themselves. Decisions on how to manipulate the environment are based on anticipated consequences. Clearly, prior conditions influence a person's choices and actions; however, as indicated in the discussion of reciprocal determinism, Bandura believes that conditions themselves are partly determined by people's actions. Individuals direct the course of action by arranging the environmental conditions most likely to elicit appropriate behavior. They also create both cognitive aids to action and reinforcing consequences. Individuals can be assisted in the process of self-regulation and can be reinforced externally by virtue of consequences they observe or experience first-hand. However, self-reinforcement is also a powerful influence on behavior. Each individual possesses a standard of acceptability for behavior and for the consequences of behavior. According to Bandura, self-reinforcement is the process in which individuals enhance and maintain their own behavior by rewarding themselves when they reach self-prescribed standards. External reinforcement and self-reinforcement are viewed as particularly important in the maintenance of newly acquired behavior.

Some recent health education efforts related primarily to smoking cessation and weight control have utilized the principles of self-regulation and reinforcement of behavior and have enjoyed varying degrees of success in engendering behavior change. Davis et al. (1984) designed a program to help smokers rearrange environmental cues and establish positive consequences for new behavior. They studied 1,237 smokers who were randomly assigned into one of four experimental groups. Compared with the average smoker described by the Public Health Service, the sample had higher levels of cigarette use and a greater proportion who had previously tried to stop smoking with a mean of 3.2 attempts to quit. One group received a package of eight leaflets on a variety of smoking topics such as health effects of smoking, impact of parental smoking on children and nonsmokers' rights. A second group received the leaflets plus a 26-page manual entitled, *A Lifetime of Freedom from Smoking*. This manual was designed to be used by ex-smokers to maintain their nonsmoking behavior. It described techniques for coping with triggers in the environment to smoking. Group members also were encouraged to dial recorded telephone messages for reinforcement available 24 hours a day. These supportive messages were played in a repeating cycle for two months after the leaflets and maintenance manual were received. A third group received a 64-page manual entitled, *Freedom from Smoking in 20 Days*. It led the reader through a series of exercises to quit smoking by the 16th day of the 20-day schedule. The exercises were designed for self-regulation: identifying triggers and cues, keeping records of smoking behavior, signing contracts to quit, using breathing and relaxation exercises to substitute for smoking behavior, and anticipating smoking situations that were likely to arise. Participants paid a $20 fee to enroll in their group.

After distribution of materials, data regarding smoking behavior were collected by telephone interview on five occasions; at 1, 3, 6, 9, and 12 months. The initial quit rate of 20 percent in the total sample was followed by substantial recidivism. The leaflet and maintenance manual group had the highest initial quit rate and the leaflets-only group the lowest. By the final follow-up period, 16 percent of the total sample were nonsmokers. Over the evaluation period, the leaflets-only group was consistently the lowest in quit rates. The cessation and maintenance manual group was the highest in quit rates by endpoint closely followed by the leaflet and maintenance group. The differences between the leaflets-only group and the other three interventions were statistically significant at the $p = .05$ level. The end point quit rate for participants in the two groups receiving the behavioral oriented maintenance manual and the opportunity for external reinforcement was approximately 16 percent. This is somewhat lower than the rate of 20 percent found by Hunt et al. (1971) to be the average quit rate across the 64 smoking cessation programs they reviewed. The leaflet group that received didactic information had a significantly lower final quit rate of just over 12 percent. In the aforementioned Davis study (Davis et al., 1984), self-help materials that gave greater attention to enabling individuals to arrange environmental inducements and produce consequences for their own actions yielded a somewhat greater behavioral change.

Strecher (1983), designed a smoking-cessation program that enabled participants to monitor and control the amount of their smoking and reinforce this positive behavior with rewards of their own choosing. He evaluated the smoking-cessation program with inpatients and outpatients at a Veterans Administration Hospital. The 216 participants were randomly assigned to a treatment or control group. The mean age of the men was 50, over 42 percent had an income below $6,000 per year, all were long-time smokers, and each participant had at least one diagnosed medical condition.

There were three components to the educational program; consultation from a health educator, a self-help smoking-cessation kit in diary format; and incentives to comply with the self-help kit. During a 20–45-minute initial consultation, each patient decided whether or not he wished to quit smoking. If he decided to quit, he then completed with a health educator's help the first series of exercises in the self-help kit. In addition, he filled out the first day of the three-week smoking diary. The remainder of the kit was completed by the patient at home. Compliance with the smoking diary was reinforced through a combination of weekly telephone calls from the health educator and the offering of a Michigan state lottery ticket for each week the diary was completed. The consultation process focused on exploring the influences on one's smoking, exploring the consequences of various smoking decisions, and developing initial awareness of one's smoking behavior. The diary self-help kit focused on developing awareness of the cues that influence smoking, developing alternative activities for coping with smoking cues, applying alternative activities to smoking cues, and using maintenance strategies for long-term smoking cessation.

Because the consultation process enabled the investigator to identify which patients had decided to quit and which wished not to quit, he could conduct three evaluations to assess the effectiveness of the health education. First, he compared the group receiving the intervention with the control group on the rate of smoking cessation for all smokers, that is, those who wished to quit as well as those who did not wish to quit. Second, he compared the experimental group smokers who were offered the intervention with control group smokers who wanted to quit smoking or were undecided. Third, he compared the experimental group smokers who accepted the intervention with the control group smokers who reported that they wanted to quit or were undecided. Self-report of behavior at the time of the posttest was used as the measure of smoking cessation.

The assessment illustrated that across all three types of evaluation, smoking cessation and reduction rates were higher among intervention groups than control groups. For all evaluation strategies, reduction rates of ≥ 25 percent were significantly higher in the intervention groups. In the third type of evaluation, reduction rates of ≥ 50 percent were significantly higher in the intervention group. Strecher's three types of evaluation separating individuals who stated a decision to quit from those who did not wish to quit allow a conservative (type one evaluation including both groups) and a liberal assessment (type three evaluation, where the control group included those who might have refused the intervention if offered, and the experimental group, which did not include those subjects) of the program. In both assessments, conservative and liberal, the intervention did better than the average 20 percent quit rate of cessation programs reviewed by Hunt et al. (1971). The more liberal assessment yielded a significantly higher quit rate than average.

Glasgow et al. (1981) evaluated the effects on smoking behavior of two self-help behavior therapy books compared with a minimal treatment program. Forty men and forty-eight women participated in the study. The two therapy books were based on self-monitoring, rearranging environmental cues, and self-rewards for positive behavior. The first by Danaher and Lichtenstein (1978) emphasized the importance of recording and combating urges to smoke. It included progressive relaxation training as an alternative to smoking. Participants selected either to set a target date for quitting and to establish a monetary contract with a friend for quitting, or to move through the manual at their own pace. The manual also included behavioral hints for managing smoking situations after quitting. The second manual by Pomerleu and Pomerleu (1977) stressed gradual reduction of smoking by eliminating it in progressively difficult situations. A number of stimulus control techniques and alternatives to smoking behavior were presented. Each reader selected a strategy from available options. An imaging exercise was included to help in the achievement of abstinence. The minimal treatment condition was the "I Quit Kit" published by the American Cancer Society. The kit was not oriented toward self-regulation and reinforcement, rather it contained motivational materials such as a poster, buttons, information on the health hazards of smoking, and a phonograph record of others' experiences in quitting. Each of the 88 participants were randomly assigned one of the above conditions to be undertaken alone (self-administered) or with the assistance of a clinical psychologist with experience in smoking cessation (therapist-administered).

Two measures of smoking were utilized: self-report of the participants and analysis of their concentration of carbon monoxide in expired breath samples. All of the treatments were effective in producing significant reductions in smoking rates from pre- to postprogram but significant relapse occurred between the posttest and follow-up test six months later. Overall, smoking rates were 48 percent at posttreatment and 75 percent at the six-month follow-up. Analysis of variance showed a significant effect of the condition of administration and type of treatment. In both behaviorally oriented treatments, the presence of the therapist yielded significantly greater reductions in smoking (47 percent vs. 8 percent). In the minimal contact condition, participants reported doing slightly better under self-administration than therapist administration. At follow-up, participants in the behaviorally oriented treatment who had received support from a therapist continued to do better in abstinence than the minimal contact group. However, analysis of data on carbon monoxide concentrations at both post-test and follow-up failed to yield any reliable differences between types of treatment or condition of administration. The investigators believed that the contradictory findings between self-report and objective data may suggest that participants felt compelled to underreport the extent of their smoking behavior.

Wheeler and Hess (1976) studied the effects of a self-regulation educational program on 40 obese children aged 2 through 11 and their mothers. The program entailed self-monitoring and self-regulation of triggers to eating apparent in the environment. Children fitting project criteria were randomly assigned to an experimental group or a control group. The mother-and-child pair was led through several behavioral steps. First, a detailed analysis of the stimuli and rewards associated with eating in the child's home environment was conducted through use of a food-intake record. Next, nutritionists worked with mother and child on an individual-pair basis to work out adjustments in a specific facet of eating behavior (e.g., limitation of TV snacking). Each counseling session was devoted to specific, manageable manipulations of behavior. Next, the effect of each manipulation on subsequent weight and behavior change was discussed by families and counselors. Any slowing of weight gain received verbal praise from the nutritionist and there was reiteration of the importance of early control of weight to fewer health problems later on. Over time, several manipulations were identified that seemed to comprise a stable and satisfactory system best suited to the long-term control of the individual child's food intake. Finally, mother and child were encouraged to assume responsibility for analysis of food intake and its control.

Evaluation data were analyzed from a matched set of 11 pairs of control and experimental children selected randomly regardless of success or failure in weight reduction. A matched pairs sign test on the change of percentage overweight over the treatment interval showed a significant improvement in the treatment as opposed to control patients. Those who remained in the treatment program for the full number of counseling sessions also outperformed those who dropped out in terms of degree of overweight at end point.

Kinsley and Shapiro (1977) also studied the effects of education on overweight children aged 10 or 11. The education entailed monitoring behavior and establishing self-inducements to increase exercise and reduce food intake. Twenty-four girls and sixteen boys were selected from respondents to a newspaper article announcing a weight-reduction program. Subjects were randomly assigned to one of four conditions: no treatment control, education for the child only, education for mother and child, and education for the mother only. Participants in the treatment groups paid an initial 30-dollar fee that was returned if all sessions were attended. The educational program, whether delivered to mother or child, was essentially the same. In the session for mothers only, the emphasis was on helping children by teaching them the necessary behavioral techniques. The education consisted of 8 weekly sessions in which participants were provided with factual information regarding obesity and nutrition. The ideal of maintaining a negative balance between reduced food intake and increased expenditure of energy was introduced. Participants used pocket calorie-counting booklets and kept daily diaries of food intake. Parents were encouraged to institute a token system in which children could earn tokens to exchange for rewards for following program instructions and procedures.

Analysis of pre- to postintervention data on weight of the children illustrated that treatment groups did not differ significantly from each other, but differed significantly from the control group. Subjects in the combined treatment groups lost a mean of 3.5 pounds, while subjects in the control group gained a mean of 2.0 pounds. Analysis also illustrated that mothers in the mothers-only group lost significantly more weight than mothers in each of the other groups. To assess maintenance of weight loss, data were collected again at six weeks and twenty weeks post-treatment. However, no control data were available for follow-up as control-group members received education immediately after post data collection. The three treatments were not significantly different in long-term effectiveness. Weight changes over the follow-up period for treatment subjects were compared with the weight table norms for 10- and 11-year-old children. Physical growth tables for children indicated a mean weight gain of about .75 pounds per month for children of this age, suggesting that normal growth weight gain for participants would be approximately 3.75 pounds over the five-month follow-up period. After significant weight loss during the treatment period, subjects in all three groups gained weight at a rate closely approximating that of non-obese children their age. No maintenance of weight loss was observed for mothers or children post-treatment. While treatment groups did not differ in outcome, some mothers in the mothers only group and some children in the children only group expressed dissatisfaction that their relatives could not participate in the educational program.

COGNITIVE RESTRUCTURING

Cognitive restructuring is not a term used originally by Bandura but has been employed by others who have accepted his descriptions of social learning. According to Bandura (1977) symbols that represent events, cognitive operations, and relationships serve as the vehicles of thought. Thinking to a large extent depends on language, numerics and other symbols. Cognitive restructuring refers to the idea that by manipulating symbols that convey relevant information, one can gain understanding of causal relationships, create new forms of knowledge, solve problems, and deduce consequences without actually performing any activities. Symbolic systems can be substituted for external events. Changes in behavior result from recognizing the association of environmental events or consequences, and rely heavily upon cognitive representations of contingencies. The capacity to represent future consequences in thought provides one a cognitively based source of motivation, that is, the incentive to act in order to attain an expected consequence. Most actions according to Bandura are thus under anticipatory control. By virtue of direct and vicarious experience, and the ability to manipulate symbols of external events, one comes to have an outcome expectancy, that is, an estimate that a given behavior will lead to certain outcomes. Through the same processes, one comes to have an efficacy expectation—that is, the conviction that one can successfully execute the behavior required to produce the outcomes. Successful performance of the behavior (mastery) and realization of the anticipated consequence, strengthens one's outcome and efficacy expectations.

Several health education programs have been based on attempts at cognitive restructuring—enabling one to manipulate symbols to anticipate the different consequences of different behavior, to increase outcome expectancy and self-efficacy. Contingency planning, anticipatory problem-solving, performance of skills, role modeling, and rehearsal have been some of the approaches used in these cognitive restructuring efforts.

Bruhn and Parcel (1982) used cognitive restructuring to encourage early childhood health promotion. They developed a health education program and implemented it with 100 four-year-olds. Seventy-three children, who did not receive the program until after evaluation data were collected, served as a comparison group. The education was delivered in the school setting and learning activities revolved around puppets that served as role models for good health behavior. Children anticipated health problems and rehearsed positive health habits via games and role plays. Ideas introduced through these activities were reinforced through songs, poems and special behavioral materials that emphasized guidelines for future behavior. These materials were provided to parents for use with the child at home.

The program was evaluated (Parcel et al., 1983) based on interview data collected from parents, children, and teachers pre- and posteducation. Children were asked to sort pictures of children exhibiting what the investigators judged to be good and bad health behaviors, and were asked, "Would you do this?" regarding each practice illustrated. In addition, children were asked to select, from a variety of options, the foods they would prefer for snacking. The evaluators reported significant differences in behavior of program children and comparison group children after the education. Mothers reported that program children were more safety conscious. They avoided sharp objects, wore seatbelts more often, stayed away from matches and chose fruit as snacks over candy. There were no significant differences in children's reports of their preferences for health or safety behavior; however, program children *were* different in their views toward smoking. These children were significantly more likely than control children to state that they would not smoke cigarettes, pipes, or cigars.

Bowler and Morisky (1983) reported on the evaluation of a small-group strategy for improving compliance behavior and blood pressure control in a low-income, predominantly black and female population: The program was developed and implemented by Green et al. (1975). It emphasized anticipating problems in managing hypertension and constructing options for responding to these problems. It also was designed to increase the participants' perceptions that they could control their medical problem. Two hundred patients were assigned at random into an intervention or control group. The education was a series of three weekly, two-hour sessions with 8 to 10 patients. It was specifically designed to increase the participants' feelings of control over their medical problem and is described as "internality training." The group facilitator was a social worker skilled in group dynamics. The program began with the facilitator eliciting from group members their expectations for the education and the priority areas of interest related to their medical condition. Agreement was reached regarding which issues would be addressed in the sessions. A videotape of each individual describing her expectations was replayed for the group so members could identify common themes and concerns. A medical regimen was constructed for each patient. These were displayed in poster form around the meeting room and blood pressure readings, taken at each session, were entered weekly. The posters were seen as a way to make the similarities and differences in patients' management problems more visible to participants. During group meetings, patients were asked to select a cognitive (I don't know how pills help my hypertension) or affective (I am nervous when I have to talk to the doctor) problem area from the list of concerns compiled initially. Two interpersonal skills methods were used by the facilitator to help the participant think about the problem she chose. One was the Reimanis and Shaefer (1970) method described by Bowler and Morisky as an attempt to help the patient see herself as having power to effect change. This was done by (1) challenging or confronting "external" statements with "internal" questions to get the patient to examine her reasons for choosing from among certain options; (2) rewarding "internal" statements; and (3) helping patients to focus on the result of behavior (what could she have done to change outcomes). The second method was Master's (1979) "behavioral reinterpretation," which attempted to get the patient to see that the way she looked at a problem or responded to a situation affected her behavior (would it help to look at the problem from a different perspective?) The Health Belief Model (Rosenstock, 1974) was used as a framework around which to organize these problem-solving discussions. At the conclusion of discussions, participants were asked to view videotapes depicting hypertension problems. Patients were asked to act as consultants and to comment on the tapes based on their own experiences with high blood pressure. This activity aimed to reinforce the participants views of themselves as knowledgeable people.

The evaluation of the effect of the program (Morisky et al., 1983) used three variables: self-reported medication compliance, appointment-keeping behavior, and blood pressure control status. The greatest impact of the program was on blood pressure control. After the "internality training," 55 percent of the experimental groups had their blood pressure under adequate control, while 44 percent of the control group were in control. This finding was not statistically significant. Follow-up data were collected on the cohort three years after the conclusion of the health education. At that time, patients in the intervention had their blood pressure under control to a significantly greater degree than did the control group (a total of 83 percent of participants; a statistically significant difference from the control group). In addition, a 53 percent reduction in hypertension-related mortality was found in the experimental group at the time of follow-up that was also statistically significant.

Hurd et al. (1980) studied a smoking-prevention program with 1,526 seventh grade students. The education was provided in the school setting. It focused on assisting children to anticipate and construct optional behaviors to smoking situations, and to formulate counter arguments when being persuaded to smoke. Four schools participated. School one served as a comparison school. School two was also a comparison school but smoking behavior of school two students was monitored via a questionnaire about cigarette use and by collection of saliva samples for thiocyanate analysis. School three was monitored and received a social pressures curriculum comprised of four sessions. The sessions were a combination of film and videotape presentations and discussion groups. Discussion sessions were led by college students who were seen by researchers as role models for the children. After media presentation, children were divided into groups of 6 to 15. Each child was asked individually to write down three things that were bad about smoking and then after group discussions to record the collective responses of group members. The process was repeated using the questions, "What are three ways to say no to smoking?" and "What are three ways people start smoking?" A second session was designed to illustrate to students that smokers are in the minority in the seventh grade and in the general population. Students were asked to estimate the percentage of smokers in each group and then were shown the actual statistics. Discussion ensued. A third session included the presentation of a videotape followed by role playing of situations similar to those depicted on tape. In the role plays, students practiced saying no to smoking in several different types of situations. A final discussion included a film showing media, family, and peer pressures on young people to smoke. In small discussion groups, students then described advertisements for smoking with which they were familiar and formulated counterarguments. In school four, students were monitored and received the social pressures curriculum plus personalization. Personalization provided students with familiar and respected role models selected from among their peers. Before initiation of the program at school four, students were asked to identify five students in their class whose opinions they respected. The three most-cited students were videotaped role playing various smoking situations. These videotapes were used for the discussion groups held at school four, replacing the unknown actors who appeared in tapes used at school three. Half the students at school four received, in addition, the commitment condition. These students were asked to complete the sentence, "I'm not going to smoke because . . . " Students rehearsed their sentence and were recorded by videotape while making their statement. Each tape was played back to the class as a whole.

Complete data were collected on 1,245 of the participating students. The number of students reporting nonsmoking declined in all schools during the study period. The decline was greatest in comparison school two and less in schools one, three and four although statistical comparisons were not significant. The trend was unrelated to level of baseline smoking. Experimental smoking increased in three of the four schools including one intervention and both comparison schools. Regular smoking increased in all schools. The increase was greatest in the comparison schools, which doubled their number of smokers. In the schools with the prevention curriculum the rate of increase was modest. An examination of comparison school two with intervention schools three and four yielded a significant difference in smoking behavior among schools. Thiocyanate analysis of saliva samples paralleled the self-report measure. The investigators concluded that the programs embodying all three elements, social-pressures curriculum, personalization and commitment, effectively reduced the onset of smoking in the seventh grade students.

Condiotte and Lichtenstein (1981) studied the effect of two smoking-cessation programs on 87 adult smokers. Treatment included a significant effort to increase participants' perceptions that they could give up smoking. Participants ranged in age from 16 to 70; 38 were male and 49 were female. The investigators were particularly interested in efficacy enhancement as a result of treatment. The subjects were recruited from two cessation programs, one a federally funded treatment clinic and the other a program conducted by a religious group. Subjects in one program ($N = 24$) were assigned to a maximal record-keeping group. All other subjects were assigned to a minimal record-keeping group. The measure of smoking was the individual's self-report. Data regarding smoking behavior and efficacy expectations were collected in a preliminary intake interview, and again during a three-month follow-up period after completion of the program.

The behavioral approaches in the two treatment programs varied in content and control techniques. Such activities as nicotine fading, normally paced vs. rapid smoking and individual and group sessions to increase feelings of self-efficacy were part of the programs. Session times varied from five consecutive days to seven once a week meetings. Subjects in the maximal record keeping group were required to monitor their smoking behavior, efficacy and mood states on a daily basis for five weeks after treatment. Subjects in the minimal record-keeping group did not monitor their behavior, but took part in telephone interviews to assess the state of their smoking behavior, self-efficacy and emotional reactions. Data analysis of pre- to postprogram data revealed that both treatment programs significantly enhanced efficacy states, and that the two programs did not differ from each other with regard to the extent of this effect. Nor were the programs different in their effect on smoking status: program one had an abstinence rate of 49 percent and program two had a rate of 42 percent. Analysis of data for the maximal record keeping group members (for whom there were complete data) illustrated nonsignificant changes in self-efficacy enhancement from pre- to midtreatment and from mid- to post-treatment. Since social learning theory suggests that only those who actually derive benefit from a program (through achieving mastery) will have improvement in the efficacy state, the investigators removed from the data pool subjects in the maximal record-keeping group who showed no behavioral improvement after the intervention ($N = 6$), and analyzed data for the remaining 18. For this subset, t-tests comparing pre- and midtreatment efficacy states revealed significant enhancement from pre- to midtreatment and enhancement from mid- to post-treatment. Analysis of relapse data on all subjects revealed that the higher the level of perceived self-efficacy at the completion of treatment, the greater the probability that the subject would remain abstinent through the entire experimental period. Relapse was defined as resumption of smoking at the rate of more than one cigarette per week. At the end of the three-month follow-up period, 44 of the 78 subjects had relapsed.

Coelho (1984) examined self-efficacy in a sample of 66 adult smokers who participated in a cessation program. Subjects, 25 males and 41 females whose mean age was 41, were randomly assigned to two treatments. Both treatments are described by the authors as having a social learning focus and increasing perceptions of self-efficacy as a goal. Seven meetings were held over a six-week period. Self-efficacy was measured by use of a questionnaire pretreatment, post-treatment, at one month and again three months post-treatment. At post-treatment, 64 percent of participants were abstinent. At the three-month follow-up, 27 percent were abstinent. Abstinent subjects had significantly higher levels of self-efficacy than those smoking. Self-efficacy increased significantly from pre- to post-treatment, and decreased significantly from that point to the three-month follow-up.

The work of Lenker et al. (1984) is interesting in light of the concept of self-efficacy (see also Yalow and Collins, in this volume). They were curious as to why participants in an arthritis self-management program who increased their ability to self-manage did not realize improvements in health status. To examine the question, the investigators reinterviewed 54 participants. Inquiries were made of individuals who had exhibited either positive or negative changes in health status after the program. Each was asked open-ended questions about whether the arthritis course components had an influence on their health. Both substantive (arthritis information) and process (e.g., modeling of behavior) components were discussed. Judges reviewed the responses of the participants to identify categories of theoretical interest. Three major categories were identified. They were perceived self-control over the disease, the current emotional status of the patient, and perceived social support received by the patient. Interviews were then coded into these categories to determine if the education had had a positive or negative effect on the category. The "perceived control" category included statements ranging from "nothing helps arthritis" to "I feel I can control the level of pain and disability." Levels of affect or emotional response ranged from "I'm extremely depressed" to "I try to do what I can to feel good about it." Interrater reliability was .62 for control and affect categories. The mean scores for each category of patient were compared (negative outcomes versus positive outcomes) by a t-test. Subjects who had experienced positive health outcomes perceived that they had significantly more self-control, more social support, and more positive emotional response than did patients who had negative health outcomes after the program. The investigators caution that this study was designed to generate and not test hypotheses related to mediating variables that influence the effects of health education. Their retrospective design did not allow investigators to identify whether self-control, social support and positive emotional responses increased from pre- to post health education, and whether increases were directly related to improvements in health status. Nonetheless, the authors suggest that this exploration is an interesting comment on Bandura's concept of self-efficacy. One can infer from study findings either that those who judge themselves able to have impact on their disease process are the ones to self-manage and have more positive health status outcomes, or that more positive self-management yields the feeling of having greater impact on disease.

EMOTIONAL COPING

According to Bandura (1977), at the initial stages of human development, environmental stimuli have no influence (except for those that are inherently aversive, e.g., hunger, or rewarding, e.g., food when hungry). However, through direct and vicarious experience a vast array of stimuli acquire the capacity to activate and guide behavior. Over time, events that were formerly neutral gain predictive value for the individual. People fear and avoid things associated with aversive experiences and like and seek those that have had pleasant associations. A person does not simply respond to stimuli, but interprets them. Experiences create expectations and these expectations can activate fear and defensive conduct. Until the individual develops effective coping behaviors, threats produce high emotional arousal and various defensive maneuvers. Emotional arousal can influence efficacy expectations in threatening situations. Individuals are more likely to expect success when they are not not beset by fear. If fear is reduced and success expected, people are more likely to attempt an action. Cognitive activity can reduce fear by providing an awareness of other contingencies. Threat is reduced when one rearranges contingencies so that different consequences can be expected. Bandura posits that cognitive activities can also produce direct physiological effects. As thoughts have the potential to activate emotions, a person can control aversive arousal generated by perturbing thoughts by engaging in serene thoughts.

One or two health education efforts have attempted to use anticipatory discussions to reduce emotional responses associated with health problems to increase efficacy expectations and one's intention to take needed action. Some, as well, have taught relaxation techniques, most of which are designed directly to reduce anxiety or to serve as a focus of activity in the face of fearful events.

Fassler (1980) designed a program for children 6 to 12 years old who were admitted to a hospital pediatric ward for tonsillectomy. The program was aimed at helping children to describe anticipated problems and to reduce their anxiety through talking over their fears and receiving reassurances from health personnel. Forty-five children were randomly assigned into an experimental group receiving information and emotional support, an experimental group receiving regular care, emotional support and no additional information, and a control group that received regular care with no additional information or support. Children in the first experimental group were read a story by a health-care provider. Parents were in the child's room, but did not participate in the education. The story, "Elizabeth Gets Well," and a series of related questions were designed to stimulate discussion and enable the child to express fears or anxieties and receive needed information. After the discussion of the story, children were given hospital toys to play with including an operating table and medical instruments. They were asked to make up a story using the toys. The child's story was used as a basis for identifying fears, answering questions and correcting misconceptions about the hospital experience. Again the child was encouraged to openly express his or her feelings. Finally the child was asked to draw a picture of himself or herself and asked to point to where the tonsils were in the picture. The child was also asked to draw a picture of the tonsils and misconceptions apparent in the drawings and in discussion of the drawings were discussed and corrected.

After the education, two anxiety scales were administered. The first was the Manifest Anxiety Test, based on the Children's Manifest Anxiety Scale (Castaneda et al., 1956), which requires that the child respond to a number of self-descriptive statements. The second was the Callahan Anxiety Picture Text (Callahan 1962), a projective test that asks children to interpret blot-type drawings.

Children in the second experimental group received additional emotional support without information concerning hospitalization. They were read a story entitled "Curious George Gets a Medal" and played with toys that did not include hospital toys. Children also were asked to make two drawings. All discussions were directed toward outside interests, school and family. Children in the regular care control condition received no additional support or information.

A three-way analysis of variance on anxiety scale data yielded a significant positive effect for the first experimental group on both scales compared to the other two conditions. The group receiving emotional support scored lower on the CAP scale than the control group receiving no intervention; however, the difference in the MAT scores was not statistically significant.

Skipper and Leonard (1968) in a much earlier study illustrated that attempts to assist mothers to anticipate and cope with the emotional factors associated with their children's hospitalization yielded both psychological benefits for mothers and physiological benefits for children. They studied 80 children between the ages of 3 and 9 who had been admitted to a hospital for tonsillectomy. Children were randomly assigned to an experimental or control group. Experimental group mothers were the target of an intervention provided by nurses at the time of admission. The nurse attempted to create an atmosphere that would facilitate the communication of information to the mother and maximize her freedom to verbalize fear, anxiety and special problems. The information given to the mother provided an accurate account of the reality of the hospital experience. The interaction was characterized by the investigators as expressive, person-oriented, and intimate. The nurse probed the mother's feelings and the background of those feelings as possible causes of stress. In each individual case, the nurse tried to help the mother meet her own individual problems and find ways to cope with them.

Parents were asked to complete a questionnaire related to the amount of stress they experienced during and after the child's operation. In addition, blood pressures, pulse rates and temperatures were taken on all study children at four periods: admission, pre-operation, post-operation and discharge. Analysis of data illustrated that mothers of experimental group children reported significantly less stress than did mothers of control-group children. More interesting, however, were the effects of the intervention on the health status of the children. Complete data were available for 48 children (referred to as Experiment I) and partial data on the remaining 32 children (Experiment II). Data for Experiment I illustrated that the mean systolic blood pressure of experimental group children was significantly lower at the three points in time after admission than was the mean pressure of control-group children. Similarly, the mean pulse rate for experimental children was significantly lower and mean temperature of experimental-group children was significantly closer to normal than was the mean rate for control children. Investigators posited that the intervention with the mothers of hospitalized children enabled the parent to cope with associated stress, and subsequently to reduce the stress felt by the child.

Gray-Toft (1980) studied the effect of a counseling-support program designed to help hospice nurses identify and discuss their job-related anxiety. The number of subjects is very small, and the study design dependent on the 17 nurses serving as their own controls. The program is included here first, because findings are interesting and, second, because there are so few interventions related to emotional coping and health care to serve as examples of theory in action.

There were two program phases. First, nurses were involved in discussion of stressful events they experienced in the week before the educational session. Participants were encouraged to verbalize their feelings of stress and anxiety and share experiences. Next, the nurses were led through a series of structured exercises for coping with stress, including conflict resolution, improving communication skills, role plays of difficult situations, and relaxation techniques. Relaxation was practiced one hour a week for nine weeks.

Data on each nurse that related to stress experienced on the job were collected. Also, a job-description index was used that required each nurse to describe job attitudes and experiences. Analysis of these data illustrated that the program had a significant pre- to post-effect on the levels of stress reported by the participants related to death and dying, the job satisfaction of the nurses, and in job turnover in the cohort.

OBSERVATIONS ON HEALTH EDUCATION BASED ON SOCIAL LEARNING THEORY AND PROBLEMS IN PROGRAM EVALUATIONS

Characteristics of Current Programs

One is struck with how few published health education programs have been organized around the principles of social learning theory. It is also clear from the examples reviewed here that no consistent pattern regarding programs or evaluation findings is apparent in current efforts. Of course, the lack of observable patterns could be a function of the small number of examples. Nonetheless, it is interesting to note that programs to date have cut across all age groups (4-year-olds in the Parcel study to military veterans, 50 years of age, in the Strecher study), all ethnicities and all income levels. In the studies on children, there has been no discussion of the problems that may exist when these theoretical principles are applied to those who may not have reached cognitive maturity.

The current health-related examples of the principles of self-regulation and reinforcement in which empirical evaluation data are available to us, center on smoking and obesity. Self-regulation and reinforcement theoretically lend themselves well to these health problems, as reversing the conditions involves mastering specific behaviors for specific situations (e.g., resisting environmental cues, controlling food intake, and taking medicines at the appropriate times). Within the context of these conditions the tasks of monitoring behavior, identifying positive and negative consequences, and replacing ineffective behaviors with effective ones, while by no means simple, are behaviorally and conceptually clear. None of the health education programs located for this review concerned disease management, where the behavioral context is less clear. If one exercises and controls food intake, for example, a fairly reliable outcome is a degree of weight reduction. A feeling of mastery is then likely, as is a positive consequence (looking or feeling better). In many disease-management tasks, however, discerning which behaviors to apply in which situations can be difficult; given behaviors are not certain to produce the expected consequences. For the sake of example, consider the tasks associated with asthma self-management. One must be able to distinguish severe wheezing episodes from minor ones, and decide which behaviors are needed given a variable situation, a variable disease, and medicines that are far from foolproof. One might carry out a set of recommended behaviors (medicine taking), yet the desired outcome (reduced wheezing) may not *always* occur. Positive consequences as a result of given disease management behaviors cannot be guaranteed. The difficulty of specifying relatively reliable cause and effect in the management of many diseases may mean that the principles of self-regulation and reinforcement may not translate easily into this area of health-education practice.

It is impossible to say, based on existing data, if self-regulation and reinforcement provide a comparable or better theoretical base for health education related to smoking and obesity than do other theories. Existing evaluations have not compared a comprehensive range of learning activities based on these social learning principles against activities based on other learning theories, for example, operant conditioning, or Freire's (1970) theory of consciousness raising. From the examples reviewed here, one might say simply that in the short run, programs using the concepts appear to yield better results than no program at all. Participants gave up smoking and lost weight. However, there was no long-term effect from these approaches. Recidivism was high. It would be unfair to suggest that the failure to realize long-term change via self-regulation and reinforcement programs related to obesity and smoking is a failure of social learning theory. It may be instead a problem of uninspired application of the theory in program activities. In addition, there may be inadequacies in the evaluative procedures used to assess program effectiveness. Further, Bandura (1977) emphasizes that external reinforcement and self-reinforcement are particularly important for newly acquired behavior. It also may be that programs failed to stay with learners long enough to reinforce change and not that the theory fails to explain the mechanism of change.

Given the very limited data, one might also say that facilitating cognitive restructuring, especially enhancing self-efficacy, is better than no program at all. No data, however, allow one to say that this theoretical notion is comparable to, or better than, other social learning theory principles or to assess how it stacks up against use of constructs from similar theories e.g., locus of control (Rotter, 1966), or quite different ones. In three studies (Condiotte & Lichenstein, 1981; Coelho, 1984; Lenker, 1984) increased self-efficacy was associated with improved health status: abstinence from smoking and functional ability in arthritis patients. In the Bowler and Morisky (1983) evaluation, long-term blood pressure control was evident after "internality training" and efforts to enhance belief in self-control. Strecher et al. (1986), in a recent review, found extensive evidence that self-efficacy and health behavior change are strongly related and that the construct deserves more study.

Unfortunately, so few data are available regarding emotional coping interventions that there is little to say about their effect. The Skipper and Leonard (1968) study is very interesting in that both psychological and physiological outcomes were assessed and improvements noted as a result of the education program. The potential for emotional coping interventions to significantly enhance management of health problems and recovery, appears to be an important area for program development and rigorous evaluation.

Problems in Program Evaluations

Findings to date suggest that social learning theory may have an important contribution to make to health education programming. To determine adequately the extent of the contribution some evaluation design and method issues must be addressed.

First is sample size. The great majority of studies regarding Bandura's learning principles beyond self-efficacy (Stricker et al., 1986) has concerned non-health issues. Most have focused on such things as phobias, lack of assertiveness or other psychological constructs. In addition, most intervention studies have involved small numbers of subjects. To assess more equitably the effects of the theory in health education practice, health-related studies with larger samples must be undertaken.

In addition, program and evaluation designs to date have made it difficult if not impossible to distinguish the effects of particular aspects of social learning theory on behavior. Programs have combined many principles into eclectic educational approaches, and evaluations have been classical black-box assessments. Furthermore, as mentioned previously, no studies have been designed to compare social-learning-based programs with programs derived from other theories. Of the programs reviewed, only two (Glasgow, 1981; Davis, 1984) use designs that tested self-regulation and reinforcement approaches against other approaches, i.e., a didactic, information-based approach, and a conventional motivational approach. More comparative studies are needed.

Measures used to assess outcomes in social-learning programs need careful consideration, especially those assessing self-efficacy. Self-efficacy is a construct that has been measured by different evaluators in their own way. One might speculate that this proclivity does not trouble Bandura (1977), as he has stated that self-efficacy is situational; one feels efficacious about a specific behavior or event. Nonetheless, there have appeared at least two articles (Lee, 1983; Sherer et al., 1982) that propose that self-efficacy is a generalizable state; one who feels efficacious in a given situation is likely to feel efficacious in general. At least one general self-efficacy index has been developed (Sherer et al., 1982). While the idea of general self-efficacy is interesting, as general locus of control is an interesting construct, neither is particularly useful in practice as they provide little specific information on which to base interventions. The development of health- and situation-specific efficacy measures would be much more instructive for health education programming. The more specific program and evaluation objectives are, the more powerful and focused the learning activities can be.

Finally, a comprehensive and systematic way to apply the variety of elements that constitute social learning theory must be devised. The theory is eclectic. Nonetheless, if it is effective in predicting and explaining how to change behavior, then it must be possible to make operational its constituent parts. As yet, practice has not adequately reflected theory.

In summary, social learning theory holds promise for health-education research and development, but the limited data available to date make it impossible even to guess how significant the contribution will be.

ACKNOWLEDGMENTS

The author is grateful to Dr. Irwin M. Rosenstock for his critical review of this chapter.

NOTE

1. The term "social learning theory" appears in lower case as Bandura and others see the theory as work in progress and tend not to use capitals when referring to it.

REFERENCES

Bandura, A. (1977a). Social learning theory. Englewood Cliffs, NJ: Prentice-Hall.
Bandura, A. (1977b). Self-efficacy: Toward a unifying theory of behavioral change. *Psychological Review*, *84*(2), 191–215.

Bandura, A. (February, 1982). Self-efficacy mechanisms in human agency. *American Psychologist*, *37*(2), 122–147.

Bandura, A. (1986). Social foundations of thought and action: a social cognitive theory. Englewood Cliffs: Prentice-Hall.

Becker, M. H. (1974). The health belief model and sick role behavior. *Health Education Monograph*, *2*, 409–419.

Bowler, M. H., & Morisky, D. E. (Spring, 1983). Small group strategy for improving compliance behavior and blood pressure control. *Health Education Quarterly*, *10*(1), 57–69.

Bruhn, J. G., & Parcel, G. S. (1982). Preschool health education program (PHEP): An analysis of baseline data. *Health Education Quarterly*, *9*(2, 3), 20, 33.

Callahan, R. (1962). Validity of the children's anxiety pictures. *Percept. Motility Skills*, *14*, 166.

Castaneda, A., McCandless, R., & Palermo, D. (1956). The children's form of the manifest anxiety scale. *Child Development*, *27*, 317–326.

Coates, T. J., & Thoresen, C. E. (February, 1978). Treating obesity in children and adolescents. *American Journal of Public Health*, *68*(2), 143–150.

Coelho, R. J. (1984). Self-efficacy and cessation of smoking. *Psychology Reports*, *54*, 309–310.

Condiotte, M. M., & Lichtenstein, E. (1981). Self-efficacy and relapse in smoking cessation programs. *Journal of Consulting and Clinical Psychology*, *49*(5), 648–658.

Danaher, B. G., & Lichtenstein, E. (1978). Become an ex-smoker. Englewood Cliffs, NJ: Prentice-Hall.

Davis, A. L., Faust, R., & Ordentlich, M. (1984). Self-help smoking cessation and maintenance programs: A comparative study with 12-month follow-up by the American Lung Association. *American Journal of Public Health*, *74*(11), 1212–1217.

Fassler, D. (1980). Reducing preoperative anxiety in children: Information versus emotional support. *Parent Counseling and Health Education*, *2*(83), 130–134.

Freire, P. (1970). *Pedagogy of the oppressed*. New York: Seabury.

Glasgow, R. E., Schafer, L., & O'Neill, H. K. (1981). Self-help books and amount of therapist contact in smoking cessation programs. *Journal of Consulting and Clinical Psychology*, *49*(5), 659–667.

Gray-Toft, P. Effectiveness of a counseling support program for hospice nurses. *Journal of Counseling Psychology*, *24*(4), 346–354.

Green, L. W., Levine, D. M., & Deeds, S. G. (1975). Clinical trials of health education for hypertensive outpatients: Design and baseline data. *Preventive Medicine*, *4*, 417–425.

Hunt, W. A., Barnett, L. W., & Branch, L. G. (1971). Relapse rates in addition programs. *Clinical Psychology*, (27), 455–456.

Hurd, P. D., Johnson, C. A., Pachacek, T., Bast, L. P., Jacobs, D. R., & Juepker, R. V. (1980). Prevention of cigarette smoking in seventh grade students. *Journal of Behavioral Medicine*, *3*(1), 15–28.

Janz, N. K., & Becker, M. H. (Spring, 1984). The health belief model: A decade later. *Health Education Quarterly*, *11*(1), 1–48.

Kingsley, R. G., & Shapiro, J. (1977). A comparison of three behavioral programs for the control of obesity in children. *Behavioral Theory*, *8*, 30–36.

Lee, C. Self-efficiency and behavior as predictors of subsequent behavior in an assertiveness training program. *Brit. Res. Ther.*, *21*(3), 225–232.

Lenker, S. L., Lorig, K., & Gallagher, D. (1984). Reasons for the lack of association between changes in health behavior and improved health status: An exploratory study. *Parent Education and Counseling*, *6*(2), 69–72.

Masters, K. (1970). Treatment of adolescent rebellion by the reconstruction of stimuli. *Consultan. Clinical Psychology*, *6*, 567–572.

Morisky, D. E., Levine, D. M., Green, L. W. Shapiro, S., Russell, R. P., & Smith, C. R. (February, 1983). Five year blood pressure control and mortality following health education for hypertensive patients. *American Journal of Public Health*, 73(2), 153–162.

Nye, R. D. (1979). *What is B. F. Skinner really saying*. Englewood Cliffs, NJ: Prentice-Hall.

Parcel, G. S., & Baranowski, T. (1981). Social learning theory and health education. *Health Education*, 12(3), 14–18.

Parcel, G. S. Bruhn, J. G., & Murray, J. L. (Fall/Winter, 1983). Preschool health education program (PHEP): Analysis of education and behavioral outcomes. *Health Education Quarterly*, 10(3, 4), 149–172.

Pomerleau, O. F., & Pomerleau, C. S. (1977). Break the smoking habit: A behavioral program for giving up cigarettes. Champaign, IL: Research.

Reimanis, G., & Schaeffer, M. (April, 1970). Effects of counseling and achievement motivation training on locus of reinforcement control. Paper presented at the EDA Convention, Atlanta City.

Rosenstock, I. M. (1974). Historical origins of the health belief model. *Health Education Monogr*, 2, 328–335.

Rotter, J. B. (1966). Generalized expectancies for internal versus external locus of reinforcements. *Psych. Monogr.*

Sherer, M., Maddux, J. E., Mercandante, B., Prentice-Dunn, S., Jacobs, B., & Rogers, R. W. (1982). The self-efficacy scale: Construction and validation. *Psychological Reports*, 51, 663–671.

Skinner, B. F. (1976). About behaviorism. New York: Vintage Books.

Skipper, J. K., & Leonard, R. C. (1968). Children, stress, and hospitalization: A field experiment. *Journal of Health and Social Behavior*, 9, 275–287.

Strecher, V. J. (1983). Effect of a minimal-contact smoking program in a health care setting. Unpublished Doctoral Dissertation, University of Michigan.

Strecher, V. J., DeVillis, B. M., Becker, M. H., & Rosenstock, J. M. The role of self-efficacy in achieving health behavior change. *Health Education Quarterly*, 13(1):73–92.

Wheeler, M. E., & Hess, K. W. (1976). Treatment of juvenile obesity by successive approximation control of eating. *Journal of Behavioral Therapy and Experimental Psychiatry*, 7, 235–241.

THE CONCEPT OF CONTROL:
A TYPOLOGY AND HEALTH-RELATED VARIABLES

Frances Marcus Lewis

ABSTRACT

The concept of control is a dominant theme in Western culture and a major
component of the practice ideology of the health professions. As a tenet of
their profession, health educators are often socialized to believe in the patients' rights to control their own situation and in clinicians who adopt a
mutual-participation model of practice and advocate for clients' rights to
control their environment. Despite the theoretical importance of the concept
of control, its meaning is often assumed but undefined. Furthermore, control
is often treated as a unidimensional concept, not a complex one. Thus, there
is considerable need for a conceptual typology that makes clear the different
types of control, an analysis of their relationship to health, and the implications for the practice of health education.

The purposes of this chapter are to organize an integrative typology of
control and to examine selected research with clinical populations that links
the different types of control to health determinants and health outcomes.
The integrative typology differentiates five types of control: processual con-

Advances in Health Education and Promotion, vol. 2, pages 277–309
Copyright © 1987 JAI Press Inc.
All rights of reproduction in any form reserved.
ISBN: 0-89232-617-4

trol, contingency control, cognitive control, behavioral control and existential control.

INTRODUCTION

The patient's right to personal control is endorsed in the patient education literature (D'Altroy, Blissenbach, & Lutz, 1978; Thornbury, 1982; Morisky, Bowler, & Finlay, 1982; Duryea, 1983; Hamrick, Anspaugh, & Smith, 1980; Mullen, 1980); the patient decision making literature (Szasz & Hollender, 1956; Jamison & Mueller, 1979; Schain, 1980); the chronic illness and rehabilitation literature (Feldman, 1974); the hospice and thanatology literature (Benoliel, 1978; Benoliel & McCorkle, 1978; Skorupka & Bohnet, 1982; Krant, 1974); patient advocacy models (Nowakowski, 1977; Fiore, 1979; 1984), and the self-care literature (Green & others, 1977; Hayes-Bautista, 1976; Orem, 1971, 1979). Western ideology dictates that children be reared in ways that foster their sense of personal efficacy and control and that adults believe in control over their environment (Averill, 1973).

Patient statements, heard on a regular basis, remind us of the importance of control to them. "I'm going to lick this thing." "She has a fear of losing control in her life." "It's all right—things are under control." "It's very unsettling to have your body do these things when it's unrelated to whatever you do." Analyses of common situations by some health-care workers reinforce the dominant position that the concept of control maintains in their practice perspectives. As one health educator commented, "Although control over disease may decrease in the later stages of illness, the client can still be assisted in maintaining control over interpersonal relationships and, to some extent, the physical environment" (Thornbury, 1982, p. 6).

Despite the presence of the concept of personal control in professional ideology, closer examination reveals a conceptually primitive and undefined term. Empirical studies of control often depend on an assumed understanding of the concept. Perhaps even more typically, studies suffer from severe operationalism; the measurement of the concept suffices to define it (Lewis, 1982a, b). When health educators want to foster control in a client population, their health education program may be well-intentioned but potentially mistargetted if the concept and meaning of control are left undeveloped.

INTEGRATIVE TYPOLOGY OF PERSONAL CONTROL

An analysis of the control literature reveals five types of control: processual control, contingency control, cognitive control, behavioral control and ex-

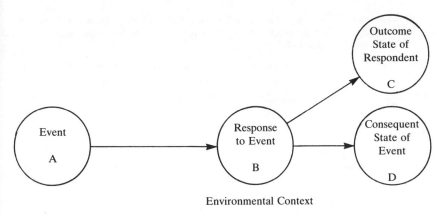

Figure 1. Structural elements in a control situation.

istential control. Before reviewing these types of control, it is important to adopt a set of terms that help us to define the different types of control. These terms also make clearer the distinctions between the different types of control and increase the precision of their definitions. Terms used to define and to clarify these types of control are summarized in Figure 1 and define the structural elements in any potential control situation.

In Figure 1, elements within a potential control situation are labeled the event (A), the response to the event (B), the outcome state of the respondent to the event (C), the consequent state of the event (D), and the environmental context in which the respondent experiences the event. Other labels for the event include stressor, aversive stimulus, threat, or stimulus event. Responses to the event (B) are the types of control exercised by the individual to be developed in the current typology. Outcome states of the respondent (C) are the consequences in the individual who responded to the event and may include health determinants like perceptions or attitudes as well as long-range outcomes like morbidity or mortality. Consequent states of the event (D) include the degree and type of alteration of the event caused by the individual's response to it. Because control experiences of greatest interest to health educators are those that occur in the turbulence of natural field settings, the event (A) is probably best viewed as multidimensional. For purposes of analysis we focus on singular index events. The properties or characteristics of the aversive event to which the individual responds are either the objective or the subjective characteristics of an event. The five types of control are defined next; summaries of these definitions are presented in Figure 2.

Processual Control	Processual control is the participation by the individual in discussions or decisions affecting the event, the response, the outcome, or the environmental context.
Contingency Control	Contingency control is the individual's perception that her/his response to the event controls the individual's outcomes.
Cognitive Control	Cognitive control is the individual's intellectual management of the event so as to reduce its perceived threatening properties.
Behavioral Control	Behavioral control is the individual's possession of a behavioral repertoire that alters the objective qualities of an aversive event.
Existential Control	Existential control is the individual's imposition of meaning and purpose on an event so as to reduce its perceived threatening properties.

Figure 2. Typology of control.

PROCESSUAL CONTROL

Processual control is the participation by the individual in discussions or decisions affecting the event, the response, the outcome, or the environmental context.

Processual control is characterized by interactions or communication individuals have with health educators regarding options for their lifestyle management, adherence to a prescribed medical regimen, or self-care management. In these discussions the individual can initiate requests for additional information, clarification, or may even confront the provider (Mills & Krantz, 1979; Roter, 1977). The critical element in processual control is the element of exchange between the individual experiencing the stressful event and a relevant other who has the power to affect the event (A), the response options (B) available to the individual, or the environmental context.

The definition of processual control has its origins in the group dynamics literature (Cartwright & Zander, 1968; Bales & Borgatta, 1965; Bales, 1951); the patient participation literature (Szasz & Hollender, 1956); and the human relations school of complex organizations (Likert, 1967; Argyris, 1957). These literatures distinguish between participation, influence, and decision-making. Participation and discussion imply involvement, but do not require the actual exercise of influence or decisions. Influence implies affecting an altered state, but does not necessarily imply a final decision. Decisions involve acts of selection and choice carried to completion in the mind of the individual. Discussions do not require that individuals actually make decisions, nor do these discussions necessarily influence the final decisions. Discussions may offer a sense of participation and involvement, but they may not be linked to any final decision. Decision-making definitionally requires that the individual select and decide from among alternatives. Definitionally, behavioral acts or skills are not required, but communication is essential. Decision-making includes the decision to *not* participate and to decide *not* to decide. Such decisions represent acts of choice. Decisions vary to the extent that they are binding, i.e., affected by someone else's approval or clearance before they can be implemented (Stinchcombe, 1968).

Processual control encompasses aspects of what Thompson (1981) and Averill (1973) labeled earlier as decisional control, but is broader in scope than decisional control. By distinguishing decision-making, participation, and influence, processual control includes more than merely a final decision about an aversive event. It also includes verbal exchanges comprising communication in which ideas, options, and issues can be shared. These exchanges are especially relevant to people and clinical patient populations in which the final technical decision may rest with the health educator or some other provider, but in which the patient may participate or influence that final decision (Powers & Wooldridge, 1982; Szasz & Hollender, 1956).

Interest in processual control is consistent with Green's and Mullen's recent critique of mediocentricism (Green, Werlin, Schauffler, & Avery, 1977; Mullen, 1980). Rather than view the patient as a passive, uninformed person, they instead argue for the patient's self-determination and view the patient as an active, processing, and self-reflective individual in search of meaning and understanding in life experiences (Mullen, 1980).

Earlier work by Roy (1977) included the measurement of processual control in her questionnaire, the "Hospitalized Patient Decision-Making Instrument." Applications of her work are represented in more recent research by Eagle (1983). Emphasis in Roy's work was on the identification of decision-making by hospitalized patients and preferences for decision-making in the activities of daily living. Her scale measures decision-making in broad terms but does not differentiate participation, influence and decision-making.

Research completed by Ushigusa (1984) and Surla (1984) has extended and refined Roy's definition of decision-making by distinguishing between decision-making, influence, and participation. Surla (1984) developed a scale of current and preferred decision-making for late-stage cancer patients; Ushigusa and Lewis developed a scale of processual control for hospitalized cancer patients (Ushigusa, 1984).

Chang's (1978b) current research on decision-making and the institutionalized elderly is also relevant to processual control and includes the development of a questionnaire, the Situational Control of Daily Activities Questionnaire (Chang, 1978). The items in the questionnaire include indicators of processual control as defined in the current typology. Additional research by Langer and Cassileth's teams and Rodin, Schulz, and Levin all relevant to processual control (Langer & Rodin, 1976; Rodin & Langer, 1977; Schulz, 1976; Levin, 1982).

CONTINGENCY CONTROL

Contingency control is the individual's perception that his or her response to the event controls the outcome state of the individual.

Contingency control involves the individual's perception of a direct relationship between the individual's response to the event and the outcome state of the individual (Hamburg, Elliot, & Parron, 1982, p. 81). The person perceives that his or her response matters, that the reinforcement or outcome follows from one's own direct actions.

Rotter's Social Learning Theory (Rotter, 1954, 1966, 1975; Lefcourt, 1966; Joe, 1971) and extensions into generalized health expectancies by Wallston and Wallston's team (Wallston et al., 1976; Wallston & Wallston, 1978; Wallston, Wallston, & DeVellis, 1978) are relevant to the current definition of contingency control. Rotter hypothesized that individuals develop general and specific expectancies about the causes of their reinforcements based on their learning. Locus of control is a construct reflecting an individual's belief about a perceived contingency relationship between the individual's own behavior and the outcomes or reinforcements of that behavior (Joe, 1971; Lefcourt, 1966). Over time, individuals develop an understanding of the self as causing or not causing the outcomes that follow their behavior. They learn that reinforcements are a result of their own behavior or of forces external to themselves or outside their control (Rotter, 1966). Recent research in the use of education as a strategy has perhaps been dominated by this type of control (Lewis, 1982b; Lowery, 1981). In addition, policy emphasis in health promotion is often predicated on the concept of contingency control.

Seligman's theory of learned helplessness also relates to contingency control (Seligman, 1975). Under conditions of learned helplessness, the theory states that the individual perceives that his or her response to the event has no effect on the event. The event is perceived as uncontrollable and inescapable, and therefore the outcomes are not perceived as being linked to the individual's own behavior. The theory hypothesizes further that individuals who perceive a link between their own behavior and their outcome state experience higher levels of motivation and lower levels of anxiety and depression (Seligman, 1975).

Self-efficacy theory, explicated by Yalow and Collins in the current volume, is also relevant to contingency control and may be found in the

Research and Evaluation section. Multiple measures of contingency control exist in the literature. One of the earliest measures offered is the Internal-External (I-E) Scale (Rotter, 1966). Later work by Wallston and Wallston's team built upon Rotter's work and resulted in the development of the Health Locus of Control Scale (HLC) and the Multidimensional Health Locus of Control Scale (MHLC) (Wallston & Wallston, 1978; Wallston, Wallston, Kaplan, & Maides, 1976; Wallston, Wallston, & DeVellis, 1978). Recent work has included contingency control scales for specific clinical populations; see, for example, Saltzer (1982) for the Weight Locus of Control (WLOC) Scale. Analysis of the psychometric properties of the HLC and the MHLC for clinical populations was reported recently by Larde and Clopton (1983), Lewis (1982a), Meyers, Donham, and Ludenia (1982), Snow and Thurber (1983), and Thomas and Hooper (1983). Additional measures of contingency control are offered by Ziegler and Reid (1979), Nowicki and Duke (1974), and Lau and Ware (1981).

COGNITIVE CONTROL

Cognitive control is the individual's intellectual management of the event so as to reduce its perceived threatening properties.

Intellectual management is probably best understood as an orienting strategy the individual uses to handle affectively or emotionally the event in ways that mitigate the emotional trauma of the aversive properties (Thompson, 1981). This orienting strategy may be characterized by information gain (Averill, 1973); an appraisal-reappraisal process (Lazarus, 1974; Folkman & Lazarus, 1980; Cohen & Lazarus, 1983); cognitive predictive control (Haberman, 1984; Wortman, 1974; 1976); or a mobilization of intellectual coping strategies or styles (Sidle et al., 1969; Averill & Rosenn, 1972; Lipowski, 1970; Cohen & Lazarus, 1973; Pearlin & Schooler, 1978). In the process of denaturing the stressful characteristics of the event, the event is redefined as manageable. Cognitive control is one of the bases for anticipatory guidance (Aguilera, Messick, & Farrell, 1970); preoperative instruction (Lindeman & VanAerman, 1971) and sensory and informational instruction (Padilla & others, 1981; Johnson & Leventhal, 1974; Hartfield, Cason, & Cason, 1982; Hill, 1982).

Cognitive control is relevant to both acute and chronic illnesses in which aspects of the experience can be potentially redefined in the minds of the individual as nonthreatening or manageable. For example, a patient can redefine aspects of an intrusive diagnostic procedure as tolerable. Similarly, insulin-dependent diabetics can find ways to think about multiple injections as important or acceptable experiences.

Currently there are no known measures of the appraisal-reappraisal component of cognitive control. Most typically, cognitive control is inferred as operating in experimental studies designed to manipulate levels of cognitive control (Johnson & Leventhal, 1974; Hill, 1982) or is reduced to a measure of coping behaviors or strategies. Coping scales are offered in the published literature by Pearlin and Schooler (1978); Lazarus and Launier (1978); Folkman and Lazarus (1980); Sidle et al. (1969).

BEHAVIORAL CONTROL

Behavioral control is the actual alteration of the objective qualities of the event by the individual's own behavior.

Behavioral control involves the possession of a behavioral or motor repertoire that the individual uses to manipulate the observable and objective qualities of the stressful event. With behavioral control such factors as the intensity, duration, and visibility of the event can be modified (Schmidt & Keating, 1979). Modification of the event's properties is able to be determined by an objective observer and is not merely dependent on the subjective assessment of the individual doing the modification. Experimental research with presumed healthy adults has demonstrated that an absence of behavioral control is linked to impaired performance in solving conceptual tasks, lower skin conductance levels, smaller phasic skin conductance responses, and more spontaneous electrodermal activity compared to individuals experiencing the event as controlled by their own behavior (Gatchel & Proctor, 1976).

Behavioral control is relevant to pain-related events in which the individual can pace or self-administer the stimulus. For example, a dental patient could be given control over the amount of time the dentist continues to drill a tooth; a patient with a severe burn undergoing a painful dressing change could be instructed to raise a hand to interrupt, at least temporarily, the removal of the dressing.

No measures of behavioral control were identified in the published literature. Rather, behavioral control is often inferred by direct observation of the behavior, or by verbal report by the individual that he or she possesses the behavior. Health educators, for example, might debrief patients using transducers to modify their chronic pain by the frequency with which they used the transducer; hypertensive clinic patients may be asked about the self-care behavior they practiced that controlled their blood pressure.

EXISTENTIAL CONTROL

Existential control is the individual's imposition of meaning and purpose on an event so as to decrease its perceived threatening properties.

Existential control is the attribution of meaning on an event in a way that diminishes its threat potential. Some would argue that existential control is basic to struggling with the meaning of life (Yalom, 1980). The definitional roots of the meaning of existential control derive from the Myth of Sisyphus. In this myth, the individual ardently struggles to push a large rock up a steep mountain only to have it inevitably fall down again. It is at the moment of awareness of the inevitability of the travail that the individual overcomes the rock. By imparting meaning to the experience the individual gains control over it. The rock no longer threatens; rather the situation is understood. Threat is reduced even though the rock will roll down again. Technically the individual does not physically control the rock, rather the individual controls the threat value of the rolling stone by imposing meaning on it. By being aware and by imparting meaning, we overcome the threat initially associated with the event.

Antonovsky's (1980) concept of coherence expands our understanding of existential control. Antonovsky's theoretical analysis emphasizes that the world may be perceived to varying degrees as in control, predictable, and chaote. It is not important, in Antonovsky's analysis, that the individual control the world so much as he or she perceive it as meaningful and purposeful. Furthermore, he argues, control or power can be in the hands of the legitimized and trusted other, and the world can still be experienced as meaningful (Antonovsky, 1980). That is, the world may be viewed and experienced as *in control*; it is not important that the individual maintain that control.

Existential control is also relevant in Frankl's (1958, 1962) concept, will to meaning, in which the individual strives to find purpose, a cause, or a sense of mission that gives direction to one's life and makes it comprehensible.

There is only one known questionnaire that provides an adequate measure of existential control, the Purpose-in-Life Test (PIL) developed by Crumbaugh (1968). The PIL is a 20-item, self-report questionnaire with 7-point ordinal response options that documents the extent to which an individual perceives that life has direction, purpose and meaning. Derived from Frankl's (1958, 1959) earlier work and intended to measure existential frustration (Crumbaugh & Maholick, 1963), a large proportion of the questionnaire items attain face validity for existential control. Recent work with adults with advanced cancer had linked existential control with measures of quality of life (Lewis, 1982a, 1983).

CONTROL AND HEALTH-RELATED VARIABLES

Having offered definitional distinctions of the five types of control, published research is now analyzed that relates these types of control to health

Source	Typology Categories
Averill, 1973	Three Types of Control: 1. Behavioral control 1.1 regulated adminstration 1.2 stimulus modification 2. Cognitive control 2.1 information gain 2.2 appraisal 3. Decisional control
Miller, 1979	Four Types of Behavioral Control: 1. Instrumental control 2. Self-administration 3. Predictability 3.1 actual control 3.2 potential control
Thompson, 1981	Four Types of Control: 1. Behavioral control 2. Cognitive control 3. Information 4. Retrospective control

Figure 3.   Previously developed typologies of control.

behavior, attitudes, perceptions and knowledge. The literature review is limited to empirical research on adult populations relevant to health education and health promotion. The analysis does not include a review of the therapeutic literature on control with psychiatric patients nor families (Minuchin, 1981; Meichenbaum, 1969a, 1977); experimental stress studies with presumed healthy adults, nor control studies completed on nonhuman subjects (Weiss, 1971a, c).

The goal of this analysis is to answer the following question: "When an individual experiences an uncomfortable or stressful event, will different types or levels of control influence cognitive and behavioral factors that determine health status?" To date, there has been no known attempt to answer this question for adult clinical populations in natural settings. Instead we have had to rely on analyses of research on experimental stress studies most commonly completed on presumed healthy adults experiencing an isolated aversive event in a highly controlled experimental study. Thompson (1981), Averill (1973) and Miller (1979) offer reviews of these experimental studies for the interested reader. See Figure 3 for the structure of their reviews.

PROCESSUAL CONTROL

Few studies have attempted to examine systematically and empirically the effects of processual control on health-related behavior or outcomes. Moreover, little attention has focused on the effects of consumer participation as an example of processual control in the clinical setting (Vertinsky, Thompson, & Uyeno, 1974). Instead most published discussion on processual control emphasizes the unconditional importance of client or community participation. Ideology takes over reasoning and the potentially deleterious effects of assigning choice, responsibility or decision-making are not always examined. Sechrist (1983) was one of the few health educators who raised an important caution about inappropriately endorsing personal responsibility in health education settings. Empirical studies on processual control are now reviewed.

Roter's study is an exemplary study of processual control (Roter, 1977). One of the purposes of the study was to examine the consequences of a health education intervention designed to increase levels of patient participation. Roter measured patient participation as the frequency of question asking during a regularly scheduled clinic visit. Subjects were primarily elderly Black females with chronic illness treated at an east coast community outpatient facility. Processual control was systematically manipulated in a true experimental design in which subjects were randomly assigned to the treatment or to the control group. The treatment group, i.e., those trained to carry out higher levels of processual control, consisted of 100 patients who were exposed to a 10-minute intervention conducted by a health educator. The intervention focused on a question-asking protocol that assisted patients to identify questions they might have about either their illness or treatment. A total of eight areas of patient questions was reviewed. For example, questions were identified that related to disease duration or prevention. (See Appendix B in Roter, 1977, for the detailed protocol). After covering all possible categories in the protocol, the health educator then read the patient the list of questions he or she had identified. The health educator concluded by saying, "We think that asking questions is an important part of coming to the clinic. This is the only way patients can really find out about their illness" (Roter, 1977, p. 298). Roter found that the experimental intervention increased the frequency with which patients from the experimental group asked direct questions during the next tape-recorded clinic visit. Specifically, the mean number of questions recorded by the experimental group was 2.12 compared to only 1.21 in the comparison placebo group ($t = 2.97$, d.f. 156, $p < .001$) (Roter, 1977, p. 299). Using an interactional analysis scheme to code the content of the taped patient-provider interaction, Roter also documented higher levels of patient and provider anger in the experimental group compared to the comparison placebo group ($t = 2.06$, d.f. $= 156$, $p < .02$, and $t = 2.08$, d.f. $= 156$, $p < .02$, respectively) and higher levels of patient anxiety in the experimental group compared to the placebo group ($t = 3.27$, d.f. $= 156$, $p < .001$) (Roter, 1977, p. 300). In addition, patients in the experimental group had lower satisfaction scores than patients in the placebo group. Thus, although Roter's experimental treatment raised patient participation rates, it also increased levels of anger in the patients and the providers as well as levels of patient dissatisfaction.

Using a questionnaire during a survey of 200 at-home respondents, Vertinsky et al. (1974) studied consumers' perceptions of participation in clinical decision-making. By documenting role preferences in clinical decision-making, the team argued that they could infer the role consumers themselves would like to play in the clinical decision-making process. Using a structured interview format, subjects were interviewed about a common medical situation: the respondents were asked to project themselves into the role of advisor to a fictitious patient and then to rate a number of possible alternative actions the patient might take. These actions were rated on a Likert-type scale of importance ranging from 1 (unimportant) to 5 (very important) and formed the basis for the calculation of index scores. Subjects were also asked to rate the actions the physician might take in the same situation. The rating procedure was repeated for each patient who returned for a follow-up visit.

The authors used factor analysis to identify the attitudinal dimensions of consumer participation in clinical decision-making. Index scores were then calculated for each of the separate factors. The results revealed eight dimensions or types of consumer participation. One dimension of patient participation involved supplementing the physician's orders with proprietary drugs; another dealt with seeking more information from the physician; and still another dealt with seeking an additional professional opinion. Within 7 of the 8 dimensions, obtained scores covered the entire possible range of scores, reflecting a wide diversity of attitudes. Index scores also reflected that the majority of respondents did not want to take the entire responsibility for medical decisions. They also, however, did not want to be entirely passive in the patient-provider exchange (Vertinsky et al., 1974, p. 130).

Analyses were also reported for associations between selected demographic characteristics of the study sample and the index scores on patient participation. As the respondent's age increased, there was a decreased desire for patient participation ($r = -.23$, $p = .001$) and the greater the frequency of visits to the physician or the greater the length of hospitalization experienced by the respondents, the less likely they wanted to participate in clinical decision-making ($r = -.31, p = .001; r = -.22, p = .003$, respectively) (Vertinsky et al., 1974, p. 130). The authors concluded that a guidance-cooperation model was generally acceptable when describing the respondent's preferred patient role as long as cooperation characterized the exchange (Vertinsky et al. 1974, p. 133).

Both Surla (1984) and Ushigusa (1984) studied processual control in adult cancer patients using descriptive correlational designs. Surla (1984) documented the frequency with which terminally ill cancer patients actually make binding decisions compared with their reported preference to do so about their disease and treatment. Data were obtained from 18 subjects through mail survey. The majority of individuals were currently making, and preferred to make, decisions about their disease and treatment most of the time (Surla, 1984, pp. 85–87). However, some of her subjects reported that they preferred "seldom" or "never" to make decisions about their disease and treatments. In addition, Surla correlated the length of time since the cancer diagnosis with decision-making preferences, and found that the longer patients had been diagnosed with cancer, the less they actually preferred to make decisions about their cancer management (Kendall's tau $= .39; p = .02$; Surla, 1984). (This pattern of results is similar to that documented earlier by Vertinsky's team, 1974.)

In the same study, the relationship between self-reported anxiety levels and the discrepancy between current and preferred decision-making practices was found to be statistically significant. Namely, the higher the discrepancy between the frequency with which patients reported making decisions vs. the frequency with which they preferred to make decisions, the higher their self-reported anxiety (Kendall's tau $= .30; p = .04$; Spearman's correlation $= .43; p = .04$) (Surla, 1984, p. 98). That is, higher decision-making discrepancy scores significantly covaried with anxiety levels. A detailed examination also revealed that 78 percent of the subjects experienced some degree of discrepancy between the frequency with which they actually made vs. preferred to make decisions about their disease or treatment (Surla, 1984, p. 94). Of these, 23 percent had moderate to high levels of discrepancy scores (Surla, 1984, p. 95). Similar to those results obtained from Vertinsky et al. (1974) Surla also documented a trend between the age of the patient and preferred decision-making practices. Younger patients preferred more frequently to make decisions about their disease and treatment than did older patients (Surla, 1984, p. 100).

In another study of processual control, Ushigusa (1984) measured aspects of processual control in a sample of 58 hospitalized, adult cancer patients and related levels of processual control with self-reported anxiety levels. Using correlational analysis, there was a statistical trend for higher levels of processual control to correlate with lower levels of anxiety; $r = -.17$;

$p = .10$ (Ushigusa, 1984, p. 69). The magnitude of these results, however, shows a less conclusive relationship between levels of processual control and levels of anxiety than did results obtained from Surla (1984).

Using a quasi-experimental design, Langer and Rodin (1976) measured the effects of responsibility in the institutionalized elderly on activity levels and involvement. Induced responsibility included decisions about one's self, the room in which the elderly lived, time allocation, visitation, and the care of a houseplant. Results showed that participants in the experimental group with manipulated levels of responsibility had significantly higher attendance rates at social events in the nursing home ($z = 1.71$, $p < .05$ one-tailed), and had higher levels of participation in institutional social events ($t_{50} = 5.18$, $p < .005$) compared to the comparison group. In a follow-up study, Rodin and Langer (1977) measured the long-term effects of the experimental manipulation on the nursing home residents and found that the treatment group had significantly more nurse-reported positive ratings of mood, awareness, sociability, mental attitude and physical activity ($F_{1,40} = 6.31$, $p < .05$); had higher objective health ratings ($F_{2,40} = 3.73$, $p < .05$); and had significantly lower mortality rates ($z = 1.73$, $p < .05$, one-tailed) than did the comparison group (Rodin & Langer, 1977).

Using an exploratory descriptive correlational design, Cassileth's team studied the participation preferences of 256 cancer patients and correlated participation preference with levels of hopelessness (Cassileth, Zupkis, Sutton-Smith, & March, 1980). The overall majority of patients preferred to participate even though younger and better educated patients had statistically higher levels of participation preference scores than the older and less educated participants. A stated preference for participation was also significantly associated with more hopefulness (Cassileth et al. 1980).

COGNITIVE CONTROL

The only known measures of cognitive control are questionnaires developed to measure an individual's coping strategies. Work by Folkman and Lazarus (1980) and recent work with extensions by Vitaliano (1985), Stone and Neale (1984), and Billings and Moos (1984) are exemplary. Additional coping scales are offered by Sidle et al. (1969), and Pearlin and Schooler (1978). Most typically, respondents are presented with a situation and asked to indicate, using structured response categories, the behavior they would use to manage the situation. Alternatively, respondents may be asked to identify a specific current or past problem they handled and asked to specify, again with predetermined response categories, the behavior they used to manage their situation. These questionnaires, however, do not measure threat reduction as a result of the coping strategy; they assume it. Furthermore, existing coping scales often contain measures of behavioral as well as cognitive control. In experimental studies that manipulate levels of cognitive control in the treatment groups, cognitive control is inferred, but not typically measured. For example, it is inferred that levels of cognitive control are affected through exposure to an experimental intervention in patient education studies designed specifically to affect cognitive control (Johnson & Leventhal, 1974; Hill, 1982).

Cognitive control has been linked recently to recovery from illness, including heart attack (Mullen, 1978; Johnson et al., 1978; Wood & Pesut, 1981; Krantz, 1980) as well as to symptom and distress reduction in hospitalized or diagnosed patients (Taylor, Lichtman, & Wood, 1984; Hill, 1982). The underlying assumption is that self-regulatory mental processes have the potential to influence health status.

There is a substantial number of empirical studies examining the effects of cognitive control on the individual's health outcomes. Major research programs by Johnson and Leventhal (1974) as well as seminal work by Egbert's team (1964) are representative.

In a recent study of 81 cholecystectomy patients, Johnson and colleagues used a factorial design to test the independent effects of two different types of instruction and two different types of preoperative information on immediate and long-term post-operative recovery (Johnson, Rice, Fuller, & Endress, 1978). One intervention dealt with cognitive control through the provision of information about either the usual events that are inherent in a surgical experience (procedural information) or the typical sensations experienced as part of the surgical procedure (sensory information). (The effects of the two different types of instruction will be discussed later under behavioral control.)

Results were reported separately for high and for low preoperative fear groups. Results revealed a tendency for procedural information to increase fear levels as well as positive mood states and to decrease self-reported levels of helplessness and anger compared to the no-information control group. Sensation information had a tendency to increase higher positive moods and to decrease negative moods compared to the control group. There was a trend for patients experiencing the treatment condition to have shorter post-operative hospitalizations compared to the controls, but only the sensation information condition differed significantly from the control group (Dunnett's $t_{3,64} = 3.45$, $p < .001$). Patients in the sensation information group also had significantly less time before they ventured from their homes post-hospital discharge compared to the controls (Dunnett's $t_{3,60} = 2.12$, $p < .05$).

In another intervention designed to decrease the negative aspects of experiencing an endoscopic examination, Johnson and Leventhal (1974) designed a sensory and a behavioral instruction intervention for 48 hospitalized patients. (As before, effects of the behavioral instruction will be discussed under Behavioral Control in this chapter). Patients under 50 years of age who received sensory instruction received fewer milligrams of tranquilizer than did the control group ($t_{40} = 2.10$; $p < .02$) (Johnson & Leventhal, 1974, p. 714). Heart rate changes and avoidance acts were not significantly related to experimental treatment. Sensory instruction significantly reduced the proportion of patients who gagged in the treatment group as compared to those who gagged in the control group ($p < .05$) (Johnson & Leventhal, 1974, p. 715). Sensory instruction did not significantly reduce the length of time needed to pass the endoscopic tube into the stomach (Johnson & Leventhal, 1974, p. 716).

More recent work by Hill (1982) extended Johnson & Leventhal's 1974 study by offering sensory instruction to 40 patients scheduled for unilateral cataract surgery. Sensory instruction involved a seven-minute tape-recorded message that described typical sensations cataract patients experience post-operatively. Although there was a trend for sensory information to reduce the subjects' anxiety and depression scores post-operatively as compared to the control group (control mean change = $-.03$; sensory instruction group mean change = $-.3.80$; Dunnett's $t_{4,33} = 1.93$, n.s.), the results were not statistically significant (Hill, 1982, p. 20). There was also a trend, but not a significant effect, for sensory instructed patients to venture from their homes sooner after discharge compared to the control group (mean change for control group = 5.6; mean change for sensory group = 4.0) (Hill, 1982, p. 20).

Extending Johnson's paradigm to patients undergoing a nasogastric intubation procedure, Padilla's team (Padilla et al., 1981) compared the distress-reducing effects of four different types of information interventions. Using a true experimental design, 50 patients were shown filmstrips depicting the procedure (P); or the procedure along with common distressful sensations (PS); or the procedure with comfort-inducing coping behavior (PB); or the procedure with coping behavior for relieving distress (PSB). Self-reported distress levels were measured by an author-constructed, 10-item scale for 10 specific distressful intubation experiences and subjective measures of pain, discomfort, and anxiety. Results revealed that subjects in the PSB condition experienced the least amount of discomfort compared to the other three groups ($F_{1,42} = 18.42$, $p < .001$, Padilla et al., 1981, p. 381).

In a case-intensive interview study of 148 adult hospitalized patients experiencing pain, Copp (1974) used an inductive method to summarize concept categories from the data and documented five forms of cognitive control that patients reported they used to respond to their pain. These were counting, deep thinking and visualization, separation, distraction and word use (Copp, 1974, p. 494). No specific data were reported; only summary statements were provided in the study. Patients reported they counted everything and anything to cope with their pain. Patients used prayer, imagery, concentration, focusing, and other forms of deep thinking and visualization to respond to their pain (Copp, 1974, p. 494). Patients also reported deliberate attempts to "separate mind and body," including denial of being a part of the body and the use of absolute silence (Copp, 1974, p. 494). Patients offered multiple examples of using distraction, including smoking and asking others to talk or to read to them (Copp, 1974, p. 494). Finally, patients reported using seven major types of words or phrases to respond to their pain. These control words and phrases included, "I won't scream;" "I can stand this;" supplication, "Let it be over soon;" intercession, "Help me, Jesus," memorized words, prayers, repetitive words, multiple syllabled words, derisive phrases, "This is ridiculous!" evaluative comment, "It hurts most now;" and anxious expressions, "I can't make it through this." (Copp, 1974, p. 494).

Taylor, Lichtman, and Wood (1984) documented a significant relationship between adjustment in women to having breast cancer and self-reported cognitive control. For subjects who reported that the cancer diagnosis had made them think about their lives differently, there was a statistically significant relationship between labeling the change as positive and standardized measures of adjustment scores ($F_{2,67} = 4.09$; $p < .03$) (Taylor, Lichtman, & Wood, 1984, p. 496). These same authors examined the association between information control and adjustment and found no linear relationship. Rather, information and adjustment had a curvilinear relationship; respondents with moderate levels of information reflected slightly better adjustment scores but the relation was nonsignificant.

Using open-ended interviews to study self-regulatory mental processes in 26 adult postsurgical patients, Wood and Pesut (1981) found that patients attributed their own postoperative recovery to their "positive thinking" as well as to resources and support offered by others (Wood & Pesut, 1981, p. 264). The authors reported the patients' use of "attention/awareness deployment" strategies (Wood & Pesut, 1981, p. 265). Attention/awareness deployment involved the internal strategies of visual imagery, future time projection, imagining, and internal auditory dialogue, e.g., "keep hangin' on, it will be over soon" (Wood & Pesut, 1981, p. 265). External strategies were also used as part of attention/awareness deployment. Patients used environmental resources to divert and to distract themselves, e.g., worked a crossword puzzle (Wood & Pesut, 1981, pp. 265–266).

In a study involving case-intensive interviews with 57 pre-cachectic terminally ill adult cancer patients, Lewis, Haberman and Wallhagen (1986) found repeated evidence of the patients' use of cognitive strategies to manage the uncertainty of their illness trajectory.

CONTINGENCY CONTROL

Empirical work with contingency control represents a dominant research tradition in health education. Predominantly represented in the work by Wallston and Wallston's team and their followers, the major hypothesis across studies is that higher levels of internal contingency control are related to more positive health outcomes for both well and ill individuals. Empirical results, however, between contingency control and health-related outcomes are anything but conclusive (Lewis, Morisky, & Flynn, 1978). Although a number of studies show statistically significant relationships between higher levels of contingency control and more positive health outcomes in selected populations, there are many studies the results of which fail to reach statistical significance. Earlier Wallston and Wallston (1978) summarized the published literature on health locus of control and concluded that internally oriented subjects may be more likely to participate in positive health-seeking behaviors, including smoking reduction or cessation, weight loss, and preventive health behavior than more externally oriented subjects. Our purpose here is to integrate literature published since 1978.

Based on observational and self-report data from 101 dental outpatients treated in a Veterans Administration dental clinic, Ludenia and Donham (1983) reported statistically significant negative relationships between the internality subscale of the Multidimensional Health Locus of Control (MHLC) and trait anxiety and anger scores on the Spielberger State-Trait Personality Inventory ($r = -.43$, $p < .001$; $r = -.27$, $p < .01$, respectively) and the Beck Depression Scale ($r = -.40$, $p < .001$) (Ludenia & Donham, 1983, p. 856). That is, the more subjects were internally oriented, the less anxious, angry or depressed they were. Degree of periodontal disease did not significantly correlate with any of the MHLC subscales. Only the "powerful others" subscale score was significantly correlated with the status of oral hygiene ($r = -.19$, $p < .05$) (Ludenia & Donham, 1983, p. 856).

In a recent study by Gierszewski (1983), the relationship between contingency control and actual weight loss was examined in a sample of 46 female employees of an insurance company who participated in a weight control program. The MHLC Scale (Form A) measured contingency control and Feinstein's Reduction Index measured weight loss. Contrary to prediction, subjects with higher internality scores actually had less weight loss and more weight gain than those with higher externality scores.

Studying 94 randomly selected mothers of preschool children, Rosenblum's team found no statistically significant association between MHLC total scores or subscale scores and levels of the mothers' compliance to their child's immunization schedules (Rosenblum et al., 1981). In fact, there was a tendency for the externally scoring, not the internally scoring, to be more compliant with the child's immunization schedule.

To study the relationship between contingency control and levels of independent living, Currie-Gross and Heimbach (1980) administered the MacDonald and Tseng Locus of Control Scale and a seven-item scale on independent living to 90 former vocational rehabilitation clients. Sixty subjects were used for purposes of data analysis, the most external one-third and the most internal one-third. Statistically significant differences were reported for the internals and externals for levels of self-care ($t_{58} = 1.73$, $p < .05$); employment ($t_{58} = p < .05$); and mobility ($t_{58} = 1.76$; $p < .05$). In all of these cases, subjects with higher internality scores demonstrated higher levels of independent living.

Contingency control may be represented by a belief that one can control the reinforcements one receives or one's own outcome state, not just a score on a locus of control scale. Using case-intensive interviews conducted in the homes of 78 women with Stages I and II breast cancer, Taylor's team found that a single item that documented "a personal belief that one could control one's own cancer significantly" predicted adjustment scores ($F_{1,68} = 6.03$; $p < .02$) (Taylor, Lichtman, & Wood, 1984, p. 496). This relationship was unchanged when controls were made for both prognosis and for socioeconomic status.

In a recent study of 57 terminally ill at-home cancer patients, Lewis (1982a) examined the relationship between a modified version of the HLC and self-reported measures of self-esteem and anxiety. It was hypothesized that cancer patients with a higher sense of personal control over their health (more internal subjects) would experience lower levels of anxiety and higher self-appraisal. Unexpectedly, the results showed that there was no significant relationship, or statistical trend, between HLC scores and anxiety nor self-esteem scores. The relationships between HLC and self-esteem and anxiety were essentially random. Concurrently, Lewis (1982a) offered a single-item, ordinal measure of contingency control that read, "I have control over my life" and correlated the indicator with both self-esteem and anxiety. As predicted, this single item indicator of contingency control significantly correlated with both self-esteem (Kendall's tau $= -.33$; $p = .001$) and with anxiety (Kendall's tau $= -.30$; $p = .001$); higher control was associated with lower anxiety and higher self-esteem (Lewis, 1982a, p. 116).

BEHAVIORAL CONTROL

Behavioral control is involved in situations in which individuals possess motor behavior that actually changes the objective characteristics of a stressful event. Extensive empirical research with behavioral control has been carried out under tightly controlled experimental conditions with presumed healthy adults but only a few studies are available with patient populations. Published studies with patient populations are now reviewed.

Johnson and Leventhal's (1974) experimental intervention with 48 hospitalized patients undergoing an endoscopic examination is an exemplary study of instruction designed to maximize behavioral control in the field setting. Behavioral preparation consisted of detailed instructions on how and when to act when the endoscopic tube was inserted and passed as well as prior rehearsal of the specific actions until their mastery was achieved. The investigator's assumption was that demonstration of the instructional behavior actually altered the objective properties of the tube insertion process. A smaller proportion of the patients who received the behavioral instruction gagged compared to the control group but the result did not reach statistical significance (Johnson & Leventhal, 1974, p. 715). Contrary to prediction, the behavioral instruction group had a longer mean time required to pass the endoscopic tube than did the control group (Johnson & Leventhal, 1974, p. 716).

In another experimental intervention study on a group of presurgical patients, Johnson's team documented that behavioral control, as represented by instruction on deep breathing, coughing, leg exercises, turning and ambulating, affected post-operative doses of analgesic as compared to a no-instruction control group ($F_{1,68}$ = 3.83, p = .06) (Johnson et al., 1978, p. 10). That is, patients who received behavioral instructions received fewer doses of analgesics than did patients who were not instructed. In addition, there was a trend for instruction to decrease negative mood states and to increase positive mood states compared to the non-instructed control group. Results reached statistical significance for anger (Dunnett's $t_{1,65}$ = 3.32, p < .001) and for happiness (Dunnett's $t_{1,65}$ = 3.35, p < .001).

Building on Johnson's work, Hill (1982) studied the effects of behavioral instruction on post-operative well-being in a sample of 40 patients who had cataract surgery. Behavioral instruction involved rehearsal of behavior designed to reduce discomfort in the post-operative period as well as self-care skills, e.g., getting out of bed (Hill, 1982, p. 18). Contrary to prediction, behavioral instruction did not significantly influence postoperative anxiety, depression, ambulation or length of postoperative hospitalization as compared to the control group (Hill, 1982, p. 20).

As part of a larger randomized factorial design, Morisky, Bowler, and Finlay (1982) studied the effects of three weekly two-hour sessions of behavioral instruction on levels of contingency control and blood pressure control for a sample of 200 Black, primarily female hypertensives. This study is interesting in many respects, one of which is the assumption that instruction in behavioral control methods can affect an individual's level of contingency control as well as long-range health outcomes. The behavioral intervention involved small face-to-face groups of diagnosed hypertensives and emphasized the acquisition of problem-solving skills, provided role-taking experiences, and covered general content on hypertension. The group's overall purpose was to enhance and to reinforce concrete behavioral examples of management in the antihypertensive regimen. Data analyses were reported for a combination of both the behavioral instruction intervention and a family-level intervention (statistics were not reported on only the behavioral instruction intervention.) The authors reported statistically significant differences in blood pressure control status for the experimental versus the control group ($X^2 = 4.22; p < .05$) but nonsignificant results for the compliance and the contingency control measures. That is, neither self-reported medication compliance nor HLC scores were significantly affected by the interventions even though blood pressure control was significantly affected.

Taylor, Lichtman, and Wood (1984) examined the relationship between self-reported behavioral control and adjustment in a sample of women with breast cancer. In their sample, 22 percent of the 78 subjects reported making no changes in their health-related behavior since their cancer diagnosis; 55 percent had made 2 or more changes; and 23 percent had made 3 or more changes (Taylor, Lichtman, & Wood, 1984, p. 497). Effects of the different types of behavioral control were variable. Increased exercise and leisure activities were significantly associated with better adjustment ($r = -.23, p < .03; r = .26, p < .02$, respectively).

EXISTENTIAL CONTROL

The concept of existential control is the least well developed in the published literature. Although we understand the concept in terms of the client's attempts to attribute meaning and purpose on a stressful experience to make it more tolerable, little empirical work has been reported on either the meaning or the correlates of existential control. The few known relevant studies are now reviewed.

Seminal research with severely injured accident victims adds to our understanding of existential control (Bulman & Wortman, 1977). To gain insight into the subjects' ascriptions of meaning, 29 victims of spinal cord injuries were interviewed and asked whether they had ever asked themselves the question, "Why me?" and how they had answered the question. All respondents claimed that they had asked themselves that question; 18 had identified a single explanation and 10 had identified two explanations of their victimization (Bulman & Wortman, 1977, p. 358). Only one person stated he had not identified an answer to the question. Six categories of ascribed meanings were identified by the subjects: predetermination, probability, chance, "God had a reason," deservedness, and reevaluation of the event as positive (Bulman & Wortman, pp. 358–360, 1977). (This latter ascription reflects cognitive control as defined in the current typology.) These categories of ascribed meaning were used next in a regression analysis to predict both nurses' and social workers' reports of the individual's level of coping with their injury. None of the categories of ascribed meaning significantly predicted coping scores (Bulman & Wortman, 1977, p. 358), i.e., no particular category of ascribed meaning predicted how well the patients were currently coping with their injury. The authors concluded that their data may reflect more a "need for an orderly and meaningful world than a need for a controllable one" (Bulman & Wortman, p. 362, 1977). This interpretation moreover is consistent with that offered by Frankl (1959) and by Antonovsky (1980).

Studying adult patients with rheumatoid arthritis, Lowery, Jacobsen, and Murphy (1983) documented that patients who were able to make causal attributions for their disease, i.e., to explain them, were significantly more adjusted than arthritics who could not make attributions. The positive effects of these attributions occurred regardless of their medical accuracy. In another study Mullen used grounded field theory methodology to obtain data from 100 myocardial infarction patients using a semi-structured interview approach (Mullen, 1978). Interviewees included the diagnosed patient and various combinations of couples and groups as well. Although correlates or outcomes of control were not examined, Mullen's study helps us to understand part of the processes myocardial infarction patients experience as they develop existential control. Like participants in Bulman and Wortman's earlier study, patients in Mullen's study needed to cast some meaning or explanation on their experience; they developed answers to the question, "Why me?" or "Why now?" (Mullen, 1978, p. 300). These explanatory searches for meaning often involved comparisons with others with similar experiences. Mullen claimed that the patient's assigning cause, gathering and processing information and making comparisons are the basis for the patient's sense of control (Mullen, 1978, p. 300).

Work by Lewis (1982a, 1983) extends our understanding of the effects of existential control on the psychosocial well-being of patients. Studying 57 late-stage adult cancer patients, Lewis (1982a) found that a self-report measure of existential control significantly correlated with both self-esteem scores ($r = -.44$; $p = .001$) and with health locus of control scores (Kendall's Tau $= -.18$; $p = .05$) (Lewis, 1982a, pp. 115, 117). That is, the more patients perceived their world as meaningful and purposeful, the more positively they evaluated themselves and the more internally oriented they were about their own health.

Copp (1974) interviewed 148 hospitalized adult patients to understand better a patient's response to pain. The patients' attempts to ascribe meaning, to explain and to make sense out of their pain experiences were evident in the study results. Eleven percent of the patients described pain and suffering as a challenge and thought that there would be positive effects on their health as a result of the experience (Copp, 1974, p. 492). Ten percent blamed themselves and viewed pain as a personal weakness; thirteen percent perceived pain as punishment (Copp, 1974, p. 492). Twenty-six percent of the patients claimed value in their pain experiences, including an opportunity for such things as "creative expression, self-searching and self-testing" as well as "fostering an appreciation of what less fortunate patients had gone through" (Copp, 1974, pp. 492–493).

DISCUSSION AND CONCLUSIONS

Control is a complex and multidimensional concept, not a simple unidimensional term. Five types of control are distinguished for heuristic purposes: processual control, contingency control, cognitive control, behavioral control, and existential control. Processual control is the participation by the individual in discussions or decisions affecting the event, the response, the outcome, or the environmental context. Contingency control is the individual's perception that his or her response to the event controls the outcome state of the individual. Cognitive control is the individual's intellectual management of the event so as to reduce its perceived threatening properties. Behavioral control is the actual alteration of the objective qualities of the event by the individual's own behavior. Existential control is the individual's imposition of meaning and purpose on an event so as to decrease its perceived threatening properties.

Empirical research with the five types of control offers conditional support for the underlying assumption that achievement of higher levels of control results in changed health outcomes or their determinants. Empirical evidence reviewed on processual control informs us that clients or community members want to be active participants in health and treatment-related discussions but do not necessarily want to assume total responsibility for medical decisions (Vertinsky et al., 1974; Surla, 1984). There is also a trend for the older, sicker, and less educated to exercise or to want to exercise lower levels or processual control compared to their younger, healthier and better educated counterparts (Vertinsky et al., 1974; Cassileth et al., 1980; Surla, 1984). This highlights a potential need to focus attention on the aging, elderly and poorer clients as well as to empirically document reasons for this difference in levels of processual control. Roter's (1976) seminal study on processual control reminds us of the potential recoil, to both clients and to providers, of increased levels of processual control in health care systems which may have no expectations nor structural provisions for it. There is preliminary evidence that links levels of processual control with health determinants or health outcomes. Ushigusa's (1984) results show a trend for higher levels of processual control to correlate negatively with self-reported anxiety levels. Rodin and Langer's (1977) studies offer strongly suggestive evidence of the importance of increased choice and responsibility for the aging elderly. Clearly there is a need for additional research on the consequences of processual control in health education studies.

Results from empirical studies with cognitive control reveal that many patients spontaneously initiate cognitive control mechanisms to manage their environments even in the absence of formal instruction or intervention (Copp, 1974; Lewis & Haberman, 1984; Wood & Pesut, 1981). The cumulative evidence in the experimental studies manipulating levels of cognitive control highlights the potential importance of sensory and procedural instruction in affecting distress levels or recovery rates (Johnson & others, 1978; Padilla & others, 1981). Admittedly, though, results across intervention studies are not consistent and future research in this area needs to consider both theoretical and methodological refinements that might yield more consistent results.

The results of studies with contingency control are inconsistent in linking internality with better health outcomes (for a possible explanation, see Becker and Rosenstock in this volume). Although the driving assumption of these studies is that internality results in health determinants or better health outcomes, there is building evidence that externality may yield better results under some conditions (Rosenblum et al., 1981; Lewis, 1982a; Giersyewski, 1983). These latter results raise additional questions that beg addressing in future studies, including under what conditions does externality result in better health outcomes? Under conditions of failing health or an irreversible disease course, externality may protect one's self-concept and one's self (Lewis, Morisky, & Flynn, 1978; Lowery & Jacobsen, 1985). As a result, the uninformed valuing of higher levels of contingency control by health educators must give way to more conditional statements and the active valuing of lower levels of control under certain conditions (Bazerman, 1982; Lewis, 1982a, 1983). The latter seems particularly relevant to situations in which the disease is objectively uncontrollable, e.g., in a rapidly declining disease trajectory, or when the available behavioral or processual responses are extremely limited (Lewis, 1982a).

Results of studies on behavioral control, like with cognitive control, are mixed. In some studies behavioral control resulted in positive outcomes (Johnson et al., 1978) and in other studies the link between behavioral control and outcomes was more tenuous (Hill, 1982; Johnson & Leventhal, 1974). Results may be inconsistent partly because the criterion outcome variable may be mistargetted and results reflect a false negative error. Speed of endoscopic tube passing, for example, may not be an appropriate criterion variable for the benefits of a behavioral instruction.

The accumulated evidence on existential control is still extremely limited but the initial studies provide beginning evidence that individuals with chronic, debilitating or life-threatening diseases or those with pain are in the process of developing existential control, even in the absence of intervention or instruction (Bulman & Wortman, 1977; Copp, 1974; Lewis, Haberman & Wallhagen, 1986). If individuals are indeed continually in the process of making meaning, this raises a host of questions about the potential role health educators can play in facilitating the individual's imposition of meaning under such aversive conditions. The preliminary evidence from correlational research suggests that existential control, instead of contingency control, may be a more powerful predictor of health determinants in patients with life-threatening illness (Lewis, 1982a, 1983).

The five-dimensional typology forces us to distinguish between the types of control that a particular health education program or intervention is targetting. This helps us to clarify and to specify both the theory motivating the program as well as the health-related consequences we should expect as outcomes. Surla's (1984) work on processual control also points out the importance of measuring the degree of congruence between actual and valued or preferred levels of control.

Theoretical work underlying each type of control ought to inform both the choice of measures for that particular type of control and the predicted consequence for that type of control. Using the HLC or MHLC Scales makes no sense when behavioral, existential, processual or cognitive control are involved. The HLC and MHLC scales measure only contingency control as defined in the current typology. As Lowery (1981) also pointed out, the locus of control construct fails to address both the stability and the control dimensions.

Within the tradition of experimental stress research with nonclinical populations, distinctions are made between the anticipatory period—the time before experiencing the actual event; the impact period—the time during the actual experience of the threat; the immediate postevent period—the time immediately after the experience with the stressful event; and the long-range postevent period, i.e., the time after which the immediate postevent reaction occurred. Differential effects for these different time periods have been documented in the experimental stress research and reported elsewhere (Thompson, 1981) but typically these time periods have not been part of the designs of the health education studies reviewed in this chapter. Padilla's study provided one of the few exceptions (Padilla & others, 1981). Health educators may do well to specify precisely when measurement of program effects should be done and to attend to the possibility of differential outcomes at different points in time after the health education intervention. For example, studies in experimental stress research reveal that behavioral control and cognitive control affect physiological arousal and anxiety during the anticipatory period and have reliable effects for increased tolerance during the impact period. Behavioral control, however, has unreliable effects for arousal during the impact period for distress or for pain. Cognitive control, however, has reliable effects for pain during the impact period. An absence of behavioral control in the immediate post-event period has adverse effects (Thompson, 1981).

Clearly, health educators need additional research and evaluation of the short- and long-term effects of the different types of control. Even existing classic studies in health education leave unanswered the important question, what type of control worked and why. In our early research we may have been justified to package an intervention, to document its effects, and to assign a value to its contribution to practice. We can no longer afford such an approach. Egbert's study, for example, documented the significant effects of a preoperative intervention package, but we still do not know what parts of the package caused the effects, or why (Egbert et al., 1964). As a result, we really do not know the meaning of the treatment variable even though the treatment had effects. This makes it difficult to systematically attain repeated effects across different studies.

An emphasis on the provision of information by some health educators as the major form of intervention with cognitive control needs to give way to programs that provide sensory, procedural, processual or behavioral instruction as well. There is some preliminary evidence that it is not the main effects of informational or behavioral instruction that are effective in changing health outcomes so much as it is the combination or interaction between the two types of intervention that results in statistically significant health changes (Hill, 1982; Johnson et al., 1978). In addition, the arousal caused by the provision of information needs to be linked with multiple ways to manage the threat. Although the provision of information may increase an individuals' sense of predictability, and thereby affect their level of cognitive control, information without ways to use it may also increase distress levels.

The inconsistent relationships between cognitive preparation and short- and long-term outcomes in the experimental interventions with hospitalized patients raises issues worthy of reflection. The provision of cognitive instruction (e.g., sensory or procedural information) does not guarantee that the individual acquires cognitive control. Instead there are two additional issues that need to be checked. First, do instructed individuals "take" or otherwise integrate the information into their cognitive repertoire? This issue is testable through disclosure of the cognitive repertoire in a debriefing session. Second, the possession of a cognitive repertoire does not definitionally mean that the person has cognitive control according to the definition in the current typology. To have cognitive control, the individual must perceive that the possessed cognitions reduce the aversiveness of their situation. If there is no such perception, the person can have the necessary cognitions, but not necessarily experience them as control. Denaturing the threat associated with the aversive event is key to the definition of cognitive control.

In conclusion, we can no longer assume that the common sense or everyday meaning of control suffices; neither can we broadly claim that health educators or health education programs are helping individuals gain control. Further clarification and specificity are needed to advance empirical work and clinical practice with the concept of control. The salient issue for clinical practice and research on control is: Do we know what we mean when we say it and can we say what we mean when we know it?

ACKNOWLEDGMENTS

Preparation of this manuscript was supported in part by BRSG S07 RR05758 awarded by the Biomedical Research Support Grant Program, Division of Research Resources, National Institutes of Health and by a grant from the Division of Nursing, R01 NU–01000. The author expresses appreciation to Mel R. Haberman, Ph.C., and Margaret I. Wallhagen, Ph.C., for their comments on selected aspects of earlier versions of the typology.

REFERENCES

Aguilera, D. C., Messick, J. M., & Farrell, M. S. (1970). *Crisis intervention, theory and methodology*. St. Louis: C. V. Mosby.
Antonovsky, A. (1980). *Health, stress, and coping*. San Francisco: Jossey-Bass.
Argyris, C. (1957). *Personality and organizations: The conflict between system and the individual*. New York: Harper & Row.
Averill, J. R. (1973). Personal control over aversive stimuli and its relationship to stress. *Psychological Bulletin, 80*(4), 286–303.
Averill, J. R., & Rosenn, M. (1972). Vigilant and nonvigilant coping strategies and psychophysical stress reactions during the anticipation of electric shock. *Journal of Personality and Social Psychology, 23*(1), 128–141.
Bales, R. F., & Borgatta, E. F. (1965). Size of group as a factor in the interaction profile. In *Small groups*. Hare, A. P., Bales, R. F., & Borgatta, E. F. (Eds.), New York: Alfred A. Knopf, pp. 495–512.
Bales, R. F. (1951). Appendix: Definitions of the categories. In *Interaction process analysis*. Cambridge, MA: Addison-Wesley, pp. 177–195.
Bazerman, M. H. (1982). Impact of personal control on performance: Is added control always beneficial? *Journal of Applied Psychology, 67*(4), 472–479.

Benoliel, J. Q. Care, communication and human dignity. (1978). In Garfield, C. A. (Ed.), *Psychosocial care of the dying patient*. New York: McGraw-Hill.

Benoliel, J. Q., & McCorkle, R. (1978). A holistic approach to terminal illness. *Cancer Nursing*, *1*(2), 143–149.

Billings, A. G., & Moos, R. H. (1984). Coping, stress and social resources among adults with unipolar depression. *Journal of Personality and Social Psychology*, 46, 877–891.

Bugaighis, M. A., & Schumm, W. R. (1983). Alternative measures of perceived locus of control. *Psychological Reports*, *52*, 819–823.

Bulman, R. J., & Wortman, C. B. (1977). Attributions of blame and coping in the "real world": Severe accident victims react to their lot. *Journal of Personality and Social Psychology* 35(5): 351–355.

Cartwright, D., & Zander, A. (1968). *Group Dynamics, Research and Theory*, 3rd Ed. NY: Harper & Row.

Cassileth, B. R., Zupkis, R. V., Sutton-Smith, K., & March, V. (1980). Information and participation preferences among cancer patients. *Annals of Internal Medicine*, *92*, 832–836.

Chang, B. L. (1980). Black and White elderly: Morale and perception of control. *Western Journal of Nursing Research*, *2*(1), 371–387.

Chang, B. L. (1979). Locus of control, trust, situational control and morale of the elderly. *International Journal of Nursing Studies*, *16*(2), 169–181.

Chang, B. L. (1978). Perceived situational control of daily activities: A new tool. *Research in Nursing & Health*, *1*(4), 181–188.

Chusid, W. (Jan/Feb/Mar, 1981). The paradoxical nature of helpless behaviour: Control through helplessness. *Canadian Journal of Psychiatric Nursing*, *22*(1), 12–13, & 15.

Cohen, F., & Lazarus, R. S. (1983). Coping and adaptation in health and illness. In Mechanic, D. (Ed.) *Handbook of health care and the health professions*. New York: The Free Press, pp. 608–635.

Cohen, F., & Lazarus, R. S. (1973). Active coping processes, coping dispositions, and recovery from surgery. *Psychosomatic Medicine*, *35*(5), 375–389.

Copp, L. A. (1974). The spectrum of suffering. *American Journal of Nursing*, *74*(3), 491–495.

Crumbaugh, J. C. (1968). Cross-validation of Purpose in Life Test based on Frankl's concepts. *Journal of Individual Psychology*, *24*(1), 74–78.

Crumbaugh, J. C., & Maholick, L. T. (Summer, 1963). The case for Frankl's "will to meaning." *Journal of Existential Psychiatry*, *4*(13), 43–48.

Currie-Gross, V., & Heimbach, J. (April/May/June, 1980). The relationship between independent living skills attainment and client control orientation. *Journal of Rehabilitation*, *46*, 20–22.

D'Altroy, L. H., Blissenbach, H. F., & Lutz, D. (November, 1978). Patient drug self-administration improves regimen compliance. *Hospitals, JAHA*, *52*, 131–132, 134–136.

Duryea, E. J. (January, 1983). Decision making and health education. *Journal of School Health*, *53*(1), 29–32.

Eagle, F. K. (August, 1983). The relationship between decision-making control and purpose-in-life for the hospitalized client with a diagnosis of cancer. Unpublished Masters' thesis, The University of Texas Health Science Center at Houston.

Egbert, L. D., Battit, G. E., Welch, C. E., & Bartlett, M. K. (April 16, 1964). Reduction of postoperative pain by encouragement and instruction of patients. *New England Journal of Medicine*, *270*(16), 825–827.

Feldman, D. J. (1974). Chronic disabling illness: A holistic view. *Journal of Chronic Disease*, *27*, 287–291.

Fiore, N. (1979). Fighting cancer—one patient's perspective. *New England Journal of Medicine*, *300*, 284–289.

Fiore, N. (1984). *On the road back to health: Coping with the emotional side of cancer.* New York: Bantam Books.

Folkman, S., & Lazarus, R. S. (1980). An analysis of coping in a middle-aged community sample. *Journal of Health and Social Behavior, 21,* 219–239.

Frankl, V. E. (1962). *Man's search for meaning: An introduction to logotherapy.* Boston: Beacon Press.

Frankl, V. E. (1958). The will to meaning. *Journal of Pastoral Care, 12,* 82–88.

Frankl, V. E. (1959). The spiritual dimension in existential analysis and logotherapy. *Journal of Individual Psychology, 15,* 157.

Gatchel, R. J., & Proctor, J. D. (1976). Physiological correlates of learned helplessness in man. *Journal of Abnormal Psychology, 85,* 27–34.

Gierszewski, S. A. (1983). The relationship of weight loss, locus of control and social support. *Nursing Research, 32,* 43–47.

Green, L. W., Werlin, S. H., Schauffler, H. H., & Avery, C. H. (Summer, 1977). Research and demonstration issues in self-care: Measuring the decline of mediocentricism. *Health Education Monographs 5,* 161–189.

Haberman, M. R. (May, 1984). Dimensions of cognitive control. Paper presented at Seventeenth Annual Communicating Nursing Research Conference. Western Society for Research in Nursing, San Francisco, CA.

Hamburg, D., Elliott, G., & Parron, D. (Eds.) (1982). *Health and behavior: Frontiers of research in the biomedical sciences.* Washington, DC: National Academy Press.

Hamrick, M. H., Anspaugh, D. J., & Smith, D. L. (October, 1980). Decision-making and the behavior gap. *Journal of School Health, 50*(8), 455–458.

Hartfield, M. T., Cason, C. L., & Cason, G. J. (1982). Effects of information about a threatening procedure on patients' expectations and emotional distress. *Nursing Research, 31*(4), 202–206.

Hayes–Bautista, D. E. (1976). Modifying the treatment: Patient compliance, patient control and medical care. *Social Science and Medicine, 10,* 233–238.

Hill, B. J. (1982). Sensory information, behavioral instructions and coping with sensory alteration surgery. *Nursing Research, 31*(1), 17–21.

Jamison, H., & Mueller, D. P. (1979). Patient initiative and responsibility: The potential effect on treatment and control of disease: The case of gonorrhea. *Social Science and Medicine, 13A*(3), 303–311.

Joe, V. C. (1971). Review of the internal-external control construct as a personality variable. *Psychological Reports, 28,* 619–640.

Johnson, J. E., Fuller, S. S., Endress, M. P., & Rice, V. S. (1978b). Altering patients' responses to surgery: An extension and replication. *Research in Nursing and Health, 1*(3), 111–121.

Johnson, J. E., Rice, V. H., Fuller, S. S., & Endress, M. P. (1978a). Sensory information instruction in a coping strategy and recovery from surgery. *Research in Nursing and Health, 1*(1), 4–17.

Johnson, J. E., & Leventhal, H. (1974). Effects of accurate expectations and behavioral instructions on reactions during a noxious medical examination. *Journal of Personality and Social Psychology, 29*(5), 710–718.

Johnson, J. E., Dabbs, J. M., & Leventhal, H. (1970). Psychosocial factors in the welfare of surgical patients. *Nursing Research, 19*(1), 18–29.

Krant, M. J. (1974). *Dying and dignity: The meaning and control of a personal death.* Springfield, IL: Charles C. Thomas Publishers.

Krantz, D. S. (Spring, 1980). Cognitive processes and recovery from heart attack: A review and theoretical analysis. *Journal of Human Stress,* 27–38.

Krause, N., & Stryker, S. (1984). Stress and well-being: The buffering role of locus of control beliefs. *Social Science and Medicine, 18*(9), 783–790.

Langer, E. J. (1983). *The Psychology of Control*. Beverly Hills: Sage.

Langer, E. J., & Rodin, J. (1976). The effects of choice and enhanced personal responsibility for the aged: A field experiment in an institutional setting. *Journal of Personality and Social Psychology, 34*(2), 191–198.

Larde, J., & Clopton, J. R. (1983). Generalized locus of control and health locus of control of surgical patients. *Psychological Reports, 52*(2), 599–602.

Lau, H. R., & Ware, J. F., Jr. (November, 1981). Refinements in the measurement of health-specific locus-of-control beliefs. *Medical Care, 19*(11), 1147–1157.

Lazarus, R. S., Averill, J. R., & Opton, E. M. The psychology of coping: Issues of research and assessment. In Coelho, G. V., Hamburg, D. A., & Adams, J. E. (Eds.), *Coping and adaptation*. New York: Basic Books, pp. 249–315. 1974.

Lefcourt, H. M. (1976). *Locus of control: Current trends in theory and research*. New York: Wiley. p. 154.

Levin, R. F. (Feb/Mar, 1982). Choice of injection site, locus of control, and the perception of momentary pain. *Image, 14*(1), 26–32.

Lewis, F. M. (1983). The concept of personal control: Specification and measurement. Paper presented at Sixteenth Annual Communicating Research Conference, Western Society for Research in Nursing. Portland, Oregon, May 4–6.

Lewis, F. M. (1982a). Experienced personal control and quality of life in late-stage cancer patients. *Nursing Research, 31*(2), 113–119.

Lewis, F. M. (1982b). Health Locus of Control. *Oncology Nursing Forum, 9*(3), 108–109.

Lewis, F. M., Haberman, M. R. & Wallhagen, M. I. (1986). How late-stage cancer patients experience control. *Journal of Psychological Oncology, 4*(4), in press.

Lewis, F. M., Morisky, D., & Flynn, B. S. (Spring, 1978). A test of the construct validity of health locus of control: Effects on self-reported compliance for hypertensive patients. *Health Education Monographs, 6*(2), 138–148.

Likert, R. (1967). *The Human Organization*. New York: McGraw-Hill.

Lindeman, C. A., & Van Aerman, B. (1971). Nursing intervention with the pre-surgical patient: The effects of structured and unstructured pre-operative teaching. *Nursing Research, 20*, 319–332.

Lipowski, Z. J. (1970). Physical illness, the individual and the coping process. *Psychiatry in Medicine, 1*, 91–102.

Lowery, B. J. (1981). Misconceptions and limitations of locus of control and the I-E scale. *Nursing Research*, 30(5), 294–298.

Lowery, B. J., Jacobsen, B. S., & Murphy, B. B. (1983). An exploratory investigation of causal thinking of arthritics. *Nursing Research, 32*, 157–161.

Ludenia, K., & Donham, G. W. (November, 1983). Dental outpatients: Health locus of control correlates. *Journal of Clinical Psychology, 39*(6), 854–858.

McCusker, J., & Morrow, G. (1979). The relationship of health locus of control to preventive health behaviors and health beliefs. *Patient Education and Counseling, 1*(4), 146–150.

Meichenbaum, D. (1977). *Cognitive-behavior modification: An integrative approach*. New York: Plenum Press.

Meichenbaum, D. H. (1969). The effects of instructions and reinforcement on thinking and language behavior of schizophrenics. *Behavior Research and Therapy, 7*, 101–114.

Meichenbaum, D., & Goodman, J. (September, 1969). Reflection-impulsivity and verbal control of motor behavior. *Child Development*, 40, 785–794.

Meyers, R., Donham, G. W., & Ludenia, K. (1982). The psychometric properties of the health locus of control scale with medical and surgical patients. *Journal of Clinical Psychology, 38*(4), 783–787.

Miller, S. M. (1979). Controllability and human stress: Method, evidence and theory. *Behaviour Research and Therapy, 17*, 287–304.

Mills, R. T., & Krantz, D. S. (1979). Information, choice and reactions to stress: A field experiment in a blood bank with laboratory analogue. *Journal of Personality and Social Psychology, 37*, 608–620.

Minuchin, S., & Fishman, H. C. (1981). *Family therapy techniques.* Cambridge: Harvard University Press.

Morisky, D. E., Bowler, M. H., & Finlay, J. S. (Spring, 1982). An educational and behavioral approach toward increasing patient activation in hypertension management. *Journal of Community Health, 7*(3), 171–182.

Mullen, P. D. (1978). Cutting back after a heart attack: An overview. *Health Education Monographs, 6*(3), 295–311.

Mullen, P. D. (1980). The (already) activated patient: An alternative to mediocentricism. In Squyres, W. D. (Eds.), *Patient Education: An Inquiry into the State of the Art.* New York: Springer, pp. 271–298.

Murray, J. E. (July/August, 1974). Patient participation in determining psychiatric treatment. *Nursing Research, 23*(4), 325–333.

Nowakowski, L. (1977). A new look at client advocacy. In Hall, J. E., & Weaver, B. P., (Eds.), *Distributive nursing practice: A systems approach to community nursing.* Philadelphia: J. B. Lippincott, pp. 227–238.

Orem, D. E. (Ed.). (1979). Nursing Development Conference Group. *Concept formalization in nursing, process and product.* 2nd ed. Boston: Little, Brown, & Company.

Orem, D. E. (1971). *Nursing: Concepts of practice.* New York: McGraw-Hill.

Padilla, G. V., Grant, M. M., Rains, B. L., Hansen, B. C., Bergstrom, N., Wong, H. L., Hanson, R., & Kubo, W. (1981). Distress reduction and the effects of preparatory teaching films and patient control. *Research in Nursing and Health, 4*, 375–387.

Pearlin, L., & Schooler, C. (1978). The structure of coping. *Journal of Health and Social Behavior, 19*, 2–21.

Pohl, J. M., & Fuller, S. S. (1980). Perceived choice, social interaction, and dimensions of morale of residents in a home for the aged. *Research in Nursing and Health, 3*(4), 147–157.

Powers, M. J., & Wooldrige, P. J. (December, 1982). Factors influencing knowledge, attitudes, and compliance of hypertensive patients. *Research in Nursing and Health, 5*(4), 171–182.

Rodin, J., & Langer, E. J. (1977). Long-term effects of a control relevant intervention with the institutionalized elderly. *Journal of Personality and Social Psychology, 35*, 897–902.

Rosenblum, E. H., Stone, E. J., Skipper, B. E. (Nov/Dec, 1981). Maternal compliance in immunization of preschoolers as related to health locus of control, health value, and perceived vulnerability. *Nursing Research 30*(6), 337–342.

Roter, D. L. (Winter, 1977). Patient participation in the patient provider interaction: The effects of patient question asking on the quality of interaction, satisfaction, and compliance. *Health Education Monographs, 5*(4), 281–312.

Rotter, J. B. (1975). Some problems and misconceptions related to the construct of internal versus external control of reinforcement. *Journal of Consulting and Clinical Psychology, 43*(1), 56–67.

Rotter, J. B. (1966). Generalized expectancies for internal versus external control of reinforcement. *Psychological Monographs, 80*(Whole No. 609): 1–28.

Rotter, J. B. (1954). *Social learning and clinical psychology.* Englewood Cliffs, NJ: Prentice-Hall.

Roy, Sr. C. (1977). Decision-making by the physically ill and adaptation during illness. Unpublished doctoral dissertation, University of California, Los Angeles.

Saltzer, E. B. (1982). The weight locus of control (WLOC) scale: A specific measure for obesity research. *Journal of Personality Assessment, 46*, 620–628.

Schain, W. S. (August, 1980). Patients' rights in decision making. *Cancer*, 46(4), 1035–1041.

Schmidt, D. E., & Keating, J. P. (1979). Human crowding and personal control: An integration of the research. *Psychological Bulletin*, 86(4), 680–700.

Schulz, R. (1976). Effects of control and predictability on the physical and psychological well-being of the institutionalized aged. *Journal of Personality and Social Psychology*, 33(5), 563–573.

Sechrist, W. (1983). Causal attribution and personal responsibility for health and disease. *Health Education*, 14(2), 51–54.

Seligman, M. E. P. (1975). *Helplessness: On depression, development and death*. San Francisco: W. H. Freeman.

Sherrod, D. R., Hage, J. N., Halpern, P. L., & Moore, B. S. (1977). Effects of personal causation and perceived control on responses to an aversive environment: The more control the better. *Journal of Experimental Social Psychology*, 13, 14–27.

Sidle, A., Moos, R., Adams, J., & Cady, P. (February, 1969). Development of a coping scale. *Archives of General Psychiatry*, 20, 226–232.

Skorupka, P., & Bohnet, N. (1982). Primary caregivers' perceptions of nursing behaviors that best meet their needs in a home care hospice setting. *Cancer Nursing*, 5(5), 371–374.

Snow, M., & Thurber, S. (Fall, 1983). Factorial validity of the health locus of control (HLC) scale. *Educational and Psychological Measurement*, 43(3), 893–895.

Stinchcombe, A. (1968). The conceptualization of power phenomena. In *Constructing social theories*, pp. 149–200.

Stone, A. A., & Neale, J. M. (1984). New meaure of daily coping: Development and preliminary results. *Journal of Personality and Social Psychology*, 46, 892–906.

Surla, J. (1984). Health decision making practices of people with advanced cancer. Unpublished Master's thesis, University of Washington.

Szasz, T., & Hollender, M. (1956). A contribution to the philosophy of medicine. *Archives of Internal Medicine*, 97, 585–592.

Taylor, S. E., Lichtman, R. R., & Wood, J. V. (1984). Attributions, beliefs about control and adjustment to breast cancer. *Journal of Personality and Social Psychology*, 46, 489–502.

Thomas, P. D., & Hooper, E. M. (March, 1983). Healthy elderly: Social bonds and locus of control. *Research in Nursing and Health*, 6(1), 11–16.

Thompson, S. C. (1981). Will it hurt less if I can control it? A complex answer to a simple question. *Psychological Bulletin*, 90(1), 89–101.

Thornbury, K. M. (1982). Coping: Implications for health practitioners. *Patient Education and Counseling*, 4(1), 3–9.

Ushigusa, K. K. (1984). Cancer knowledge, anxiety and processual control in cancer patients. Unpublished Masters' thesis, University of Washington.

Vertinsky, I. B., Thompson, W. A., & Uyeno, D. (Summer, 1974). Measuring consumer desire for participation in clinical decision making. *Health Services Research*, 121–134.

Vitaliano, P. P., Russo, J., Carr, J. E., Maiuro, R. D., & Becker, J. (1985). The Ways of Coping Checklist: Revision and psychometric properties. *Multivariate Behavioral Research*, 20, 3–26.

Wallston, B. S., & Wallston, K. A. (Spring, 1978). Locus of control and health: A review of the literature. *Health Education Monographs*, 6(2), 107–117.

Wallston, K. A., Wallston, B. S., & DeVellis, R. (Spring, 1978). Development of the multidimensional health locus of control (MHLC) scale. *Health Education Mongraphs*, 6(2), 160–170.

Wallston, B. S., Wallston, K. A., Kaplan, G. D., & Maides, S. A. (1976). Development and validation of the health locus of control (HLC) scale. *Journal of Consulting and Clinical Psychology*, 44(4), 580–585.

Weisman, A. D. (1979). *Coping with cancer*. New York: McGraw-Hill.

Weiss, J. M. (1971a). Effects of coping behavior in different warning signal conditions on stress pathology in rats. *Journal of Comparative and Physiological Psychology, 77*, 1–13.

————. (1971b). Effects of punishing the coping response (conflict) on stress pathology in rats. *Journal of Comparative and Physiological Psychology, 77*(1), 14–21.

————. (1971c). Effects of coping behavior with and without a feedback signal on stress pathology in rats. *Journal of Comparative and Physiological Psychology, 77*(1), 22–30.

Wood, D. J., & Pesut, D. J. (1981). Self-regulatory mental processes and patient recovery. *Western Journal of Nursing Research, 3*(3), 263–271.

Wortman, C. B. (1976). Some determinants of perceived control. *Journal of Personality and Social Psychology, 31*(2), 282–294.

Wortman, C. B. (1974). Causal attributions and personal control. In Harvey, J., Ickes, W., & Kidd, R. (Eds.), *New Directions in Attribution Research*. Vol. I. New York: Wiley.

Yalom, I. D. (1980). *Existential psychotherapy*. New York: Basic Books, pp. 419–460.

SOCIAL NETWORKS AND SOCIAL SUPPORT:
A SYNTHESIS FOR HEALTH EDUCATORS

Barbara A. Israel and Kathleen A. Rounds

INTRODUCTION

Over the past 15 years, empirical evidence increasingly suggests a positive relationship between social networks and social support and physical and mental health. The growth in the number of studies conducted is substantial. House & Kahn (1985) report that in the Social Science Citation Index the number of articles with the term "social support" in their titles grew from two in 1972 to fifty in 1982. This research has involved diverse populations, study designs, conceptual frameworks, measurement instruments, outcome variables, data analyses, findings, implications for practice, and limitations. These investigations have been carried out by persons representing numerous disciplines, including health education, epidemiology, social psychology, gerontology, sociology, anthropology, psychology, and social work. As a result of this broad examination of social networks and social support, there has been an accompanying increase in the number of literature reviews of this area. These reviews have represented many perspectives and contain varied suggestions for future directions. The expan-

Advances in Health Education and Promotion, vol. 2, pages 311–351
Copyright © 1987 JAI Press Inc.
All rights of reproduction in any form reserved.
ISBN: 0-89232-617-4

sion of the literature is continuing. For example, within the last two years, three journals, *Health Education Quarterly* (Israel & McLeroy, 1985), the *Journal of Social Issues* (Brownell & Shumaker, Part I 1984, Part II 1985) and the *Journal of Counseling and Clinical Psychology* (Heller, in press), have devoted entire theme issues to the topic of social networks and social support, and three edited books have a similar focus (Cohen & Syme, 1985; Sarason & Sarason, 1985; Sauer & Coward, 1985).

Given the extensiveness of the subject and the discrepancies within the field of study, a person interested in but relatively new to the area is faced with the difficult task of reviewing the literature. This is perhaps even more problematic for health educators concerned with organizing, synthesizing and integrating diverse theoretical perspectives and empirical findings into the design, implementation and evaluation of interventions. The purpose of this article is to provide a guide for identifying and understanding the social network and social support literature. The article is written primarily for health educators who are relatively new to this area; however, others may find the article to be a useful review. In an attempt to provide an integration of relevant theoretical and conceptual considerations, empirical findings and issues, and practice implications, this article will build upon the existing literature by presenting a *review of reviews*. Hence, the focus of this chapter will be on summarizing and analyzing literature reviews that have examined the concepts of social networks and social support.

The review articles were located through a computerized search using Social Science Citation Index and Psychological Abstracts and through personal networks. Journal articles and book chapters written from 1980 to early 1985 are included. Although the reviews are not all-inclusive, they comprise an extensive representative sample that reflects the interdisciplinary nature and multiple perspectives found in the topic area. The studies reviewed in these articles have included diverse adult populations and have examined both physical and mental health outcomes.

Thirty-three review articles were selected for examination in this chapter. (See References for complete listing.) Over half of the articles review the empirical evidence regarding the relationship between social networks and social support and health status or health behavior (e.g., Antonucci, 1985; Berkman, 1984; Broadhead et al., 1983; Cohen & Wills, 1985; DiMatteo & Hays, 1981; Kessler & McLeod, 1985; Leavy, 1983; Levy, 1983; Mueller, 1980; Thoits, 1982; Wallston et al., 1983). Approximately one-third of the articles present conceptual frameworks from which social networks and social support are viewed (e.g., Cohen & McKay, 1984; Heller & Swindle, 1983; House, 1981; Kahn & Antonucci, 1980; Moos & Mitchell, 1982; Norbeck, 1981). Several of the articles focus on applying social support and social network concepts in the analysis of interventions (e.g., Gottlieb, 1981b; Minkler, 1981; Pilisuk & Minkler, 1980). Additionally, several of these review articles have integrated the presentation of empirical evidence, the development of a conceptual framework, and the discussion of practice considerations (e.g., Ell, 1984; Israel, 1982; Mitchell & Trickett, 1980; Norbeck, 1981).

It is useful to mention types of review materials that were not selected for this article. There are numerous important literature reviews written before 1980 and thus are not included (e.g., Caplan, 1974; Cassel, 1976; Cobb, 1976; Dean & Lin, 1977; Hamburg & Killilea, 1979; Heller, 1979; Kaplan, Cassel, & Gore, 1977; Mitchell, 1969; Pilisuk & Froland, 1978; Sarason et al., 1977). Entire books on social support or social networks written by a single author were not examined here (e.g., Biegel, 1984; Gottlieb, 1983; Maguire, 1983), and may be of interest to the reader. Literature reviews that focus on social networks and social support in relation to only one specific disease entity, for example, schizophrenia (e.g., Hammer, 1981; Marsella & Snyder, 1981) or cancer (e.g., Wortman, 1984) are not included. Articles in which the emphasis in the review is on the application of social network and social support concepts to the treatment of chronically mentally ill persons, are not examined (e.g., Greenblatt et al., 1982; Cuter & Tatum, 1983). Finally, there are articles that were not selected that present a conceptual framework and review empirical studies, but are primarily a report of the author's own research (e.g., La Rocco et al., 1980; Lieberman, 1982; Schaefer et al., 1981).

This chapter focuses on describing and analyzing previous reviews of the social network and social support literature. The similarities and differences of topics and findings addressed in these reviews will be highlighted along with issues considered to be particularly important for health education. First, the definitions and concepts that describe the terms "social networks," "social support," "social support system" and "social support networks" will be examined. Next, the theoretical underpinnings and conceptual frameworks applied to social networks and social support will be reviewed. Third, a summary of the major empirical findings will be reported. After that, some of the methodological issues that the review articles address will be presented. Fifth, important practice implications will be reviewed. A summary of each section will be followed by conclusions and future directions suggested by the present authors.

SOCIAL NETWORKS AND SOCIAL SUPPORT: DEFINITIONS

Both of the terms "social networks" and "social support" have been defined and conceptualized differently by various authors. Furthermore, the terms "social support network" (McKinlay, 1980; Minkler, 1981; Pilisuk & Minkler, 1980) and "social support system" (Cohen & McKay, 1984; Ell, 1984; Thoits, 1982) are sometimes used in place of the term "social network." This section presents some of the more frequently used definitions and discusses the distinction between social networks and social support as found in these reviews.

Of the thirty-three review articles, over half discuss both social networks and social support (e.g., Ell, 1984; Heller & Swindle, 1983; Kahn & Antonucci, 1980). While most of these attempt to integrate the two concepts, authors usually emphasize either social networks (e.g., Mueller, 1980) or social support (e.g., Turner, 1983). Of the remaining half of the review articles, most focus primarily on the concept of social support (e.g., Broadhead et al., 1983; DiMatteo & Hays, 1981; Kessler & McLeod, 1985). Very few of the reviews examine only social networks (e.g., McKinlay, 1980; Pilisuk & Minkler, 1980).

There is more conceptual agreement with the way the term "social network" is defined than with the term "social support." In those articles where the major emphasis is on social networks the definitions of Mitchell (1969) and Walker and MacBride (1977) are most frequently used. Mitchell (1969) defines a social network as "a set of linkages among persons in which the characteristics of the linkages are useful for understanding the behavior of the persons involved" (p. 2). Walker and MacBride (1977) define social network as "that set of personal contacts through which the individual maintains his social identity and receives emotional support, material aid, services, information and new social contacts" (p. 35). Hence, a social network refers to the existence and nature of social ties. The concept is frequently further specified by defining the personal (Wellman, 1981) or egocentric network as that part of the network, where "the individual subject is the point of anchorage from which all network linkages can be traced" (Mueller, 1980, p. 147).

To explain social networks further, several authors (e.g., Israel, 1982; Mitchell & Trickett, 1980) have categorized network characteristics along three dimensions. These are: (1) structural characteristics: size (the number of people in a network) and density (the extent to which people who could know one another, do know one another); (2) interactional characteristics, such as reciprocity (the mutuality within a relationship, the extent to which functions are both given and received); durability (the extent of stability of a person's ties with other network members), frequency of interaction, and dispersion (the ease with which a person can make contact with network members); and (3) functional characteristics: affective support (caring, love), instrumental support (tangible aid and services), cognitive support (information, advice), maintenance of social identity, and social outreach (access to social contacts and social roles). Thus, one function of social network ties is the provision of social support.

In addition to the term "social network," Kahn and Antonucci (1980) refer to a "convoy" as the personal network over the life-course of an individual. Thoits (1982) uses the term "social support system" to describe "the subset of persons in the individual's total social network upon whom he or she relies for socioeconomic aid and/or instrumental aid" (p. 148). The terms "social support networks" and "social networks" are used interchangeably by McKinlay (1980) adding to the lack of clarity among these terms. Wellman (1981) takes issue with the use of the term "support system," arguing that it oversimplifies the nature of social networks by assuming that ties between certain network members are supportive.

The literature reviews examined in this article cite numerous definitions of social support. (For a comprehensive discussion and review of social support definitions, refer to Antonucci, 1985; House, 1981; Leavy, 1983; and Turner, 1983.) The definitions most often cited are those of Caplan (1974), Cobb (1976), House (1981), and Kahn and Antonucci (1980). Of these definitions, the House taxonomy is most frequently cited by other authors of these review articles as the most comprehensive (e.g., Cwikel & Israel, 1985; Jung, 1984; Leavy, 1983). House (1981) includes four broad types of supportive behaviors or acts in his conceptualization of social support: (1) emotional support (esteem, affect, trust, concern, listening); (2) appraisal support (affirmation, feedback, social comparison); (3) informational support (advice, suggestion, directives, information); and (4) instrumental support (aid, money). While these four support functions can be conceptually differentiated, Cohen and Wills (1985) note that "in naturalistic settings they are not usually independent" (p. 313).

Different researchers have used the term "social support" to refer to a variety of processes (Jung, 1984). House and Kahn (1985) refer to three ways that social support has been defined and measured and suggest that each is a part of the overall domain of social support. They describe these three aspects in terms of: (1) the existence or *quantity* of social relationships, e.g., marriage or organizational membership; (2) the nature of the *structures* among a person's social relationships, e.g., size, density, usually referred to as an individual's social network; and (3) the *functional content* of the relationships, usually referred to as social support. Because these three aspects are closely interrelated (e.g., the structure of an individual's social relationships may determine how much or what type of social support he/she receives), House and Kahn (1985) recommend that in a research study at least two if not all three of these aspects be conceptualized and measured. Another useful conceptualization of social support proposed by Leavy (1983) has two interrelated components: structure (network characteristics) and content (the form that help takes, i.e. types of support) that interact with a third component, process ("the way an individual develops, nurtures, and uses supportive ties," p. 17). He argues that all three components need to be included in conceptualizing social support to understand its complexity fully.

The distinction between social networks and social support is an important one (Berkman, 1984; Ell, 1984; Gottlieb, 1981a, b; Heller & Swindle, 1983; Israel, 1982; Mitchell & Trickett, 1980; Moos & Mitchell, 1982), but one that is not always made. Social network refers to the linkages among persons and social support refers to some of the functions that may or may not be provided by these linkages. The advantages of using a social network approach to study social support are presented by several authors (Gottlieb, 1981a; Israel, 1982; Mitchell & Trickett, 1980; Wellman, 1981). According to these authors, a network analysis approach provides for (1) a neutral approach that does not assume that ties are necessarily supportive; (2) an examination of network characteristics and their relationship to health status; (3) an examination of the different types of support that might be provided by different types of relationships; (4) the study of the interconnectedness of relationships, for example, how network linkages and structure affect the flow of social support; and (5) an assessment of network characteristics that might be important in the development of interventions.

The lack of consensus regarding the terms "social network" and "social support" is a major problem. As will be discussed later, it creates difficulty in measurement as well as in summarizing study findings regarding the relationship between social networks, social support, and health. Any effort to improve conceptual clarity requires that the distinction discussed here between the concepts of social network and social support be made and that the terms not be used interchangeably. As mentioned earlier, it is important that the existence, structure, and functions of social relationships be conceptualized and measured (House & Kahn, 1985). We suggest that social network is a broader concept than social support and that it encompasses social support as defined by the House (1981) typology (emotional, appraisal, informational, and instrumental support). Thus social support is a functional characteristic of a social network. We agree with the advantages presented earlier of using a social network approach. We do not view this as an either/or choice (i.e., social networks or social support), rather as a matter of emphasis. When making such decisions for practice, of whether to examine numerous characteristics of social networks, including social support, or to focus on social support functions, consideration needs to be given to theoretical and empirical findings, the needs of the target population, intervention goals and objectives, and pragmatic issues such as funding, staff, and available time.

THEORETICAL AND CONCEPTUAL CONSIDERATIONS

Before examining the empirical evidence regarding the association between social networks, social support, and health, it is important to understand the theoretical and conceptual contexts within which social networks and social support have been discussed. This task is made difficult because of the different interpretations of what constitutes a theory and what comprises conceptual issues. For example, some authors present the definitions of network characteristics as theory; others suggest that the topic of social support does not yet constitute a theory, and instead use the term "theory" to refer to a broader explanatory schema, e.g., exchange theory. Some authors also refer to theoretical issues when they are actually discussing methodological concerns, e.g., operational confounding.

This chapter in no way purports to untangle this inconsistent use of terms. However, to compare reviews, we have attempted to apply a common, although not totally satisfactory, definition. Hence, the summary of *theoretical considerations* described in the literature will refer to comprehensive explanations that address the nature and processes of how people and social systems relate (Snow & Gordon, 1980). *Conceptual issues* will be those associated with an explanatory model or framework that identifies numerous variables and hypothesizes how they are related to one another and with what effects. The relationships posited in such conceptual frameworks can be tested empirically.

Theoretical Considerations

Approximately half of the articles reviewed make no, or only brief, mention of theoretical considerations. Of the other articles that do discuss theories to some extent, numerous theories are applied in different ways. For example, some authors describe a given theory as an antecedent to social networks and social support (e.g., crisis theory, Moos & Mitchell, 1982). Other authors discuss theoretical underpinnings that help explain why and how social networks and social support operate (e.g., social comparison theory: Cohen & McKay, 1984; exchange theory: Israel, 1982; symbolic interactionism, Israel, 1982; Thoits, 1982; theory of anomie: Thoits, 1982; Turner, 1983). Several of these theories that are most frequently mentioned in the review articles will be briefly examined below.

After an extensive review of studies on social support and physical health, Wallston et al. (1983) suggest that social support may have its effect on health by influencing the state of learned helplessness (i.e., exposure to unpredictable, uncontrollable aversive events), which has been associated with illness outcomes. They discuss several mechanisms whereby social support could contribute to reducing the state of learned helplessness. For example, social support could provide information that assists an individual in feeling a greater sense of predictability; or it could influence a person to respond in a way that produces desirable outcomes and an accompanying increase in sense of control.

Cohen and McKay (1984), in their interpretation of how social support may be responsible for its presumed buffering effects, describe a possible relationship between learned helplessness, self-esteem and social support. They suggest that the type of social support that enhances one's self-esteem might be effective in encouraging a person to cope when exposed to uncontrollable stressors (a component of learned helplessness) that may otherwise result in feelings of inadequacy.

An interpretation of the major components of exchange theory is suggested by Israel (1982) as a theoretical underpinning to the network characteristic of reciprocity. Exchange theory posits that social interactions are influenced by a desire to obtain maximum rewards (e.g., respect, money, information, advice) at minimum costs. Therefore, relationships are established in which there are valued reciprocal transactions between the persons involved.

Hansson et al. (1984), in their discussion of the influence of personality on maintaining relationships and support networks, suggest that some people have dispositions important to a social exchange framework (e.g., sensitive to the needs of others, sense of equity and personal responsibility). Drawing from equity theory, they posit that those people who are able to maximize the rewards of all network members are able to maintain cohesive and stable support networks.

Heller and Swindle (1983) examine social comparison theory in their presentation of social psychological antecedents to social support. The main premise of social comparison theory is that people assess their opinions and attitudes through a comparison of either how others behave or by objective standards. Since objective standards are usually not available, the theory postulates that people use the behavior of others as a comparison. Heller and Swindle suggest that the relevance of social comparison theory to social support is that it states that under situations of uncertainty or stress people affiliate with others to gain a better idea of how to act. The theory posits that people will choose for comparison people who are similar to themselves.

Cohen and McKay (1984) elaborate on social comparison theory in their discussion of social support and the assessment of situations as threatening. Concerning the selection of similar others for comparison information, the theory states that the important aspects of similarity include similarity of personality, attitudes, and experience. Cohen and McKay build upon the assumption that social support serves as a buffer against stress by helping people reassess a situation as less threatening. They suggest that from a social comparison theory perspective, social support will have the effects of reducing stress only when certain conditions exist; for example, when the supportive comparison person responds to a potential stressor in a relatively calm way.

Thoits (1982) discusses symbolic interactionism as a theoretical basis for why social support should have a direct relationship to psychological well-being, separate from the presence of stressful life events. Symbolic interactionism postulates that social identity and self-evaluation, important components of psychological well-being, come from social interactions. Since social support serves to enhance or maintain social identity and self-esteem, then one would expect it to be directly related to well-being.

Israel (1982) examines symbolic interactionism as an explanation for the importance of the quality (perceived meaning, intensity, mutual sharing) of social interactions and their association to well-being. The theory emphasizes that human behavior is based on the meaning that people assign and derive from social interactions with others. To understand these social interactions, one must obtain the meanings that people give to their actions, which is based on ongoing perceptions and interpretations. Therefore, drawing upon this theory, one would expect that it is not the objective characteristics of social networks (e.g., size, frequency of interaction) but the subjective or qualitative characteristics (e.g., strength of ties and reciprocity), as interpreted by the individual, that are most strongly related to well-being.

In addition to the theories discussed above, numerous others are applied to social networks and social support in the review articles. Some of the theories mentioned are: role theory (Kahn & Antonucci, 1980); attachment theory (Kahn & Antonucci, 1980); reference group theory (Heller & Swindle, 1983); social facilitation theory (Heller & Swindle, 1983); and helping theories (Jung, 1984).

In summary, not only are theoretical considerations often not discussed at all in articles reviewed, but also when they are, no single theoretical perspective is suggested for understanding social networks and social support. Furthermore, the various theories discussed are interpreted differently. This diversity is not surprising given the lack of clarity and agreement on the concepts of social networks and social support. Also, given the various disciplines of the authors, the tendency, for example, of sociologists to apply sociological theory and social psychologists to apply social psychological theory, is somewhat predictable.

There is a need for determining the extent to which a given theoretical perspective helps explain and guide future research in the area of social networks and social support. Building upon these theories, and as more multidimensional studies are conducted, it may be possible to synthesize more clearly these theoretical considerations. Such a synthesis may move us toward the development of a theory of social networks and social support. Although such a theory does not exist to date, several recent articles (e.g., Cohen & McKay, 1984; Hansson et al., 1984) have made important contributions toward this end.

Conceptual Issues

Of the thirty-three articles being reviewed, over two-thirds present an explanatory model or conceptual framework in which the relationships between numerous variables are identified. These articles will be the focus of this discussion. Approximately half of these articles provide a visual representation of the model being discussed (e.g., House, 1981; Kahn & Antonucci, 1980; Norbeck, 1981), and the remaining half provide a verbal description (e.g., Cohen & McKay, 1984; Moos & Mitchell, 1980).

There is considerably more consistency in the literature regarding conceptual issues than was found for theoretical considerations. Of the review articles that examined conceptual issues to a great extent, most present one or the other of two frameworks. Before examining these two specific frameworks, it is important to summarize the more general conceptual underpinnings of social networks and social support.

Almost every article reviewed either refers to, or provides an in-depth explanation of, the early conceptual considerations put forth by the late epidemiologist, John Cassel (1974, 1976). These reviews describe Cassel's thinking concerning the relationship between stress and "psychosocial processes" and health. Drawing from numerous animal and human studies, Cassel (1976) argued that psychosocial variables are associated with disease susceptibility. He elaborated on two sets of psychosocial factors. Cassel (1976) states that at least one of the properties of the stress factor that could affect health status might be that the individual "is not receiving adequate evidence (feedback) that his actions are leading to anticipated consequences" (p. 113). With regard to social support, Cassel explains that there is another set of factors that "might be envisioned as the protective factors buffering or cushioning the individual from the physiologic or psychologic consequences of exposure to the stressor situation. It is suggested that the property common to these processes is the strength of the social supports provided by primary groups of most importance to the individual" (p. 113).

As these review articles emphasize, Cassel provided an early conceptual framework for understanding the relationship between stress and health. Social support is posited as a key psychosocial factor that can potentially have either a direct positive effect on well-being or can serve as a buffer or mediator of the effects of stress on health status. Furthermore, these psychosocial factors are related to both physical and mental health outcomes in a nonspecific way. That is, the effects of this stress process may be different for different individuals. For example, one individual exposed to certain stressors and with certain social supports may be at risk of negative mental health consequences, another individual may experience poor physical health outcomes, and another may have no deleterious effects. Cassel's conceptual framework has provided an important foundation from which other more detailed models have evolved.

The two conceptual models most frequently discussed in these review articles can be roughly categorized along two dimensions. First, there are models of the stress process in which stress is viewed as the central component and social support is referred to as a conditioning or moderating variable (e.g., Cohen & McKay, 1984; Cohen & Wills, 1985; House, 1981; Thoits, 1982). A major aspect of these models is the hypothesized role of social support as a buffer against stress or as having a direct effect on stress or well-being. Along a second dimension, conceptual frameworks are presented that place social networks as the central component with their determinants and effects as important variables (e.g., Israel, 1982; Kahn & Antonucci, 1980; Mitchell & Trickett, 1980; Moos & Mitchell, 1982). Social network characteristics (including structure and functions) are viewed as key variables in the relationship between psychosocial factors and health and disease; and stress is usually an implicit not explicit component of these models. Further brief explanations of each of these two models will be provided below. Although within these review articles there are some differences concerning which variables are included in the models and their suggested associations, for the purposes of this article, one model from each category will be described to exemplify the major conceptual issues.

Conceptual Framework: The Stress Process

The chapter by House (1981) provides a "Paradigm of Stress Research" (p. 36). He visually presents several major dimensions in the stress process and depicts their hypothesized relationships as having potential direct (main) effects and buffering (interactive) effects on health status. The major dimensions are: "stressors," defined as objective social conditions conducive of stress; which may lead to "perceived stress," defined as appraisal of a given condition as stressful. These may in turn lead to "short-term responses to stress," defined as the resultant short-range physiological, psychological or behavioral responses to perceived stress, e.g., tension, use of alcohol; which may lead to "enduring health outcomes," defined as long-term physiological, psychological or behavioral outcomes, e.g., depression, alcoholism. House (1981) suggests that the level and effect of each of these dimensions may be influenced by "conditioning variables" defined as individual or situational factors, e.g., social support.

In this model, the hypothesized *buffering effect* of social support suggests that the negative impact of stress on health is reduced as social support increases, and thus, support will have its most beneficial effect on health among people who are experiencing stress. For example, social support could buffer the effect of a stressor by influencing an individual to perceive the condition as less threatening or stressful. Additionally, social support could help people adapt to perceived stress, thereby reducing or eliminating short-term responses that are productive of disease. In this framework, the hypothesized *direct effect* of social support suggests that as social support increases it seems to improve health (regardless of level of stress) and to reduce stress (regardless of level of health). Thus, everyone could potentially benefit from increases in social support.

Although this is an oversimplification of House's (1981) model, there are several points that are of most importance for this article. First, stressors and perceived stress are major variables in understanding short-term and long-term disease outcomes. Second, there are numerous factors including social support, which may serve to have a direct effect or to buffer against the possible deleterious effects of stress, short-term responses and enduring outcomes. Therefore, based on this model (and the others that fit into this category), it is necessary to examine social support within a broader stress paradigm; and within this paradigm a key concern is the hypothesized buffering effects versus main effects of social support. These hypothesized relationships, especially the buffering hypothesis, have guided much of the research and are a focus of several of the review articles (e.g., Cohen & McKay, 1984; Cohen & Wills, 1985; Thoits, 1982). That is, within this broad stress paradigm, the relationship between stress and social support with regards to the buffering hypothesis is emphasized.

Cohen and McKay (1984) argue for a conceptualization of the buffering process that considers both the diversity of coping strategies that may be called upon in a stressful situation, and the different types of support (e.g., emotional, tangible, appraisal) that may or may not be provided by one's social network. Therefore, the effectiveness of social support in buffering one against stress depends upon a match between the type of support provided and the coping requirements. Cohen and McKay (1984) give the example that after the death of a spouse several coping requirements may be elicited (e.g., need to obtain income, need to feel one belongs) in which different types of support are needed (e.g., tangible, emotional) in order for support to serve as an effective buffer against stress. Therefore, Cohen and McKay's (1984) model is an elaboration and further specification of the buffering hypothesis component of the broader stress paradigm (as presented by House, 1981).

Conceptual Framework: Determinants and Effects of Social Networks

The second type of conceptual framework presented in several of these review articles places social networks as the central component from which their determinants and effects are posited (e.g., Israel, 1982; Kahn &

Antonucci, 1980; Moos & Mitchell, 1982; Norbeck, 1981). The model discussed by Kahn and Antonucci (1980) will be described below to exemplify this category.

Kahn and Antonucci (1980) provide a visual representation of an explanatory framework of "Hypothetical Determinants and Affects of Convoy Properties" (p. 270). As defined earlier, they use the term "convoy" to refer to supportive networks over the life course. They regard convoy structure (network characteristics such as size, reciprocity, durability) as the core of this model and "the remainder of it consists of the hypothesized causes and consequences of convoy structure, including its moderating or interactive effects as well as its direct outcomes. The model emphasizes interactions . . . " (p. 271). The major dimensions and their hypothesized relationships are: a person's "requirements for social support" that are jointly determined by "properties of the person" (e.g., age, other demographic characteristics, needs, abilities) and "properties of the situation" (e.g., role expectations, opportunities, demands, resources). In turn, "convoy structure" is jointly determined by these three dimensions. (i.e., requirements for social support, personal, and situational properties). The "adequacy of social support" that a person receives is determined by convoy structure and the properties of the person and situation; this leads to the "outcomes" (e.g., well-being, individual performance), which are jointly determined by the adequacy of support, and personal and situational factors. Finally, convoy structure and adequacy of social support moderate the effects of personal and situational properties on the outcome.

In summary, Kahn and Antonucci (1980) posit that the structural and interactional characteristics of social networks (convoy structure) are the key variables associated with health, disease and performance outcomes. The model suggests that the causes and consequences of convoy structure are interactive, and include personal and situational factors and a person's need for and adequacy of social support. Network characteristics, including types of support given and received, change over the life course. Furthermore, the role of stress in this framework is implicit not explicit. As mentioned previously, models similar to this one are the focus of several of the other review articles (e.g., Norbeck, 1981).

In addition to the two types of conceptual frameworks described above, several somewhat different models are discussed in some of the articles reviewed. Heller and Swindle (1983) present a model of social support and the coping process, which emphasizes social networks and their determinants, stress, perceived social support, and coping behaviors. Hansson et al. (1984) suggest a conceptual model, which posits that relational competence (defined as "characteristics of the individual that facilitate the acquisition, development and maintenance of mutually satisfying relationships," p. 7) affects the quality and effectiveness of social support. Furthermore, several articles consider social support within the conceptual framework of person-environment fit (e.g., Broadhead et al., 1983; Gottlieb, 1981a).

Section Summary and Suggestions

In summary, over two-thirds of the articles reviewed include a fairly extensive discussion of conceptual issues. Of those that do not, there is usually brief reference to the perspective that social networks and social support are only part of a more encompassing framework comprised of numerous variables. Clearly, the development and presentation of a conceptual framework can serve as an important guide for understanding the concepts, reviewing the empirical findings, and planning for future research and interventions. Not only do such models guide researchers and practitioners in examining the relationship between social networks and social support and health, but they also provide a direction for addressing the interconnectedness between social networks and social support and other key variables, e.g., stress, personal and situational factors (Moos & Mitchell, 1982).

It is useful to recognize that the two most frequently presented types of models (described above) are not contradictory, but rather one can be considered as a subset or expansion of a key variable of the other. That is, the overall stress paradigm highlights the stress process and includes social support or social networks as a conditioning variable. Social networks and social support can, in turn, be considered in more depth through a conceptual model in which they are the central component and their determinants and effects are included. A combined model that incorporates both types is conceptually feasible. However, since no one research study or intervention can examine all the variables within either one of these models, it is perhaps more useful to identify the major aim of and theory behind a given study or program, and to determine the most appropriate conceptual framework. For example, if exchange theory is posited as a major perspective, social network characteristics, especially reciprocity, will be key factors to consider. An appropriate conceptual model might focus on the determinants and effects of network characteristics. If stress is hypothesized to be of primary importance, then social support may be included as one of numerous variables influential in understanding the relationship between stress and health. Both perspectives recognize the complex, interactive nature of these relationships, and thus are not linear cause-and-effect models. Both perspectives also consider the consequences of these relationships as being nondisease-specific, suggesting the importance of examining psychological and behavioral outcomes as well as physical ones.

The design and use of a conceptual framework both for research and practice is recommended. In addition to the points discussed above, there are several other issues to consider when developing such a framework. In that theory and empirical evidence guide conceptual development, as further or different findings are substantiated, it is necessary to incorporate them into a conceptual model. In this regard, several of the articles reviewed offer some suggestions with which we concur. Within the broad stress paradigm, the frequently hypothesized buffering relationship between social support and stress may be due to another variable, such as social competence (e.g., Cohen & Wills, 1985; Heller & Swindle, 1983; Jung, 1984; Moos & Mitchell, 1982; Turner, 1983), and hence the inclusion of social competence may strengthen a conceptual model. Also, the relationship between social networks, social support and health status may be different at various stages of an illness or problem (e.g., Berkman, 1984; Jung, 1984; McKinlay, 1980; Wallston et al., 1983), and at various points in time over the life course (e.g., Kahn & Antonucci, 1980), and therefore, this needs to be reflected in a conceptual framework. Many of the conceptual models include personal and situational factors as determinants of social networks and social support. It is also suggested that it may be the interaction of personal and situational characteristics that has the most influence on well-being (e.g., Leavy, 1983; Mitchell & Trickett, 1980; Norbeck, 1981), and thus needs to be considered. Another variable that needs further study for possible inclusion in a conceptual framework is one's orientation toward using network resources (Moos & Mitchell, 1982).

Another issue to consider in developing conceptual models relates to the earlier discussion on definitions. How one defines social networks and social support, and which concept is included in a model, will influence which other variables are selected and the nature of their relationships. That is, a model highlighting social networks will probably include the structural, interactional and functional characteristics of networks as defined here, whereas a model emphasizing social support may only include functional characteristics.

RESEARCH FINDINGS

The research on social networks, social support and health includes the study of a wide range of populations, from large study samples of the general population to small samples of individuals experiencing a specific life transition such as widowhood or recovery from a serious illness. DiMatteo and Hays (1981) describe the following problems encountered in reviewing the research: lack of consensus regarding the concept of social support; measurement problems; and a paucity of empirical findings. These problems are compounded when one attempts to review and summarize these 33 literature reviews because the authors organize and approach the research in different ways. Some authors report findings without critiquing the studies; others critique individual studies but do not summarize findings; and approximately one-third of these literature reviews report, critique, and summarize findings (e.g., Cohen & Wills, 1985; Kessler & McLeod, 1983; Leavy, 1983). Because reviews in the latter group tend to be more comprehensive in their treatment of empirical findings, this section will draw primarily, but not exclusively, from them.

Another difficulty with summarizing findings discussed in these 33 review articles is that some authors examine both studies of social networks and of social support, while others include only studies that deal with one or the other of these two concepts. Rather than discuss research findings from studies of social networks separately from those of social support, we have chosen to combine the two. The findings regarding specific network determinants and characteristics are covered in a separate subsection.

These 33 reviews include research that examines a variety of physical and mental health outcomes. Approximately two-thirds of the articles review both studies involving mental health outcomes and studies of physical health outcomes (e.g., Broadhead et al., 1983; Norbeck, 1981; Turner, 1983). The remaining one-third focus on studies involving mental health outcomes ranging from psychiatric disorder to psychological well-being (e.g., Kessler, Price, & Wortman, 1985; Leavy, 1983; Mueller, 1980), or on studies of individuals with physical health problems and examine physical and/or mental health outcomes (e.g., DiMatteo & Hays, 1981; Wallston et al., 1983; Wortman & Conway, 1985). While it can be argued that making a separation between mental health and physical health is not valid because of the "reciprocal influence of the two" (Jung, 1984, p. 144), it is one way that some authors have used to narrow the focus of their review. The major emphasis of a few of the reviews is the examination of studies that test the buffering hypothesis (e.g., Cohen & Wills, 1985; Kessler & McLeod, 1983; Thoits, 1982). Some of the reviews discuss studies that examine the determinants and characteristics of social networks (e.g., Antonucci, 1985; Israel, 1982; Mitchell & Trickett, 1980). Thus, this section is organized to reflect the major ways that the authors have approached and summarized their findings: social networks and social support and their relationship to physical health, mental health or psychological well-being; tests of the stress-buffering hypothesis; and social-network determinants and characteristics. In addition, the findings on two other issues of interest, the negative effects of social support and gender differences in social support, will be discussed.

Physical Health Status and Health Behavior

The six reviews (Berkman, 1984; Cwikel & Israel, 1985; DiMatteo & Hays, 1981; Levy, 1983; Wallston et al., 1983; Wortman & Conway, 1985) that focus primarily on studies concerning specific physical health problems categorize their findings in a variety of ways. Any discussion of these findings is not completely straightforward because, while the reviewed studies are of individuals with physical health problems or who are at risk for such, the examined outcomes include both physical and mental health outcomes. For example, DiMatteo and Hays (1981) limit their review to studies of serious physical illness and injury that examine the outcome variables of physical, social role and socioemotional recovery. These three outcome factors were created by asking a panel of eleven psychologists to group eighteen general outcomes into three to five conceptually related factors. The review is organized according to the categories of serious illness and injury, and "at risk," which includes new parenthood and hypertension. The authors draw the following conclusions: (1) social support may be associated with rehabilitation, compliance, and adjustment during terminal illness; and (2) "taken as a whole, the research suggests that social support may, in fact, be associated with recovery, and coping with serious illness and injury" (p. 121). It is unclear from the text what the conclusions are regarding social support and at-risk populations.

Wallston et al. (1983) organize their review of the relationship between social support and physical health according to stages of health and illness: illness onset; utilization of health services; adherence to medical regimens; and recovery, rehabilitation, and adaptation to illness. The authors make the following conclusions: (1) overall, findings differ based upon the stage of illness and the type of research study; (2) the evidence is neither strong nor adequate enough to suggest a direct link between lack of support and the onset of illness; (3) there appears to be some evidence for a relationship between social support and compliance to prescribed medical regimens, although the evidence is stronger for intervention studies than for correlational studies; (4) the strongest evidence for the social support—health relationship is found in studies on recovery, rehabilitation, and adaptation to illness. This latter conclusion appears to be consistent with the findings of others. Wortman and Conway (1985) also conclude that "the majority of studies show that support facilitates recovery from health problems" (p. 284). The studies that Wortman and Conway are referring to are generally of interventions using health care professionals, support groups, or lay persons with similar health problems, not of interventions using members of the individual's naturally occurring social network.

The article by Cwikel and Israel (1985) reviews experimental and quasi-experimental studies that examine the effects of social network and social support interventions on individuals who are experiencing or who are at risk for a physical health problem. They categorize studies according to the type of preventive effort (primary, secondary, and tertiary). Based on their review of studies, Cwikel and Israel make the general conclusions that the interventions that seem to have a stronger effect are those that use emotional support rather than informational support, those that use a combination of different types of support, and those that use lay counselors to deliver the intervention rather than professionals.

One of the reviews specifically focuses on the effect of social networks and social support on adherence to medical regimens (Levy, 1983). The review examines experimental studies that are categorized into four groups based on the nature of the intervention: home visits, training of significant others outside the home, structured reinforcement and contracting, and group support. Levy concludes that, on the whole, the evidence suggests a positive association between social support and compliance, but that it is difficult to draw conclusions regarding the specific effects of social support. While a positive association may exist, it should be viewed cautiously because many of the studies use health outcomes rather than measures of compliance, and it is difficult to determine whether or not social support was actually provided (Levy, 1983). Another problem with studies of this type is that many of the supportive interventions are multifaceted, which makes it difficult to assess what part of the treatment caused the effect (Wortman & Conway, 1985).

Several of these reviews discuss findings from studies that examine the relationship between social networks and health care utilization or help seeking (e.g., McKinlay, 1980; Mitchell & Trickett, 1980; Wallston et al., 1983). One problem in summarizing such studies is that they use different definitions of "help." However, there appears to be evidence that social-network characteristics "influence the degree and mode of help seeking behavior" (Mitchell & Trickett, 1980, p. 36). Wallston et al. (1983) note that the characteristics that influence utilization may differ between women and men. They also conclude that the social network's norms or values regarding help-seeking have a greater effect on utilization than whether or not one's network consists predominately of kin vs. non-kin.

Mental Health or Psychological Well-Being

While several of the articles discuss the research on the relationship between social networks, social support and mental health, three reviews in particular comprehensively review this research (Kessler, Price, & Wortman, 1985; Leavy, 1983; Mueller, 1980). These reviews examine studies of populations ranging from psychiatric patients (e.g., schizophrenics, depressives) to individuals in the general population dealing with a life crisis. Although each review approaches the research differently, the overall findings and conclusions among the articles are fairly consistent.

The information summarized here from the Kessler, Price, and Wortman (1985) review is contained in the section on social support from their more extensive article on social factors in psychopathology, which include stress, social support, and coping processes. They discuss findings from both research studies and other review articles and group the research according to: studies of clinical samples, normal population, and case-control studies, studies on reactions to life crises, and experimental support interventions. Leavy (1983) reviews 46 studies on informal social support and psychological disorder, 80 percent of which were conducted since 1978. The review is organized according to five different research strategies: (1) comparison between the "informal support systems" of clinical and nonclinical populations; (2) studies of clinical populations with a specific type of disorder; (3) studies of the support systems of the general population; (4) studies of individuals dealing with specific life crises; and (5) gender differences in support. Using social networks as a framework, Mueller (1980) organizes his review of the research according to the relationship between network structure and psychiatric disorder, the relationship between supportiveness of network ties and disorder (specifically depression), and how change or disruption in the network affects psychiatric disorder.

As noted earlier, the findings among these three reviews are fairly similar. All three conclude that there is consistent evidence supporting the finding that there are differences between the networks of psychiatric patients and "normals." Generally speaking, individuals with psychiatric disorders have networks that are smaller, more asymmetric (less reciprocal) and with fewer multiplex relationships (Mueller, 1980). Also, clinical populations tend to rely more on nonfamily ties than normal populations (Leavy, 1983). However, it remains unclear whether there is a causal relationship between network characteristics and psychiatric disorder and, if so, what the direction of this relationship might be.

After reviewing the research on the effects of lack of support or the supportiveness of network ties, Mueller (1980) concludes that there is considerable evidence for the relationship between lack of social support and psychiatric impairment. This relationship appears to be particularly evident in the case of depressive symptoms, especially among women. Kessler, Price, and Wortman (1985) also note that there is evidence that suggests a negative relationship between the supportiveness of family members and relapse among schizophrenics. Leavy (1983), however, states that while lack of emotional support seems to be positively related to psychiatric impairment among a clinical population, this association is significant, but weaker among the general population.

Regarding the impact of stressful life events on well-being, Kessler, Price, and Wortman (1985) state that most of the longitudinal studies on reactions to major life events provide evidence for a positive relationship between support and emotional adjustment. Mueller (1980) notes that many stressful life events involve changes or disruption (loss) in the social network, and that there appears to be a positive relationship between loss in the social network and psychiatric disorder (Mueller, 1980). However, it is difficult to draw any clear conclusions from this literature because the differences among the stressful situations and various populations studied make it hard to compare findings (Leavy, 1983).

Stress-Buffering Effects

Several reviews examine studies that test the buffering hypothesis, i.e., the hypothesis that social support mediates or buffers the effects that stress has on well-being (e.g., Cohen & Wills, 1985; Kessler & McLeod, 1985; Thoits, 1982). Conclusions regarding the buffering hypothesis vary considerably, with some authors stating that the findings are strongly supportive of the buffering hypothesis, and others asserting that such conclusions are overstated. Kessler & McLeod (1985) discuss and critique 25 studies that demonstrate either clearly positive or negative results of the stress-buffering effect of social support, and find evidence for buffering in two-thirds of the studies. When they compare the results of studies that examine "membership in affiliative networks and a life-event inventory in predicting psychological distress" (p. 232) with the results of studies that examine "interactions between emotional support and a life event inventory" (p. 233), they conclude that emotional support has a buffering effect, while membership in "affiliative networks" does not. Membership in affiliative networks is determined by scales that measure the number of friends and relatives, membership in clubs and church, and frequency of interaction. Studies that examine interactions between perceived availability of support and life events are also reviewed; these findings are inconclusive. They also examine studies that use measures of chronic strain rather than life events, and conclude that there is evidence that social support buffers the impact of chronic strains.

Heller and Swindle (1983), on the other hand, conclude that there is little evidence to support the buffering hypothesis. They review 15 articles that are frequently cited as evidence of stress buffering, and conclude that only six demonstrate effects of buffering. Because of the conceptual and methodological problems inherent in many of these studies, Heller and Swindle call for a moratorium on "classical buffering studies." Thoits (1982) seems to concur; she notes that while there appears to be some evidence of stress buffering, because of the problems in methodology these findings have to be interpreted cautiously. Thoits argues that buffering effects may be a result of a statistical artifact resulting from the confounding of social support and life events such as losses from the social network. However, findings of others (Cohen & Wills, 1985) do not support the statistical artifact argument.

Evidence for buffering may, in part, be dependent upon the type of study conducted and measures used. Wallston et al. (1983) note that while retrospective studies that test for interaction between stress and social support usually provide evidence for buffering, prospective studies do not. Cohen & Wills (1985) organize their review of the research on the buffering effect according to the type of measurement of social support that is used in the study. They use a typology based on (1) structural (the existence of relationships) versus functional (the degree to which support functions are provided by relationships) measurements; and (2) specific measures of structures or functions versus global measures (the combination of structures or functions in a global index). They suggest that to find a buffering effect, specific measures of support functions that are relevant to a particular stressor need to be used. Findings suggestive of a stressor-buffer specificity model are discussed in detail by Cohen and McKay (1984). They found that in studies where social support is measured by assessing how well individuals are integrated into a larger social network, there is evidence for a main effect, rather than a buffering effect.

Social Network Determinants and Characteristics

Several authors review studies that examine the determinants of social networks (e.g., Antonucci, 1985; Kahn & Antonucci, 1980; Mitchell & Trickett, 1980). Mitchell and Trickett (1980) organize their review of this research according to three categories of network determinants: environmental factors, individual characteristics, and the interaction of environmental and individual influences. Three environmental determinants are listed as having an important effect on network development: the influence of family characteristics, physical proximity or access to social interaction, and the individual's experience of and participation in community processes. Individual determinants that may influence the social network include expectations about relationships and the individual's behavior. Mitchell and Trickett note that there have been few studies that assess the role that individuals play in determining their networks, and in particular that examine the effect of social competence on network development and maintenance. (For more on social or relational competence see Hansson et al., 1984). Because few studies have been conducted that examine the effect of the interaction between environmental and individual influences on the network, these studies are not summarized by Mitchell and Trickett.

However, they assert that interactional approaches to assessing network development are the most useful.

The importance of an interactional approach is also emphasized by Kahn and Antonucci (1980) who state that an individual's convoy (social network over the lifespan) is "determined jointly by enduring properties of the person, by the person's requirements for social support, and by properties of the situation" (p. 269). Antonucci (1985) reviews the research on the effect of individual characteristics (e.g., age, sex, ethnicity, marital and family status), and situational characteristics (e.g., living arrangements, role changes, organizational membership) on a person's convoy (structure, function, and adequacy). The findings from these studies are too diverse and numerous to summarize here. However, it is important to note that while extensive research has been conducted on the determinants of networks, investigators rarely take an interactional approach in assessing the determinants of networks.

The limited body of research that examines the relationships between specific social network characteristics and health and well-being is reviewed by a number of authors (e.g., Antonucci, 1985; Israel, 1982; Mitchell & Trickett, 1980; Mueller, 1980) and has primarily focused on structural and interactional network characteristics (Israel, 1982) such as size, density, intensity, and reciprocity. Findings regarding structural and interactional characteristics and their relationship to well-being are conflicting and difficult to summarize (House & Kahn, 1985; Israel, 1982). For instance, evidence suggests that, in general, a network characterized by high density (that is, one in which a high percentage of people in the network know one another) is positively related to perceived support; but specific studies, for example, of women in transition (e.g., recently widowed or returning to college) indicate that density is negatively related to perceived support and adaptation. However, there seems to be evidence to suggest that intensity (Israel, 1982) and reciprocity (House & Kahn, 1985; Israel, 1982; Mitchell & Trickett, 1980) within networks are positively related to well-being.

Other Issues

While the research findings on the negative effects of social networks and social support are sparse and inconclusive, several reviews discuss this issue as one that holds promise and needs further investigation. Wortman & Conway (1985) cite several reasons why it is important to assess negative effects, especially in the context of physical illness. In the studies that they review, negative effects are generally the result of supportive others having misperceptions about coping with physical illness and thus, while trying to provide support, may be increasing the patient's stress. DiMatteo & Hays

(1981) cite several studies where the social support provided by family members is overprotective and has a negative impact on the individual's recovery and return to work. Social support may have a negative impact on individuals recovering from illness by reducing their self-esteem; however, there are no findings to support this (DiMatteo & Hays, 1981; Wallston et al., 1983). A number of reviews (Jung, 1984; Wortman & Conway, 1985) cite studies that found the association between the negative aspects of social relationships and mental health outcomes to be stronger and more consistent than the association between positive aspects and mental health.

A number of these reviews cite evidence of gender differences in the role of social support and the composition of social networks. The social networks of women tend to be larger and more multifaceted and the nature of these ties seem to be different from those of men (Antonucci, 1985). Findings from studies of normal populations suggest that women have more supportive relationships than men (Leavy, 1983). Norbeck (1981) cites a number of studies that indicate that men and women have different social-support needs and receive different amounts of social support. However, she states that it is difficult to conclude from the research evidence whether women actually need more support or whether they are able to obtain more than men. Cohen and Wills (1985) conclude that there may be gender differences in whether or not certain support functions act as buffers against stress. They suggest that these differences may be related to the differences in the content of supportive interactions among men and women. Some evidence supports the fact that "relationships with women may be more supportive and health promotive than relationships with men" (House & Kahn, 1985, p. 93).

This section has summarized the research findings presented in these review articles along the categories of: social networks and social support and their relationship to physical health, mental health or psychological well-being, tests of the stress-buffering hypothesis, and social network determinants and characteristics. Findings regarding the negative effects of social support and gender differences in social networks and social support have also been discussed. Despite the fact that study populations, measurement of key variables, and methodologies vary across studies, there appears to be sufficient evidence to suggest a positive relationship between social networks, social support (especially affective support) and health and well-being. This relationship seems to be most consistent in the evidence presented regarding psychiatric populations, and recovery from physical illness. Several promising issues warrant considerably more research: gender differences, the negative effects of ties, the role of social competence, and reciprocity. As noted earlier, the findings regarding specific network characteristics and their relationships to health and well-being are limited and conflicting; the network characteristics of reciprocity, sex composition, and density seem to be the most promising for further research (House & Kahn, 1985). Finally, social support needs to be investigated as a dependent variable. Broadhead et al. (1983) suggest that findings from such research would assist in the development of prevention and intervention strategies.

METHODOLOGICAL ISSUES

Approximately three-fourths of the 33 review articles address methodological issues to some extent; of these, numerous articles strongly emphasize methodological issues (e.g., Berkman, 1984; Broadhead et al., 1983; Cohen & Wills, 1985; House & Kahn, 1985; Jung, 1984; Kessler & McLeod, 1985; Thoits, 1982). There appears to be general agreement on the main methodological concerns surrounding the research on the relationship between social networks and social support and well-being. Several key issues emerge from this literature: problems in the measurement of the social network and social support constructs, the preponderance of cross-sectional studies and the lack of studies designed to assess causality, the problem of operational confounding, and issues regarding the study population and sample size.

The methodological issue most frequently referred to in these review articles is the problem with measurement of social networks and social support. The lack of agreement and specificity surrounding the definition of the terms "social network" and "social support" is reflected in their measurement. (For a comprehensive critique of measurement issues see House & Kahn, 1985.) Imprecise and inadequate measures appear to be a major concern (e.g., Berkman, 1984; Leavy, 1983). Several authors cite the lack of measurement standardization across different studies as creating a difficulty in comparing research findings (DiMatteo & Hays, 1981; Jung, 1984; Wallston et al., 1983). Others raise the problem of low reliability or validity of support measures (Cohen & Wills, 1985; Leavy, 1983) resulting in part from the use of single item measures or scales created for secondary data analysis of large data sets (Berkman, 1984; Cohen & Wills, 1985). Thoits (1982) and Mueller (1980) discuss the need for measures that reflect the multidimensional nature of social support. Mueller suggests that measures should include the dimensions of source (i.e., who is providing the support: a relative, friend, or professional), type (e.g., emotional, instrumental), and the intensity of the relationship (e.g., whether or not it is a confiding relationship). For each source of support the occurrence or availability should be assessed (House & Kahn, 1985). Concerning types of support, it is suggested that a distinction be made among emotional support, informational support, instrumental support and affirmation or appraisal support (House, 1981; House & Kahn, 1985; Kahn & Antonucci, 1980). By assessing these dimensions, researchers may be able to determine what type(s) and source(s) of support have what effects on health behavior, stress, and physical and mental health status.

Several authors discuss the importance of making a distinction between perceived and objective social support, and the need to measure both (Antonucci, 1985; DiMatteo & Hays, 1981; Jung, 1984). Perceived or subjective support is from the frame of reference of the receiver; whereas, objective support is measured from the viewpoint of an outside observer (Caplan, 1979). Most measurement of social support is based on self-report and therefore, is perceived support. Because the perception that social support is available may mediate one's perception of a stressful event, a measure of perceived availability of support is especially important to show evidence of a buffering effect (Cohen & McKay, 1984; Cohen & Wills, 1985). Heller & Swindle (1983) define perceived social support as "the appraisal that one is supported" and describe it as a function of the "availability of social networks" and "interpersonal skills in accessing and maintaining supportive relationships" (p. 35). While obtaining measures of objective support is highly desirable, it is also very time-consuming and costly because it requires interviewing providers as well as receivers of support or observing actual behaviors.

There are a number of different measurement approaches that are used to assess social networks. In part, the difference in approach is the result of how the term social network is conceptualized and subsequently operationalized. Mitchell and Trickett (1980) list a number of diverse operational definitions that vary based upon how social network membership is defined. For example, membership criteria might be based on the frequency of interaction or strength of the relationship. Antonucci (1985) discusses several ways of assessing the social network. Two of these are (1) by asking about formal (or categorical) relationships such as relatives, friends, and neighbors; and (2) by asking the respondent to list those individuals who perform or can be counted on to help with supportive acts. As Antonucci notes, the disadvantage of the first method is that important network members may be left out because they do not fit into a particular category. The problem with the second method is that it only obtains membership of a support network and not of the entire network. Therefore, it excludes negative interactions which may have an important effect on well-being. House and Kahn (1985) point out several problems with network measurement. One of these is the amount of time and cost required to fully measure the structure of an individual's social network. Since evidence has not indicated that assessment of a total network is critical, they suggest limiting the network size to 5 to 10 persons.

The use of weak study designs, primarily cross-sectional and retrospective, is a criticism frequently raised in the discussion of methodology. Several authors discuss the need for conducting longitudinal studies (Cohen & McKay, 1984; Ell, 1984; Mueller, 1980) to make causal inferences. The problem with cross-sectional study designs is that the relationship between social support and health is open to several interpretations: social support affects well-being (health status), well-being affects social support, and/or another usually unmeasured variable affects both social support and well-being (Cohen & Wills, 1985). The difficulty in determining the direction of causality is especially problematic in studies of the chronically ill. The problem of the "third variable" (Wortman & Conway, 1985) affecting both social support and well-being can arise when variables that are closely related to social support are not measured or controlled. Social competence or skill and neuroticism have been proposed as such plausible underlying variables (e.g., Cohen & Wills, 1985; Heller & Swindle, 1983; Jung, 1984; Wortman & Conway, 1985).

A number of authors address the problem of confounding in their discussion of methodological concerns (e.g., Broadhead et al., 1983; Kessler, Price, & Wortman, 1985; Thoits, 1982). Thoits (1982) suggests that life events (as a measure of stress) may be seriously confounded with support. The occurrence of a major life event, such as the death of a spouse, divorce, or job loss, could be interpreted as an indicator of change in social support. This is especially a problem in research that measures social support after a major life event. Thus, Thoits concludes that to adequately test the buffering hypothesis, social support needs to be measured at more than one point in time. Other ways to deal with confounding *post hoc* are suggested by Cohen and Wills (1985). They recommend that the correlation between stress and social support be examined (*post hoc*), and that a finding of a significant negative correlation would suggest confounding. If confounding exists, a modified life-events score should be created by removing the "social-exit events" from the total stress score.

Confounding of the independent and dependent measures may also be a problem (Heller & Swindle, 1983). For instance, individuals' perception of amount and adequacy of support may be influenced by their psychological state (Berkman, 1984). That is, depressed persons might be more likely to report low levels of support when their support may actually be adequate. Confounding may also exist between the independent and dependent variables in the research on social support and health behaviors, specifically regarding adherence to medical regimens. Individuals who tend to be compliant may also be more attentive to family relationships, thus promoting a more supportive environment (Levy, 1983).

In their critique of research on the buffering hypothesis, Heller and Swindle (1983) propose three types of studies of social support that need to be conducted: (1) exploratory research involving individuals at risk for stress, to generate hypotheses about how individuals cope over time and what types of support are beneficial; (2) longitudinal design studies with assessments at repeated time intervals to look at the sequential effects of stressful events, social support, symptoms and coping; and (3) laboratory studies using both cross-sectional data and randomized experiments. Cohen and Wills (1985) note that one of the problems with prospective, longitudinal designs is that they assume that social support is stable over time, which is often not the case. Therefore, they recommend that in evaluating prospective research, one examine "the correspondence between longitudinal intervals, the time-course of the criterion disease, and the stability of social support in the population under study" (p. 21).

Broadhead et al. (1983) review research findings and methodologies in the context of Hills' (1965) criteria for causality and assert that few studies use adequate randomized clinical trials and pre- and post-intervention measures. Several other authors emphasize the need for experimental interventions (House & Kahn, 1985; Jung, 1984; Kessler, Price, & Wortman, 1985; Turner, 1983). Kessler & McLeod (1985) conclude that evidence for a causal influence of support will more likely come from intervention experiments than from surveys of normal populations.

Another methodological issue that is raised by a few of these authors concerns the nature of the study population and size of the study sample. Berkman (1984) addresses the "well-integrated communities problem" that she describes as the problem of using the number of social contacts and social activities as measures of social support in studies of populations in well-integrated communities. Berkman reviews studies of well-integrated populations, where the differences in risk between isolated and nonisolated individuals is not significant. One explanation that she presents is that in such communities, the overall level of social support is so high that "very few people are isolated severely enough to reveal significant increases in risk" (Berkman, 1984, p. 427). In a review of studies testing the buffering hypothesis, Cohen & Wills (1985) discuss the problem of using a young healthy population or a clinical sample, in which there is little variability in stress levels because most subjects are experiencing high levels of stress. With such populations, the probability of finding relationships between stress, support, and symptoms is statistically less than in a sample with broad ranges of these variables. Regarding the issue of sample size, after reviewing 25 normal population surveys that examine support, stressful life experiences, and mental health outcomes, Kessler and McLeod (1985) conclude that several studies fail to find a significant buffering effect, in part due to small sample size.

In summary, the methodological problems in the research on social networks and social support and their relationship to health and well-being are well-documented in these review articles. While the problems are numerous and difficult to resolve, it is encouraging to note that many of them are being addressed presently in current research efforts. We especially concur with the conclusions of several reviewers (e.g., Broadhead et al., 1983; Kessler & McLeod, 1985) regarding the need for and potential contribution of intervention studies that can address some of these methodological issues. In the field of health education, such intervention and action-research studies are of critical importance and should focus on prevention as well as treatment.

PRACTICE IMPLICATIONS

Of particular interest to the health educator is to what extent and how are the theories, conceptual issues, and empirical evidence concerning social networks and social support applicable to the practice of health education? The integration of the existing work on social networks and social support can enrich the development, implementation, and evaluation of health education interventions. However, of the 33 articles reviewed here: one-third discuss to some extent implications for practice; slightly fewer than one-third make only brief mention of practice considerations, and in the remaining one-third, there is no reference to practice. Not surprisingly, the extent to which theory and research are applied to practice often is related to the purpose of the review article, the background and training of the author(s), and the focus of the journal in which the article is published.

This section will summarize and analyze the major points linking theory and research to practice as reviewed in those articles (approximately one-third) that emphasize such points. Of these articles, several present an extensive review of theoretical, conceptual and empirical findings concerning social networks and social support and then discuss implications for practice (e.g., Ell, 1984; Israel, 1982; Mitchell & Trickett, 1980; Norbeck, 1981). Several of the articles (e.g., Gottlieb, 1981b; Minkler, 1981; Pilisuk & Minkler, 1980) summarize major findings from the field (e.g., importance of reciprocity) and describe and analyze specific interventions in light of these findings (e.g., the extent to which a program enhanced the development of reciprocal ties). Additionally, several of these articles are reviews of intervention studies and hence practice issues are addressed, directly or indirectly, throughout (e.g., Cwikel & Israel, 1985; DiMatteo & Hays, 1981; Levy, 1983; Wortman & Conway, 1985). The articles differ whether their primary emphasis is on social support (e.g., DiMatteo & Hays, 1981; Levy, 1983; Wortman & Conway, 1985), social networks including social support functions (e.g., Ell, 1984; Gottlieb, 1981b; Israel, 1982; Jung, 1984; Mitchell & Trickett, 1980; Moos & Mitchell, 1982), or social support networks (e.g., Minkler, 1981; Norbeck, 1981; Pilisuk & Minkler, 1980). These articles also vary in their focus on health education practice (e.g., Israel, 1982; Minkler, 1981; Pilisuk & Minkler, 1980) social work practice (e.g., Ell, 1984); medical settings (e.g., DiMatteo & Hays, 1981; Norbeck, 1981; Wortman & Conway, 1985), and community mental health (e.g., Gottlieb, 1981 a, b; Mitchell & Trickett, 1980).

Given the diversity and inconsistencies of the empirical evidence concerning social networks and social support, and the methodological limitations discussed above, any discussion of practice implications will be somewhat tentative. Several authors caution that, given the present research findings, it is too early to suggest specific factors that would be most effective in the design of social network interventions (e.g., DiMatteo & Hays, 1981; Jung, 1984; Wortman & Conway, 1985). Although we concur with the need to apply these concepts cautiously, the following discussion provides some evidence of the appropriateness of linking current knowledge to the development of health education programs.

Drawing from the literature, the review articles present several overall points that are important for practitioners to consider when developing social network interventions. The choice and effectiveness of any given intervention strategy will depend upon a number of these general factors, including: the kind of problem or crisis and stage at which it is occurring (Ell, 1984; Israel, 1982; Moos & Mitchell, 1982); the individual's need for social support (Israel, 1982; Norbeck, 1981); the availability of different types and sources of support (Moos & Mitchell, 1982; Norbeck, 1981); the presence of certain network structural characteristics and norms appropriate for resolving a given problem (Gottlieb, 1981b); the individual's orientation toward using network resources (Israel, 1982); availability of broader socioeconomic resources and conditions (Minkler, 1981; Mitchell & Trickett, 1980); and the theoretical and ideological perspective of the practitioner (Mitchell & Trickett, 1980). Given these numerous factors, it is apparent that the integration of social network and social support concepts into practice extends beyond any one strategy, purpose or target population, problem area, or professional role. Hence in the following discussion, it is important that the practitioner keep in mind these general considerations.

The selection of a target population for an intervention involving social networks can be made in accordance with the conceptual framework presented earlier, concerning the relationship between stress, social support and health. Gottlieb (1981b) discusses interventions that are intended to enhance the quality of social support within existing ties, which are aimed at "promoting the health" (p. 211) of the targeted individuals, without reference to specific stressors. This identification of program recipients without emphasis on a given stressful experience or situation, is consistent with the conceptually founded and empirically tested hypothesis that social support has a direct positive effect on health. Gottlieb (1981b) also analyzes interventions that are intended to strengthen new or existing social ties, which are aimed at "protecting the health" (p. 211) of individuals experiencing certain life events and transitions. This selection of program participants considered to be at risk because of exposure to stressful conditions, is consistent with the conceptually founded and empirically tested hypothesis that social support has a buffering effect on stress and health. Moos and Mitchell (1982) suggest that the attitudes of practitioners about which of these processes is operating influences their design of programs. They state that those practitioners who believe that generally beneficial effects come from strengthening network resources (i.e., direct effect hypothesis) are more likely to develop broad-based interventions. Practitioners who believe that strengthening network resources will have the greatest effect on people experiencing stress (i.c., buffering effect hypothesis) are more likely to develop programs that are targeted at people undergoing a life crisis or transition (Moos & Mitchell, 1982). As presented earlier, the research evidence to date would support the design of programs targeted at both populations.

This discussion is also congruent with the distinctions made between social network and social support programs aimed at primary prevention (including health promotion), secondary prevention, and tertiary prevention (e.g., Broadhead et al., 1983; Cwikel & Israel, 1985; Ell, 1984; Gottlieb, 1981a; Israel, 1982). Broadly defined, programs aimed at primary prevention may include the population at large (i.e., direct effect hypothesis), or persons considered to be at risk (i.e., buffering effect hypothesis), but without as yet experiencing any negative health outcome. Programs aimed at secondary and tertiary prevention would include persons experiencing stress (i.e., buffering effect hypothesis) who also have an identifiable illness.

Types of Social Network and Social Support Interventions

In examining the various types and purposes of interventions that have integrated social network and social support concepts, one finds diverse approaches toward categorizing program examples. Levy (1983), in her review of interventions concerning social support and compliance, describes programs according to how social support is manipulated (e.g., home visits, significant-other training, structural reinforcement, group). DiMatteo & Hays (1981) divide the studies that they review according to recovery from serious illness (e.g., myocardial infarction, cancer) and recovery from risk states (e.g., hypertension, new parenthood). Cwikel & Israel (1985) analyze intervention studies by prevention category, e.g., primary prevention—widowhood, transition to parenthood; secondary prevention—compliance, acute illness; and tertiary prevention—rehabilitation from myocardial infarction, chronic illness.

Program examples have also been discussed with an emphasis placed on the type of network linkages and sources of support involved. One typology (Israel, 1982) that includes four broad categories of interventions, will be briefly presented here. Review articles that describe programs that fit into each category are cited. An elaboration of the specific strategies used (e.g., training, consultation, group discussion) within each of the four categories will not be provided here, but is included in some of the review articles (e.g., Gottlieb, 1981b; Israel, 1982; Minkler, 1981; Pilisuk & Minkler, 1980).

The first category refers to interventions that focus on strengthening already-existing network ties. The emphasis here is usually on identifying individuals with particular needs and then involving significant members of their network in the process of meeting those needs. For example, family members involved in a program to get hemodialysis patients or hypertensives to follow prescribed medical regimens, or close friends participating in an intervention aimed at getting clients to stop smoking. Several of the articles reviewed here describe such programs (e.g., Cwikel & Israel, 1985; Ell, 1984; Gottlieb, 1981b; Israel, 1982; Levy, 1983; Norbeck, 1981; Pilisuk & Minkler, 1980). There are numerous important questions to consider in designing this type of intervention: To what extent does the client have already-existing network linkages? What is the nature of these relationships, e.g., types of support provided, reciprocity, negative aspects? To what extent are network members available and able to enhance their involvement with the targeted individual? Hence, this type of intervention may be most effective for an individual who has existing network ties that are capable of providing different types of support, are reciprocal, and not overburdened.

A second category of programs is often referred to as including those that are aimed at developing and enhancing new network linkages (e.g., Cwikel & Israel, 1985; Ell, 1984; Gottlieb, 1981b; Israel, 1982; Norbeck, 1981; Pilisuk & Minkler, 1980). The focus here is on linking a given individual in need with another person or persons, previously not a part of the given individual's network, in a way that will provide new network resources. For example, a program that brings together parents of children with cancer to form a mutual-aid group, or an intervention in which recently widowed individuals are contacted by someone who has effectively handled the experience. Frequently, these types of programs develop new linkages between persons who share a common situation. Important questions to consider in planning this type of intervention include the following: What are the limitations of a client's already existing network relationships? What additional network resources are available in the community? What is the nature of the problem situation and to what extent might others experiencing similar problems benefit from establishing interpersonal ties? Thus, this type of program may be particularly effective for individuals whose existing network relationships are limited, destructive, overburdened or not able to provide the type of support needed (e.g., appraisal support).

A third category of interventions involves enhancing the total network through natural helpers (see Israel, 1982, for program examples). The emphasis here is on identifying natural helpers—lay people to whom others naturally turn for advice, emotional support and tangible aid—and involving them in a training or consultation capacity to further strengthen and extend the provision of social support. For example, a neighborhood-based program that identifies persons who frequently provide information and advice on health matters and involves them in training concerning health and disease and how to make appropriate referrals. This type of program is often developed within a neighborhood or geographic community. Some of the questions to be addressed in designing such a program are as follows: To what extent do natural helpers exist within a given target area? What is the nature of the help they provide and how does it relate to the needs identified? How can a program involve natural helpers without negatively altering the "naturally occurring" benefits that they provide? To what extent is this strategy understood and valued by the agency to be involved? Therefore, the careful selection of these natural helpers and the strategies for collaborating with them are most important for program success.

A fourth category of programs involves bringing together overlapping networks/communities in meeting identified needs. The development of network linkages occurs as a secondary aim of this type of program (e.g., Israel, 1982; Pilisuk & Minkler, 1980). The focus is on people joining together to engage in cooperative problem-solving strategies around the issues identified by the people themselves. A program in which community members organize and engage in income-generating projects is an example. There are numerous questions to be considered in developing this type of program. To what extent does communication, influence, help-giving and problem-solving exist across overlapping networks? In what ways might the strengthening of network linkages be given more direct program emphasis? Thus, the extent to which such programs directly emphasize enhancing social networks might result in increased benefits for the persons involved.

Although these intervention categories are often presented as if they are separate and discrete, it is useful to recognize that programs that combine strategies have the potential for complementing each other. For example, a stroke patient may benefit from both involvement in a mutual-aid group of other stroke patients (i.e., developing new network linkages) and having family members assist in health maintenance activities (i.e., strengthening already existing ties). The latter might be accomplished by family members periodically participating in the mutual-aid group or perhaps organizing a mutual-aid group for family members of the stroke patients. Additionally, a community-based program focused on the development of jobs and job skills (i.e., in which network strengthening is a secondary aim) may involve natural helpers in the provision of informational and affective support to unemployed workers. In deciding which approach might be most appropriate and effective for a given population or problem area, the health educator is encouraged to consider the general points for practice discussed earlier in this section.

Program Implications of Assessment Issues and Research Findings

Regardless of which type of intervention is used, the issue of how to assess social networks and social support is important for program planning and evaluation. Since a summary of and recommendations for measurement were presented in the section on Methodological Issues, the discussion here will focus on suggested uses of assessment tools for interventions, not the specific content of the measurement instruments.

Several of the review articles describe the usefulness in clinical interventions of assessing social network characteristics (e.g., Ell, 1984; Israel, 1982; Mitchell & Trickett, 1980; Norbeck, 1981). Mitchell & Trickett (1980), in their discussion of individual and family-focused treatment interventions, suggest that conducting a social network analysis as part of an intake interview allows the clinician "to focus attention more clearly on the interpersonal and social context within which behavior occurs" (p. 38). This information in turn can be used to determine how and when to involve the client (e.g., skill training on maintaining network ties), to engage network members for what ends, or to seek new social ties. Thus, a clinical assessment of social networks can determine an individual's need as compared to availability of support as a means of assessing the adequacy of interpersonal relationships, that in turn will be helpful in planning interventions (Norbeck, 1981).

Application of social network analyses within the context of a community needs assessment is also recommended by several authors (e.g., Ell, 1984; Israel, 1982; Mitchell & Trickett, 1980). An examination of social networks within a given neighborhood could provide information on: the existence of natural caregivers; the extent and nature of interpersonal helping, communication, and influence patterns; and problem areas and at-risk groups. Mitchell & Trickett (1980) describe an example of conducting a needs assessment of the elderly within a given neighborhood, in which the analysis of social network patterns might reveal problems of isolation and failure to use existing formal services. This same analysis might indicate that the elderly frequently mention church membership as an important link, which may suggest disseminating information and developing programs through the church and clergy to strengthen social ties and enhance community integration (Ell, 1984; Mitchell & Trickett, 1980).

Many of the review articles discuss the application of research findings to the development and critique of interventions (e.g., Cwikel & Israel, 1985; Gottlieb, 1981b; Pilisuk & Minkler, 1980). These discussions often focus on the evidence regarding the effect of a given network characteristic, for example reciprocity or density on health status or health behavior. Minkler (1981) defines seven network characteristics (i.e., size, geographic dispersion, density, member homogeneity, strength of ties, reciprocity and multiplicity) as having important implications for the development of interventions. She documents the significance of network size, strength of ties and reciprocity, particularly for elderly persons, and then describes examples of health education programs that have applied these network properties. Minkler (1981) suggests that health educators involved in designing programs for the elderly "should take into account the various properties of social networks which may then help to increase program responsiveness to the possibility of increasing network opportunities" (p. 160).

A slightly different approach to applying the research evidence regarding network characteristics has also been used. Characteristics frequently cited as being significantly related to various health outcomes include: reciprocity, size, density, strength of ties, and affective support. Program examples are then described in some detail and assessed with regards to the extent to which these interventions have emphasized and brought about changes in each of these network characteristics (e.g., Cwikel & Israel, 1985; Gottlieb, 1981b; Pilisuk & Minkler, 1980). A more general discussion of the importance of and how to integrate such network characteristics into practice is also provided by some authors (e.g., Israel, 1982; Norbeck, 1981). Consistent with the research evidence presented earlier, the network characteristics of reciprocity and affective support are most frequently mentioned as important properties to consider in designing health education interventions.

Issues regarding the role of the professional in linking formal and informal sources of help are mentioned only briefly in a few of the review articles (e.g., Israel, 1982; Gottlieb, 1981a; Minkler, 1980). Such role issues are concerned with the extent to which the responsibility for and control of activities and decision-making is separate or shared by the professionals and the lay persons involved. More in-depth analysis of these important issues can be found in numerous other sources (e.g., Collins & Pancoast, 1976; Froland et al., 1981; Gartner & Riessman, 1977; Kleiman et al.,

1976; Lenrow & Burch, 1981). A common thread linking many of these discussions is an emphasis on the need for a professional role that does not interfere with nor co-opt the already existing capacity of the network to provide support.

Social Network and Support Interventions: Cautions and Limitations

In addition to the enthusiastic application of network concepts to practice, there are also cautionary points or caveats presented in the review articles. Several of these considered by us to be particularly salient are mentioned below. This will be followed by a discussion of future directions for practice.

Gottlieb (1981b), in his description and critique of preventive interventions that involve training of natural helpers, emphasizes the need to examine the position in the helpee's network occupied by the natural helper. That is, the extent to which the helper is a member of a local, grass roots network, and how much influence the helper actually has on the behavior and problem-solving efforts of the helpee, will have an impact on program effectiveness. Furthermore, Gottlieb (1981b) stresses the importance of providing training that is congruent with the norms and expectations of helping that already exist within the informal system. For example, training helpers in professionally determined skills (e.g., reflective listening) may not be appropriate for many situations. Additionally, Gottlieb (1981b) cautions that the use of close-ended surveys to carry out network analyses may not be adequate for gaining an understanding of when, how, and with what effects helping networks operate.

When designing social network interventions, the practitioner is also urged to not only consider individual characteristics but also to examine broader socioeconomic, political, and environmental forces. Such forces may weaken already-existing supportive ties and serve as a barrier to the development of new supportive, reciprocal relationships (e.g., Ell, 1984; Kahn & Antonucci, 1980; Minkler, 1980; Mitchell & Trickett, 1980). So, for example, it may not be enough to organize a support group for at-risk elderly within a nursing home, when simultaneously the nursing home is adopting a policy in which Medicaid patients are no longer accepted, resulting in relocation of such patients with the concomitant change in network ties of the elderly and their families. Health educators need to recognize the potential impact on social networks of these broader forces and policies, and to engage in strategies that address these issues. (See Pilisuk & Minkler, 1985, for an elaboration of this discussion.)

Another potential limitation of network interventions involves the problems sometimes associated with obtaining adequate social support. Wortman and Conway (1985) describe situations where well-intentioned attempts to provide support are not considered to be helpful by the recipient. Similarly, Gottlieb (1981b) suggests that programs aimed at strengthening existing network resources could backfire if network members are not able to provide support or if they recommend inappropriate coping strategies.

The practitioner is also cautioned to be aware of possible negative consequences for the provider of social support. This may be particularly problematic for individuals required to provide high levels of support over a considerable time period, but where the recipient of the support is unable or unwilling to reciprocate (Wortman & Conway, 1985). The development of network interventions that further overburden such support providers could have deleterious effects on all persons involved, and thus, health educators need to design programs that minimize or ameliorate this problem. (See Rounds & Israel, 1985, for an in-depth discussion.)

Future Directions for Practice

In reviewing the literature on social networks and social support, it is apparent that a gap frequently exists between the work being conducted by those who consider themselves primarily researchers and those who consider themselves primarily practitioners. Several of the review articles recognize this gap as they discuss the need for integrating theory, research and practice (e.g., Cwikel & Israel, 1985; Ell, 1984; Israel, 1982; Norbeck, 1981). Many of these reviews recommend evaluation research and action-research which, within the context of an intervention, would examine both the effectiveness of the processes and outcomes of the program, and the relationships between major variables, e.g., social support, stress, health (e.g., Ell, 1984; Gottlieb, 1981b; Israel, 1982; Jung, 1984; Pilisuk & Minkler, 1980; Norbeck, 1981). As discussed earlier, to make causal inferences from the findings of such evaluation research, there is a need for both longitudinal studies (e.g., Cohen & Wills, 1985; Levy, 1983; McKinlay, 1980) and experimental studies (e.g., Broadhead et al., 1983; DiMatteo & Hays, 1981; Ell, 1984; Kessler & McLeod, 1985; Levy, 1983; Norbeck, 1981). Additionally, the published results of intervention research need to respond to the frequent critique regarding the lack of information in articles specifying the details of a given intervention (e.g., Cwikel & Israel, 1985; Levy, 1983; Wortman & Conway, 1985). That is, it is not enough to know whether a program successfully enhanced network ties and with what effects. Also needed is a well-documented assessment of how program activities were carried out and the specific processes involved, including information on other factors that may have influenced program outcomes.

There are numerous questions that evaluation research could appropriately address. Many of these are similar to the general research issues discussed earlier, and thus, only a few are mentioned here. For example, an intervention could assess the relationship between network structural (e.g., size), interactional (e.g., reciprocity) and functional (e.g., affective support) characteristics and health behavior and health status. The program could, in turn, be evaluated as to its effectiveness in changing such network characteristics and accompanying health behavior and well-being (e.g., Ell, 1984; Gottlieb, 1981b; Moos & Mitchell, 1982).

Intervention research can also be used to examine the roles of helpers within naturally occurring networks—their impact on help-seeking, utilization and compliance behavior (e.g., Ell, 1984). This information could be used to design and evaluate an appropriate program aimed at, for example, increasing compliance with medical advice. Such an effort could also examine what people actually do when providing support and the extent to which it is perceived by the recipient as supportive, nagging, patronizing or overprotective (Wortman & Conway, 1985).

Additionally, an evaluation-research approach is most appropriate for assessing the relationship between occupational stress, social support and physical and mental health status. Here again, data gathered can be used to develop network-related interventions aimed at reducing stress.

This section has summarized how the concepts of social networks and social support have been applied to different types of practice situations; discussed limitations and cautions in carrying out network interventions; and described future directions for more effectively linking theory, research and practice. Although it is apparent that there are many opportunities for the health educator to apply social network concepts, it is most important that these types of interventions neither be considered "the answer" for successful programming nor as an alternative to providing existing and needed services (Israel, 1982; Minkler, 1981).

CONCLUSION

As we stated at the beginning of this article, the concepts of social networks and social support have received increasing attention as major variables positively related to health behavior and physical and mental health status. Given the extensive theoretical perspectives, empirical findings and practice implications, the aim of this chapter has been to provide health educators with a guide to the social network and social support literature through a review of 33 review articles.

As this review has highlighted, there are numerous limitations and inconsistencies in the conceptualizations, applications of theory, measurements, research designs, outcomes, and interventions concerning social networks and social support. However, even with this diversity, there is notable constancy that suggests that this is a viable area in need of further refinement and expansion. To that end, we have made concluding remarks and suggestions for future directions at the end of each section of this article.

We particularly advocate the conduct of intervention research. Such studies could draw from different conceptual frameworks, research designs, and program strategies, as appropriate to the needs and objectives of the people involved. The complexity of the social network and social support constructs suggests the use of multidisciplinary teams to carry out successful intervention research. Such teams, involving researchers, practitioners, and members of the lay system have the potential to contribute not only to our understanding of social networks and social support and to improved health status, but also to the development of collaborative mechanisms that strengthen interdependence and mutual assistance. In this regard, we can engage in efforts that will enhance our own social networks as well as those with whom we work.

ACKNOWLEDGMENTS

Preparation of this Chapter has been supported in part by Grant #5 T32 MH16806-04 from the National Institute of Mental Health. We would like to thank Toni Antonucci and Noreen Clark for their helpful comments on an earlier draft, and Edward Surovell for his editorial assistance.

Reprint requests should be sent to Barbara A. Israel, Department of Health Behavior and Health Education, School of Public Health, The University of Michigan, 1420 Washington Heights, Ann Arbor, MI 48109-2029.

REFERENCES

The 33 review articles that are the focus of this chapter are preceded by an asterisk.

*Antonucci, T. C. (1985). Personal characteristics, social support, and social behavior. In Binstock, R. H., & Shanas, E., (Eds.), *Handbook of aging and the social sciences*, 2nd ed. New York: VanNostrand Reinhold.
Biegel, D. E., Shore, B. K., & Gordon, E. (1984). *Building support networks for the elderly; Theory and applications*. Beverly Hills: Sage.
*Berkman, L. (1984). Assessing the physical health effects of social networks and social support. *Annual Review of Public Health*, 5, 413–432.
*Broadhead, W., Kaplan, B., James, S., Wagner, E., Schoenbach, V., Grimson, R., Heyden, S., Tibblin, G., & Gehlbach, S. (1983). The epidemiologic evidence for a relationship between social support and health. *American Journal of Epidemiology*, 117, 521–537.
Brownell, A., & Shumaker, S. A. (Eds.), (1984, 1985). Social support: New perspectives in

theory, research and intervention. *Journal of Social Issues*. Part I, Volume 40; Part II, Volume 41.

Caplan, G. (1974). *Support systems and community mental health*. New York: Behavioral Publications.

Cassel, J. C. (1976). The contribution of the social environment to host resistance. *American Journal of Epidemiology*, *104*, 108–123.

Cassel, J. C. (1974). Psychosocial processes and 'stress': Theoretical formulations. *International Journal of Health Sciences*, *4*, 471–482.

Cobb, S. (1976). Social support as a moderator of life stress. *Psychosomatic Medicine*, *38*, 300–314.

*Cohen, S., & McKay, G. (1984). Social support, stress and the buffering hypothesis: A theoretical analysis. In Baum, A., Singer, J. E., & Taylor, S. E. (Eds.), *Handbook of psychology and health*, Volume 4, Hillsdale, NJ: Erlbaum.

Cohen, S., & Symes, L. (Eds.) (1985). *Social support and health*. New York: Academic Press.

*Cohen, S., & Wills, T. A. (1985). Stress, social support and the buffering hypothesis. *Psychological Bulletin*, 98:310–357.

Collins, A. H., & Pancoast, D. L. (1976). *Natural helping networks: A strategy for prevention*. New York: National Association of Social Workers.

Cuter, D. L., & Tatum, E. (1983). Networks and the chronic patient. *New Directions for Mental Health Services*, *19*, 13–22.

*Cwikel, J., & Israel, B. A. (1985). Practice applications of health related intervention studies of social support and social networks. Submitted for review.

Dean, A., & Lin, N. (1977). The stress-buffering role of social support. *Journal of Nervous and Mental Disease*, *165*, 403–417.

*DiMatteo, M., & Hays, R. (1981). Social support and serious illness. In Gottlieb, B. H. (Ed.), *Social networks and social support*. Beverly Hills: Sage.

*Ell, K. (1984). Social networks, social support and health status: A review. *Social Service Review*, *58*, 133–149.

Froland, C., Pancoast, D. L., Chapman, N. J., & Kimboko, P. J. (1981). *Helping networks and human services*. Beverly Hills: Sage.

Gartner, A., & Riessman, F. (1977). *Self-help in the human services*. San Francisco: Jossey-Bass.

*Gottlieb, B. H. (1981a). Social networks and social support in community mental health. In Gottlieb, B. H. (Ed.), *Social networks and social support*. Beverly Hills: Sage.

*Gottlieb, B. H. (1981b). Preventive interventions involving social networks and social support. In Gottlieb, B. H. (Ed.), *Social networks and social support*. Beverly Hills: Sage.

Gottlieb, B. H. (1983). *Social support strategies: Guidelines for mental health practice*. Beverly Hills: Sage.

Greenblatt, M., Becerra, R., & Serafetinides, E. (1982). Social networks and mental health: An overview. *The American Journal of Psychiatry*, *139*, 977–984.

Hamburg, B. A. & Killilea, M. (1979). Relation of social support; stress, illness and use of health services. In *Healthy people: Background papers*. The Surgeon General's Report on Health Promotion and Disease Prevention, Washington, DC: U.S. Government Printing Office.

Hammer, M. (1981). Social supports, social networks and schizophrenia. *Schizophrenia Bulletin*, *7*, 45–57.

Hammer, M., Makiesky-Barrow, S., Gutwirth, L. (1978). Social networks and schizophrenia. *Schizophrenia Bulletin*, *4*, 522–545.

*Hansson, R. O., Jones, W. H., & Carpenter, B. N. (1984). Relational competence and social support. In Shaver, P. (Ed.), *Review of personality and social psychology*. Volume 5, Beverly Hills: Sage.

Heller, K. (Ed.) (in press). Social support theme issue. *Journal of Counseling and Clinical Psychology*.

*Heller, K., & Swindle, R. W. (1983). Social networks, perceived social support and coping with stress. In Felner, R. D., Jason, L. A., Moritsugu, J., & Farber, S. S. (Eds.), *Preventive psychology: Theory, research and practice in community intervention*. Elmsford, NY: Pergamon Press.

Heller, K. (1979). The effects of social support, prevention and treatment implications. In A. P. Goldstein, A. P., & Kanfer, F. H. (Eds.), *Maximizing treatment gains: Transfer enhancement in psychotherapy*. New York: Academic Press.

*House, J. S. The nature of social support. In *Work stress and social support*. Reading, MA: Addison-Wesley, 13–30.

*House, J., & Kahn, R. (1985). Measures and concepts of social support. In Cohen, S., & Syme, L. (Eds.), *Social support and health*. New York: Academic Press.

*Israel, B. A. (1982). Social networks and health status: Linking theory, research and practice. *Patient Counselling and Health Education*, *4*, 65–79.

Israel, B. A., & McLeroy, K. (1985). Social networks and social support: Implications for health education. *Health Education Quarterly* theme issue, Volume 12.

*Jung, J. (1984). Social support and its relation to health: A critical evaluation. *Basic and Applied Social Psychology*, *5*, 143–169.

*Kahn, R. L., & Antonucci, T. C. (1980). Convoys over the life course: Attachments, roles and social support. In Baltes, P. B. & Brim, O. (Eds.), *Life span development and behavior*. Volume 3, New York: Academic Press.

Kaplan, B. H., Cassel, J. C., & Gore, S. (1977). Social support and health. *Medical Care*, *15*, 47–58.

*Kessler, R. C., & McLeod, J. (1985). Social support and mental health in community samples. In Cohen, S. & Syme, L. (Eds.), *Social support and health*. New York: Academic Press.

*Kessler, R., Price, R., & Wortman, C. (1985). Social factors in psychopathology: Stress, social support and coping processes. *Annual Review of Psychology*, *36*, 531–572.

Kleiman, M. A., Mantell, J. E., & Alexander, E. S. (1976). Collaboration and its discontents: The perils of partnership. *Journal of Applied Behavioral Science*, *12*, 403–410.

LaRocco, J. M., House, J. S., & French, J. R. P., Jr. (1980). Social support, occupational stress and health. *Journal of Health and Social Behavior*, *21*, 202–218.

*Leavy, R. L. (1983) Social support and psychological disorder: A review. *Journal of Community Psychology*, *11*, 3–21.

Lenrow, P. B., & Burch, R. W. (1981). Mutual aid and professional services: Opposing or complementary? In Gottlieb, B. H. (Ed.), *Social networks and social support*. Beverly Hills: Sage.

*Levy, R. (1983). Social support and compliance: A selective review and critique of treatment integrity and outcome measurement. *Social Science and Medicine*, *17*, 1329–1338.

Lieberman, M. A. In Goldberger, L., & Breznitz, S. (Eds.) (1982). *Handbook of stress: Theoretical and clinical aspects*. New York: Free Press.

Maguire, L. (1983). *Understanding social networks*. Beverly Hills: Sage.

Marsella, A. J., & Snyder, K. K. (1981). Stress, social support and schizophrenic disorders: Toward an interactional model. *Schizophrenia Bulletin*, *7*, 152–163.

*McKinlay, J. (1980). Social network influences on morbid episodes and the career of help seeking. In Eisenberg, L., & Kleinman, A. (Eds.), *The relevance of social science for medicine*.

*Minkler, M. (1981). Applications of social support theory to health education: Implications for work with the elderly. *Health Education Quarterly*, *8*, 147–165.

Mitchell, J. C. (1969). The concept and use of social networks. In Mitchell, J. C. (Ed.), *Social networks in urban situations*. Manchester, England: Manchester Press.

*Mitchell, R. E., & Trickett, E. J. (1980). Social networks as mediators of social support. An analysis of the effects and determinants of social networks. *Community Mental Health Journal, 16*, 27–44.

*Moos, R. H., & Mitchell, R. E. (1982). Social network resources and adaptation: A conceptual framework. In Wills, T. (Ed.), *Basic processes in helping relationships*. New York: Academic Press.

*Mueller, D. (1980). Social networks: A promising direction for research on the relationship of the social environment to psychiatric disorder. *Social Science and Medicine, 14A*, 147–161.

*Norbeck, J. S. (1981). Social support: A model for clinical research and application. *Advances in Nursing Science*, 43–58.

Pilisuk, M., & Minkler, M. (1985). Supportive ties: A political economy perspective. *Health Education Quarterly, 12*, 93–106.

*Pilisuk, M., & Minkler, M. (1980). Supportive networks: Life ties for the elderly. *Journal of Social Issues, 36*, 95–116.

Pilisuk, M., & Froland, C. (1978). Kinship, social networks, social support and health. *Social Science and Medicine, 12B*, 273–280.

Rounds, K. A., & Israel, B. A. (1985). Social networks and social support: Living with chronic renal disease. *Patient Education and Counseling, 7*, 227–247.

Sarason, S. B., Carroll, C. F., & Matton, K. (1977). *Human Services and Resources Networks: Rationale, Possibilities and Public Policy*. San Francisco: Jossey-Bass.

Sarason, I. G., & Sarason, B. R. (Eds.), (1985). *Social support: Theory, research and application*. The Hague: Martinus Nijhof.

Sauer, W., & Coward, R. (1985). *Social support networks and the care of the elderly: Theory, research, practice and policy*. New York: Springer.

Schaefer, C., Coyne, J. C., & Lazarus, R. S. (1981). The health-related functions of social support. *Journal of Behavioral Medicine, 4*, 381–406.

Snow, D. L., & Gordon, J. B. (1980). Social network analysis and intervention with the elderly. *The Gerontologist, 20*, 463–467.

*Thoits, P. (1982). Conceptual, methodological and theoretical problems in studying social support as a buffer against life stress. *Journal of Health and Social Behavior, 23*, 145–159.

*Turner, R. J. (1983). Direct, indirect and moderating effects of social support on psychological distress and associated conditions. In Kaplan, H. B. (Ed.), *Psychosocial stress: Trends in theory and research*. New York: Academic Press.

Walker, K., MacBride, A., & Vachon, M. (1977). Social support networks and the crisis of bereavement. *Social Science and Medicine, 11*, 35–41.

*Wallston, B., Alagna, S., DeVellis, B., & DeVellis, R. (1983). Social support and physical health. *Health Psychology, 2*, 367–391.

*Wellman, B. (1981). Applying network analysis to the study of support. In Gottlieb, B. H. (Ed.), *Social networks and social support*. Beverly Hills: Sage.

Wortman, C. B. (1984). Social support and the cancer patient: Conceptual and methodological issues. *Cancer, 53*, 2339–2360.

*Wortman, C. B., Conway, T. L. (1985). The role of social support in adaptation and recovery from physical illness. In Cohen, S., & Syme, L. (Eds.), *Social support and health*. New York: Academic Press.

RECONCILING CONCEPT AND CONTEXT:

THEORY OF IMPLEMENTATION

Judith M. Ottoson and Lawrence W. Green

INTRODUCTION

How do concepts, ideas and policies get transformed into practice? How do concepts materialize in the context of professional and administrative behavior? How one answers this question—indeed, how one asks the question—depends in large part on one's theoretical perspective. An economist for example, asks how the manifestation of ideas affects or is affected by the distribution of scarce resources (Stokey & Zeckhauser, 1978). Philosophers have grappled with the question for centuries as a problem of the value formation of ideas (Adler, 1957; Durant, 1961). Health educators have treated it as a question of innovation and diffusion (Kolbe & Iverson, 1981), and a problem of evaluation (Basch, 1986; Green & Lewis, 1981, 1986), of participation in planning (Green, 1986) and of organizational development (Ross & Mico, 1980).

This chapter will draw primarily from sociological theory. Sociology arose as a science of social motion. It attempts to discover the laws of interpersonal and intergroup behavior (Zollschan & Perrucci, 1964). From

Advances in Health Education and Promotion, vol. 2, pages 353–382
Copyright © 1987 JAI Press Inc.
All rights of reproduction in any form reserved.
ISBN: 0-89232-617-4

this perspective, the general problem of concern for education and health promotion is how the manifestation of ideas (policies, theories, principles) in practice affects various types of human interaction (political, organizational, and interpersonal).

The Practitioner's Dilemma

This chapter addresses that specific problem of educational or public health practice that presents itself as a dilemma for the practitioner trying to implement an innovative idea as social action. Because ideas and actions are distinguishable entities, ideas necessarily change in form (not to say become accommodating) during implementation. Ideas, as policy, usually hatch in some central governmental or organizational headquarters, but they must be implemented in varied local circumstances. Ideas as innovations usually hatch in some innovative local situation, but must diffuse to less innovative situations. Ideas as theories often hatch in one type of organization (e.g., a university), and may be implemented in another type (e.g., a health department).

Various organizational, economic, political, and human factors shape the meaning and direction of the idea as it is transformed into action. During implementation, the practitioner must cope with discrepancies among these various forces and arrive at an idea that is "reasonable" (Williams, 1976a), "realistic" (Williams, 1976b), or "productive and workable" (Rabinovitz et al., 1976) in practice.

McGowan (1976) captured some of the elements of the practitioner's dilemma in what she described as the paradox central to implementation of social innovations: programs that are likely to appeal to varied constituencies are often broad and vague, but this imprecision makes the programs less workable and more problematic for executive agencies. As a result, implementors feel caught: on one hand they have their own weak grasp of the ideas, looseness of the developmental process, and limited control; on the other hand they have their accountability to concept developers and oversight agencies and frequently their own desires for social reform. This dilemma, combined with a passion for rationality, produces a series of mismatches between innovative ideas and the policy-makers' influence, and between each of these and rational management.

These issues reflect the heart of the implementor's dilemma: both the concept and the context must change for implementation to occur. Nonimplementation is the lack of change or adjustment by either the project or the setting (Berman & McLaughlin, 1976). Total fidelity to the concept means the idea remains virginal and of limited value in the field, the classroom or the clinic. Having a good idea is not enough; the value and meaning of an idea, as Aristotle insisted, derives from its interaction with the concrete world (Adler, 1957). The overzealous implementation of an idea even as sound as health promotion can lead to disrepute for the idea (Goodman & Goodman, 1986).

Total fidelity to the context means there is nothing to implement. The context remains unchanged, the policy is co-opted, as seen in the early failure of civil rights regulations (Lazin, 1973). Implementation becomes perfunctory, an end in itself, when there is no commitment to changing the implementing environment. Finding a feasible middle ground between the intent of the concept and realities of the context becomes the main task of implementation, and therefore the main challenge for program administrators and practitioners attempting to carry out policies.

Implementation achieves feasibility through a series of trade-offs among various political, organizational and interpersonal factors. The rules for achieving "acceptable" trade-offs, however, cannot be formulated before practice (Rein & Rabinovitz, 1977). As a result, they are left to the practitioner to negotiate during the confusing process of implementation. The process is so "slippery" (Pressman & Wildavsky, 1973) as to make it conceptually difficult to distinguish inputs and independent effects from each other (Williams, 1976b). Neustadt and Fineberg (1978) went so far as to subtitle their case study, *The Swine Flu Affair: Decision-Making on a Slippery Disease*.

In the midst of such conceptual confusion, it is not only difficult for the practitioner to know how to negotiate trade-offs, but to know what there is to trade.

Purpose and Scope

Sorting out this dilemma and illuminating the elements and process of policy implementation trade-offs should be of interest to administrators and health educators in practice, policy-making, and evaluation. By understanding the dilemma of implementation, the practitioner is less likely to be buffeted by it and, therefore, more constructive in its resolution (Cleary et al., 1985). For policy-makers, an understanding of implementation trade-offs can contribute to more rational policy choice (Elmore, 1976), and can lead to the design of more implementable programs (Berman & McLaughlan, 1976) and contribute to an analysis of implementation feasibility (Chase, 1979).

Because implementation dominates the innovative process and its outcomes (Berman & McLaughlin, 1976), it should be of interest to evaluators. A study of implementation explores how program activities and objectives change during implementation and helps differentiate whether a program fails because it was based on a poor idea or because it was poorly executed (Basch, 1986; Green & Lewis, 1986; Weiss, 1972).

The following review encompasses primarily sociological, but also political, philosophical, and organizational theories and concepts concerned with the transformation of ideas into action. The review is divided into two sections. The first analyzes various perspectives on the meaning of implementation. The second describes the four major factors that shape implementation: the policy, the implementing organization, the political milieu, and the environment. We then conclude with some theoretical generalizations and conclusions of our own, suggesting implications for theory, research, policy and practice in health education and health promotion.

PERSPECTIVES ON IMPLEMENTATION

If it is true that "what you see is what you get," then one should expect many things from implementation. After reviewing the definitions and research approaches taken by other analysts, we will offer a theatrical metaphor for understanding its elements and process and an operational definition of implementation.

Definitions

Implementation is that vague area somewhere between idea development and program outcomes. It has been defined, researched, and engaged in by people who have different (or vague) ideas of what it means. Hargrove (1975) finds it important to study the various definitions of implementation; otherwise, different " . . . characters are likely to act in the play using the same word with different meanings without mutual awareness of that fact." A sample of the definitions of implementation that surfaced in this literature reviews reveals varying assumptions about what implementation is, when it begins and ends, how it works, and who is involved. Implementation is variously described as a stage, a process, or as actions. For Williams (1976b), implementation ends when program operations begin, but for Weiss (1972) implementation *is* program operations. For Pressman and Wildavsky (1973), implementation is a process of interaction; for Berman and McLaughlin (1976), implementation is more specifically an organizational process.

Research

Alternative definitions of implementation lead to varying research approaches. Implementation has been studied from the top down (Derthick, 1972) and from the bottom up (Green, 1986; Weatherley & Lipsky, 1977), at macro and micro levels (Berman, 1978; Green & McAlister, 1984), as progressing in stages and different kinds of stages (Berman & McLaughman, 1976; Rein & Rabinovitz, 1977), and as part of larger processes such as change (Ginzberg & Reilly, 1957), innovation (Berman & McLaughlin, 1976; Kolbe & Iverson, 1981), and policy development (Hargrove, 1975).

Implementation has been described as a process that is chiefly organizational (Berman & McLaughlin, 1976) or political (Bardach, 1977), interpersonal and motivational (Williams, 1976b). It has been analyzed as an assembly line (Bardach, 1977), as mutual adaptation (Berman & McLaughlin, 1976), and as evolution (Pressman & Wildavsky, 1973). One particularly mind-twisting view describes implementation as a circular process in which policy is initiated from the bottom up (Rein & Rabinovitz, 1977). This latter view corresponds with the participatory theories of community health education and health promotion (Green, 1986).

It is not clear from implementation research which variables influence implementation the most (Hargrove, 1975). Some of the variables identified as most important include the implementing organization (Berman & McLaughlin, 1976), instability of the innovation (McGowan, 1976), the political environment (Bardach, 1977), the disposition of key actors (Parkinson et al., 1982) or some combination of these. Effective implementation contradicts itself; it is both devoted and unfaithful to the original policy intent (Pressman & Wildavsky, 1973).

The Actors in Implementation

Implementation has variously been considered by some a ubiquitous problem that is the analytic equivalent of "original sin" (Pressman & Wildavsky, 1973) and by others a select problem primarily of concern to third world countries (Smith, 1973). Some consider the implementation process inherent to all organizations (Van Meter & Van Horn, 1975), while others consider it primarily a governmental process (Smith, 1973).

Huysmans (1970) sees only managers as the actors in implementation; Van Meter and Van Horn (1975) cast decision-makers both within and outside the organization, and Bennis (1966) includes "client-systems" as actors in implementation.

Key implementation actors within systems are identified as the chief executive officer (Ginzberg & Reilly, 1957; Williams, 1976b), intended beneficiaries (Gustafson, 1979), or the implementor as key translator (Hargrove, 1975). To make matters more complex, key factors and actors are thought to change with the stage, timing, and context of implementation (Berman & McLaughlin, 1976; Rein & Rabinovitz, 1977).

Much of the relevant literature is concerned specifically with the implementation of ideas expressed as social policy. Weiss (1977) ventures a characterization of the policy-implementation nexus that places the onus for the development and implementation of policy at high levels of decision-making power: " . . . we are clearly concerned here with matters of moment, with decisions that go beyond the routine . . . under conditions of complexity and uncertainty."

The results of implementation research can hardly be described as conclusive. Perhaps the best summary of the implementation literature comes from Pressman and Wildavsky (1973) when answering the question, "What has policy wrought?: Having tasted of the fruit of the tree of knowledge, the implementor can only answer, and with conviction, it depends. Health educators will be comfortable with this summary, having found from research, experience, or both, that the success of any health education method, strategy or program depends on a broad array of variables.

Policy as the Plot

One thing on which implementation does seem to depend is an understanding of what sort of entity a policy is before trying to implement it (Van Meter & Van Horn, 1975). Is it a detailed and finished product, like a script, or a general direction such as a set of goals, or an irrelevant idea? Understanding the nature and intent of policy is one way of arriving at an operational approach to implementation. The *Objectives for the Nation* in health promotion and disease prevention, for example, provide general policy directions (PHS, 1980), but their implementation depends on adaptation to special populations (PHS, 1981) and to state and local levels with quite distinct implementation plans in each state and locality (PHS, 1983b, 1985).

The implementation literature contrasts two general views of decision-making in policy development: the traditional "fundamental choice" model (Stokey & Zeckhauser, 1978) and the "resultant" model (Allison, 1971).

In the traditional model, the main task of implementation is protecting the policy. Policy is considered a real entity before implementation; it is a fully articulated plan, needing only enforcement through various control and compliance measures (Pressman & Wildavsky, 1973; Rabinovitz et al., 1976; Van Meter & Van Horn, 1975). Interaction during implementation that results in unprescribed changes equates with interference.

In the resultant model, the main task of implementation is nurturing interaction. Policy, in this model, is a real entity after implementation. Interaction does not destroy policy, it gives birth to it. Policy provides the plot for implementation, not the script.

The debate over whether policy is real before or after implementation has its roots in a classical philosophical argument between Plato and Aristotle about the nature of ideas. In the *Doctrine of Ideas*, Plato argued that ideas are real things in themselves. The *Idea* might be a class to which something belongs, a law by which the thing operates, or the ideal to which it may develop. The *Idea* is conceived by reason and thought, and is more real than the particular things perceived by the senses. Aristotle argued against this realism of universals, contending that ideas are real only when actualized as actions or tangible objects.

What is perhaps more important to an understanding of implementation is not that about which these philosophers disagreed, but that on which they agreed: the importance of interaction of an idea with the concrete world.

The Context as the Stage

It is through interaction or application that ideas became "real" to Aristotle and gained "worth" to Plato. The generalizations and abstractions that give meaning to ideas were for Plato " . . . worthless except they be tested in the concrete world" (Durant, 1961). By addressing the value of ideas and coming to consensus on interaction as the test of value and reality, philosophy provides a way of bridging the gaps among some of the contrasting models of policy implementation. The bridge of interaction is a welcome one since there is substantial *prima facia* evidence to suggest that policy is real not only before or after, but during implementation.

Whether it is a product of choice or interaction, policy is real before implementation. It contains the ideals, intent, and expectations of its proponents and developers (Derthick, 1972; Smith, 1973). Before implementation, policy has value in its transformation of wants, needs, demands and resources into intent (Van Meter & Van Horn, 1975) and in the inspiration of its ideals (Rein & Rabinovitz, 1977). Policy merges into and emerges from the interaction that shapes it. This was the thesis of David Stockman's (1986) analysis of what went wrong with "Reagonomics." The "supply-side" concept was not policy until it interacted with politics, but it was politics that triumphed leaving the concept still an untested idea. Acknowledging policy as a real entity before implementation, however, does not make policy a finished product. Policy is a *proposal* for change; not a detailed map (Gross et al., 1971).

The details of the map only become apparent during implementation. Policy cannot be understood in a value-free form in isolation from its means of execution (Elmore, 1976; Titmus, 1972). Policy before implementation is a hypothesis containing initial conditions (independent variables) and predicted consequences (dependent variables); policy in practice, as John Dewey characterized educational policy in 1898, is an experiment in adjustment (Dewey, 1976). Implementation is not always a fair test of the hypothesis because the independent variables cannot always be controlled.

The problem-solving process in the adjustment of policy during implementation may be rational (Stokey & Zeckhauser, 1978), entrepreneurial (Stockman, 1986), or interactive in nature (Lindblom, 1965; Lindblom & Cohen, 1979). Adjustment means putting something into working order. The interaction of the implementation context puts policy into working order by determining its value. The process of adjustment, therefore, should not be viewed as an aberration, but as a goal (McLaughlin, 1976).

Policy is the plot of implementation; the rest is context. Policy contains the plan or scheme that is gradually developed over time on the stage of implementation. Various scripts determine the roles played during implementation: concept developers are the producers, the chief implementor is the protagonist, and intended beneficiaries are the audience. The interaction among these parties to the play is guided by the potentials and limitations of the plot and the stage. Collectively, these elements provide the drama that is implementation.

Toward an Operational Definition

Drawing on the definitions and research of the implementation literature and philosophical insights about the nature of ideas, the following conclusions about the nature of implementation are derived.

Process

Implementation is a process, not an event (Gross et al., 1971). Although analysts may vary in their view of implementation as an organizational, political, or interpersonal process, they generally agree that implementation represents a series of actions, not a single occurrence. We can think of no health education or health promotion policy or program that is implemented with a single stroke.

The series of actions required for implementation indicates that it is a segmented, rather than unitary, process. Different foci, tasks, and outcomes may occur at different times during implementation. To speak of implementation as a single process is to ignore or lump under a single rubric all the nuances of different activities during different stages. For example, administrative guidelines are developed in early stages and resources distributed in later stages (Rein & Rabinovitz, 1977). Health education tasks must be described and assigned before staff can be asked to devote time and effort to the tasks.

Change

Implementation is not an isolated process; rather it is part of some larger process of change, such as innovation adoption (Berman & McLaughlin, 1976). During implementation both concept and context are changed. Bending one to fit the rigidity of the other is co-optation, not implementation.

As part of a larger process of change, implementation connects and responds to the ideals and intents of those who initiated it, the values and interaction of those who shaped it, and the needs and circumstances of those who are to benefit from it.

Beginning and Ending

Implementation is not spontaneously combustible; policy precedes implementation and serves as its catalyst. The origins of implementation lie in the interaction that gives birth to policy, and its legacy lies in the actions that follow. It is not an end in itself. There must be some goal or ending point by which to judge the success of implementation (Pressman & Wildavsky, 1973). Ignoring the concept while transversing the context of policy is like driving without a destination; ignoring the context in pursuit of the concept is like driving in new territory without a nap.

Feasibility

Feasibility signals anticipated implementation. When policy has been deemed feasible, it has been judged implementable. The objective of implementation is "performance, not conformance ... implementation should consist of a realistic development of the underlying decision in terms of the local setting" (Williams, 1976b). There is no one right solution to the implementation puzzle. Instead, there are potentially feasible alternatives or clusters of potential policies. The number of possible alternatives depends on such factors as how vaguely or specifically the policy is stated, and the creativity and resourcefulness of the implementor.

Mutual Adaptation

"Although the literature is rich in examples of implementation failure (or, at least, outcomes that do not meet certain standards, though they may be functional on other grounds), implementation monsters—policy outcomes bearing no recognizable relationship to the original idea—seem to be rare" (Pressman & Wildavsky, 1973). Adaptation means that the policy and context have adjusted to each other in arriving at social action, yet retain a recognizable relationship to their original states.

Own Focus

Implementation has its own focus beyond that of policy. Practitioners are warned that the separation of program design from implementation may be "fatal." It can be equally lethal for a practitioner not to know whether he or she is designing or implementing programs. Although related, program design and implementation differ on three criteria: primary focus, principal actors, and conditioning climate. The strategy and plan of implementation take place at different times and engage the attention of different actors (Hargrove, 1975). Table 1 differentiates implementation from related processes.

In general, the table shows implementation to be focused on action rather than ideas, more concerned with local realities than with the big picture, and eclectic in a search for feasibility rather than clear-cut and analytical. The main actors of implementation are more likely to be at lower rather than higher management levels, and more effective as artists and politicians than theorists and technicians. The climate of implementation is slippery, subjective, dynamic, less inclined toward solitary action, and more toward coalition building than protection of self-interests.

Operational Definition

Considering these understandings of implementation, the following operational definition will be used in this chapter:

> *Implementation* is an iterative process in which ideas, expressed as policy, are transformed into behavior, expressed as social action.

FACTORS THAT SHAPE IMPLEMENTATION

The dynamics of implementation make it difficult to capture the factors that shape its course. Four general factors are identified in this literature review: the policy, the implementing organization, the political milieu, and the surrounding environment. Each of these will be analyzed for the specific variables that affect implementation.

Table 1. Differentiating Implementation From Related Processes by Primary Focus, Actors, and Climate

RELATED PROCESS	CRITERION: PRIMARY FOCUS	
	Other Process	Implementation
1. Antecedent Processes		
a. Decision-Making	Analytical	*Ad hoc* search for feasibility
	Decisions	Actions
	Knowing what	Knowing how
b. Policy Adoption	Developing Intentions	Carrying out Practicality
c. Strategic Planning	Big picture	Local focus
	Future	Now
	Constraints hidden	Constraints discovered
	Deliberate search	Trial and error
2. Concurrent Processes		
a. Management	Organizational objectives	Interorganizational objectives
b. Operations	Tasks	Actions and interactions
3. Subsequent Processes		
a. Evaluation	*A priori* goals	Translated goals
	Measuring effects	Producing effects
RELATED PROCESSES	CRITERION: MAIN ACTOR	
1. Antecedent Processes		
a. Decision-Making	Upstairs	Downstairs
b. Policy Adoption	Various groups	Implementing organization
c. Strategic Planning	National Organizational	Organizational Unit
2. Concurrent Processes		
a. Management	Top management	Middle Management
b. Operations	Management	Labor

Table 1.   Continued

RELATED PROCESS	CRITERION: MAIN ACTOR	
	Other Process	Implementation
3. Subsequent Processes		
a. Evaluation	Theorist Technician	Artist Politician

RELATED PROCESSES	CRITERION: CLIMATE	
1. Antecedent Processes		
a. Decision- Making	Open	Restrictive
b. Policy Adoption	Coalition building	Self-interest
c. Strategic Planning	Linear	Iterative
2. Concurrent Processes		
a. Management	Effective	Messy
b. Operations	Efficient Rigid protocol	Slippery Flexible protocol
3. Subsequent Processes		
a. Evaluation	Objective	Subjective

Factor 1: The Policy

The basic preconception for any study of implementation is a detailed knowledge of the essential components of what is to be implemented (El-more, 1976). The previous section discussed the nature of policy; this section identifies the hypothesized characteristics of policy that affect its interaction with the implementation context. Nine such characteristics or variables are discussed below. Reference will be made for examples to counterpart documents that illustrate their application in relation to the national policy in disease prevention and health promotion initiated with the U.S. Surgeon General's Report in 1979, under the direction of Julius Richmond and Michael McGinnis.

Theory

A policy decision implies theory. It points to a chain of causation between initial conditions and future consequences (Berman, 1978; Pressman & Wildavsky, 1973). The hypothesis to be tested may be expressed as an organizational or resource support, a regulation, a program or a project that the decision-maker puts in place to cause predicted effects or outcomes (Williams, 1976b). If the theory on which policy is based is either non-existent or not sound, the expected outcomes may not be achieved (Weiss, 1972). Theory failure differs from implementation failure in that the former implies wrong thinking; the latter implies wrong doing (Green & Lewis, 1981, 1986; Weiss, 1973). Examples of the theory relating causes and effects in the U.S. national disease prevention and health promotion policy initiative can be seen in various documents describing the sequence of proposed inputs, hypothesized processes of change, short-term objectives, intermediate objectives, and long-term (1990) goals (Green, 1979, 1980, 1982, 1986; Green, Wilson, & Bauer, 1983; McGinnis, 1980).

Supporting Assumptions

The assumptions and research underlying a policy need to be examined. Prior research may not support program activity; policy decisions are frequently based on overly optimistic assumptions about or interpretations of the state of knowledge (Elmore, 1976). Much of this research on assumptions preceded the Surgeon General's Report (PHS, 1978) and was summarized in background papers to the Surgeon General's Report (1979b). Efforts to confirm or to fill gaps in the assumptions continue during implementation through research, national surveys, and other data collection, synthesis and review activities.

Goals and Objectives

Policy contains a general statement of purpose (Rein & Rabinovitz, 1977) that gives implementation direction. One characteristic of goals and objectives is their level of specificity. For some analysts, more specific program-related objectives are an essential constituent of policy implementation (Pressman & Wildavsky, 1973). Lack of such specification is a major implementation problem (Elmore, 1976; Williams, 1976b). Another relevant characteristic is the level of goal consensus. Some analysts have found goal consensus a facilitator to implementation (Van Meter &

Van Horn, 1975). The most dramatic and effective step taken in the national disease prevention/health promotion initiative was the formulation of 226 specific, quantified objectives for 1990 through a consensus-development process, thereby giving the policy both credibility as a feasible and concrete plan with broad-based political support (PHS, 1980).

One tricky issue of policy purpose is the difference between that which is overtly and covertly expressed. If one only pays attention to the general, overt purposes that are widely acceptable, it is easy to miss the true policy intent or to ignore competing self-interests (Weiss, 1973). Consensus on more specific objectives helps iron out the competing self-interest.

There is, however, a point of diminishing returns in continuing to multiply and specify centrally defined objectives. Beyond the point of clarifying vague policy goals, they begin to constrain the imagination and limit the prerogatives of those who must implement the policy. Regarding the nation's disease prevention/health promotion initiatives, special populations (e.g., minority groups and the elderly) insisted on setting their own priorities and objectives (PHS, 1981), and states, one by one, have repeated the process of decentralized priority-setting and adjustment of the objectives (e.g., PHS, 1981; Texas Department of Health, 1984).

Change Proposed

Policies are intended to produce change (Smith, 1973). The kinds of changes proposed by policy are defined, in part, by the following:

- *Nature of the Innovation.* Although policy does not necessarily contain an innovation, when it does, it contributes to implementation success or failure. McGowan (1976) identifies the instability of the innovation, not program size nor sponsor control, as one chief barrier to implementation. The type of innovation affects how it is carried out (Derthick, 1972).
- *Amount of Change.* The scope of change proposed by the project design "greatly" affects implementation outcomes (Berman & McLaughlin, 1976). Programs that require major changes frequently lead to goal conflict among major actors and this, in turn, affects implementation (Van Meter & Van Horn, 1975).
- *Rate of Change.* Incremental change is easier to implement than are ambitious nonincremental changes (Smith, 1973; Van Meter & Van Horn, 1975).
- *"Radicalness."* Is this a familiar change to those involved or is it a radical departure (Gustafson, 1979). The more radical the change, supposedly the more difficult it is to implement. On the other hand,

recommending a large change is more likely to get at least a small change than recommending only a small change to start with.

- *Centrality or Congruence.* Some changes determine an agency's primary responsibilities, while others may affect its responsibilities peripherally (Baum, 1980). The effect of centrality on implementation outcomes is not clear. One clue about its effect, however, comes from research analyzing the congruence of project goals and values. When values and goals inherent in project designs are not congruent with those of project participants, implementation may at best be symbolic or at worst nonexistent (Berman & McLaughlin, 1976).
- *Complexity.* A complex change that involves numerous transactions or discrete functions is more difficult to implement than one that is relatively simple (Berman & McLaughlin, 1976; Pressman & Wildavsky, 1973). A related issue is the amount of coordination the complex change requires (Chase, 1979).
- *Form.* The change may be expressed as a formal decisional statement, law, or program (Smith, 1973). It may be either positive or negative in nature (Chase, 1979). Although considered a "relevant" variable, it is unclear how form affects implementation outcomes.

Resources

Resources may or may not be attached to policy. If attached, they may be in the form of money, personnel, space, or supplies (Chase, 1979). The "Objectives for the Nation in Health Promotion and Disease Prevention" have stimulated widespread implementation of policy with very few resources specifically earmarked for implementation (PHS, 1983b, 1984).

Debate exists about how the nature, amount, and availability of resources affect policy. On one hand, Gross, et al. (1971), indicate that funding is a facilitator of implementation. Gustafson (1979) identifies funding assurance as a strong indicator of implementation success. On the other hand, Murphy (1976) found that money is not the key to reform that some would like to believe. Berman and McLaughlin (1976) support Murphy's finding in their research where, other things being equal, variation in the funding level and the concentration of funding had small and generally not significant effects on project outcomes.

One might conclude from this debate that although monetary resources alone are not responsible for implementation success or failure, the right resources at the right time in the right amount are more likely to facilitate than to hinder implementation.

Specification

Clarity and precision are considered by some to be essential ingredients of policy (Williams, 1976b; Gross, 1971; Van Meter & Van Horn, 1975). Specificity means that the purpose, characteristics, and resources of policy are identified in an unambiguous manner. Specificity can set the course, clarify expectations, rally resources, prevent avoidable interpersonal conflicts, ease the burden of supervision, and assure uniformity and continuity of implementation (Schaefer, 1985).

Specificity can also erode shaky coalitions that support policy and, thereby, undermine implementation. Different perceptions of program purposes can lead to tension about specification (Elmore, 1976). Policy needs to balance the specificity that defines direction with the ambiguity that molds coalitions and spans innovation.

Flexibility

Policy is actually a cluster of potentialities (Pressman & Wildavsky, 1973). A policy that can give birth to any one of these clusters and still be considered successful is flexible. A policy that has only one cluster is inflexible. Flexibility is important because it is not possible to know in advance all the problems and opportunities that may arise during implementation (Rein & Rabinovitz, 1977).

Effect

Policies do not equally affect all stages of implementation. One study found that policies have their most important influence on the adoption of innovations, an indirect effect on implementation, and an insignificant effect on actual outcomes (Berman & McLaughlin, 1976). Van Meter and Van Horn (1975) corroborated the finding that the standards and objectives of policies have an indirect effect on implementation performance.

Developers

The motives, intent, position, resources, and support of those who developed the policy may affect implementation. Baum (1980) found that there may be considerable value in comparing implementation in different contexts on variables such as the policy enactor's influence over implementation.

In sum, policy affects implementation, but is not its sole determinant. A policy that is based on theory and supported by assumptions; contains identifiable purposes; proposes changes that are small, incremental, non-radical, and simple; attaches resources; balances specificity and ambiguity; and maintains flexibility, is more likely to facilitate, rather than hinder, implementation.

Factor 2: The Implementing Organization

The implementing organization is concerned with the administration, as opposed to the making, of policy. For those analysts who consider implementation an organizational process (Berman, 1976), the key to understanding implementation lies in the structure, technology, and people of the organization primarily responsible for implementing policy (Allison, 1971). The following section analyzes these three broad variables and their more specific characteristics which are hypothesized to effect implementation.

Organizational Structure

The organizational structure has been suggested as the "biggest hurdle" to implementation (Williams, 1976a). Failure of the organizational structure to adjust to policy has been identified as a contributing factor to implementation failure (Gross et al., 1971).

The organizational structure exists at both formal and informal levels. The formal structure includes organizational goals, tasks, size, roles, and standard operating procedures (Bolman & Deal, 1979a; Ginzberg & Reilly, 1957; Moore, 1979; Pincus, 1976). The informal structure consists of organizational culture, climate, and orientation (Murphy, 1976; Berman, 1978; Bolman & Deal, 1979a). The overall structure, as well as these individual components, affects implementation.

- *Goal.* Unless policy goals, stated or unstated, are relevant to organizational goals, overt or covert, implementation may be delayed or halted.
- *Task.* Different organizations have different approaches to programs in the same area (Rein & Rabinovitz, 1977). These approaches, or tasks, vary with the organization if the policy is held constant. For example, legislative and judicial branches of the government approach policy development differently (Baum, 1980), and both differ from the administrative branch in their expectations for implementation (Stockman, 1986).
- *Scale and Complexity.* Moore (1979) identifies these variables in a study of implementation feasibility. As with the policy, the more complex the organizational setting, the more complex and poten-

tially less successful the implementation (Green & McAlister, 1984).

* *Roles.* Debate exists about whether the chief executive officers of the organization or the front line workers have more effect on implementation. To some, implementation is hindered without administrative participation (Ginzberg & Reilly, 1957; Smith, 1973; Gross et al., 1971; Williams, 1976b). To others implementation may be hindered by the personal policy interpretations of "street-level bureaucrats" (Weatherley & Lipsky, 1977; Schaeffer, 1985).

The inconclusiveness of the implementation research on roles leads to a conclusion that both administration and staff affect implementation. The real issue may lie not in the relative *strength* of their effects, but in the timing of their involvement.

* *Standard Operating Procedures (SOPs).* These are the rules and regulations that identify usual organizational procedures. Relying on SOPs inappropriate to a specific policy has been identified as a factor contributing to implementation failure (Derthick, 1972). By using the discretion that resides in SOPs, it is possible to reshape routine procedures to policy (Elmore, 1976). A change in SOPs, however, does not necessarily alter actual practices (Lazin, 1973; Schaeffer, 1985).

The climate and culture express the informal organizational structure. This includes the needs, beliefs, orientation, affective ties, patterns of interaction and communication, and leadership among organizational members (Bolman & Deal, 1979a). The formal characteristics of the organization may find complementary or contradictory counterparts in the informal structure.

Approaching an understanding of implementation through organizational structure assumes that changes in structure affect people and ultimately the task, i.e., if people know their role and the organizational goal, they will accomplish it. Order, discipline, and authority acceptance are valued in a structural approach to implementation (Leavitt, 1965). Failure of implementation from this perspective is bad management (Elmore, 1976).

Technical Capacity

The technical aspects of implementation have been found to be less complicated than political and administrative changes (Radin, 1976). In fact, Williams (1976b) finds technical questions "trivial" when compared to political questions. Nevertheless, technical capacity does affect implementation (Leavitt, 1965) and is shaped by the specific technology and resources.

- *Technology.* Technology comes in different forms, such as, machines, programs, and services (Leavitt, 1965). In the social sciences, however, people are processed more often than materials. As a result, social or organizational technology lacks the kind of exactness found in the physical sciences (Lindblom & Cohen, 1979). This makes it not only difficult to determine what the organizational technology is, but how it affects implementation.
- *Resources.* To be able to apply technology, the organization needs resources. These might be in the form of space, personnel, supplies, or funding (Chase, 1979). The resources here differ from those attached to policy. The former exist within the organization and the latter are additions.

Timing and staff orientation are two resource considerations. Resources that are not readily available or cannot be obtained without a minimum of complexity and additional layers of bureaucracy may impede implementation (Gustafson, 1979; Chase, 1979). The inadequate preparation of staff to implement policy is also a hindrance.

Employees

McLaughlin (1976) argues that we should shift the primary focus of change-agent policies from the delivery system to the persons designated as deliverers. Individuals working for the implementing organization affect implementation through their disposition, professional affiliation, and behavior. Disposition includes the approaches, motivation, support, value, attitude, and beliefs that people bring to their work in general and the specific implementation task in particular. It can be affected positively or negatively by prior experiences with implementation (Smith, 1973; Ginzberg & Reilly, 1957). Behavior is studied as a separate phenomenon because disposition does not necessarily indicate behavior. The age, ambition, and professional socialization of workers determine their disposition. The following are characteristics of disposition:

- *Approach.* A problem-solving approach, rather than an opportunistic approach, may be necessary for the kind of mutual adaptation that facilitates implementation (Berman, 1976).
- *Morale.* A decline in staff motivation has been identified as a factor contributing to implementation failure (Gross et al., 1971).

- *Support.* Acceptance, support, and commitment to the need for change from chief administrators facilitate implementation (Basch, unpublished paper; Berman & McLaughlin, 1976; Cataldo et al, 1986; Gross et al, 1971).
- *Value.* Implementation is facilitated when project goals and values are congruent with those of the participants (Berman & McLaughlin, 1976).
- *Attitudes.* One analyst found that failure of implementation lies more with the attitudes of the agency and administration than the content of regulations (Lazin, 1973). Williams (1976b) reinforces this point, by noting that changing the attitude of management is the most important factor in improving implementation.
- *Confidence.* When people do not believe that ideal goals can be carried out, implementation is hindered (Derthick, 1972).
- *Professional preparation.* The various professions embody distinctive orientations toward action and knowledge that affect their behavior during implementation. The delegation of a service to a profession is one way to predict reliably how that service will be delivered (Hargrove, 1975). Physicians, nurses, and dieticians would implement the same patient education policy in distinct ways.
- *Other characteristics.* The above are just some of the characteristics of disposition that are identified in the implementation literature. This list fails to include several other potentially important characteristics, such as faith, loyalty, esprit de corps, cohesiveness, comraderie, and peer pressure and support.

When going into implementation, whatever the nature of these dispositions, the essence of successful change is not the design of the plan. It lies, instead, in the ability of those involved to alter their behavior in accordance with new principles. Effecting change means altering behavior (Ginzberg & Reilly, 1957). Changing the behavior of individuals, however, is not to be equated with changing the organization (Katz & Kahn, 1966).

In sum, the implementing organization plays a major role in affecting implementation through its structure, technology, and employees. In general, implementation is facilitated when the organizational structure changes with the policy, technical capacity is available, and individuals involved are positively disposed toward the policy and are willing and able to change their behavior accordingly.

Factor 3: The Political Milieu

The political milieu concerns itself with the making as opposed to the administration of policy. By addressing the issue of power and control, this factor attends to the messier aspects of implementation (Bolman & Deal, 1979). Policy research that does not consider politics is criticized as academic (Hargrove, 1975).

The political milieu can be analyzed at both the intraorganizational level (Allison, 1971; Elmore, 1976; Bolman & Deal, 1979) and the interorganizational level (Hargrove, 1975; Bardach, 1977). For some, implementation *is* a political process (Bardach, 1977). That is, the political perspective assumes that multiple, independent actors are in conflict over goals, resources, and actions. Their perceptions are determined by parochial priorities and perceptions, goals and interests, stakes and stands, deadlines and the faces of issues (Allison, 1971). Actors have a stake in making the most out of the conflict, even creating it, for their own self-interest (Alinsky, 1972; Bolman & Deal, 1979). Sometimes the chief policy-maker is the one who turns the policy around to fit political needs (Stockman, 1986).

In exploring the politics of policy, the central question is one of obedience and coercion (Titmus, 1972). From this follows a central question for implementation: "Why should I implement the policy as it is rather than as I would like?" In trying to answer that question, it becomes evident that knowledge about power and responsibility are basic to a study of implementation (Williams, 1976a).

Power is defined by one analyst as a blend of bargaining advantages, skills, and the will to use them, and the other players' perceptions of these (Allison, 1971). The primary variables to include in a political analysis are four aspects of power: form, strength, use, and distribution (Bolman & Deal, 1979; Elmore, 1976).

- *Form.* Power may be expressed in different forms: authority, expertise, control of rewards, coercion, and personal power (Bolman & Deal, 1979). It may also be expressed in the size and share of resources one controls (Williams, 1976a) or in one's position and ability to mobilize external support (Elmore, 1976).
- *Strength.* Some implementation participants are more effective or potent with their power than others. In general, those with more power are more likely to affect implementation positively or negatively than are those with little or no power.
- *Use.* Use involves the ability and willingness to make power serve a particular end or purpose. Those who use their power either for action or inaction (to support or resist) are more likely to affect implementation than those who do not use their power.
- *Distribution.* Power may be concentrated or dispersed. It is unclear how either affects implementation. A related variable in the implementation literature is "support" as expressed by a critical

mass (Berman, 1976), alliance formation (Gustafson, 1979), and the endorsement of key influentials (Gustafson, 1979).

The inclusion of the political milieu in implementation analysis assumes that the making of policy extends into the implementation of policy. There is much in the implementation literature to suggest that this is true. Actors, for instance, stay involved in the policy process after their main input has occurred. One criticism of the exclusive use of this perspective is that it denies rational aspects of implementation (Rein & Rabinovitz, 1977).

In sum, it is possible to conclude that those who have power are more likely to affect implementation—either positively or negatively—than those who do not have power.

Factor 4: The Environment

"The environmental factor includes those variables which can influence or be influenced by the policy implementation" (Smith, 1973). They include everything "out there" (Bolman, 1979a, Chin, 1966). Generically this means the cultural, social, political, and economic conditions that may differ with different policies (Smith, 1973). The most important elements of the immediate environment are diversity, activity, stability, and predictability (Bolman & Deal, 1979a).

Three important environmental variables are identified in the implementation literature: timing, intended beneficiaries, and participating organizations.

Timing

Time is one of several strategic factors identified as relevant to organizational change (Ginzberg & Reilly, 1957). Because implementation is a process, not an event (Gross et al., 1971), it involves the passage of time. Common wisdom has it that in policy implementation "timing is everything." The assumption underlying such wisdom implies that there is a "right" and a "wrong" time for implementation. The overall timing of a policy may affect implementation, i.e., the point in time a policy was developed, as well as the specific timing of implementation components, such as the availability of resources.

Intended Beneficiaries

Along with concept developers and organizational implementors, discussed in previous sections, the intended beneficiaries are part of the cast of characters in policy implementation (Hargrove, 1975). The inclusion of beneficiaries is based on the idea that those who are affected by innovations should have a chance to make known to others their own needs, ideas, group standards, and suggestions (Fine, 1981).

A review of the implementation literature would lead one to believe that the intended beneficiaries do not play any role in implementation other than a "dim figure" in the background (Hargrove, 1975) or "watchdogs" (Bardach, 1977). When "target" or "user" groups (Smith, 1973) are identified in the literature, they refer to the end-line organizational member who must change to meet the demands of policy (McLaughlin, 1976). One reason for overlooking beneficiaries is that policy-makers and program officials take their participation for granted (Bardach, 1977).

Despite their general exclusion, some analysts identify the ways in which intended beneficiaries affect implementation (Gustafson, 1979; Pencus, 1976; Chase, 1979). Consumers can withdraw from use of services or act openly to get service producers to change their ways (Hargrove, 1975). Furthermore, Williams warns: "The recipients whose welfare is ostensibly the main thrust of the innovation cannot be expected to accept passively what is offered" (Williams, 1976b).

The ultimate consumers' needs and interests are the starting point for any planning activity (Fine, 1981), especially in health education (Green et al., 1980). As useful as needs are, they are often ambiguous. They change over time (Bardach, 1977), people may not be aware of their needs (Bolman & Deal, 1976b), and methods of ascertaining them are questionable. Whatever the difficulty with beneficiary needs, they do serve an important role: legitimization of policy. Self-interests can be disguised in alleged consumer needs.

Participating Organizations

Although that organization responsible for implementation gets most of the attention, other organizations also play a major role either by participation or nonparticipation. One major criticism of the perspective taken in the organizational literature about implementation is the limited focus on intraorganizational issues at the expense of interorganizational influences. Chase (1979) notes that some of the toughest obstacles in implementation are the actors and organizations not controlled by those responsible for implementation, but whose cooperation or assistance is required.

Four general factors affect implementation: the policy, the implementing organization, the political milieu, and the environment. Each factor contains multiple variables, with varying degrees of evidence about how they affect implementation.

A forty-four-item check list developed by Chase (1979) to examine obstacles to the implementation of human service programs seemed overwhelmingly long and complicated at first. As we complete this review, however, such a check list seems simplistic and insufficient in the variables included and excluded.

Furthermore, the static nature of any list makes it comforting to hold in hand, but of questionable use in determining the feasibility of implementation. The value of having generated such a list of variables in Table 2 lies, not in its predictive powers, but in its revelation of the complexities of implementation.

Most of the theory implied by the structure of this list holds immediate utility for the practitioner who faces, and to some degree manages or maneuvers around, the variables listed. For the policymaker, too, the mere classification and recognition of these factors can guarantee better policy.

CONCLUSION

As Mazmanian and Sabatier (1983) argue for their list of sixteen variables influencing public policy implementation, "the original policymakers can affect substantially the attainment of . . . objectives by utilizing the levers at their disposal to coherently structure the implementation process." But trying to control implementation with more detailed policy is like trying to control the growth and development of a child with more rules and restrictions. The program, like the child, needs room to breathe, to experiment, to adapt to new circumstances and people. Policy in health education and health promotion can provide greater protection, greater resources, and greater clarity of purpose for the programs it spawns, but it cannot mark every step of implementation without retarding the very growth of people it is intended to promote.

ACKNOWLEDGMENTS

This chapter is based on the senior author's doctoral work at the Harvard Graduate School of Education, and the experience of both authors in the federal Office of Disease Prevention and Health Promotion with special thanks to Michael McGinnis and Julius Richmond. We are indebted to Carol Weiss, David Cohen and Jerry Murphy at Harvard; Roger Bulger and Ruby Isom at the University of Texas Health Science Center at Houston, and Sarah Jean Jackson formerly at the Houston Academy of Medicine/Texas Medical Center Library, now with the University of Texas System Cancer Center/M.D. Anderson Hospital Library. William Ward and Jennie Kronenfeld provided helpful comments. Preparation of this manuscript was supported by National Institutes of Health postdoctoral research training grant No.

Table 2. Summary of the Effects of the Policy, Implementing Organization, Political Milieu, and the Environment on Implementation

	EFFECTS ON IMPLEMENTATION		
FACTOR/VARIABLES*	Positive/ Facilitating	Negative/ Hindering	Uncertain
1. Policy			
a. Theory	solid	unproven	
b. Assumptions	defined	unclear	
c. Goals	stated	nonexistent	
d. Change			
nature			?
amount	small	large	
rate	incremental	ambitious	
radicalness	familiar	unfamiliar	
centrality	central	peripheral	
complexity	few transactions	many transactions	
form			?
e. Resources	available	nonexistent	
f. Specification	some	none	
g. Flexibility	possible solutions	one right answer	
h. Impact	early stages	later stages	
i. Developers			?
2. Implementing Organization			
a. Structure			
goal	relevant to policy	irrelevant to policy	
task	suitable	unsuitable	
scale	small	large	
roles			?
SOPs			?
b. Climate	supportive	unsupportive	
c. Technical Capacity			
technology	appropriate	inappropriate	
resources	available	unavailable	
d. Employee Disposition			
approach	problem solving	opportunistic	
motivation	maintained	declines	
support for change	supportive	unsupportive	
values	congruent	incongruent	
attitudes	favorable/ changeable	unfavorable/ unchangeable	
beliefs	faith in policy	no faith in policy	

Table 2.   Continued

| FACTOR/VARIABLES* | EFFECTS ON IMPLEMENTATION | | |
	Positive/ Facilitating	Negative/ Hindering	Uncertain
e. Employee Behavior	changes	no changes	
3. Political Milieu			
a. Power			
form			?
strength	strong	strong	
use	use	use	
distribution			?
b. Support	present	absent	
4. Environment			
a. Timing	"right"	"wrong"	
b. Intended Beneficiaries	needs	no needs	
c. Other Organizations	controllable	uncontrollable	

Note:
*See text for description of variables.

HL07555–02A1 to the University of Texas Center for Health Promotion Research and Development.

REFERENCES

Adler, M. (1957). *Aristotle for everybody*. New York: Macmillan.
Alinsky, S. D. (1972). *Rules for radicals: A pragmatic primer for realistic radicals*. New York: Vintage Books.
Allison, G. (1971). *Essence of decision*. Boston: Little, Brown.
Bardach, E. (1977). *The implementation game: What happens after a bill becomes a law*. Cambridge: MIT Press.
Basch, C. Implementation analysis: A neglected phase of curriculum evaluation. Assistant Professor, Department of Health Education, Russell Sage College, Troy. New York: undated and unpublished paper.
Baum, L. (1980). Comparing the implementation of legislative and judicial policies. In Sabatier, P., & Mazmanian, D. (Eds.), *Effective policy implementation*. Lexington, MA: Lexington Books.
Bennis, W. (1966). *Changing organizations*. New York: McGraw Hill.
Berman, P. (1978). The study of macro- and micro-implementation. *Public Policy, 26*, 157–184.

Berman, P., & McLaughlin, M. (1976). Implementation of educational innovation. *The Educational Forum, 40*, 347–370.

Bolman, L., & Deal, T. (1979). *The political frame*. Boston: Harvard Graduate School of Education.

Bolman, L., & Deal, T. (1979a). *A structural perspective*. Boston: Harvard Graduate School of Education.

Bolman, L., & Deal, T. (1979b). *The human resource frame*. Boston: Harvard Graduate School of Education.

Carlaw, R. W. (1982). *Perspectives on community health education: A series of case studies: Vol. 1. United States*. Oakland: Third Party Publishing Co.

Cataldo, M. F., Green, L. W., Herd, J. A., Parkinson, R. S., & Goldbeck, W. B. (1986). Preventive medicine and the corporate environment: Challenge to behavioral medicine. In Cataldo, M. F., & Coates, T. J. (Eds.), *Health and industry: A behavioral medicine perspective*. New York: Wiley.

Chase, G. (1979). Implementing a human services program: How hard can it be? *Public Policy, 27*, 385–435.

Chin, R. (1966). The utility of system models and developmental models. In Finkle, J., & Garble, R. (Eds.), *Political development and social change*. New York: Wiley.

Cleary, H. P., Kichen, J. M., & Ensor, P. G. (1985). *Advancing health through education: A case study approach*. Palo Alto: Mayfield.

Derthick, M. (1972). *New towns in-town*. Washington, DC: The Urban Institute.

Dewey, J. (1976). In Koch, D. (Ed.), *Lectures on psychological and political ethics: 1898*. New York: Hafner Press.

Durant, W. (1961). *The story of philosophy*. New York: Washington Square Press.

Edwards, G. C., III (1980). *Implementing public policy*. Washington, DC: Congressional Quarterly Press.

Elmore, R. (1976). Follow through planned variation. In Williams, W., & Elmore, R. (Eds.), *Social program implementation*. New York: Academic Press.

Fine, S. (1981). *The marketing of ideas and social issues*. New York: Praeger.

Ginzberg, E., & Reilly, E. (1957). *Effecting change in large organizations*. New York: Columbia University.

Goodman, L. E., & Goodman, M. J. (1986). Prevention—how misuse of a concept can undercut its worth. *Hastings Center Report, 3*, 26–38.

Green, L. W. (1979). National policy in the promotion of health. *International Journal of Health Education, 22*, 161–168.

Green, L. W. (1980). Healthy people: The Surgeon General's report and the prospects. In McNerney, W. K. (Ed.), *Working for a healthier America*. Cambridge: Ballinger.

Green, L. W. (1982). Reconciling policy in health education and primary health care. *International Journal of Health Education, 24*, 1–11 (Suppl. 3).

Green, L. W. (1986). The theory of participation: A qualitative analysis of its expression in national and international health policies. *Advances in Health Education and Promotion, 1*, 211–236.

Green, L., Kreuter, M., Deeds, S., & Partridge, K. (1980). *Health education planning: A diagnostic approach*. Palo Alto: Mayfield.

Green, L., & Lewis, F. (1981). Issues in relating evaluation to theory, policy and practice in continuing education and health education. *Mobius, 1*, 46–58.

Green, L., & Lewis, F. (1986). *Measurement and evaluation in health education and health promotion*. Palo Alto: Mayfield.

Green, L. W., & McAlister, A. (1984). Macro-intervention to support health behavior: some theoretical perspectives and practical reflections. *Health Education Quarterly, 11*, 323–339.

Green, L. W., Wilson, R. W., & Bauer, K. (1983). Data required to measure progress on the objectives for the nation in disease prevention and health promotion. *American Journal of Public Health, 73*, 18–24.

Gross, N., Giacquinta, J., & Berstein, M. (Eds.) (1971). *Implementing organizational innovations: A sociological analysis of planned change in schools.* New York: Basic Books.

Gustafson, D. (1979). *An approach to predicting the implementation potential of recommended actions in health planning.* Madison, WI: The Institute for Health Planning.

Hargrove, E. (1975). *The missing link: The study of the implementation of social policy.* (Paper 797–1). Washington, DC: The Urban Institute.

Huysman, J. (1970). *The implementation of operations research.* New York: Wiley.

Lazin, F. (1973). The failure of federal enforcement of civil rights regulations in public housing, 1963–1971: The co-optation of a federal agency by its local constituency. *Policy Sciences, 4,* 263–273.

Leavitt, H. (1965). Applied organizational change in industry: Structural, technological, and humanistic approaches. In March, J. (Ed.), *Handbook of Organizations.* Chicago: Rand McNally.

Lindblom, C. (1965). *The Intelligence of Democracy.* New York: The Free Press.

Lindblom, C., & Cohen, D. (1979). *Usable knowledge.* New Haven: Yale University Press.

Katz, D., & Kahn, R. (1966). *The social psychology of organizations.* New York: Wiley.

Kolbe, L., & Iverson, D. (1981). Implementing comprehensive health education: Educational innovations and social change. *Health Education Quarterly, 8,* 57–80.

Mazmanian, D., & Sabatier, P. (1983). *Implementation and public policy.* Glenview, IL: Scott, Foresman.

McGinnis, J. M. (1980). Trends in disease prevention: Assessing the benefits of prevention. *Bulletin of the New York Academy of Medicine, 56,* 38–44.

McGowan, E. (1976). Rational fantasies. *Policy Sciences, 7,* 439–454.

McLaughlin, M. (1976). Implementation as mutual adaptation: Change in classroom organization. In Williams, W., & Elmore, R. (Eds.), *Social program implementation.* New York: Academic Press.

Moore, M. (1979). A feasibility estimate of a policy decision to expand methadone maintenance. *Public Policy, 26,* 285–304.

Murphy, J. (1976). Title V of ESEA: The impact of discretionary funds on state education bureaucracies. In Williams, W., & Elmore, R. (Eds.), *Social Program Implementation.* New York: Academic Press.

Neustadt, R. E., & Fineberg, H. V. (1978). *The swine flu affair: Decision-making on a slippery disease.* Washington, DC: U.S. Department of Health, Education, and Welfare.

Parkinson, R. S., et al. (1982). *Managing health promotion in the workplace: Guidelines for implementation and evaluation.* Palo Alto: Mayfield.

Pincus, J. (1976). Incentives for innovation in the public schools. In Williams, W., & Elmore, R. (Eds.), *Social program implementation.* New York: Academic Press.

Pressman, J. , & Wildavsky, A. (1973). *Implementation.* 2nd. ed. Berkeley: University of California Press.

Public Health Service, Office of Disease Prevention and Health Promotion (1978). *Disease prevention and health promotion: Federal programs and prospects.* Washington, DC: Department of Health, Education and Welfare.

Public Health Service, Office of Disease Prevention and Health Promotion (1979a). *Healthy people: The Surgeon General's report on health promotion and disease prevention.* Washington, DC: Department of Health, Education and Welfare.

Public Health Service, Office of Disease Prevention and Health Promotion (1979b). *Healthy people: The Surgeon General's report on health promotion and disease prevention-background papers.* Washington, DC: Department of Health, Education and Welfare.

Public Health Service, Office of Disease Prevention and Health Promotion (1980). *Promoting health/preventing disease: Objectives for the nation.* Washington, DC: U.S. Department of Health and Human Services.

Public Health Service, Office of Disease Prevention and Health Promotion (1981). *Strategies for promoting health for specific populations.* Washington, DC: U.S. Department of Health and Human Services.

Public Health Service, Office of Disease Prevention and Health Promotion (1983a). *Prevention '82.* Washington, DC: U.S. Department of Health and Human Services.

Public Health Service, Office of Disease Prevention and Health Promotion (1983b). Promoting health/preventing disease: Public health service implementation plans for attaining the objectives for the nation. *Public Health Reports,* (Supplement to the September/October 1983 issue).

Public Health Service, Office of Disease Prevention and Health Promotion (1984). *Prevention profile.* Washington, DC: U.S. Department of Health and Human Services.

Public Health Service, Office of Disease Prevention and Health Promotion (1985). *Proceedings of prospects for a healthier America: Achieving the nation's health promotion objectives.* Washington, DC: U.S. Department of Health and Human Services.

Public Health Service, Office of Disease Prevention and Health Promotion (1986). *A review of state activities related to the public health services' health promotion and disease prevention objectives for the nation.* Washington, DC: U.S. Department of Health and Human Services.

Rabinovitz, F., Pressman, J., & Rein, M. (1976). A plethora of forms, authors, and functions. *Policy Sciences, 4,* 399–416.

Radin, R. (1976). The implementation of SSE: Guaranteed income or welfare? In Williams, W., & Elmore, R. (Eds.), *Social program implementation.* New York: Academic Press.

Rein, M., & Rabinovitz, F. (1977). Implementation: A theoretical perspective. Working Paper No. 43. Cambridge, MA: Joint Center for Urban Studies of MIT and Harvard University.

Ross, H. S., & Mico, P. R. (1980). *Theory and practice in health education.* Palo Alto: Mayfield.

Schaeffer, M. (1985). *Designing and implementing procedures for health and human services.* Beverley Hills: Sage.

Smith, T. (1973). Policy roles: An analysis of policy formulators and policy implementors. *Policy Sciences, 4,* 297–307.

Stockman, D. A. (1986). *The triumph of politics: How the Reagan revolution failed.* New York: Harper & Row.

Stokey, E., & Zeckhauser, R. (1978). *A primer for policy analysis.* New York: W. W. Norton.

Texas Department of Health (1984). *Proceedings of the Texas conference on disease prevention and health promotion 1990 objectives.* Austin: Texas Department of Health.

Titmus, R. (1972). *The gift relationship from human blood to social policy.* New York: Vintage Books.

Van Meter, D., & Van Horn, C. (1975). The policy implementation process: A conceptual framework. *Administration and Society, 6,* 445–488.

Weatherley, R., & Lipsky, M. (1977). Street-level bureaucrats and institutional innovation: Implementing special-education reform. *Harvard Educational Review, 47,* 171–197.

Weiss, C. (1972). *Evaluation research.* Englewood Cliffs, NJ: Prentice-Hall.

Weiss, C. (1973). Evaluation research in the political context. Paper presented at the annual meeting of the American Psychological Association, Montreal, Canada.

Weiss, C. (Ed.) (1977). *Using social research in public policy making.* Lexington, MA: Lexington Books.

Williams, W. (1976a). Implementation problems in federally funded programs. In Williams, W., & Elmore, R. (Eds.), *Social program implementation.* New York: Academic Press.

Williams, W. (1976b). Implementation analysis and assessment. In Williams, W., & Elmore, R. (Eds.), *Social program planning*. New York: Academic Press.
Zollschan, G., & Perrucci, R. (1964). Working papers in the theory of institutionalization. In Zollschan, G., & Hirsch, W. (Eds.), *Explorations in social change*. Boston: Houghton Mifflin.

BIOGRAPHICAL SKETCHES OF
AUTHORS AND EDITORS

Marshall H. Becker, PhD, MPH, is Professor and Chairperson of the Department of Health Behavior and Health Education at the University of Michigan's School of Public Health. He has had recent articles in *Social Science and Medicine, Patient Education and Counseling*, and the *American Journal of Public Health*. Becker is currently doing research in the areas of education of health care professionals to increase patient compliance, development of health beliefs in children, and determinants of contraceptive continuation among teenage women.

Noreen M. Clark, PhD, is a Professor of Health Behavior and Health Education at the University of Michigan School of Public Health. Clark has published recently in the *Journal of School Health, Nursing Outlook, Patient Education and Counseling*, and the *Journal of Allergy and Clinical Immunology*. She is a co-author of *Evaluation of Health Promotion and Education Programs* published by Mayfield in 1984. Her current research is in the family management of asthma in low-income children and the family management of heart disease in an elderly population. Clark is former Chair of the Public Health Education Section of the American Public Health Association (APHA), former President of the Society for Public Health Education, and a member of the Pulmonary Diseases Advisory Committee for NHLBI. In 1985, she received the Mayhew Derryberry Award for Outstanding Contribution to Health Education in Behavioral Science from APHA.

Janet L. Collins, PhD, is an Assistant Director at IOX Assessment Associates in California and a lecturer in the Education Department at the University of California at Los Angeles. She works on evaluation of health promotion programs, research on motivation and behavior change, self-efficacy in achievement settings, and cognitive, affective and behavioral assessment. She wrote her doctoral dissertation on self-efficacy and ability in achievement behavior. Her research includes validation of behavioral self-report measures in smoking, exercise, and stress management and intervention research on adult immunization.

Leonard H. Dawson, MSPH, is a clinical Associate Professor and Director of the Masters Programs in the Department of Health Education in the School of Public Health at the University of North Carolina, Chapel Hill. He specializes in rural health and community organization. He has an upcoming book entitled Participatory Planning in Community Health Education. His current research includes evaluation of adolescent pregnancy prevention and the analysis of the North Carolina Child Safety Restraint Legislation and its implementation.

Rocco DePietro, PhD, is an Adjunct Associate Professor in the Department of Communication at the University of Michigan. His main areas of study are market research, focus-group studies, product development, and clinic-utilization studies. Among his works are those specifically of interest to those in health education and promotion that have been published in the *Health Education Quarterly*, and in a report to the Michigan Department of Public Health. He is currently developing a computerized market scan survey for hospitals. DePietro belongs to the American Public Health Association and the International Communication Association.

Nancy E. Epstein, MPH, is presently coordinator of indigent health care. She works in the areas of health education and health policy. Currently she is focusing her studies on indigent health care, hunger and malnutrition, health policy, and public policy analysis. Her most recent work was published in a report to the Texas Senate. She is affiliated with the Texas Health and Human Services Coordinating Council and the Texas Legislature.

Brian R. Flay, D.Phil., is an Associate Professor and the Deputy Director of the Health Behavior Research Institute at the University of Southern California. He has expertise in smoking and drug-abuse prevention, mass media for health promotion, attitude and behavior change, and program evaluation. Flay's recent works have been published in *Pediatric and Adolescent Behavioral Medicine, Evaluation and the Health Professions*, and *Preventive Medicine*. Flay was the Principal Investigator on a study of the relative efficacy of classroom and televised drug-abuse prevention programs, funded by NIDA.

Robert M. Goodman, MPH, is a doctoral candidate at the University of North Carolina's School of Public Health in the Department of Health Education. He works with community health development and organizational theory. Goodman's doctoral dissertation is on the variables that facilitate and inhibit the institutionalization of health promotion programs.

Lawrence W. Green, DrPH, is Director of the Center for Health Promotion Research and Development and Professor of Family Practice, Community Medicine and Behavioral Sciences in the School of Public Health and the Medical School at the University of Texas Health Science Center, Houston. Green's areas of expertise include health education, health promotion, health policy, international health, behavioral sciences, and evaluation and research. Green is currently involved in research in the meta-analysis of 102 experimental studies of patient drug information transfer. The research is supported by the Pharmaceutical Manufacturers' Association. The March of Dimes is funding a study of the assessment of risks in women of reproductive ages. The U.S. Office of the Assistant Secretary for Planning and Evaluation is supporting, through the Research Triangle Institute, a review of evaluations of health promotion in worksites, and a National Cancer Institute grant funds work with Alfred McAlister on the impact of mass media and community organization for reduction of smoking in border communities in Texas. Green is senior author of books published by Mayfield Publishing—*Health Education Planning: A Diagnostic Approach* (1980) and *Measurement and Evaluation of Health Education and Health Promotion* (in press), and a book by the C. V. Mosby Co. (1985)—*Community Health*, 5th edition. He has currently in press a book published by the World Health Organization, *New Policies for Health Education in Primary Health Care*. Green has received a Presidential citation, the Distinguished Career Award from APHA and many other national recognitions.

Alan C. Henderson, DrPH, MSPH, is Professor and Chairperson of the Health Sciences Department at California State University, Long Beach. He focuses his studies in the areas of health education manpower development, patient education, and health behavior. Henderson has written two federal reports on role delineation for health education. The first was on initial role delineation, and the second on role refinement and verification. Currently he is analyzing statistical techniques in reported health education research and studying medication compliance using a computerized medicine dispenser.

Barbara A. Israel, DrPH, is Assistant Professor, Department of Health Behavior and Health Education in the School of Public Health at the University of Michigan. Her responsibilities include teaching, research, and community service in the areas of group dynamics, organization development, social networks and social support, community organization, occupational stress, international health, and social change. She is Principal Investigator of an NIAAA-funded study to evaluate action research for the prevention of occupational stress-related disorders and coinvestigator in the development of an interdisciplinary program in conflict management alternatives. She has published recently in the *Journal of Consulting and Clinical Psychology, Patient Education and Counseling*, and *Health Education Quarterly*.

Frances M. Lewis, PhD, is a Professor in the Department of Community Health Care Systems, School of Nursing at the University of Washington, Seattle. She has had her works published in *Patient Counseling and Health Education, Journal of Psychosocial Oncology*, and *Family Relations*. She co-authored *Evaluation and Measurement in Health Education and Health Promotion* with Lawrence W. Green. She also contributed two chapters to *Issues and Topics in Cancer Nursing*. Lewis is a member of the American Nurses' Association, American Public Health Association, Sigma Theta Tau, and the Society of Public Health Educators. She is guest editor of the Research and Evaluation Section of Volume 3 of *Advances in Health Education and Promotion* (forthcoming).

Patricia Dolan Mullen, MLS, DrPH, is Associate Director, Center for Health Promotion Research and Development and Associate Professor, School of Public Health, University of Texas Health Science Center, Houston. Mullen has recent publications in the *International Quarterly of Community Health Education*, the *Journal of Nurse Midwifery, Patient Education and Counseling, Geriatric Consultant*, and the *Journal of the American Diabetes Association*. Mullen wrote Guidelines for Health Promotion and Education Services in HMOs with Jane Zapka (Government Printing Office, 1982). Her areas of expertise include qualitative approaches to research and evaluation, meta-analysis, patient education and health promotion in medical care settings, and the behavior of health professionals and their communication with patients. Current research is in the meta-analysis of evaluations of patient education programs, effects of training and educational outreach on the physician in health promotion counseling, and arthritis self-management.

Judith M. Ottoson, MPH, EdD, is with the Center for Health Promotion Research and Development at the University of Texas in Houston. She has published recently in the *Journal of Continuing Education in Nursing* and the *American Journal of Nursing*. Ottoson has considerable international experience in the development of training programs, project management, communications and marketing, and policy analysis.

Gilbert Ramirez, MPH, is a doctoral candidate in the School of Public Health at the University of Texas in Houston. He is an Environmental Science Officer and in the U.S. Army. His areas of expertise are environmental health, information synthesis and health services organization. His current research is on occupational physical activity and pregnancy outcome.

Irwin M. Rosenstock, PhD, is a Professor in the Department of Health Behavior and Health Education at the University of Michigan. His main areas of study are program evaluation, lifestyle modification strategies, and the determinants of health-related behavior change. He has published works in *Diabetes Care, Health Psychology* and *Health Education Monographs*. Rosenstock is presently focusing his research on relapse prevention in lifestyle modification and enhancing compliance with weight-loss programs.

Kathleen Rounds, PhD, is an Assistant Professor at the School of Social Work, University of North Carolina. She received her PhD and MPH from the Department of Health Behavior and Health Education, The University of Michigan, School of Public Health and her MSW from the University of Washington, School of Social Work. Her research interests include social networks and social support and interventions to assist individuals and families coping with chronic disease.

Scott K. Simonds, DrPH, is a Professor in the Department of Health Behavior and Health Education and the Assistant Dean of the School of Public Health at the University of Michigan. He has expertise in policy development and administration, patient education and human resource development and continuing education. He has published works in the *SOPHE Heritage Collection of Health Education Monographs, Patient Counseling and Health Education*, and the *International Quarterly of Community Health Education*. He contributed a chapter to *A Handbook of Health Enhancement and Disease Prevention*. Currently, Simonds is involved in research in the assessment of exit competencies in professional education. He was awarded the Distinguished Fellow Award from the Society for Public Health Education in 1983.

Allan Steckler, DrPH, MPH, is an Associate Professor and the Acting Chairman for the Department of Health Education in the School of Public Health at the University of North Carolina. He focuses his studies on community health education, program evaluation, and social policy. His works have been published in the *Southern Medical Journal, Health Education Quarterly*, and the *International Quarterly of Community Health Education*. He is serving currently as the Chair of the Five Year Plan Committee for the American Public Health Association. His present research is on the evaluation of health promotion programs.

Cynthia J. Stewart, PhD, MPH, is an Assistant Professor at the University of Michigan's School of Public Health. She was formerly the director for the Center for Continuing Education of Public Health Professionals in the School of Public Health at the University of Michigan.

William B. Ward, DrPH, MA, is Associate Professor at the University of South Carolina in the Department of Health Education and Coordinator of International Studies in the School of Public Health and holds an adjunct appointment in the Department of Anthropology. Ward is series editor of *Advances in Health Education and Promotion* (JAI Press, Inc.). Recent publications are in the *International Quarterly of Community Health Education, Social and Economic Planning Studies* (in press), and the *International Journal of Health Education*. He is first author of a chapter in *Perspectives in Health Education, Vol. I: the United States* (Third Party Publishing, 1982) and is co-editor of *Perspectives in Health Education, Vol. II: the African Experience* (Third Party Publishing, in press). He is author of a chapter in that same volume. Ward's recent research includes community resources for oral rehydration therapy in rural Haiti, factors influencing breast self-examination education, social network analysis, and risk factors in pregnancy. He is involved in funded research in African health behavior assessment for the Centers for Disease Control and the development of an automated data base for health promotion programming.

Elanna S. Yalow, PhD, is an Associate Director for IOX Assessment Associates in California. She has expertise in the evaluation of health promotion programs, validation of assessment strategies, individual differences in information processing, and cognitive, affective, and behavioral assessment. She has recently published works in the *Handbook of Human Intelligence, Educational Researcher*, and the *Journal of Allergy and Clin-*

ical Immunology. Yalow's current research is in the areas of intervention research on adult immunization, assessment strategies for teacher and student competencies, instructional materials development for childhood asthma and validation of behavioral self-report measures in smoking, exercise, and stress management.

INDEX